PRAISE FOR *THE MAN WHO FLEW THE* MEMPHIS BELLE

"Fans of military memoirs will like the first-person straight talk and action. . . . Morgan's personal life . . . is presented with ease and relative candor."
—*Publishers Weekly*

"This book unashamedly sports a Greatest Generation aura as it sings a love song to the B-17 that aviation buffs at least should find irresistible. It also provides an invaluable participant's view of a major aspect of the U.S. experience of World War II—the strategic bombing campaign—and as such is definitely a book that needed to be written while the best man could still write it."
—*Booklist*

"Morgan (Colonel, USAFR, Ret.) and Powers (Pulitzer Prize–winning journalist and coauthor of James Bradley's *Flags of Our Fathers*) bring a new perspective to World War II literature. Written in a chatty style that is easy and exciting to read, this book is recommended."
—*Library Journal*

"A chronicle of loyalty, love, and heroism under fire."—*Air Classics*

"Well written."
—*Greensboro News & Record*

"Readers cannot escape the fear felt by Morgan and his crew as he describes the bombing missions in fascinating detail, explaining how each crew member is a vital part of a team, counting on each other for survival."
—*The Anniston Star*

The Man Who Flew the

MEMPHIS BELLE

Memoir of a WWII Bomber Pilot

Col. Robert Morgan, USAFR, Ret.,
with Ron Powers

NAL
CALIBER

NEW AMERICAN LIBRARY
Published by New American Library, a division of
Penguin Group (USA) Inc., 375 Hudson Street,
New York, New York 10014, USA
Penguin Group (Canada), 90 Eglinton Avenue East, Suite 700, Toronto,
Ontario M4P 2Y3, Canada (a division of Pearson Penguin Canada Inc.)
Penguin Books Ltd., 80 Strand, London WC2R 0RL, England
Penguin Ireland, 25 St. Stephen's Green, Dublin 2,
Ireland (a division of Penguin Books Ltd.)
Penguin Group (Australia), 250 Camberwell Road, Camberwell, Victoria 3124,
Australia (a division of Pearson Australia Group Pty. Ltd.)
Penguin Books India Pvt. Ltd., 11 Community Centre, Panchsheel Park,
New Delhi - 110 017, India
Penguin Group (NZ), 67 Apollo Drive, Rosedale, Auckland 0632,
New Zealand (a division of Pearson New Zealand Ltd.)
Penguin Books (South Africa) (Pty.) Ltd., 24 Sturdee Avenue,
Rosebank, Johannesburg 2196, South Africa

Penguin Books Ltd., Registered Offices:
80 Strand, London WC2R 0RL, England

Published by NAL Caliber, an imprint of New American Library, a division of Penguin Group (USA) Inc. Previously published in Dutton and New American Library editions.

First NAL Caliber Printing (reissue edition), July 2011
10 9 8 7 6 5 4 3 2 1

NAL Caliber Trade Paperback ISBN: 978-0-451-23352-3

The Library of Congress has cataloged the hardcover edition of this title as follows:

Morgan, Robert.
The man who flew the Memphis Belle: a memoir of a WWII bomber pilot/Robert Morgan, with Ron Powers.
p. cm.
ISBN 0-525-94610-1
1. Morgan, Robert. 2. Memphis Belle (B-17 bomber). 3. World War, 1939–1945—Personal narratives, American. 4. Bomber pilots—United States—Biography. 5. United States. Army Air Forces—Biography. 6. World War, 1939–1945—Campaigns—Western Front. 7. World War, 1939–1945—Aerial operations, American. I. Powers, Ron. II. Title.
D790.M615 2001
940.54'4973'092—dc21
00-065857

Set in Sabon
Designed by Julian Hamer

Printed in the United States of America

PUBLISHER'S NOTE
While the author has made every effort to provide accurate telephone numbers and Internet addresses at the time of publication, neither the publisher nor the author assumes any responsibility for errors, or for changes that occur after publication. Further, publisher does not have any control over and does not assume any responsibility for author or third-party Web sites or their content.

To the late Mabel Morgan, who was my inspiration

To Linda Morgan, without whose perseverance
and assistance this book would have never been written

To Peggy Morgan Partin, without whom I would
not have been here to write this book

To Earl Friedell, who started it all in flying
with his instruction

ACKNOWLEDGMENTS

While not quite as big an operation as commanding a bomber squadron, putting a book together still involves a lot of very dedicated and helpful people, all of whom deserve credit and my heartfelt thanks. At the top of my list is Ron Powers. Without him, this book never would have gotten off the ground. I also salute Cindy Kimball of Kimball Office Services in Bristol, Vermont, whose rapid tape transcriptions kept Ron well supplied with copy. Of course, there is also the crew on the *Memphis Belle* and *Dauntless Dotty,* who made it possible for me to come home and be here today. Then there is my editor at Dutton/NAL, Doug Grad, who kept me on a straight line to the finish, and his assistant, Ron Martirano, who provided help on the photo research. And I thank Jim Hornfischer of The Literary Group International, who believed in my story and helped steer it into book form. I'm grateful to Ed Frank, Curator of Special Collections at the University of Memphis Libraries, for furnishing copies of the letters Margaret Polk and I wrote to one another. The staff at the Smithsonian Institution's Air and Space Museum was tremendously helpful, digging out many great photos from the USAF collection. More thanks for their help on providing photos go to Dasha Morgan for the family photos, Brian Woodcock, S/Sgt. Angela Stafford at the United States Air Force, and Frank Donofrio at the *Memphis Belle* Association. Robert Morgan Jr. also gets my thanks for supplying important family information. Credit goes to Peggy Evans for providing all the information on Vince Evans, and to Brent Perkins for keeping me updated on the current status of the *Memphis Belle.* Finally, I have to acknowledge Jim Verinis for being the best friend in the world.

—Col. Robert K. Morgan, USAFR (Ret.)
Asheville, North Carolina,
December 21, 2000

The Man Who Flew the
MEMPHIS BELLE

PROLOGUE

I still go over to Memphis and see her once in a while. She looks pretty good for an old girl. We've both been through a lot since we first met back in 1942, and I'm always amazed at how well she's held up through it all. After more than half a century she's still about the most gorgeous thing I ever saw. She's had a little help in that department from some specialists in the field, but then you name me one great beauty that has not.

I look at her and the memories come flooding back. I can stand there at her side and all of a sudden an hour has passed and it has all streamed through me again at high speed, the images and the noises and the terror and the ecstasy and the grief and the triumph. And then all the decades since.

And maybe when I come out of that reverie I have to put my hand against her for a minute to steady it. That cool smooth exterior. And her? Not a tremor. Nothing ever seemed to bother her much. Nothing ever brought her down.

I come to visit her at least once a year from my home in Asheville, North Carolina. "Visit" isn't quite strong enough a word. It's a pilgrimage. I still enjoy being with her. Of course, things will never be the same between us as back then, but that doesn't matter. Hell, we'd all be in a pretty pickle if they were. No, what matters is that she is not forgotten—not by me, and not by the country she helped save. That, and the fact that she has a good, secure place to spend the rest of her days, even if it is in a theme park. Damn, I whisper to her sometimes. Could either of us ever have predicted this? That you'd end up in a theme park on an island in the Mississippi River? With 150,000 people coming to admire you each year, there amidst all the gift shops and the restaurants and the children's playground and the musicians blowing jazz in the summer?

Sometimes, maybe on a Saturday or a Sunday when the crowds are biggest, I stand off to one side and watch the people drift into the little domed museum on Mud Island, where she's been housed since 1987. I watch them as they form a circle around her and take off their sunglasses and look up at her—perhaps aim a flash camera in her direction—and try to hear what they have to say. Or to read their thoughts—most of them have fallen silent.

Silent in the presence of the *Memphis Belle*.

Very few of them look my way. To them, I'm half-invisible, just another senior citizen out to enjoy the weekend sunshine and a few minutes of nostalgia for a time that is fast fading from America's firsthand memory.

It's mostly the old and the very young who come to see the *Belle*: groups of retirees on bus tours and whole classes of schoolchildren with their teachers and chaperones still excited from their ride over the river on the Monorail. Maybe this is just one stop on a busy schedule that will include a look inside the Mississippi River Museum, a few minutes on board the full-scale reproduction of an 1870s-era steamboat, a souvenir T-shirt; then back to the Monorail and out onto I-55 for a visit to Elvis Presley's Graceland, a quick stroll and a barbecue sandwich on Beale Street, the Home of the Blues; a pilgrimage to the Lorraine Hotel, where Martin Luther King was shot.

Lots of American history in Memphis.

I enjoy watching these folks come and go. I enjoy eavesdropping on the questions they ask the two or three World War II veterans who serve as guides inside the dome. I am moved by how they are moved, watching it dawn on them that they have wandered into the presence of something huge and mysterious and fascinating.

This quaint-looking but still elegant and splendidly designed flying war machine rose from a field in England again and again to rain down fiery destruction on occupied France and Nazi Germany in a war that pitted America's and the world's common people against the forces of unspeakable tyranny. In doing so, she flew through torrents of gunfire and flak that kept her crew in constant jeopardy as plane after plane burst into flames in the Allied formations around the *Belle*.

This B-17 airplane became a wartime legend for surviving twenty-five brutal missions over western Europe in 1942 and 1943, and returning to America with its crew. The *Belle* was the first bomber to accomplish that feat in an Allied campaign that sacrificed two out of every three young fliers to the cause of turning back Adolf Hitler's aggression: 26,000 boys killed or missing in action, another 28,000 taken prisoner.

This airplane, with its beautiful pinup girl painted on each side of its nose, symbolized not only the valor of all American wartime fliers, but also a wartime romance that caught the imagination of the American people back home, a romance between its pilot and the young Memphis girl for whom the *Belle* was named.

I watch the good folks drift in and out of the dome, in and out of the *Memphis Belle*'s silent yet magnetic aura. From my half-invisible vantage point I observe them putting on their holiday faces again, after those few moments of unexpected solemnity; watch them make ready to enjoy the wonders of this island theme park, of the city, of America in these first moments of its new century. This is as it should be. This is what we fought to allow them to do.

It's hard to tell where each departing group of visitors to the Memphis Belle Museum is headed. But there are two places where I am sure they will not go.

One place is a certain address on an older residential street in Memphis called Patricia Drive. Just a whiteframe bungalow with a small swimming pool in the back, where more than sixty-five summers ago people from the whole neighborhood would come over for a dip. That house was the family residence of Margaret Polk, the *Belle* pilot's sweetheart and the airplane's namesake. The young girl whose photograph is still taped to the instrument panel of the cockpit of the *Memphis Belle*. Where I put it.

The other place they will never go is into that cockpit. That cockpit belongs to history now.

And in my heart, it still belongs to me. My name is Robert Morgan. I was the pilot of the *Memphis Belle*.

Sometimes I can't help asking history to move over. Let me be honest about it: I get up into that cockpit every time I go over there. I sit there with my hands gripping the yoke and my feet on the rudder pedals, and I close my eyes and everything we lived through together overwhelms my consciousness. I'm there again. I can hear the sounds of machineguns firing. I can actually feel the vibrations of a great warplane thumping along through the high winds over Europe, buffeted by flak bursts and the slipstreams of German fighters. These sensations are beyond description, more real to me than anything in my present world. I look at the instruments on the panel in front of me. They're all still there. I look at the picture of Margaret, still right where I taped it. In the photograph she's still young and beautiful, though she's been dead these many years.

I whisper to her briefly. I say, "Hi, Gal. We did it, didn't we? We did it together. You, me, the airplane, the crew. All of us working together."

Yes, sir. This senior citizen knows what it was like to have been inside that cockpit, to have heard those four engines come alive and roar, and then to push the throttles forward. I know what it was like to have given up a life of Southern affluence and rakehell glamour for the privilege of flying that airplane into combat.

I also know what it was like to return and find that my pre-war life did not exist any longer, that it had been transformed, like the rest of America, by the war the *Belle* and my crew and I helped fight and win.

So, yes, I still go over to Memphis and see her once a year. After all, she has been a part of my life since I was twenty-two, and I'm in my eighties now. I don't really know where she stops and I begin. She sure made me a different person than I started out to be. She made me look at life in a different way, and value life more.

Yet she's not mine. She doesn't belong to anybody. A lot of people, a lot of groups, would like to claim her, but she's not for sale. She's America's airplane, and that's the way it ought to be.

If you have a little time to spare before heading off to the next attraction, stay awhile. I'll tell you all about it.

CHAPTER

1

First thing you do is, you sit there.

You sit there.

You don't move. You let it wash over you for two, or three, or four, or five minutes. You've come through it again. You've got at least one more night of poker ahead of you. One more morning when you won't wake up dead. Maybe one more red-hot date in London.

It doesn't matter if it's the first time or the twenty-fourth, which this one was. What matters is that you're down out of the sky. Your wheels are on the tarmac. You've brought your crew back safe.

You take a big deep breath. You feel the sweat that has soaked through your long underwear and your tunic and lubricated the fleece lining of your leather jacket, plastering it to your shoulders and back and chest. Maybe you clench and unclench your hands a few times. Man, it feels good to have turned loose of that yoke. You've held on to it for maybe six, eight hours, knuckles white, keeping thirty-two tons of bomber steady at 25,000 feet, your hands wrapped around that shuddering yoke, your feet tensing against the rudder pedals. Your margin of error is down to feet, from the wingtips of the bomber on your left and the bomber on your right. All this with deadly antiaircraft fire and cannon and machinegun rounds from hostile fighter planes and the smoke and debris from your comrades' planes around you cracking your universe apart just as the trip started to get dull.

Now maybe you start to slide your feet off those pedals, let your legs go limp a little, and here comes the pain from those relaxing muscles, shooting all the way up your calves and thighs clear to your hips. Feels good, that pain. It means you're still alive.

You sit there for your two or three or four or five minutes. They say DiMaggio liked to do that in the Yankee clubhouse before a game, just sit there by himself with his cup of coffee. But this is after the game, if "game" is the word for what went on up there over Germany and was going to keep going on for God knew how long.

You let the rest of the crew get out ahead of you. Luxury. You've heard about "luxury" all your life. Thought you'd seen it firsthand, even. How come nobody ever told you what real luxury is? It's sitting in your cockpit for a little while after the big Wright Cyclone engines have shut down and the propellers have stopped turning. Just sitting there looking out through your scarred and milky Plexiglas windshield at the airfield and the English countryside beyond it, at the fine rain that always seems to be falling, at the wind sock on the control tower, at those black English bicycles strewn everywhere. Now the other planes come droning in, some of them shot up and wobbling over on one wing, their pilots fighting for control with their yokes and rudders. Seems like always a few less coming in than went out that morning.

Yes, you're just sitting there with nothing more on your mind than, Oh boy, I'm lucky again.

Finally you unstrap yourself and swing down through the hatch, and you feel the built-up tension shooting through your joints again as you amble over to where the boys are standing huddled around the fuselage: Quinlan the tailgunner and Harold Loch the serious-minded flight engineer and the rest. It's always kind of an awkward moment. You're all standing there in a little knot, feeling as though there ought to be something to say, but at the same time knowing that to say anything would be to ruin it. Hard to describe those emotions, exhilarated and sad at the same time, and sometimes a little angry too, although it's tough to know at what, exactly. Maybe at anybody who's not a part of your little circle just then, maybe at the people who decided there had to be a war.

Here comes the ground crew already, on the run, primed to jump in and start caulking up the bullet holes in the wings and tailfin and the body of the *Belle*. They all want to know what it was like, what happened up there today. The crew chief is up on a stepladder with his paintbrush, slapping the next cartoon bomb at the end of the row with all the others. Number 24.

There's nothing left to do out there, so you turn and start the long ambling walk across the shiny tarmac toward the Interrogation Room. The boys fall into stride around you—Robert Hanson the radio man, and waistgunner Tony Nastal and the rest of that great crew. They're the best in the business, individually and as a team, but they look up to you. Hell, you're the pilot, the one that has to do his job before any of them can do theirs. They've come to believe in you absolutely. They believe that you will get them to the target and then get them back here safely every time. That's something to live up to. You've done it twenty-four times and there's one more mission left to go, one more round-trip in the Belle, and if you make it, you can all go home.

No pilot and full crew have done that yet—survived twenty-five missions and been sent home with their bomber—in the eight months that the hundreds of American B-17 bombers of the Eighth Bomber Command, taking off without fighter-plane escorts from bases carved out of the English countryside, have been rumbling and droning across the Channel and over the fortified fields of occupied France, and Belgium, and later on over the Fatherland itself—Adolf Hitler's Germany. The first Allied force of any kind to carry the hell-fire of World War II into the Führer's own territory.

In the first three months of that great offensive, beginning in November 1942, you've seen a loss rate of more than 80 percent from your Bomb Group, the 91st. You know that other groups are catching the same kind of hell from those slashing Messerschmitts and Focke-Wulfs and the endless square miles of bursting flak. You know you and your crew could catch it at any instant of any day you're up there. You know you haven't flown one mission yet without taking some kind of hit. A few weeks back they damn near took your whole tail-section off, and Quinlan with it.

Hell, look at today, as far as that went. You'd hit a heavily fortified target, so you came back a little beat up. A few holes in the right wing, some damage to the underpart of the bomb bay over the target—luckily, Vince Evans, your ice-cool bombardier, had got the bombs away before the flak hit. Your group as a whole had lost three planes. Three crews, thirty-odd boys you'd had breakfast with and wouldn't see for dinner.

You know all this. And still you go up there every day they tell you to.

The attrition rate got so high so fast, and the horror of it grew so haunting for each crew that survived a run, that before long the generals decided to build in a little incentive, sort of like the Fuller Brush Company did for its salesmen. Twenty-five missions, and your war is over.

And now, on this day, this fifteenth of May 1943—this time of year when the dogwood and the redbud would be out in full force through the Blue Ridge Mountains above Asheville, North Carolina—you and your boys are one workday shy of that goal: the only bomber crew in the Mighty Eighth within reach of finishing their twenty-five and being sent home with their airplane.

What does a fellow think about at a moment like that, ambling across the tarmac toward Interrogation?

I was that fellow. I was thinking a lot of things, and I'd continue to think about them that afternoon when I took a pass on having the customary few beers with some of my crew members in the lounge at Bassingbourn air base, and I'd think about them on into that night, and the next day, and right up to the moment when I swung back up through that hatch to rev up the engines on the *Memphis Belle* and point her toward the continent and our twenty-fifth mission.

I thought about a lot of things. But here is one damn thing I knew for sure. I knew I was a long way from Beaucatcher Mountain.

I go by a lot of names. I was "Morgan!" to various redfaced colonels and majors who wanted to chew me out about not bothering to wear my uniform cap, or about my incurable taste for buzzing airstrips and swanky beaches where the top brass were having their cocktail parties. Some of my fellow pilots knew me as Floorboard

Freddie, which I guess must have had something to do with my style of landing a Flying Fortress. I was Dennis in a 1990 movie made about me and the crew. My family and closest pals back in North Carolina used to call me Bobby, at least until I told them to stop. Sounded a little sissy to me. My official designation in the U.S. Air Force Reserve lists is Col. Robert K. Morgan, USAFR/Ret.

To the crew of the *Memphis Belle* I was The Chief, and that handle has meant more to me than any other. And to a certain other belle, one Margaret Polk of Memphis, Tennessee, I was "Jug Head." That meant quite a bit as well.

But in May of 1943, to tell the truth, I was essentially a serial number, and proud of it. The same was true of all the nearly two and one-half million men and women who wore the uniform of the United States Army Air Corps—as combatants, but also as ground crew and mechanics, clerk-typists, bookkeepers, instructors. We were serial numbers, but we were special serial numbers.

The world war that had swept us all out of our ordinary lives, the most terrible ever fought in human history, was far from being decided. In the spring of that year, near the war's midpoint as far as America was concerned, the Axis Powers dominated Europe, Nazi U-boats terrorized shipping convoys in the North Atlantic, and German industrial cities poured out an unending supply of tanks, planes, weaponry and ammunition. On the other side of the world most of the southwestern Pacific islands still lay heavily fortified in the hands of their Japanese conquerors, defiantly awaiting the massive Allied—and mostly American—counteroffensive just then gaining momentum under Gen. Douglas MacArthur and Adm. William F. Halsey.

The huge tide of Axis aggression had begun to buckle against its outer limits by that year. Allied air power had played its part in the turning. The battle of Midway in May 1942 was decided at the last moment when a gallant squadron of Dauntless dive-bombers closed in on three Japanese carriers and incinerated them, finally turning back the slashing advance of the Rising Sun through the Pacific. Just a little more than a year before that, the outnumbered Royal Air Force had destroyed Hitler's plans for invading England in the historic Battle of Britain, shooting down nearly 1,400 Luftwaffe fighters and bombers in four hellish months of dogfighting, while taking more than 800 fighter-losses itself.

In February 1943 Hitler's reckless invasion of the Soviet Union collapsed at Stalingrad with the surrender of the German Sixth Army and what was left of its 1.5 million troops. Just two days before the *Memphis Belle* touched down from its twenty-fourth mission, the Allies won a great victory in North Africa, accepting the surrender of 275,000 German and Italian troops and paving the way for an Allied invasion of Sicily. Heavy bomber groups, two of them diverted to Africa from the Eighth, played a prominent role in that breakthrough.

Yet it was far from over. The great Channel-based invasion of the European continent, just now beginning to form its mass in England, was more than a year in the future. The final subjugation of Imperial Japan by nuclear explosion was two years away. Even the missions we crewmen of the Eighth Air Force had been flying over Europe these past six months were but a prelude, an opening phase. The first of the Eighth's B-17s had touched down on British soil less than a year earlier, in July 1942. Only eighteen Fortresses participated in the first raid, some railroad marshaling yards near Rouen on August 17. Through that fall and winter—the bulk of the *Belle*'s career—a mission at peak force might amount to some 90 planes.

The size and strength of the Eighth were still increasing in those months, and the great massed missions were still to come—the famous "Little Blitz Week" of July 1943, when it struck at sixteen industrial targets; the buildup to twenty-two bombardment groups in the British Isles by the end of that year; the 600-bomber run of January 1944; the formations of 1,000 and then 2,000 planes shortly afterward.

What a stupendous thing it was to have been a part of all that.

Those of us who were there lived through our share of pain and loss and sacrifice. But we had this knowledge to help us through— we represented a kind of fighting force that the great armies of the past could never have comprehended. Those warriors who fought under the banners of Hannibal, and Genghis Khan, and Napoleon, and Robert E. Lee, and even General Pershing—how could they have predicted a time when thousands of men would launch massive offensives and fight titanic battles in machines soaring five miles above the surface of the earth?

We were participants in a style of warfare that had been made technically feasible less than half a century before it took form in the skies over Europe and the Pacific Ocean. We, and our enemies, were still improvising rules and tactics every time we left the ground for a new day of confrontation above the clouds. The air war demanded skills that even its best surviving practitioners found hard to communicate to their families, friends, and historians—levels of competence, concentration, physical endurance, discipline, and teamwork bordering on brotherhood. Over it all was the constant grim prospect of a sudden helpless spiraling descent to violent death that was simply beyond the range of experience available to most people who had ever lived.

Ironically—given how futuristic this style of warfare seemed in its time—it is a mode that today seems as enshrouded in the mists of the past as the jousting of knights in the courtyard of some medieval castle. Propellers! Leather helmets!

The breakthroughs in science and engineering that created the means for long-range strategic bombing and fighter-plane combat in World War II didn't stop with our Allied victories in 1945. Chuck Yeager test-flew his Bell X-1 faster than the speed of sound just two years after that, and my era was ready for the museum crowds. Within another four years, American F-86 Sabrejets were battling it out against Russian-made MiG-15s over Korea. The Vietnam War, the "Living-Room War," brought high-tech Delta Daggers and Super Sabres and Stratojet bombers.

I heard once that some Hollywood producer had compressed the entire Vietnam War into a music video. Well, by 1991, it was all starting to look like a video game. We were punching up smart bombs against Iraqi forces in the Persian Gulf and reducing the fourth-largest army in the world to the second-largest army in Iraq within forty-eight hours. How could we old-time warriors have predicted a computerized mode of combat that could inflict 100,000 casualties while losing just 148 of our own, and only 458 wounded?

Hell, some of our pilots of the '40s honed their skills by sitting on back porches swiveling broomsticks around between their knees!

Still and all, the surviving airmen of my generation are proud of what we accomplished. Our technology was the very best that America could produce at the time, and besides, nobody has invented a piece of technology yet that's any more advanced than the human heart. I flew with men whose hearts were the finest kind. We must have done something right, in the end. We won.

So who were we, this motley, exhausted little knot of serial numbers ambling across the wet tarmac on this day in mid-May 1943, a time when the whole world seemed to be engulfed in orange flames and billowing black smoke? That was the question that had started to play at the corners of my mind.

Individually we were about as unlikely a gaggle of warriors as you were liable to come across in a week's time—a business-administration student at the University of Connecticut, a chemistry student at Ohio Wesleyan, a stevedore from Wisconsin, a kid who ran a fleet of trucks in Texas, a North Carolina good-time Charlie (me), a Spokane construction worker, an employee in a Yonkers carpet company, a washing-machine repairman from Detroit, a pressman at a rubber company in New Jersey, a chemist for a paint company in Chicago. Not the sort of crowd you might think would cause Herr Hitler to lose any sleep.

As a unit, though—well, that was something different. As a unit I have to confess that we raised a little hell.

As a unit, in the space of ten months from November 7, 1942 until May 15, 1943, the crew of the *Memphis Belle* flew about 20,000 miles and dropped some sixty tons of bombs on military and industrial targets in France, Belgium, and Germany. Flying in tight formation with clusters of our sister Fortresses, we droned heavily above the clouds to pulverize airplane-assembly installations, railway centers, docks and shipbuilding plants, submarine pens, naval shipyards and power-generating factories. To reach these targets we had to survive skyfulls of lethal bursting metal flung at us from above, below, and to either side. Vast carpets of exploding flak were calibrated with demonic precision by the Germans four and five miles below us, to burst within yards of our exposed fuselages. If we survived the flak—no small feat, as thousands of American widows and fatherless children could attest—we still had to contend with the furious swarms of attacking fighter planes, which could swell from tiny dots in the distance to giant hulks of bullet-spraying intruders in the space of two or three seconds, then vanish just as suddenly. Our gunners managed to shoot down at least eight of these banshees and probably five others, and damage about a dozen. It was harder than I've just made it sound.

For our trouble we received sixty-one decorations. Every man in that crew took home a Distinguished Flying Cross, an Air Medal and four Oak Leaf Clusters. However, I don't think you can measure our accomplishment in decorations, or even in the total miles we flew or the tonnage of bombs we dropped. What made the *Belle* crew special—I'm sure this could apply to the many hundreds of bomber crews who made it through that war, as well as the many hundreds of crews that didn't make it—was a quality of brotherhood.

Or something that went even beyond brotherhood. I don't know that anybody has ever invented a word that fits what I'm trying to say. Our crew sure as hell never tried to describe it. It was too sacred to have a name, so we played poker and drank whiskey instead. I mean it was something that took us over when we first came together as a bunch of young strangers and began our training, and that had us firmly in its spell by the time we took off on our first mission to Brest, France, on November 7, 1942, and that continued to grow in us on every new sortie afterward, something that melted down our individual personalities and differences of upbringing and education and temperament, something that flowed through us as surely as our voices flowed through our headphones, something that blended all our different skills and duties. Whatever it was turned us into a single functioning organism of war up there in those clouds.

It was intelligence, and it was instinct, and it was alertness, and it was technical prowess, and it was superhuman concentration, and it was a way of setting fear aside, and it was interdependence—a way of knowing at every instant under extreme duress what the other fellow's function was, and how he was handling it—and it was faith, if you will pardon that particular expression. It was all those things, and yet all those things don't begin to describe it.

I'm not much of a mystic, but maybe it was history itself that had called us beyond ourselves. They say that most great works of science and music and literature get produced at the beginning of an epoch, before the rules have been set in stone and all the tricks and secrets of the process have been studied and analyzed and made apparent for any fool to see. Maybe war works that way too. Here we were, ten boys from an America that still relied on horse-drawn ploughs and buttermilk churns, thrust into a kind of warfare that ran on tachometers and super-turbochargers and Norden bombsights and ball-turrets and VHF transmissions. It was a war that left no doubt as to which side was fighting for the good of mankind and which side was fighting for evil.

There was one more element—one more personality—in this mystical mix that melded all of us into one seamless entity. That was the bomber itself, the *Memphis Belle*. That magnificent specimen of a B-17, the F model, the Flying Fortress, was perhaps pound for pound and bolt for bolt the most elegant war machine ever designed.

You couldn't walk past a B-17F on the ground, if you were like I was, and not want to get in her and fly her right on the spot. She was a Stradivarius of an airplane, a masterpiece of balance and range and response and survivability in combat. She was pure geometry in motion with her great wide slices of wing and tailfin, her four thousand-horsepower engines capable of keeping her aloft for four thousand four hundred miles at a maximum ceiling of thirty-seven thousand feet—more than seven miles above the ground—at a maximum speed of 325 miles an hour. Here was a big plane built so well that she was almost a liability to herself. Early in the war she could outdistance her fighter escorts, and so she had to approach enemy territory naked, utterly exposed to fire.

Plenty of B-17s went down. Too many times my crew and I had to look on while flak or cannon rounds took one of these beautiful planes in our vicinity, riddled a wing or pierced the fuel line, and turned her fuselage into an incinerator for our buddies. How awful it was to see one of them begin that dreaded downward spiral, hear one of my crewmen urging helplessly over the phones, "Get out! Get out!" and then—if they were able—to watch those parachutes blossom through the smoke.

Many more of these aircraft, including the *Belle,* took heavy damage and survived, getting back to base riddled with holes or with so many missing parts that she seemed outside the laws of gravity. Although she was mostly unescorted by fighters until later in 1943, the B-17 was not exactly easy prey. She bristled with guns. Half my crew were gunners; top turret, ball-turret, tailgunner, two at the waist, back to back. They fired 50-caliber machineguns, one or two muzzles apiece, in every direction, and that close formation we pilots had to maintain, flying in clusters of four planes nearly wingtip to wingtip, created a concentrated source of fire that made many hundreds of enemy fighter pilots pay with their lives for homing in.

No wonder those bombers became like living extensions of their crews. No wonder we gave them sweetheart names and had beautiful, leggy women painted on their noses. They were everything to the young airmen inside them. They were hope, they were victory, they were nothing less than life and death.

Just nine years before this day—at a time when I was tooling around the Great Smokies in my father's Buick, dreaming about nothing more warlike than how fast I could get to my girlfriend's house—the B-17 had not even existed. Nothing like it had. In military terms, America then was in the final stages of its ancient history.

Strategists had started speculating about the combat uses of flying machines almost before Wilbur and Orville Wright had stripped off their goggles at Kitty Hawk in my home state in 1903. Sure enough, by the advent of World War I a decade later, both sides had managed to throw several thousand machinegun-armed monoplanes, biplanes and triplanes, even some multi-engine bombers, into the European skies—German and British planes mostly with some French and Italian planes mixed in, Fokkers going up against Sopwith Camels. A few folk-heroes emerged—Manfred von Richthofen, the legendary Red Baron from the German side and stylish Eddie Rickenbacker among the Americans—but personal glamour aside, air combat had almost no effect on the outcome of the Great War.

Nor would it ever, if some of the greatest military minds of the era had their way. The preeminent American General John J. "Black Jack" Pershing stoutly declared that the battleship, not the airplane, would remain the great bulwark of national defense. Second to the Army, of course.

Luckily, a few stubborn rebel visionaries thought otherwise. The most influential was Billy Mitchell. This outspoken aviator, who'd won a Distinguished Service Cross for his own exploits over France and later commanded all U.S. air units under Pershing, was the first to comprehend that air power could be a decisive offensive force in future wars. This was shocking heresy to the Army and Navy establishments. Mitchell shocked their sensibilities a little further by daring to sink a couple of former German battleships with a squad of eight biplanes, just to prove it could be done. When that failed to budge the tight-lipped Pershing and the others—after all, the damn ships weren't moving!—Mitchell turned himself into a one-man truth squad, railing to anybody who would listen that the U.S. was failing to exploit the most potent new weapon in all of warfare. He received a court-martial for his troubles and resigned the service in 1925, but his ideas echoed, and steadily gained credibility.

Charles Lindbergh didn't harm the cause any when he flew the Atlantic in 1927. The country was all agog about pushing the limits of aviation. That pitch of excitement prompted a couple of air transport pioneers to tinker with a bigger, stronger, smoother model than Lindy's rig, one that might carry mail and passengers across the ocean routinely. Their names were Clair Egtvedt and Edward Hubbard, and you probably never heard of them. You've heard of their Seattle-based company—Boeing. Within a few short years they perfected a prototype design that would soon help save Western civilization from Fascist tyranny.

That design took shape under peaceful intentions at first—Boeing test-flew a "Monomail" air transport in 1931—but its military contours were always just below the surface, waiting to be recognized. By 1934, when the Army was finally waking up to the need to repel an enemy invasion from overseas—maybe the reports of German throngs parading to the popular Nazi song, "When Blood Flows From Our Knives," had something to do with that—Boeing's fast-maturing prototype earned it a contract. Its product, labeled Model 299, would be the largest landplane yet built in America, all-metal, with a wingspan of over 100 feet, an unprecedented four engines and a 2,000-mile range. A Seattle newspaperman, beholding her sleek length for the first time, gave her the nickname that would quickly enter American folklore: "Why," he exclaimed, "it's a flying fortress!"

Before the war was over, almost thirteen thousand Fortresses would be built, under steadily improving specifications. About a third of them—some 4,750—would be lost in action. But to say they made a difference would be an understatement. Billy Mitchell never lived to see his prophecy come true; he died in 1936. He would have relished the words of Gen. Carl A. Spaatz, commander of the U.S. Army Air Forces in the British Isles, when the greatest conflagration in history was finally over. "Without the B-17," the General said, "we might have lost the war."

No such grandiose thoughts were on my mind as I left Interrogation after an hour or so of debriefing and headed thankfully to my quarters at Bassingbourn, the 91st Bomber Group's base fifty miles north of London. The fate of the world wasn't uppermost in my concerns just then. My thoughts were personal, and they clustered around a simple, yet gigantic fact: twenty-four missions down, one more mission to go. Then home. If we survived.

Uncharacteristically, I wanted to be alone. I had a lot of thinking to do—about places like Beaucatcher Mountain and the other landmarks of the life I'd left behind.

Bassingbourn was a long way from Beaucatcher, but it served pretty well as a home away from home. It was probably the cream of all the American bases in England, to tell the truth about it. To tell the honest and complete truth, the 91st didn't exactly belong at Bassingbourn, but as long as nobody was going to run us out—and it didn't seem like anybody was going to—we were staying put.

A far cry from the usual dreary assemblage of Quonset huts and bare ground, Bassingbourn was a cluster of elegant, landscaped country manors. It had belonged to some members of the British aristocracy, but when the American Eighth Bomber Command began to spread itself across the English countryside in early 1942, the lines between British aristocracy and Allied military began to blur pretty quickly. Actually the British had thrown together a base for the 91st, but its runways proved inadequate, and we had to find a suitable replacement.

Our commander, Col. Stanley Wray, took on the task of scouting out that replacement site, and when he beheld the baronial splendors of Bassingbourn he acted with dazzling dispatch. He hurried us onto the premises without even checking in with his superior, Gen. Ira Eaker, commanding general of the Eighth Bomber Command. When the General finally did learn of Colonel Wray's lightning strike, he sputtered, "You can't move into that base! That's a British base! That's not one that we can use without their permission."

The Colonel proved cool under fire.

"General, I'm sorry," he replied, "but we've already moved in."

"Well, you may get moved out again, too," fumed the General, who then bowed to the realities. "Until you hear from the British, you can go ahead and stay there." The 91st stayed there for the rest of the war. Bassingbourn became known as a showcase for VIP visitors. Well it should have, with its fine mess halls, its comfortable rooms, its workout facilities and ballfields and its comfortable bars for officers and enlisted men. Reporters, visiting politicians, visiting generals—everyone, it seemed, wanted to come to Bassingbourn.

Normally after a mission, I looked forward to savoring Bassingbourn's delights to the maximum, especially the delights associated with good whiskey and good comrades, but not on this day. On this afternoon of May 15, 1943, I closed the door to my quarters and stretched out on my bed and began to daydream.

How did I get here? How did my life ever take me from a carefree, even fabulous Southern boyhood in the Blue Ridge Mountains, a life with servants and fast touring cars and beautiful girls and adventures inside what was perhaps the most sumptuous mansion in the United

States, to this reckoning, this point in which one upcoming airplane ride could change my whole life, or end my life?

Bob Morgan? I kept asking myself, all that long afternoon and evening and into the night—Bob Morgan, who are you anyhow? And just what do you think you're doing flying a B-17 bomber in the middle of World War II?

CHAPTER

2

The kind of war I fought—several miles above the surface of the Earth—could scarcely have been dreamed of by the America that I was born into. I came along even before such science-fiction heroes as Buck Rogers and Flash Gordon were invented to wage their comic-strip battles in the stars. The world was moving pretty fast in that direction by the time I arrived.

I was born in Asheville, North Carolina, on July 31, 1918, the first true Southerner of my family line. I was the third child, behind my sister Peggy and my brother David, but the first to be born south of the Mason-Dixon line. My father, a businessman named David Morgan Sr., had just moved his family down there from Chicago to take a job as manager of a furniture manufacturing plant called Carolina Wood Products, on the outskirts of the city in a little community named Woodfin.

Big things were happening in the world far from where I made my appearance. In France, the month-long Battle of the Marne had reached its halfway point, that legendary counterattack by a quarter of a million United States doughboys that drove the German army back to the Vesle river and turned the tide in favor of the Allies in World War I. The Meuse-Argonne lay just ahead, in the fall, with 1.2 million American troops, the largest assault force in American army history to that time, smashing the Germans all along the Hindenburg Line and forcing the Armistice of November 11 that would conclude their war and set the conditions for mine.

Through my early years, I knew only peace—peace, and a kind of wonder. The terrain of my boyhood was probably as close to a time-less mythical kingdom as any you could find in America. I grew up in a gracious and proud old Southern town with narrow, oddly jut-ting streets, surrounded by the majestic Blue Ridge Mountains, the tallest range east of the Rockies. Mount Mitchell, the crowning spire, is more than 6,000 feet high. One of those mountains, which slopes right down on the edge of town, is named Beaucatcher, and you can see why. In the springtime it fairly drips with dogwood and forsythia and azalea blossoms. Local legend has it that a belle of the mid-nineteenth century, one Charlotte Kerry, used its paths for so many strolls with her suitors that a relative dubbed the mountain "Charlotte's beaucatcher."

Charlotte's ghost is supposed to be up there too, but I never per-sonally came across her.

My boyhood kingdom even had its palace, inhabited by royalty. The palace, a great limestone chateau built into the vast forested wilderness south of Asheville, was the largest residential house on the American continent. My family, and my mother Mabel espe-cially, enjoyed the radiance that emanated from its ballrooms and terraces for many carefree years. Eventually, though, the estate came to symbolize for me the greatest loss, and the abiding sorrow, of my long life.

I spent my earliest years in a house my father built in 1919 on the opposite side of town, the northern edge, on Sunset Parkway, a fash-ionable neighborhood of leafy sloping lawns. That house stands yet today, 4,000 square feet, still graceful behind its shutters after more than three-quarters of a century. It is a happy reminder of Dad's value to the company. Carolina Wood Products manufactured furni-ture, and also contracted to put up residential houses. Being allowed to build one of his own was one of my father's perks.

It was a fine time and place to be a boy. America was booming and my father was a success and we lived well. We had a manservant and woman servant and a cook, and a man who waited on our table and cleaned the house and did the yard work. All sorts of wonders lay within walking distance. The French Broad River, for instance, lazy and curving, drifted along not too far from the house. It carried small boats under the willow trees in the warm months—some commercial, some occupied by men in straw hats and ladies with parasols. Running right alongside the river was the railroad track. It brought trains through Asheville from the east from cities like Greensboro, and even beyond Greensboro, though we could hardly imagine it—all the way from New York City, headed for Knoxville and the great Southern metropolises. I used to wonder if I'd ever make it as far away from home as Knoxville.

The first incident that I can remember happened when I was four or five years old, and it will give you some idea of what times were like then. I overheard my mother and daddy talking about a stranger that had come to the house that day. A stranger to me, that is; he wasn't a stranger to them. They didn't know I was listening when dad said to mother, "He's probably the best bootlegger in town, and I trust him." This was during Prohibition in the early 1920s.

A few days after that the doorbell rang, and I ran downstairs as I usually did to open it and see who was there. It was this gentleman, the gentleman that Dad and Mother had been talking about. Just then Dad called to me, "Son, who's down there?" And I hollered back upstairs, "SAM, THE BOOTLEGGER, DAD!" Well, I got a little lecture on why I should try to not pass that around all over town.

The other thing I remember about that house was that it had a clothes chute that went from the upper levels down to the laundry room. At four or five years old, I could fit inside that chute. It was my favorite hiding place. If anybody would be looking for me, I'd probably be in that laundry chute. I could spend hours in there, just daydreaming and inching my way up and down. It's a wonder I never got stuck in there. Maybe it was those hours that prepared me years later for the narrow confines of a bomber's cockpit.

In 1927, when I was nine years old, Charles Lindbergh ushered in the era of long-range aircraft with his nonstop transatlantic flight from New York to Paris. In that same summer, while Babe Ruth was swatting sixty home runs for the Yankees, my family got drawn into that fantastical kingdom in the big forest southwest of Asheville.

That kingdom belonged to one of America's wealthiest families, the Vanderbilts. Cornelius Vanderbilt—"the Commodore"— amassed a legendary fortune in railroad acquisitions after the Civil War, established Vanderbilt University and founded a long line of philanthropists and social aristocrats who enriched America in many ways. In 1888 his grandson George Vanderbilt, captivated by a visit to the alpinelike wilderness of western North Carolina, decided to acquire a souvenir—he bought 125,000 acres of it. The following year droves of workers descended on Asheville to start work on George's idea of a summer getaway house, a 250-room mansion of imported Indiana limestone modeled on the sixteenth-century French Renaissance chateaux, containing thirty-five bedrooms, sixty-five fireplaces, three kitchens, a treasury of tapestries, furniture, paintings, and sculpture, and commanding a terrain of gardens and parks designed by the great Frederick Law Olmsted, who was best known for designing New York City's Central Park.

He named it Biltmore. Six years in the making and $3 million in total costs, it received its first guests on Christmas Eve 1895. President McKinley visited two years later. A year after that George Vanderbilt married Edith Dresser, and in 1900 the couple's only child and my mother's future great friend, Cornelia Vanderbilt, was born.

That astonishing friendship took hold after the Morgan family found itself right smack dab in the kingdom. George Vanderbilt died unexpectedly in 1914. A year later his widow sold most of the tremendous estate—some 87,000 acres—to the U.S. government, which used it as the base purchase for the half-million-acre Pisgah National Forest. A few years after that the family sold about 1,500 additional acres for residential development by friends of the family and by the local gentry. Known as Biltmore Forest, its lots went on the market around 1925. My father, whose fortunes were rising as fast as the celebrated stock market, was eighth in line for a tract of that real estate. He supervised the construction of a graceful, gabled white house with five bedrooms and large living and dining rooms that commanded a high swell of land on Vanderbilt Road. The house carried a big mortgage, but what did that matter? These were flush times. We moved there from Sunset Parkway when I was nine years old.

The next few years of my life were magical. Looking back across most of a century, I still find it hard to believe that a boy could be surrounded by so much enchantment and pure simple happiness, and that I was that boy. Thomas Wolfe found words for it. Wolfe was Asheville's famous native son who made great American literature out of that town and the people in it, some of whom my father knew. He beautifully captured the ache that this region could instill in a young fellow. "He believed himself at the centre of life," Wolfe wrote in *Look Homeward, Angel*; "he believed the mountains rimmed the heart of the world . . . And the air will be filled with warm-throated plum-dropping bird-notes. He was almost twelve . . ."

That about summed it up for me, though I can't match my fellow townsman for words. Still, when the time came, several years into the future, for me to put aside my hellraising habits and risk my life defending America, I drew on feelings very similar to what Mr. Wolfe expressed.

The new house and grounds alone were enough to satisfy my boyish explorer's appetite for weeks on end. I can still see and hear the player piano in the living room that my father bought for my mother. Mabel Morgan was an educated woman who loved music, and I learned to love it too, with her. We'd go through rolls and rolls of those perforated music sheets, devouring everything from popular tunes to the classics. Dad was never much interested in music, but I was fascinated.

Upstairs in my bedroom, I'd sit at night propped up by my pillows fiddling with the crystal radio set that my brother built for me. David was six years older, and we didn't have that much in common, but this radio set was one of the best gifts he ever gave me. I'd sit there far into the night with my headphones on, tuning the knobs, trying to pick up a ball game or a prizefight, maybe Jack Dempsey vs. Gene Tunney.

The new house needed two servants to cook and keep it up, and they lived glamorously, in my estimation, in quarters directly over our garage. Inside that garage were two shiny black Packards. We even had a horse barn, complete with horse. My sister Peggy made good use of that horse. She swung into the spirit of our new upper-crust neighborhood by taking up polo, which scared our dad half to death. I guess he hadn't counted on the children adapting to the good life quite *that* quickly! He didn't care much for horses in general—he seemed to prefer Packards—but he took it a little better when Peggy moved over to straight-out show riding and brought home a good supply of blue ribbons for her bedroom walls.

My own tastes in recreation were a lot less fancy. Just below our house stretched a big green recreation field where my new friends and I soaked up countless hours playing ball—baseball in the summer, football in autumn. Even more than ballplaying, we liked to ride our bicycles. There wasn't much car traffic on those rhododendron-bordered streets in those days, and we could race along the winding macadam pavement as fast as we pleased. If we were feeling brave we'd pedal all the way up into Asheville itself, to see a western at the movie house. Or we'd descend on the police station right there in Biltmore Forest. We were knocked over by those big old boys in their uniforms and shiny belts and pistols—they seemed real to us in a way the tuxedoed men at the country club did not. Sometimes the officers would let us ride around in their squad cars for a little while, and even take us with them to their favorite coffee and breakfast spot, the Hot Shot, down by the railroad tracks—a place I still stop in several times a year to this day.

I decided right then that the policeman's life was going to be the life for me.

Often we kids were content to stay in the Forest. We were happy to prop our bikes against a tree when we got tired of cycling and slip inside those dense fragrant woodlands to scout for grazing stags along the deer parks, or marvel at the daffodils and tulips and roses that brightened the flower beds of the Biltmore Estate's well-tended gardens, or loaf beside the well-stocked bass pond and lagoon, looking for the quiver of fish and enjoying the reflected beauty of the surrounding woods, always with the spires of Biltmore within our sights.

My best friend of all was Eddie Nash. He was my bicycling buddy as a boy, and we dated girls together as young men. How Eddie came to live in the Forest is one of those stories that I think could only have happened in the South in the sweet long ago. A wealthy couple, the Ellises, were neighbors of ours. Mrs. Ellis traveled to Madison, Virginia, one summer, to visit relatives, and encountered Eddie there. He was a small boy from a poor family, but sharp and engaging. Mrs. Ellis was so taken with Eddie that she persuaded his parents to let her bring him home with her to Biltmore Forest and rear him without formally adopting him. She took very good care of him, put him in a good school. He was just a great kid. I felt so close to him that for years, I incorporated his first name into my own. I called myself Robert Edward Knight Morgan.

I was always glad that Mrs. Ellis brought Eddie home. It's not often you can have a best friend delivered that way. As I think back on it, the way she just *selected* him was a clue to just how exclusive a world it was that we Morgans had inserted ourselves into. One of my other new friends, a boy named Baxter Taylor, had a pony named Bubbles. That should give you some idea. Baxter is still around Asheville as I write this, a retired successful road contractor.

Another sign of our rarified status was the way our mothers dressed us. I'm talking about knickers. Knickers, and shorts, and wide, fluffy collars. You wouldn't call it lace, exactly, but it was that kind of idea. I remember being very uncomfortable in those clothes. They were just too fancy. Let me be frank—I thought they were a little sissy. That's why, to this day, I resent people calling me Bobby. It reminds me of those damn fluffy collars.

If anything, I was a little—what would you call it?—romantically precocious for my age. I've had a lot of romances in my life, and the first one happened when I entered my new school, the Newton School, in third grade. I fell in love with my third grade teacher. She made an instant impression on me. She had a very nice figure, for one thing. I forget now what the other things were. The romance was quite serious, even though it was one-sided. I began to realize this when she got married that fall to a man named Mr. McKay, who ran a dry cleaning establishment. I was a good sport about it. I sent my clothes to his cleaners for years and years before the war, and even after the war. Anyway, Mrs. McKay was my first love, and she was a wonderful teacher besides. Maybe that was the other thing.

I felt a love of a far more rarified sort for my mother. Everybody was fond of Mabel Morgan. She had a way of savoring the good things in life, the good and beautiful things, and I learned a lot from just being around her. And she was fun, too. She liked to wear big dramatic hats with wide brims, and she loved music and parties and organizing scavenger hunts, and she smoked Camels with a cigarette holder. I remember hearing people call our place the House of Camels, and not being able to figure that out until Mother explained that it was a scavenger-hunt clue.

One of the best places where we spent time together was in the little garden that Mother kept behind our house. Only about a quarter-acre in size, it was filled with brilliant color all spring and summer long, and into the fall— irises, roses, tulips, poseys, all bordered with honeysuckle that gave off that heavy sweet aroma. There were vegetables, too—tomatoes, carrots, beans, beets. My mother tended all of these, and I was her helper.

She talked to me while we were working in the garden. She'd tell me stories about the fantastic places the two of us would visit together someday. Spain, England, Germany, France. I couldn't wait to grow up and make those journeys with her. The ironic thing, I guess, is that I eventually did get to most of those places and some others besides, but not with Mabel along.

It wasn't long before my mother's vivacious charm got her connected to the very highest circle of the Vanderbilt kingdom.

Biltmore Forest had a country club, and the Morgans were charter members. My father had changed jobs about the time we moved there, and had gone into business for himself. He and a group of his friends invested their money in a new plant that they called the Dimension Manufacturing Company. It sat out to the east of Asheville on the Swannanoa Valley near a little town called Black Mountain. Dad was the president of it. Dimension was to be a forward-thinking company, organized along Henry Ford's principles of mass production. Instead of making finished furniture, it would turn out furniture parts, to be assembled by the people who bought them. In those days the automobile industry used a lot of wood in making cars—floorboards and such—and one of Dad's customers was the Packard Motor Company of Detroit. Maybe that explained the makes of those shiny black cars in our garage. At any rate, the prospects looked good. Herbert Hoover was President, Dad was making the unheard of salary of $12,000 a year, and it seemed the most natural thing in the world—it seemed ordained in the stars—that we join the Biltmore Forest Country Club.

That is where my mother met Cornelia Vanderbilt. After all these years it still seems overwhelming when I think about it—my iris-tending mom with her piano-roll music and her Camel cigarettes, becoming best friends with a leading light of American society. Up close, it made a lot of sense. In 1924 Cornelia had married the Honorable John Francis Cecil, a rail-thin Englishman with an even thinner mustache and a fondness for tuxedos and a clipped accent that was about as upper-class British as it ever got. My sister Peggy was a flower-girl at the wedding. Lord Jack was a fine man and did much for the local community, but like most gentlemen of his era, he was quite fond of his evenings at the country club and a glass or two of bootleg champagne and whiskey. Cornelia, tall and elegant with fine dark hair, lived in a world of endless luxuries. But she began to pine for something simple, something money couldn't buy: a close friend. When she met up with my spunky mother—whose own husband, while he worshipped her, was a workaholic—all the class distinctions melted away. The two women became inseparable. And the great storybook adventure of Mabel Morgan's life commenced.

I remember the swanky dances on summer nights at that club, lit by Japanese lanterns and featuring crackerjack orchestras with glittering trombones, the dances that my mother and Cornelia presided over in their sculpted hats and strings of pearls and flapper dresses that were all the rage at that time. Sometimes the dances were so big they were held at a boxy old tobacco warehouse nearby, all festooned with lights and decorations. Sometimes they were held at the Estate itself. It was an awesome house. Edith Wharton and Henry James had visited there, although I personally could not have picked them out of a crowd. What I could appreciate, even as a shirttail boy, were the Entrance Hall with its high limestone arches, the Winter Garden with its huge central fountain sculpture of marble and bronze, and the Banquet Hall, the seat of all festivities under its 70-foot-high ceiling. And of course all the elegant costumed men and women swirling through those rooms, figures in a genteel version of America that was about to end more suddenly and painfully than any of them could realize.

I, meanwhile, was doing my best to ease into the suave mannerisms of the young country club squire, but for some reason I just never got it exactly right. While I was languorously learning to swim in the club pool, for instance, I nearly drowned. I never even made it to the languorous part. I'd started to ease myself down the steps into the shallow end of the pool—I was probably around nine or ten—and I slipped and fell in. I'd gone down twice when an attendant named Tom Foster happened to walk into the pool area from the locker room, and he reached down and fished me out with one big, strong black fist. I remember that incident very well. I guess that even back then, long before I started dodging flak and fighter planes, I was guarded by a special force.

They never talked about it around the house when it hit, not openly anyway. It was whispers, glances between the two of them, long silences at dinner where there had always been lively conversation. My brother and sister and I never officially learned what had happened. You couldn't not know, of course. Not even as a shirttail kid, you couldn't not know for very long. I knew it emotionally, if not in all the details, when my pal Baxter no longer had a pony named Bubbles. Or later, when the father of a pal of mine, a bank president, committed suicide.

Dad tried to keep his new business afloat after the stock market crashed in 1929, tried to keep our lives the same as they had been, but he never had a chance. The Depression struck the South especially hard, with all its textile mills that depended on a robust economy. Dad threw himself into the survival of Dimension for three agonizing years before the stockholders advised him that it was no use. The company shut down, but the plant and grounds still needed some security, so the stockholders hired my father to guard the facilities as a night watchman, for $50 a month.

We had to sell our house, of course. The crisis exposed our true financial state. We were not at all the landed gentry we'd been pretending to be. Dad's salary was a good one, but it was a salary, and we had been living on that paycheck of his, and now that it was gone, that huge mortgage we were floating was no longer an amusing abstraction.

Dad realized a little money out of the sale, but hardly enough to put us in another house, much less build one. As we waited for the closing, we had no idea where we were going to live next, or what we were going to do. Like millions of distraught Americans, we were suddenly facing oblivion.

Enter Cornelia Vanderbilt.

She called on my mother one day with an amazing invitation. "We have some empty property on the Estate," she told Mabel, "and we'd be very glad to let you live in one of our homes." We went to look at it and were charmed on the spot. It sat on top of a knoll with a beautiful view, not far from the Vanderbilt dairy farms. We moved in. Because we had no mortgage concerns we even got to keep one of the servants. We had some room over the garage which he could live in rent free, so it was practically a swap deal. His name was Alfonso Owens. Alfonso and I had great adventures together over many years. We hunted and fished together on the Estate. He taught me how to drive a car well before I was sixteen, and he and I remained friends until well after the war, when he came to work for my wife and me.

Why did Cornelia Vanderbilt come to our rescue? Human kindness, I'm sure, but it was also for the same reason she befriended my mother in the first place. She was lonely, walled off from Jack Cecil, isolated by her social class from most of the world—certainly from Asheville—and she needed a companion. Cornelia was traveling a lot then in Europe. She invited Mother to travel with her, at no personal expense. Mabel didn't have to think it over too hard. It was fine with Dad. It was sure fine with Peggy, who got to go along. Cornelia and Mabel would let Peggy sail with them on the Cunard Line, deliver her to Switzerland so she could get some schooling there, then travel in England and France for a few months, and pick up Peggy when they were ready to come home.

Thus my mother finally got to realize those fantasy travels to distant lands that she and I had talked about in her flower garden. Without me. I missed her.

Slowly, we Morgans recovered from catastrophe. After a while, Dad was even able to get Dimension Manufacturing started up again. He found his own rescuer, a good friend from Boston named Kent Smith, who'd been a schoolmate when they were kids. This friend put up some money, and Dad secured a loan from President Roosevelt's Reconstruction Finance Corporation, and the two of them got those furniture-making machines turning again.

The hardships we went through changed me for life, and not necessarily for the worse, either. As a little boy I'd thought it was great to live on the Biltmore Estate. But when we lost our money I could see that the really rich folks started to treat Dad in a different way. He'd never gone to college, he was never really in their income bracket, and now it started to show. I could see people look down their noses at him. I found I didn't care too much for that.

I started to see life in the Forest in a whole new light. I realized how much was just written all out for you. Go here and you swim two hours, play tennis for an hour, go back home, come back in the afternoon, swim a while longer, play some more tennis, eat a hamburger. I mean, it was monotonous.

On top of that, I started to realize for the first time what kind of reputation Biltmore Forest had with the rest of the city and county. The Depression really devastated Asheville. The city had just put up a big new City Hall and courthouse, and now it, and most of the people in it, were deep in debt. It was natural that they'd see the Biltmore Forest crowd as being a snobbish group of people, high and mighty, with our noses stuck up in the air.

I started to drift away from all that. I entered the David Millard Junior High School in the fall of 1931, and started to figure out who

I really was. I gravitated toward some of the other people who lived on the Estate—the everyday workers for the Vanderbilts and their families. I started making friends with the kids of those families. We did real things. We hunted, and fished, and hiked, and generally broke a sweat. And we had picnics. I turned into a champion picnic-thrower, and presided over some of the greatest picnics in the world. Everybody in Asheville became my friend because I could invite them onto Biltmore Estate for a picnic.

One of the greatest things about a picnic, you see, was that girls came to them. I was waking up to girls in those days. I had a lot of girlfriends, mainly because I could take them onto Biltmore Estate for picnics and—well, in those days we called it spooning.

Another sign of my new regular-guy attitude was my status as a junior-high-school crossing guard. Now here was an activity that my high-toned Biltmore friends would probably not be caught dead at, but I dived into it. Man, I really loved getting up every morning and putting on that spiffy white shoulder-band and badge they gave you, and standing out there directing traffic in front of school so the kids could get across the street. This was a step closer to that boyhood dream of mine, becoming a law-enforcement officer.

After junior high I found myself in Indianapolis, of all places. Dad thought it would be a good thing for me to test my wings outside the family household. He sent me up to Indiana in the fall of 1933 to live with his sister, my aunt Mary Wilson, and attend Short Ridge High School there. When I reported for classes at Short Ridge, the faculty took one look at my six-foot-three frame and, in effect, handed me a basketball along with my textbooks. The problem was that height alone didn't guarantee a fellow success in what was then, and still may be, the most basketball-happy state in America. I played some intramural ball, but left the varsity stardom to the guys who were born and bred for it.

I was homesick for North Carolina, and Dad relented. Thus it was that in the fall of 1934 I entered one of the most peaceful and beautiful and humane communites I've known in my long life.

After all these years I can still close my eyes and be walking the wooded trails and hailing my classmates at the Christ School, nestled in the mountains southeast of Asheville. Founded in 1900 as a mission school for poor children by the Episcopal Church, Christ School became a prep academy for boys after the spread of public education in the 1920s. It was, and still is, a wonderful place, a haven of scholastic rigor and sports and hard work and the instilling of civic and moral duty.

Here among those handsome sandstone buildings and playing fields and tillable fields I found the ideal outlet for my new restless energies. Every boy worked at Christ School. It could be washing dishes, serving at the dinning room table, cleaning classrooms, working the grounds, anything. The mentoring by the faculty was genrous, and the penalties for misbehaving were severe. If a boy broke the rules, he could look forward to receiving the Three C's. He was campused, he had to "crumb," which meant he had to wait tables at dinner and do dishes for 200, and he got a "claim." The claim was to a tree stump somewhere on the property. The guilty boy "owned" this claim until he finished digging it out with hand tools, such as a shovel, a pick, and an ax.

Did I rack up many "Three C's" at Christ School? Well, I helped build a football field with the many yards of dirt I freed from tree stumps. I even helped build a tennis court—one of several that got installed while I was there. I didn't mind that duty because I was an avid tennis player. The problem was that Christ School didn't have a tennis team. There were two or three other tennis players going to school besides me, though, and now we had some courts. And so we started a campaign with our headmaster to form a team.

Our headmaster didn't need much encouraging. David Harris— Mr. Dave, we called him—was a superb tennis player. He spearheaded the formation of a school tennis squad, and we acquitted ourselves pretty well. I was number three or four man, dueling my best friend Pete Little for that ranking. The highlight of our season was our victory over Asheville High School, which had been a tennis powerhouse for years. Mr. Dave threw us a victory party and let us drive his Model A Ford into town. He never let anybody drive that Model A Ford before us. I'll always remember that, along with many other highlights of my golden year at Christ School.

*　　*　　*

Only one regret clouded my days as I approached my mid-teens—I hardly ever saw my mother anymore. Mabel and my sister Peggy had opened up a dress shop in Washington, D.C., when they returned home from Europe. It was very fashionable, a custom shop in the ritzy heart of Connecticut Avenue, at M Street. They designed and made their clients' dresses and gowns right on the premises. And they were making money at it. Peggy lived there, and Mom spent most of her time there as well. Those great travels we'd imagined together in the garden got pushed back a little further.

I got shipped off in the fall of 1935 to Episcopal High School in Alexandria, Virginia. I hated to leave Christ School, but David, my older brother, had gone to Episcopal and was now enrolled at the University of North Carolina. So my mother and dad thought it would be a good place for me.

And it was. I was a pretty good student. I broke my arm playing football and gave that up. I still wasn't a very good basketball player. But my tennis skills earned me a place on the team. I even earned a letter my first year.

And then I absorbed the hardest blow of my life—harder than the Depression, harder than anything I would experience as a bomber pilot over Europe or Japan. I've not recovered from it yet. I don't imagine that I ever will.

I'd come down with tonsilitis in January of 1936, and had my tonsils removed across the Potomac in Washington. But while I was recovering in the hospital, something far worse was discovered in my mother—cancer of the thyroid.

She knew that there was no cure, and no hope for recovery. Mabel Morgan decided one day that she had to deal with her fate in her own way. She took the .410 shotgun that I'd used to hunt squirrels and rabbits with on the Biltmore Estate, and she turned it toward herself and pulled the trigger.

My father called me with the news. I went directly from the hospital in Washington to the funeral back home. They had a lovely service for her in Asheville, in the home of her close friends the

Thomas Raouls and their daughters Jane and Kathleen, but that didn't erase one iota of the pain.

I'll never know the full mystery of why my mother did what she did. It must have been the cancer. What else had she been feeling? She never complained outwardly about the plunge we took, never talked about how our going bust affected her relations with Cornelia, or whether it caused her great embarrassment. I'll never know. But I know this. I've had a lot of romances with women in my life, several marriages and several more affairs—more than my share of all these, I'll admit. The romance with the Memphis Belle, the real Memphis Belle, was only the most famous of quite a number. Sometimes people have wondered about it, about how I have always seemed to need a woman, quite often a new woman, to make my world complete.

The answer is really quite simple. The answer is Mabel Morgan. Mabel Morgan, who went on her ultimate journey without me. I guess I never stopped looking for the right companion after she went away.

CHAPTER

3

It was a good thing my tastes had taken a turn away from elite society and toward the company of "real" folks—an attitude that would serve me well in wartime with my redblooded *Memphis Belle* crew—because just before I went off to Episcopal High School in 1935, and several months before my mother's death, we Morgans got a reminder of how coldhearted could be the pretenders to wealth and power. We got bumped out of the house that Cornelia had provided us on the Estate, not by a Vanderbilt but by an ambitious attorney of the family.

Before Cornelia left on her Grand Tour of Europe with Mabel and Peggy in tow, she appointed a prominent local lawyer named Junius Adams and known to all and sundry by his Southern honorific, The Judge, as attorney for the Biltmore interests. One of The Judge's first important decisions was that he would move out of his mansion by the golf course in silk-stocking Biltmore Forest—he'd been a little jostled by the Depression, too—and onto the less pricey precincts of the Estate. Our house was the one that caught The Judge's eye. In the summer of 1935, when I was seventeen, we suddenly found ourselves in what had been the gardener's cottage, just on the other side of the wall from the lavish Biltmore gardens.

It was fairly primitive, in certain respects. There was no electricity and no central heating—we depended on fireplaces and kerosene and gas lamps. On the other hand, many Americans were routinely living that way in the 1930s. It had its cozy charm. With my brother David away at school, and mother and my sister gone so often, my dad and I didn't feel a bit cramped in this little four-bedroom jewel.

I dwell on this gardener's cottage partly because it was where the "new" Bob Morgan swam into focus in the years just prior to World War II. I went back to Episcopal High School in Washington after my mother's funeral in January of '36, but I was not destined to stay there very long. When I returned to Asheville and the cottage the following summer, I was not the same person at all.

I'd passed my courses, but I got into other mischief and problems at Episcopal. Something wild in me was stirring. The grief, I guess. I'd grown restless, and a little reckless. I needed outlets for these new energies and emotions, and Episcopal just wasn't the kind of place that was suited to them.

One outlet was good hard physical labor. My dad spotted this right away. He'd taken refuge in his work, too, after Mom died—he'd worshipped Mabel, just as I had. He put me to work, starting me out at the lumber yard. I got splinters in my hands unloading freight cars, stacking planks of wood for the factory. Before long I was working inside as an apprentice. I worked with machinists and got acquainted with the way cogs and cylinders and driveshafts operated. I got to know the equipment and I got to know the people who made the equipment run. We got along fine. I ate with the workmen, going to their houses for lunch. It was damn hard work, but it was good for me, like a dress rehearsal for bonding with my bomber crew.

It was also good for me because it took the edge off another outlet that I found I needed very badly, and one that Episcopal was never going to provide me. Women. Sex.

It wasn't just sex, but intimacy, closeness. Someone to help keep the ache of Mabel's death at bay. Then, and for the rest of my life, I would always need a girlfriend, or a wife. Somebody special. It was right there in the gardener's cottage where I first learned what that sort of thing was all about.

I mentioned those picnics I used to throw on the Estate. Well, before long, I graduated to parties at the cottage. With my brother and sister gone, and Dad himself pursuing an active social life outside the house, I could throw some parties that were pretty interesting, certainly by the standards of the genteel South in the 1930s.

One of the games my friends and I played at those parties was strip poker. It was ever so much more fun than Pin the Tail on the Donkey. I've been a lifelong poker player, killing a lot of time with it between missions over Europe and Japan. I guess those parties were where I learned to play so well—I'm a little on the modest side, you see.

It wasn't long before one of my friends introduced me to a girl named Lucille. Now, Lucille had had a lot of boyfriends. She was very good at dealing with boys, but she wasn't all that good at poker. To be honest about it, I was not exactly in the frame of mind to teach her the fine points of the game. I taught her what she needed to know about poker—enough to get her involved in our parties—and Lucille, after losing a number of hands and articles of clothing one night, took me upstairs to one of those little bedrooms and taught me the art of sex. I always considered that a fair swap.

Lucille was an interesting gal, but the fact is that I fell in love with every girl I went with that summer. At least I *thought* I was in love with them. I knew I wanted to get close, but not necessarily into bed with every one of them. There were other things to do in that leafy Carolina summer of 1936, when *San Francisco* with Clark Gable was playing at the local movie house and Jesse Owens was winning all those gold medals at Hitler's Olympics in Berlin and the Spanish Civil War was erupting across the Atlantic. In many ways, it was the last innocent summer of my life. Dad had bought a big Buick Century and he let me use it. Lucille was my main girlfriend. I didn't want her fooling around with any other guys—I didn't realize it till much later, but I had a real inferiority complex in those years—and I'd take her on wild rides around the Biltmore Estate in that Century, and we had a time. I was a helluva driver, I don't mind saying. Alfonso Owens taught me.

Then I started falling in love with other girls. One particular girl was Dorothy, who lived in Greenville, South Carolina. She came up to Asheville with her dad, a wealthy textile manufacturer, for the summer. I started dating Dorothy, and Eddie Nash started dating another girl from South Carolina, and when the summer ended and the girls went back to Greenville we were facing the end of some pretty good times.

But what the hell, I had the use of my daddy's big Buick Century, didn't I? What were fifty or sixty miles of curving two-lane highway and a few mountain passes? Eddie and I started wheeling that Century down to South Carolina pretty regularly. Sometimes we'd roar down and back on the same day. Sometimes we'd spend the night at their homes as guests of their family—all very up-and-up, mind you—and drive back early the next morning. Would you believe that a Buick Century could get up to 110 miles an hour on a mountain road in those days? That's what a highway patrolman told me one morning with his foot on my running board. If Dad hadn't been good friends with the sheriff in Asheville, I probably would have lost my license. I never had a wreck—all right, one small wreck—and Eddie and I didn't even have to find ourselves any new girlfriends. "Geographically undesirable" is not a worrisome concept when you are at the wheel of one of those babies. Hell, it was the B-17 of the highway.

Little did I know it, of course, but out in Seattle, just at that very time, the engineers and draftsmen at Boeing were working to turn out the real B-17, with its range well beyond the distance from Asheville to Greenville.

After my year at Christ School I was eligible for college. But I knew I wasn't ready—all that energy still needed burning. Dad said, "Fine, if you don't want to go to college, you come out here to Dimension Manufacturing Company and you work."

I worked, all right. I worked so hard that after a year, college was looking pretty good to me. I fortified myself with a year of "cram school" (as we called it then) at the Emerson Institute in Washington, living with my sister, who still managed the dress shop. Then, in the spring of 1938—the year that Nazi Germany devoured Czechoslovakia under that piece of failed appeasement called the Munich Pact—Bob Morgan was ready to become a college man.

But not before a little more fun in that Buick Century.

There was Dot Beattie, one of my favorite passengers, a stunning brunette from Greenville, South Carolina. She went off to Ashley Hall, a girls' prep school in Charleston, and so of course I went there too, often pushing 110 mph with my pal Eddie Nash riding shotgun—he was seeing a girl down there too. Eddie had his own car by then, as Mrs. Ellis had given him a green Dodge coupe. But mainly we cruised in the Century, me at the wheel, risking our necks at breakneck speeds. I recall one mad dash home from Greenville, trying to make it to our bedrooms before the sun was well up. Streaking through the little town of Flat Rock, we bore down on a fellow perched on his white picket fence, enjoying the peaceful dawn. He wasn't on that fence very long—the roar and blur of our car passing by scared him right off it!

Dot and I dated nearly a year. Then I met her roommate, who hailed from Rye, New York. That was the end of Dot Beattie and me, and the beginning of some hot train visits to Rye. Nice while it lasted.

Somehow, despite all my capacity for foolishness, I made valedictorian of my class at Emerson Institute. In the fall of 1938, I enrolled at the University of Pennsylvania, the Wharton School of Finance. Dad and my brother Dave were able to back me up financially—Dimension Manufacturing was Morgan Manufacturing now, with the two of them as owners along with a third financier—and it looked as though the lean years were behind us forever.

But money alone wasn't going to save me from myself. To say I was girl crazy would be like saying King Kong was a little taller than his peer group. Did I mention I'd gotten married in that summer of '38? Well, I had. Not Lucille, not Dot, not even Dot's roommate. No, it was a girl named Alice Lane. Alice was from New Jersey, but her folks had a summer residence in Asheville. That was not necessarily the best town to come to with a single daughter, as Alice's dad probably would have attested.

It was one of my famous picnics on the Estate that got Alice and me together. I'd gotten permission for the crowd to use the outdoor swimming pool at the Vanderbilt mansion just up the road from the cottage. Well, we didn't see too many Vanderbilts hanging around that day, so the notion took us to go skinny dipping.

I suppose that the home brew had something to do with that notion. I guess I have to pause now and tell you about the home brew. My dad used to make it. Bathtub gin, too, with his good buddy Dr. Ambler. Because of his friendship with Sheriff Lawrence Brown that I mentioned earlier, he also had a pretty good line on how to obtain the best corn liquor in western North Carolina. Whenever the sheriff would raid a still, why, he'd give Dad three or four gallons. Dad would get kegs and take charcoal from the furniture factory and put it in the kegs to age the whiskey. He'd have at least half a dozen of those kegs in our basement at the cottage. Well, I got into it—not to drink it, necessarily, but to sell to the caddies over at the golf course. They'd bring me empty batwings—small bottles—and I'd go and tap Dad's corn liquor and sell it for fifty cents. It took Dad a while to figure out what was going on. He kept saying, "You know, that stuff is evaporating down there more than I expected it to." He finally caught on.

Maybe it was the corn liquor, and maybe it was the skinny dipping, and maybe it was that old ache of mine, but I fell madly in love with Alice Lane in the summer of 1938. We decided, us two crazy kids, to run off and get married. All right, I decided it. I revved up the Century and we headed for Greenville, South Carolina, because you couldn't get married in North Carolina without a waiting period and a physical exam.

All the parents concerned were a little thunderstruck by this, but they decided to hope for the best. In the late summer Alice went off to school in Bennington, Vermont, and I began classes at Wharton. We rented an apartment in Philadelphia and alternated visiting one another on weekends. It was a beautiful autumn in Vermont and Pennsylvania, but it soon became clear that all the fall foliage in the world wasn't going to save us. We were strangers to one another. Alice's family came and got her and took her back to Florida and she got an annulment. That was the end of Marriage Number 1.

After that, I went into a kind of aimless drift. I worked at Morgan Manufacturing the next summer, 1939, but I played as much as I could. Quite a year, 1939, the year war broke out in Europe and *Gone With the Wind* with Clark Gable and Vivien Leigh premiered in America. I would have something to do with that war, of course, but the damndest thing was that I'd have something to do with *Gone With the Wind,* too, in a weird kind of way.

I dated Vivien Leigh. All right, not the movie star Vivien Leigh, but an Asheville girl who was chosen to represent Vivien Leigh in a local beauty contest, one of hundreds held around the country to help promote the movie.

The thing was that this girl's name was Vivien Leigh too. She was a cashier at the S&W Cafeteria, the largest cafeteria in Asheville. She was a beautiful brunette like her namesake. I fell madly in love with this Vivien. We dated the whole summer and things got a little hotter, let me tell you, than they did between Scarlett O'Hara and Ashley Wilkes. Just a few years into the future, as an Army Air Force pilot based in England, I would spend some pretty wild weekends in London with a certain waistgunner by the name of Clark Gable. And this time, I *am* talking about the movie star. Isn't life funny?

In the fall I returned to the Wharton School of Finance, but I couldn't quit playing; it was almost a compulsion. I was twenty-one, and it felt as though I'd already lived a lifetime. I'd lost a lot, and the years ahead seemed covered up in some kind of mist. The year 1939 passed in a blur. I spent a lot of money. I overdrew my checking account. Back home, my dad and my brother were steaming.

On September 1, the German Blitzkreig swept through Poland, and two days later Britain and France declared war. In the Pacific, the Japanese Imperial Navy was amassing its nonpareil force of ten aircraft carriers and twelve battleships. Its Imperial Army was still savoring its rape of Nanking, China, at a cost of 300,000 civilian lives. As if things weren't complicated enough, I started dating a young Quaker girl from the Philadelphia Main Line, still in her teens. Judy was her name. Before you could say, "Don't do it, Bob!" I'd put an engagement ring on her finger.

That was all Dad and Dave needed to hear. In January 1940 they took me out of school and shipped me off to Cleveland, Ohio, where I trained with the Addressograph Multigraph Corporation, of all things, to become a service and sales representative for their office printing machines.

I was a long way from my Quaker fiancée. A long way from the Biltmore Estate. A long way from Eddie. A long way from everything.

I got to go home exactly once, for my brother's wedding. David at least knew how to do it right. His bride, a beautiful dark-haired woman named Dolly Obolensky, was a princess from a White Russian royal family. Dolly, as warmhearted and artistically talented as she was stunning, bore David two children, and endeared herself deeply to the Morgan family until her death only a few years ago.

Just when I thought Cleveland was the place Southern boys got sent to atone for their sins, Addressograph Multigraph shipped me back down to Dixie. They gave me a territory in western Virginia. I moved to Roanoke, still supposedly engaged to Judy. Would it surprise you to learn that I met a girl in Roanoke? She worked at a bank, and I met her while I was depositing some money. My dad would have liked *that* story! Once again I was living the only life I'd cared about since boyhood—a girl, well, a couple of girls—some money, some good times. If only I'd had that Buick Century, the world would have been perfect.

But the world wasn't perfect, of course. Far from it. The world in 1940 was falling apart. The United States clung to neutrality as the Axis Powers spread destruction across two world fronts, but almost no one believed it would last. In Europe, Denmark and Norway fell to Hitler's armies, then Belgium, Luxembourg, the Netherlands and France. In May we read the horrible accounts of the evacuation of a defeated British army at Dunkirk. Less than two weeks later the Germans marched into Paris—Paris, where Mabel and Peggy and Cornelia had viewed the cathedrals and museums! Hitler made his own grand tour on June 23, his bantam chest thrust out as he stood in his open limousine. Two weeks after that, the Battle of Britain commenced, along with the Luftwaffe's nighttime bombing of London. A new phrase entered people's awed conversation.

Air raid. And Air Corps, another term no one had used much before. But in 1940, as newsreels at the movies showed sleek new experimental craft wheeling out from the hangars at Boeing and Lockheed, the tradition-bound United States Army and Navy wrestled behind the scenes with the insistent ghost of Billy Mitchell. "Air power!" that ghost raged, and "air offensive!" and "strategic bombing!" Gradually, grudgingly, then in a fury of mobilization, America's military planes hit the mass-production lines.

Not even the advent, in May, of women's nylon stockings as a substitute for silk—the good researchers at DuPont, bless 'em, had been experimenting with something a little more fun than turrets and rudders—could distract the country for very long. Everyone seemed to feel it. America was going to be in this war.

I sure felt it. I'd done pretty well in history at Emerson and the U. of Pennsylvania, I could read a map, and I could spot the inevitability as well as anybody.

Where was Bob Morgan going to be? That was the question I suddenly could not stop asking myself. I really didn't want to be in the Navy—I didn't like ships. Skinny-dipping aside, I couldn't swim all that well. I didn't think from the stories I read that I wanted to be in the infantry and crawl around on the ground while people were shooting at me.

That left one place to be. Up in the air.

I'd kept scrapbooks on airplanes like most boys of that time. I cut and pasted the newspaper clippings of Charles Lindbergh's transatlantic solo flight in May 1927 and the explosion of the passenger zeppelin *Hindenburg* at Lakehurst, New Jersey, ten years later. I had even been in a plane one time, a DC-3 flight from Philadelphia to Washington when I was at the University. Dad had arranged it as a birthday present. We met for dinner in Washington and I felt very up-to-date about it all. But I didn't come down the gangplank saying, Boy, this is what I want to do for the rest of my life—fly airplanes. I just wasn't one of those guys who hung around airports, like a lot of the great pilots did.

In late November 1940, just after Franklin Roosevelt was reelected President for an unprecedented third term, I took the big step. I applied to the Army Air Corps.

They ordered me to report to Langley Field in Norfolk for my physical. Here the first example of Robert Morgan's famous luck showed up.

One of the ironclad rules was that a pilot had to have 20/20 vision. There was no allowing for glasses to make a correction. My left eye, as it turned out, was not up to Army Air Corps standards.

I could almost smell the bad news the minute the flight surgeon walked into the waiting room. "Morgan," he said, "you didn't pass." He looked at me and I looked at him. In fact I gave him the most soulful look I could muster. There was a silence. "Morgan," the surgeon said, "your left eye just doesn't quite reach 20/20." Now I really let my face drop. There was another awkward silence. Then the surgeon cleared his throat and said, "Morgan, wait here a minute or two and I'll be back." He switched off the lights when he reentered the room. "Here's an ice bag. Put this ice bag against your eye and hold it until I come back. Maybe it will stimulate your optic nerve." He disappeared again and came back in about, oh, what seemed like a week. He said, "Let's check your eye again." He told me to wipe my eye gently with a towel, took me over to the equipment, set it to the 20/20 lines and said, "Can you read that 20/20 line?" I got every letter right. The surgeon said, "You passed." He grinned from ear to ear. I grinned from ear to ear. We both stood there grinning from ear to ear. It was clear that he wanted me to pass, because in giving me that ice pack, he had done everything short of fudging the results to get me through the exam.

And it was clear that I wanted to pass, because when he left that room, I could not help sauntering over to that 20/20 chart and doing a little on-the-spot memorization.

The surgeon took my hand and said, "Good luck to you, Morgan."

He didn't nearly know what he was saying, did he? I needed that luck he wished me and lots more.

Suddenly I couldn't think about anything else except the Army Air Corps and flying a plane. I went roaring back to Roanoke barely touching the ground. I hadn't yet told my boss in Richmond yet that I'd applied. And it wasn't a sure thing yet—they'd told me at Langley that I would hear from them when they had a vacancy.

Applied. Vacancy. Those words tell you a little about how different things were there at the dawn of the Second World War.

I tried to concentrate on my sales job, but already that was seeming like ancient history in another world. I rounded up books at the library and read everything I could about aviation, all the while waiting for that phone to ring. The recruiters at Langley had explained to me that with so many applicants and so few training fields available, things were backed up. They were building new fields and grabbing instructor pilots out of the civilian flying sector, but it could be a few months before they called me up.

I started to put my life in order. My first priority was to call Dad and tell him what I was doing. His words gave me a funny twinge of affection mixed with sadness. "Son," he said, "if that's what you want to do, well, more power to you, and congratulations for passing." My father and I had never been very close. I looked up to him, but the poor man was always working, it seemed. He never had time for sports or hunting and fishing. And of course as I'd grown older I'd nearly driven him crazy. But now, hearing those words of his on the phone, I realized how much he loved me. I made up my mind right then and there that whatever I'd face in this war that was bearing down on the world, I would do my best to be a credit to David Morgan.

Then I called Judy, my fiancée in Pennsylvania. The minute I told her, there was a long silence at her end of the phone line. Finally she said, "Bob, this means our engagement is broken."

I didn't understand. "Just because I'm going into the military, which I think is the honorable thing to do?"

She said, "It's not a case of whether it's an honorable thing to do, Bob. I'm a Quaker, and we don't believe in participation in military combat."

Well, damn. That was news to me. I'd never bothered to find out all about that Quaker stuff, but I was about to. I got a really concentrated thirty-second lesson about their beliefs in nonviolence. When Judy had finished, I thought, well, that's all right. I don't feel the same way, but I've sure got nothing against them. So, I said, "Well, can we still write?"

Judy was tactful about it, I'll give her credit for that. She said, very gently, "Bob, I think it's better not to do it while you're going to be doing your job. We'll keep in touch until you go in the military, and then gradually we'll break it off."

That hit me hard, right in the solar plexus—"break it off" was never anything I wanted to hear from a woman, given that old ache of mine—but instead of pleading with her I turned stubborn. I thought to myself, it's broken off now. No ifs, ands, or buts about it. And that was the end of that love affair.

Home for Thanksgiving and then Christmas. A curious kind of mood had gripped everybody I knew, gripped the whole town, probably even the nation. Folks were laughing a little too hard, wrapping their presents a little too brightly, straining to be festive. Everyone was trying to pretend that romance and good times would go on forever—we slow-danced to "Moonlight Serenade" by the Glenn Miller Orchestra on the radio, we laughed at Walt Disney's *Pinocchio* and *Fantasia* at the movies—but somehow we couldn't help notice that Charlie Chaplin had done *The Great Dictator,* and Alfred Hitchcock had directed *Foreign Correspondent.* And the newsreels left no doubt as to where we were headed.

I still hadn't heard from the Army Air Corps. I was getting itchy. Finally, as the first days of the fateful New Year dawned, it hit me that I had a special ally I could call on to get things moving—my dad. Dad may have been a Chicagoan by birth, but he was getting the hang of the "good ol' boy" connections in the South, and the way they worked. Dad's friendships didn't stop with the local sheriff—he had not lived all these years on the Vanderbilt grounds for nothing.

One of his good friends was North Carolina Senator Bob Reynolds. Bob was an Asheville native and owned a lot of land in the mountains around town. He was also, conveniently enough, the secretary of President Roosevelt's Military Affairs Committee. If anybody could do something to get me moving toward that Army Air Corps commission, it would be Senator Bob.

Sure enough, one phone call was all it took. In February 1941 I received my orders to report to the base at Camden, South Carolina, for primary cadet training.

This was the only time in my entire military career that I used political influence of any kind.

I was moving toward my destiny at last. And somewhere in the assembly labyrinths of the Boeing Company in Seattle, an airplane would soon materialize to take me there.

CHAPTER
4

I can still remember that sunny spring day in South Carolina when I eased the trusty old Model A Ford coupe I'd been driving across the threshold toward my part of World War II.

That sunlit training field at Camden sure didn't look very warlike. No reason it should have. America wasn't at war with anybody yet. On that first day of May in 1941, it seemed more like a fairground than anything else—no walls, no barbed wire, no security gate, no military police. Just a beautiful expanse of old-fashioned green pasture under blue skies with these bright yellow biplanes used for primary training all lined up on the ground—PT-17s—the Stearman plane, the one I'd soon learn to fly in.

Camden was only about three hours south of Asheville, so it hardly felt as if I were leaving one life behind and entering another when I rolled in around early afternoon. It felt more like a new early-summer adventure. I couldn't take my eyes off those trim little planes with their fat yellow noses pointed in the air, all gleaming in the sun and waiting to be taken aloft by my class of Army Air Corps cadets.

I wanted to jump into one right then and there, but instead I parked the Model A and walked inside the small building that served as headquarters. Hardly any military people were in sight. Just a few boys like me, hair slicked and parted down the middle, hands shoved in their pockets, wandering around wide-eyed, trying to figure out what to do next. Teenagers, most of them. At twenty-three, I was already one of the old guys. It almost felt like checking into summer camp, with me as the Eagle Scout in charge of arts and crafts.

Things weren't quite so festive, of course, in other parts of the world. England had survived the Battle of Britain only to endure waves of savage bombing raids from Hitler's enraged Luftwaffe. German U-boats were chewing up freighters and merchant-marine ships in the North Atlantic. Yugoslavia and Greece were choked with invading Nazi divisions that had poured in to establish the Axis Power's "Balkan springboard." But we had almost no sense of that. America was weeks away from President Roosevelt's "Unlimited National Emergency speech," and seven months from Pearl Harbor. Here in South Carolina it was as peaceful as a garden party.

I signed in and found a young lieutenant who told me where my barracks were and which bunk was mine. There were no specially built Army quarters, just a lowslung building that housed a long line of iron-framed cots covered with thick green woolen blankets. This would be my home for the next two and a half months.

The lieutenant's name was Tom Bonner. He was the first officer I met in my military career. I was interested to learn that although the lieutenant was a qualified flier, he would not be going up with us himself. Instead, he would check us new fellows off for appointments with one or another of the civilian instructors at Camden Field. Hence his handle—"check pilot." I was green, but even I was struck by the fact that already there was a shortage of military officers qualified to work with cadets during the primary and basic phases of our training. Things must be getting serious in a hurry, I figured, if this was the case.

I made my bunk, unloaded my suitcase and started to shake hands with the other boys who were drifting in. At mess that evening, I was surprised to discover how many of them had flying experience. Some had already soloed, and a few had logged forty or fifty hours in small craft such as Piper Cubs. Maybe I was among the oldest in years, but already I wondered whether I could ever catch up to these cocky young bucks in the ability to handle an airplane.

I also picked up on an air of excited expectation. Rumor travels fast in the military—that was my first lesson, I suppose—and I quickly learned why everybody seemed so on edge. The lawn-party atmosphere was about to end. The Army wasn't wasting any time with us. Tomorrow I'd start to know whether I was cut out for this. Tomorrow, we would all be in the air.

I slept restlessly that night. Flight-thoughts kept going through my head. I pitched and tossed, woke up early and slipped into my new Army-issue khaki fatigues. Arriving at the mess hall before it opened, I found a few other nighthawks like myself who'd lain awake waiting for dawn. We milled around for a while and finally found somebody who gave us a little breakfast. And then—it was another flawless, sun-drenched day in South Carolina—we hustled ourselves over to the part of the grounds where we'd been ordered to report to the Commandant of Cadets. Our careers as pilots were under way.

The Commandant, Major Huglin, gave us a basic pep talk, telling us how lucky we were to be chosen as candidates for Army Air Corps pilots. Then he warned us that if we didn't do exactly as the instructors told us, we would be "washed out." Washed out meant that we'd no longer be eligible for pilot training. We could become bombardiers, or navigators, maybe, but as far as our piloting hopes were concerned, we'd be through.

This sounded grim. The good news, though, was that we were going to receive very little military drill work in these first weeks. The emphasis would be on flying skills. That news suited me fine. I was not then, nor would I ever become, a spit-and-polish sort of guy. I wanted to fly airplanes as well as anybody in the world. The rest of it, the swagger-stick, hut-two-three-four stuff, they could lump, as far as I was concerned. Maybe I still had a little bit of Biltmore Forest in me. I saw myself as a gentleman flier, not a martinet.

My civilian instructor was a youngish fellow named Earl Friedell. Along with the three other boys assigned to his group, I reported to him by the nose of one of those yellow PT-17s out on the flight line. A nice spring breeze was blowing across the open field. Earl walked us around the airplane and told us about its components. I was listening, but I was mainly drinking in that little piece of aircraft. I could practically taste it. My eagerness increased when Earl took us up on a wing and let us look into the cockpit. It was an open cockpit, a two-seater. I was just about to plunk down into it when Earl said, "I'll take each of you up for an orientation flight today," and handed out the schedule for each of us. I was second on his list, so I had to fidget around on the ground, trying to control the pumping in my stomach, and watch the lucky first student climb into where I longed to be. Earl settled into the other cockpit, motioned for the rest of us to back off, and then cranked up the engine and slowly taxied out for the takeoff.

I realized right then that I'd just heard the sweetest sound I would ever know, the closeup cough, stutter, and roar of an airplane radial engine coming to life.

The other three of us had an hour to kill. We drifted back to the hangar and waited. We chatted a little, but mostly we watched all those yellow airplanes take off and disappear into the blue sky. Then we waited until we could see them coming back, one or two at a time, and landing. After about three or four weeks, it seemed, the hour was up. I walked as nonchalantly as I could out toward the plane as it taxied toward the refueling truck. I had the courtesy to wait until the other cadet was out before I climbed in the cockpit in front of my instructor.

Earl fired up the engine again, and we put on our headsets. I heard his amplified voice rasping in my ears. "Now, you just keep your feet off of the rudders," meaning the pedals controlling the rudders, "and keep your hands off of the stick. I'll tell you when I want you to touch them, but meantime, don't. You can watch the instruments. You can see the air speed and the altimeter and the needle and ball."

I got most of that. Air speed I could understand, and "altimeter" obviously had to do with how high off the ground we were. But the needle-and-ball deal had me buffaloed. Earl apparently could read my mind. "I'll explain to you later about the needle and ball," he squawked into my phones, and then we were bumping along the ground at a rate that would have done the Buick Century proud. Then we weren't bumping at all. I had the momentary sensation that I'd just stepped off a cliff, and then something invisible caught me and buoyed me up. Camden Field wasn't around me anymore, it was below me. We had taken off. What a thrill that was!

Was I scared? Nervous? I have to say, no. If I had any feelings at all, they were along the lines of, So *this* is what it's like to be where I belong. This was my true home. My briar patch. Whatever took me so many years to get here?

Earl pulled the stick backward and we climbed up slowly to 4,000 feet, nearly a mile above the earth. He said, "I'm going to just fly straight and level for a little bit so you can see what straight and level is. Look at that needle and ball and see what happens as I make a slight turn."

So that explained that mystery. I was starting to feel as though I'd have the hang of all this before lunch.

The next hour was like living inside a childhood dream. We were flying. Free. We soared all over the countryside. I was looking down at the ground, then looking up into the mirror at Earl. I wanted to memorize every minute of it. Was the military supposed to be this much fun?

Earl said, "Now, I'm going to do a little maneuvering, so be sure your seatbelt is strapped tight. Don't be concerned. We're going to do a few basic moves that will excite you a little bit. I'll explain them to you as we do 'em."

Sounded good to me. Then I heard Earl say, "First I'll do a slow roll. That means I'll bank to the left, turn the airplane upside down, and slowly come on through and right it up again. Don't be concerned when you're upside down. Nothing will happen."

Upside down? I hadn't figured on being upside down. Upside down was never in my scheme of things. But I didn't have much time to adapt to the idea. Earl just said, "Here we go!" and suddenly the horizon was spinning like the hands of a clock. I felt the blood rush to my head. I was upside down. I was upside down! I was *still* upside down! And then we rolled on through and came right backside up. Earl said, "I'll do another one." He did three or four, in fact, and by the time he did the fourth one, why, it was no more of a deal than taking a mountain curve on my way to a hot date in Greenville. What other tricks did this jaybird have to show me?

I soon found out. "Now," Earl said, "I'll do a snap roll."

"Snap roll?" I might have repeated.

"Snap roll," said Earl. "We go up, we go into a stall, and I snap the airplane under and over and we roll again, but it's a fast maneuver."

He did a snap roll. Believe me, it was everything he'd advertised, fast and topsy-turvy and then *over with*. And fun. I didn't mind it. I didn't even mind it when he said, "We'll do some basic stalls," and pulled the yellow nose up until I could see the airspeed drop, and drop, and drop until all of a sudden that nose whipped down. The airplane felt like it was going to head straight down and never change direction, but Earl casually leveled it out and then aimed the nose upward to repeat the stunt. He did it three or four times. Interesting, I remember thinking to myself along about the third one, in a detached and academic sort of way. Very interesting.

Earl took us to 7,000 feet and told me to get ready for a spin. He said, "First, I'll stall the airplane and then we'll go into a left-turn spin. The airplane will be spinning as it loses altitude." He yanked the airplane into a sharp ascent and I could feel it shudder and stall. The nose arced down and he started the spin. We whirled around and around I don't know how many times, the centrifugal force pressing in on me harder than any amusement-park Tilt-a-Whirl. As he pulled it out I glanced at the altimeter and saw that we had spun out about 3,000 feet.

"That was a maneuver you need to know because you'll get into spins and you'll need to know how to pull out of them," Earl's voice was droning at me through the phones. "I'll teach you all that later on. Right now we'll just fly around the countryside a little more and do your slow turns, your fast turns, your turns to the right and turns to the left." It took a beat or two for me to realize that my instructor was casually telling me that I was about to fly the plane. With a sense of awe, I let my feet slide onto the rudder pedals and my hands close, finally, around the stick.

"Remember, when you get ready to turn," said Earl, "as I told you on the ground, you push that left rudder to make a left turn. Just maneuver the left rudder slightly, and take the stick and turn it slightly. Push it to the left. Keep your nose straight and level. I know it's not easy. The plane will try to climb on you. But don't let it climb on you."

Well, it climbed on me. It climbed on me two or three times. Through the movements of my stick and pedals, I knew that Earl had regained control. "I'm doing this to help you," he said. "Just follow through with my maneuvers." I felt a little chastened, but I let him take the lead, and within minutes I'd got the hang of it. The next time I tried to make a left turn I did it pretty good. I lost a little altitude, but I managed mostly to keep it straight and level.

We did some right turns. Same movements in reverse. We did another left turn, then another right turn. This went on for fifteen or twenty more minutes, and by that time I was feeling as though I were guiding a pretty girl on a dance floor. It wasn't exactly complicated. Push the stick forward to go down, pull it back to come up. Push the rudder left to go left. Push the rudder right and it'll go right. Already I was thinking ahead to the more complicated maneuvers Earl had showed me—those snap rolls, slow rolls, and spins. How would I do when the time came for me to perform those? I have to admit that the thought made me a little bit woozy. But now my hour was about up; the fancy stuff would have to wait for another day. Earl dropped the PT-17 down gracefully and made a beautiful three-point landing on Camden Field. As we taxied, he asked me, "Did you notice how I let the airplane kind of float and stall out right till I reached the ground to get it three-point?"

"Yes," I said, but I really didn't have any idea what he was talking about. I figured he'd teach it to me later.

The fact was, beautiful three-point landings would never be my forte.

I jealously watched Earl take off with the next student—hell, the kid was sitting in *my* cockpit—and ambled back to the barracks with the guy who had landed ahead of me. Neither of us could stop talking about what we'd experienced. We must have gassed on about it for an hour and a half, nonstop. I learned that this guy, like so many of the others, had been up a number of times before. That knowledge didn't bother me anymore. I no longer cared how much experience any of these young recruits had. I'd been up there myself now. I'd tasted it. I knew beyond any possible doubt that they were the ones who'd better start measuring themselves against me, because piloting a military airplane was what this Southern boy had been born to do.

Over the next few days I learned that the prior experience my fellow cadets had gathered was essentially worthless anyway, if not worse than worthless. The Army Air Corps preferred recruits who had not learned to fly as civilians, so they could train them from scratch in the military way. "We have to untrain him," was what the instructors said about a cadet who had some flying time. Civilian fliers tended to pick up bad habits, from the military point of view. For instance, the Piper-Cub style of landing was to come in with the tail up, landing on the wheels only. The Air Corps insisted on the "three-point"—wheels and tail section touching the ground at the same instant. This provided extra stability and also drag, cutting down on taxiing length and the need to brake.

I had a big advantage there—it was all Greek to me. I just did what the instructor told me, and it came naturally.

The next few days floated by in a pleasant haze. In the mornings we'd sit in on some makeshift ground school classes, learning about the Army Air Corps, and in the afternoons we'd fly, or vice versa, depending on our assignments.

Earl expanded my limits a little bit each day. He was a good fellow, a slim blond-haired country boy without much education. Where he'd learned his own flying was a mystery to us. He sure didn't have a military background, but he understood the military way, and he was conscientious about teaching it right, and about "washing out" as few of the kids as possible.

With Bob Morgan, I regret to say, he had a student on his hands who was already getting a little too cocky for his own good. Flying came so naturally to me that by my third or fourth hour aloft I thought I knew it all. I don't mean that I was arrogant, exactly. It was more like being so caught up in the sheer bliss of it, the pure joy and fascination of being able to "walk around" up there in the sky, with the countryside below you looking vast and beautiful, yet somehow grayer, slower, more ordinary—so caught up in this that you couldn't help feeling almost like a god. If old Earl could have listened to the inside of my head during those early sessions he would have thought he was dealing with a crazy ten-year-old kid. "Gee whiz, this is *flying*," I kept yelling silently to myself. "I'm *something!* Boy, I'm going to be a pilot! *What* a pilot I'm going to be! I'm going to be a *good* pilot!"

Meanwhile, Earl was focused on more practical thoughts. As we ranged farther and farther from the familiar contours of Camden Field, he drew my attention to the nuances of the terrain below us. "I'm going to show you how to navigate off the ground, Morgan," he said through his intercom mike. "The landmarks. You've got to know where you've been, where you're going, how you'll get back to the field. You need to keep good contact with what headings you went out on so that you know what headings to come back on—the turns you made, the hills and rivers and towns you passed over, so that you can find yourself if you think you're getting lost."

He got me familiar with how to use a map and a compass. "You take a course east, Morgan," he'd order me. "Fly on that course and look at the landmarks as we go. Then when I tell you to make a turn, you make a turn. I may tell you thirty degrees on the compass, left, and I might tell you forty-five degrees on the right. I'm gonna get you disoriented. Then I'm going to say, okay, Morgan, take me back to the field."

If I needed a dose of humility, I was absorbing it now. Sometimes I got it right and sometimes I didn't. Sometimes I couldn't find Camden Field for anything. Earl was patient. He kept giving me tips on how to handle the art of flying off the ground. Gradually he gave me more time with the stick and the rudder.

It still amazes me how we packed all that expanding range of lore and technique into about five hours in the air. It still gives me goose-flesh to recall how, after we'd covered those five hours, I heard that casual voice of his setting me up for the biggest milestone yet.

"Now, it's about time you were getting ready to solo."

Mercifully, he took it by degrees. The first stage was learning to take off and land with Earl still onboard. The takeoffs were pretty simple. Setting it back down was something else. "Let's shoot some landings," Earl said. "I'll shoot them first and let you see what airspeed that I come in at. Get the feel of it. Keep your hands on the stick and your feet on the rudder. Don't control them, though. I'll do the controlling and that way you'll learn how it feels." We spent nearly an hour shooting the landings and takeoffs—or what you call a "go-around takeoff." He wouldn't come to a full stop. He'd just touch it to the ground, a good, solid three-point, and then he'd push the throttle forward and take off again for another go-around. As usual, I caught on pretty fast. After I'd followed him through about six or eight of those, he said, "All right, now you take over and bring her down and see if you can land it. I'm going to stay on the rudders and stick, so if I over-control you, don't fight me. If I see something that's not right, I'll talk you into guiding the plane through the landing."

I was thrilled. Five hours into my piloting career and I'm going to make a landing! I don't recall dwelling on the prospect that if I botched it, five hours would be the *sum total* of my flying career. We banked our wings, leveled off and came in on that first attempt of mine to put a heavy, fast-flying object back on Mother Earth, without putting it into Mother Earth. In my fast-developing flyboy cockiness I thought I'd nailed it pretty good, right up to the instant I touched down. But I kind of touched down too hard. And then I kind of pulled back on the stick too quick. The result was that I basically bounced off Mother Earth—eight or ten feet back into the air. I wrestled for control, tried to keep cool, and managed to get both wheels down on the second try. I throttled back, glad for the chance to collect my wits. But Earl had other ideas. Before I knew it my head was snapping back, and we were at full power, taking off again.

I repeated the landing maneuver four or five times, with considerably more respect for the process than the first, before I heard Earl drawl, "You're getting the hang of it. Couple more today then we'll knock off till tomorrow."

The next day I made a few more landing runs, with Earl behind me, ready to pull me out of disaster. We did some more the day after that. I can't say I did well enough for Earl to give me any great pats on the back, but he did allow as how, "You're catching on. You're catching on." Then he said, "I think maybe tomorrow I can let you try to solo. Do you think you're ready?"

I tried to sound offhand about it. "Yeah, I think I'm ready." Earl fixed me with a stern squinting look. "Well, you got to be sure, now. You got to be confident because if you're not confident, I'm not going to be confident." I thought this over and barked, "Yes, Sir! I'm confident!" Then I went back to the barracks and spent a sleepless night.

Solo day dawned as clear and balmy as the rest. As I throttled the PT-17 into the air—a skill already as routine to me as riding my bicycle—Earl's voice informed me, "We're going to do two landings, and if you do those good with me in here, I'm going to get out and let you do it yourself." Whew boy, I thought. For the first time, I had a sensation of how lonely the sky could be. I got down to business and shot a couple of fairly decent landings. Not perfect—I bounced a little bit. Earl said, "All right, pull over here and make a full stop." I did. He climbed out of the rear cockpit and yelled up at me from the ground, "You go around and bring her in. If you shoot one and you feel good about it, go around and shoot another one. And if you feel good about it, go around and shoot another one. If you still feel good, go around and shoot another one. Shoot four landings, if you feel all right. If you don't feel all right, come to a full stop and pick me up again."

If I'm still breathing, I muttered under my breath, *I imagine I'll feel all right.* I clamped my teeth together, took off, made a nice wide loop, and back I came. In my sudden rush of anxiety, I had made up my mind about one thing. Come what may, I was not going to put that plane into a stall. For that reason I gave it a little more juice than he'd told me to during my descent. I landed hot—a style that was to become my trademark. The plane took a bounce of about two feet, but I quickly controlled it, kissed the ground for a few hundred feet, pushed the throttle and took off again.

I shot another landing. Another hot one, another bounce. On the third try I nailed it clean—a three-pointer with no bounce at all. Throttling up for another takeoff I could see my mentor waving at me from the ground, his hands up, his fingers in a "perfecto" circle. I imagined he was grinning. I sure was. I felt great. I looped around again and made another clean landing. This time I taxied over to where he was standing straddle-legged in the field. He hopped in and I gave him a lift back to the line of yellow Stearmans.

Like the booster of cadets he was, Earl let me savor my moment. "Morgan, you did pretty good. Pretty good. I think I can trust you with the airplane now. We'll still be doing dual work. You need a little work navigating back to the airport. We'll shoot some more landings and takeoffs and maneuvers. But you've soloed. I'll give you your solo. You earned it."

When I looked at Earl's log book, I realized that the total elapsed flying time since my first liftoff in the PT-17 and my first solo was six hours and ten minutes. I didn't know what all the other guys had done, but I did know that of the four in Earl's class, I was one of two who had soloed.

I rode Cloud Nine that night at the mess hall, talking shop like a veteran. Guys would ask me how it went and we'd talk characteristics of the airplane, and in that spring evening I had my first true sense of the brotherhood of pilots. At some point that night I got to a telephone and called my dad and told him that I'd taken the airplane up by myself. I could feel his genuine pride through the receiver. I only wished I'd been able to tell Mabel Morgan the news. I went to sleep that night with the notion that somehow, somewhere, she knew.

Through the next few weeks we cadets worked at getting our hours in. The goal was sixty hours, then on from Primary to Basic Training. While we glided around the peaceful air over South Carolina and looked for girls in Camden on our weekend leaves, the European war we would soon be joining grew evermore massive and brutal. One indication came on June 20, when the Army Air Corps was renamed the Army Air Forces.

Since early spring, the outmanned Royal Air Force had been gallantly lashing back at England's tormentors with nighttime bombing raids on German naval and industrial targets. The raids had only limited success, but they pioneered the massive Allied aerial offensives that my *Memphis Belle* crew and I were destined to join. On June 22, 1941, three million German troops surged into the Soviet Union to engage a waiting Soviet army of nearly six million soldiers and ten million reservists—and the Russian winter. The million-fold loss of life on both sides over the next three years of siege and attrition would amount to one of the most somber chapters in the annals of military history.

Somber was as far from the prevailing attitude at Camden Field, though, as the Russian steppes. How innocent we young cadets were of what lay ahead for us and the world! What a chasm of unawareness lay between our lighthearted cavortings and the awesome responsibilities that loomed.

Nobody was any more unsuspecting than yours truly. I skylarked through those early-summer training days as jaunty as you please. "Well, heck fire," was my attitude, "there's nothing to this. I'm the world's best pilot there is. I could show everybody how to do it."

It took Earl Friedell, that unassuming, courtly, self-educated country pilot, to refocus my hotshot attitude toward just exactly what all of these swell new airborne games we were enjoying were ultimately about.

He was waiting for me, hands on hips, when I came bobbing across the landing field one fine afternoon from yet another carefree solo jaunt. "Morgan," he called as I climbed out of the cockpit, "I need to talk to you but I don't have time right now. After mess hall tonight, would you meet me out behind the hangar and we can chat a little bit?" An edge in his voice told me that we were not going to be swapping the latest Little Moron jokes.

He looked even more grim when I rounded the corner of the hangar toward sunset. Gone was the genial, patient amateur flying instructor. In his place was a stony military figure—in attitude, if not in actual rank.

"Morgan!" Earl Friedell barked at me in a tone far more severe than his usual polite drawl. He paused and looked away, measuring his next words. "You know you've been doing a pretty good job. But you're not doing a *top flight* job. Your precision is not excellent, like I like to see it. It's not where you really need it to qualify for the Army Air Forces."

I felt the blood drain out of my face. Here I was, a combat flying legend in my own mind. Was my instructor telling me that I was about to *wash out* before I even got my commission? I stood there nonplussed as he continued to ream me out.

I was getting sloppy. That was the thrust of it. "Sloppy with your landings. And not just your landings, your turns." Earl Friedell's soft

Southern voice tightened. *"That won't go!* You're supposed to get better all the time, not get lax!" He paused again and took a step closer to me. Now his voice dropped low, but it didn't get any gentler.

"Let me tell you something, Morgan." He eyed me up and down. "Do you know how I learned to fly?"

I managed something like, "No, Sir, I don't."

He said, "Well, I used to hang around airports. The guys would take me up and fly me around. I didn't have any money to pay for any lessons, but they kind of took a liking to me. They'd let me handle the stick a little bit, use the rudders, and I got the idea of what they were doing."

Earl Friedell bit his lip a little as he seemed to debate with himself whether to tell me the next part. "After I'd been at the field awhile," he said finally, almost to himself, "I'd go home in the evening and sit in a chair on the back porch. And I'd practice my maneuvers with a broomstick. I moved it around like you would your joystick in the PT-17. That's the way I learned to fly, Morgan. By practicing with a broomstick."

There was another silence as I tried to figure out what to do with my eyes. Earl Friedell spoke again. "The Army Air Force is spending over $30,000 to train you to fly. I don't think you really appreciate what they're doing for you. I wish you would straighten up and fly right, son, or you may not be around here much longer."

A lot of things grew clear in my mind just then. In the minute or so that Earl Friedell had been chewing me out, I think I learned more about flying, and about myself, than the whole rest of that summer put together. I suddenly saw myself as this man saw me, this hard-scrabble workingman from the other end of the social scale. He probably saw a stuck-up, cocksure kid from Biltmore Forest who'd been handed everything in life and never had to struggle for anything—the very sort of fellow I'd vowed not to become.

I heard something else in Earl Friedell's lecture to me. I heard a deep respect for the value of *precision*, getting it not almost right, but exactly right, every damn time. Earl may never have realized it—and maybe he did—but it was a dedication to precision, perhaps more than any other single virtue, that ushered me and my crews safely through fifty-one high-risk bombing missions in both major theaters of World War II.

I said, "Yes, Sir," and I walked away. I walked away from the feckless boy I had been a few moments earlier. From then on I was a dedicated military professional. I followed every order, every piece of advice that Earl gave me for the rest of my time in his care. My maneuvers up in those South Carolina skies became so precise that you could have plotted them out with a slide rule.

After another ten hours Earl ambled up to me one day and remarked, as offhand as if he were telling me how the St. Louis Cardinals did the night before, "You got the message, I can see."

So did a lot of German and Japanese, Earl. I guarantee you that.

Midsummer approached, and with it, the end of our primary instruction phase as fledgling pilots. It was really the true end of our connection with the civilian life. Ahead, for those of us who hadn't washed out, was Bush Field in Augusta, Georgia, and our first taste of the authentic military universe—Basic Training.

At Camden, we'd been spared all that hard drilling and discipline, not because we were anything special, but because the Army wanted to sort out which of us were worth bothering with as bona fide pilots.

Among the many benefits of this informal system were the casual rules about leaving the base. Most of us managed to get into the town of Camden two, three, or four times a week, and the people there could not have been kinder to us. It was Southern hospitality, I guess, reinforced with the unspoken knowledge that most of us were soon going off to war, and that many of us would not be coming back. Families would invite us into their homes for meals, the women of the town would bring us boxes of homebaked cookies, pies, and cakes, and the local country club was quite hospitable to us.

Then there were the girls of the town, those ardent Camden girls of the spring of 1941, fresh and proper in their straw hats and gloves and pretty dresses, smiling respectfully at us young boys in our scratchy khaki issue and making us feel like heroes even though we hadn't yet done anything remotely heroic. Betty was one of those girls, dimpled, brunette Betty, the laughing daughter of a local businessman. She was my summer sweetheart. I'd see her as many times a week as I could, and we grew very close. I ate dinner at her family's house, we saw movies together, and we did what young couples did in those warm cricketsound evenings. In July, just before my class was to depart for Bush Field, the local country club threw a big party for us—Japanese lanterns, an orchestra, white-jacketed waiters holding trays of drinks—and Betty was my date. We danced and kissed that night away. I vowed to her that although I was leaving for Georgia the next morning, I would find a way to keep her in my life. I did, too, for a while.

I wasn't destined to depart Camden Field quite as smoothly as I'd thought—and in that glitch was born one of my most famous, or infamous, maverick traits as an Army Air Forces pilot.

I had my suitcases all packed with the rest of the cadets that morning, preparing to get into our cars and hit the road to Bush Field, when all of a sudden Lieutenant Bonner—the officer I'd met on my first day there—hurried into the barracks. "Morgan, I've got to talk to you," he said. I was already catching on to the fact that when I heard an officer call me Morgan it generally was not good news. Sure enough, it held true this time. "We made a mistake in your flying time," Lieutenant Bonner continued. "We sent it down to Georgia at sixty hours and twenty-four minutes, but there's about half an hour, maybe more, that we're not sure of now. It may even be a little lower than that. So, just to be on the safe side, would you go out there and log another thirty minutes in the air?"

What could I say? I headed out to the field, picked up the first airplane on the line, took off and flew around until I figured that the brass down in Georgia would be satisfied. I found myself banking and looping back and forth over the small city where I'd had so many good times with Betty. It was yet another one of those beautiful days that Camden, South Carolina, seemed to specialize in, and as I started back toward the field, I suppose I got carried away with a sense of nostalgia for it all.

As I dropped into my landing approach, I glanced down and saw all those gorgeous yellow PT-17s, lined up in rows exactly as they had been on the day I arrived. Beautiful lines. Beautiful planes. Beautiful field. A mischevious voice said in my ear: "Bob, why don't you just go down and take a real close pass at those planes?" And I answered back, "Why, I believe I will."

I didn't know then that the Army Air Forces already had a term for what I was about to do, or that it was not a term of endearment. The term was "buzzing." Pilots were not supposed to do any buzzing. It was noisy, it was terrifying to anyone on the ground, and if you miscalculated a little bit you could pulverize your airplane, yourself, and any houses, cars, cows, or people who happened to be at ground zero.

This first buzz of my career was not exactly a grass-cutter. I didn't get any lower than about 200 feet before I throttled up again, came on around, landed and taxied back to park the airplane. There in my parking space was Lieutenant Bonner, and the look on his face made Earl Friedell look like the Chamber of Commerce president by comparison.

"Morgan," he intoned before I had a chance to say hello, and I knew I was in for it. "Morgan, you have just broken one of the rules of the Army Air Forces, and in fact of the entire military aviation training program." I raised my eyebrows to indicate interest.

"You buzzed this field. We talked about that in ground school. I felt sure we'd covered that pretty thoroughly."

We did? I must have been wool-gathering. I tried to fast-talk my way out. "Well, I heard you mention it, Sir, but I didn't realize that I couldn't do that at the *field*. I thought, buzzing most places is bad, sure, but over the military field was—ah—all right. I didn't realize . . ."

"No, Morgan, it's not right anywhere and you know it. I should wash you out, but you got a good record here and we need good pilots like you. I'm going to let you go. I'm warning you, you'd better not do that again, because the next person might not be as lenient. They might very well kick you out of training or the whole Army Air Force."

"Yes, Sir," I said, and I behaved myself. For a while.

*   *   *

We arrived at Augusta on July 7, 1941. Bush Field turned out to be another expanse of green pastoral ground, trimmed with another long line of neatly arranged aircraft. These babies were BT-15s, a low-wing model used for Basic Training that, compared to the stubby sedans we'd learned to fly in, looked like something out of Flash Gordon. They had those sliding Plexiglas canopies like the ones combat pilots snapped shut just before takeoff in the newsreels. Once again I was seized with a visceral wish to dive into one of those delicious-looking numbers, flip the ignition that got its propeller churning into a satisfying roar, and slice back up above the clouds where I belonged.

My other quick impression was that things were distinctly more military around here. Bush, like Camden, used civilian instructors in its flight training and ground school. However, this place was thick with men in uniform—men in uniform who looked as though they meant it. It wasn't just the commissioned officers in their creased pants and spit-shined boots. Our bunch was also going to be taking instructions, and maybe a little more, from the cadet class just ahead of us. We could see a squadron of them on the parade ground as we filed into our barracks, crisply arrayed young men lined up in strict formation.

Uh-oh, Morgan, I told myself, things are going to be different here. Get ready for that yes-Sir, no-Sir, salute-and-hut-hut routine. It didn't grab me, to be honest with you. I was there to learn to fly and fight. If the Army Air Forces wanted some saluting, I figured I could manage some of that too.

In the barracks some of the upper class guys greeted us informally and showed us around. Later on the Commandant of Cadets delivered a welcoming lecture and emphasized the military protocol here for those of us who may not have noticed. We'd be supervised not by one personal instructor but by several. Half our time would be devoted to ground school and basic training, the other half to perfecting our aerial skills.

I woke up the next morning, and from then on, to a bugle playing reveille, and went to bed by taps at night. The instructors crammed our heads with indoctrination on the BT-15s, which were fast and sophisticated, with far more instruments than we'd been used to. We shot some takeoffs and landings, but very quickly we moved into a new and thrilling phase of piloting skills—instrument flying.

Instrument flying essentially meant flying blind. We couldn't see out of the cockpit—forget those maps and compasses and landmarks. We started out with a piece of simulating equipment called a link trainer, a kind of enclosed tank with instruments mounted on its walls. Then we progressed to actual flying, backed up with instructors. Some of the boys were overwhelmed by the instrument phase, especially the landing part, but I picked it up without any problems. Every new thing I learned, it seemed, came naturally to me, as if I'd learned it a long time ago, in some other life. I couldn't wait for the next challenge.

The next challenge turned out to be formation flying. Here was another skill that unnerved some of the boys, but one that I found exciting and fun. We started out with three airplanes in a cluster, one plane leading and the other two on the leader's wings. We kept it loose in those early sessions—we didn't have to overlap wings—but months later, flying thousand-mile bombing runs over heavily defended enemy terrain in France and Germany, maintaining defensive four-plane clusters so tight that mere inches separated our wingtips, we pilots had plenty cause to be grateful that formation flying got built into us so early and so well.

We did long-range local jaunts that were called cross-country flights. We learned meteorology in ground school and applied it to various weather systems we encountered. We had signal corps training to absorb Morse code, which was still used in flying and also in other military operations. We got into advanced techniques in navagation, not a strong suit of mine, as would become apparent.

To my surprise, I was soon appointed to cadet lieutenant. I even had a specific title, Assistant Adjutant, whatever that meant. I say surprise, because the farther I got into Basic Training, the more I realized that I was kind of a nonesuch among my fellow cadets—a dedicated pilot who was at the same time distinctly non-military. I loved any duty, any challenge, that advanced my prowess in the cockpit and prepared me for war. At the same time, I couldn't have cared less about all the rules, the saluting, the spit-and-polish stuff that the life of a wartime pilot required. I had already felt the sting of a system that ran by the book, and I'd pay the price for my indifference a few times more as my military career went on.

One area in which I'd never been indifferent was with women. Through all the intense weeks down in Augusta, I managed to hang on to my love affair with Betty, from Camden, South Carolina, even though it meant a lot of feverish cross-country driving on weekends for both of us.

Just before my graduation from Basic, though, another figure from Camden decided to make that long drive. Not Betty, but her father. He took me to lunch at one of the nicer hotels in the city, the Henry. I was gratified, but it didn't take too long to figure out that he hadn't come all this way just to sample the butter curls.

"Morgan," he began, in the tone of voice that was curiously familiar to me. "Morgan, I want to know how serious you are about my daughter. You-all have had quite a courtship this summer, and I'd like to know what your intentions are."

I'd figured our chat might eventually lead in this direction. Experience told me to play it straight from the shoulder. I said, "Sir, I don't quite know what you mean by intentions. If you're thinking about Betty and me getting married anytime soon, that is not in the picture." I paused while he put down his salad fork and squinted at me, then continued. "I'm just going through my cadet training. Then I have another ten weeks at least in advanced training. Until I get my wings and my first lieutenant's bars and graduate and know where I'm going, I'm in no position to get married."

I could see that his mood was not improving any, so I tried the practical argument. "I don't have any money. I haven't saved anything from my civilian life. I've still got payments on my car. I'm not in a position to get married."

Economics didn't seem to interest him either—I was starting to wonder whether he'd tucked a pistol into his belt—so as a last resort, though in retrospect it should have been the first resort, I began to assure him of my fundamental esteem for his daughter.

"I'm crazy about Betty," I told him. "She's a wonderful gal. I hope that she and I might continue to see each other, but . . . I mean . . ."

I never got to finish. Betty's father offered me a suggestion that had nothing to do with what was on the dessert menu. Then he got up, slapped his napkin down and stalked out of the hotel dining room. I never saw either him or Betty again. On top of that, I got stuck with the tab for lunch.

I was kidding myself. That line of mine, "I'm not in a position to get married," made me sound almost rational in my dealings with women. The fact was, if I wanted a girl badly enough, I'd marry her no matter what stood in the way—money, war, or my own better judgment.

There was only one exception to that rule, only one girl I wanted badly enough, yet didn't take as my bride. I was several months, one more marriage and an entire continent away from meeting her, but I was on course toward her now, as sure as radar.

CHAPTER

5

By the late summer of 1941 no boy my age was kidding himself that a wedding would lead right to picket fences, diaper-changing and a job down at the office. Life as we knew it was about to vanish. America's immunity from the aggression sweeping across both the world's hemispheres was an illusion, a pipe dream, and just about everybody but the most diehard isolationists could see that. President Roosevelt had just frozen all the assets belonging to Germany, Italy, and Japan, and clamped an embargo on gasoline and scrap iron being shipped to the Rising Sun. We'd been sending destroyers, tanks, and ships to England under the Lend-Lease agreement since the fall of France the year before. On August 3, under the thin guise of a fishing trip to Martha's Vineyard, the President made a secret flight to Newfoundland and a meeting with Winston Churchill that produced the Atlantic Charter, which affirmed the United States's commitment to "the final destruction of Nazi tyranny."

In September 1941 America absorbed its first hostile thrust, a torpedo fired by a German submarine at the destroyer *Greer* off the coast of Iceland. FDR immediately assigned U.S. Navy warships to escort merchant fleets across the Pacific, with permission to attack any Nazi submarines in their path.

When the Germans sank our destroyer, the *Reuben James,* in October, the Battle of the Atlantic was on. Congress authorized the arming of merchant ships, and America and Germany were at war in everything but official declaration.

My fellow cadets and I followed all this on the radio, in the newsreels, and in the papers. We watched and waited, and wondered what our role would be. We worked on our formation flying, our instrument reading, our landings. We tried to take our minds off it at the movies, like *The Maltese Falcon* with Humphrey Bogart, Mary Astor, Sydney Greenstreet, and Peter Lorre, *Sergeant York,* with Gary Cooper, and *Buck Privates,* with Abbott and Costello.

But it was always there, the sense of a clock ticking somewhere. A countdown.

Things were coming to a boil with Japan, too, although Americans were not noticing it quite as much. After Japan swept through Southeast Asia in 1940 and then signed a mutual defense treaty with Germany and Italy, the President tried to drain off Tokyo's belligerence by economic tactics. He cut off vital American oil shipments to Japan. This only infuriated the warlords.

The only question was when, and from where, the inevitable flashpoint would erupt.

I left Augusta in late September for my final phase of training. I had an important choice to make now—would I complete that final phase as a fighter pilot, as most guys I knew wanted to be? Or as a bomber pilot? I made that choice in almost no time. The bomber would be my "office" in this war.

This surprised a lot of my friends back in Asheville, who figured from the way I drove a car that a fighter-plane was my logical next step. I made my choice for two solid reasons. I'd found out, in the navigational phase of my training, that I was not the world's best navigator. Far from it. Often I had trouble finding my way back to the field if there were no railroad tracks or major highways to guide me.

The second reason, equally important, was that I knew I did not want to be alone up there. I'm a convivial fellow, and I like being a team member a lot more than I like being a lone wolf. Little could I have realized, at that stage, just how magnificent a team I would soon be a part of.

My next assignment was Barksdale Field in Shreveport, Louisiana. Before reporting, I wangled a weekend of leave and made a fast car trip up home to Asheville. I discovered, a little to my discomfort, that

I was already a hero there—or at least a bona fide pilot in the Army Air Forces. That wasn't true yet. Although I'd logged a little over 130 hours, I was still a cadet. My dad and brother Dave were so tickled by the sight of me in uniform that I sort of let them enjoy their moment of pride. It would all be true enough soon enough.

I couldn't help think of my mother, and what she would have made of me. I imagined that we'd have had some talks about it all out in her garden, as she smoked her Camel cigarettes through a holder. Maybe we would have spooled a few sentimental songs into the player piano. There was so much I would have wanted to tell her.

Then I made the long drive from Asheville to Shreveport. I did it in a day and a half. Could've done it quicker, but I decided not to drive straight through. I reported at Barksdale Field on September 26. I'd been waiting for a real military atmosphere? Boy, I found it here. When I drove up to that base and stopped at the gate and found a cold-eyed MP staring me in the face, demanding to know what my business was, I knew that I had finally made it to the big leagues. Barksdale Field was all about getting ready for war.

I told him I was a cadet reporting for cadet training. He was not bowled over by the news. He was already military. From his perspective, I may as well have been a Tenderfoot Boy Scout.

Only six other of my Bush Field comrades made it to Barksdale out of our class, and they trickled in on that same day. Our new barracks were a lot more spartan than at Camden—weathered, little old buildings that dated at least to the First World War. Space was at a premium at this facility. Barksdale would serve not only as a training base for Army Air Forces cadets, but also as a permanent base for Army officers. Just what I needed, more brass to salute and take orders from. Occupational hazard, I figured.

We new arrivals found we had a day to kill before we needed to report to the Commandant of Cadets' office. Armed with maps of the base—it was that big—a few of us decided to look around. Look around, of course, meant make straight for the flight line and check out the type of craft we'd be flying. What we saw waiting for us made those BT-15s back up at Bush seem like bicycles with training wheels.

Here we got our first closeup view of the aerial weapon that already had begun to rewrite the rules and the history of warmaking: the bomber.

The specimens we saw—big silver AT-7s, AT-8s, B-18s and A-29s (better known as Lockheed Hudsons)—never actually made it to combat. They were obsolete by the time America entered the war. Still, they were faster, more deadly looking, and three times the size of those little training planes farther up north.

We'd be logging about 100 hours in these babies, we were told, and that sounded pretty good to me. Not to mention an even more concentrated dose of ground school, instrument flying, navigation, and cross-country trips.

My new flight instructor was a lieutenant named C. M. Wharton. He told me that he was relatively new in the A-29/Lockheed Hudson, and a few weeks later he would prove that point very convincingly indeed.

First, though, we cadets got acquainted with a far more ancient kind of military transportation. Marching.

Suddenly, life was all about keeping in step. We marched every day in some fashion or other. We had dress marches in front of visiting generals. We had dress marches in front of the base commander. We heard about a thousand versions of "Hut, two, three, four!" I didn't like the thousandth any more than I'd liked the first. As far as I was concerned, my feet were made for operating a pair of rudder pedals.

I told myself I had to do it. Why? Because the Army said I had to do it. End of discussion. I did it.

There was one form of marching that was forbidden to us— marching off the base and into town, unless we had specifically applied for and been granted a pass. No more dinners in family homes, no more slipping out of the barracks for dates several times a week. The bright lights of Shreveport beckoned, but we were at Barksdale to train, train, train.

My new piece of equipment up in the sky, the Lockheed Hudson, was a different proposition from anything I'd ever flown. One of the latest models off the line, it sat sleek and trim on the tarmac, as though it were waiting for a chance to go cause some trouble. It was the fastest plane on the field. It would be the first twin-engine plane I'd flown.

The Lockheed Hudson was a prickly piece of equipment. It was not meant to be a training airplane. Its primary intended use was as an observation plane, although it could function as a light attack bomber. Its high speed was offset by one great drawback, at least for training purposes. It had only one set of controls. To be precise, it had two sets of rudders, but only one yoke. The yoke could flip over. That is, it could be unlocked from the pilot's seat and transferred to the copilot seat. This presented real difficulties at Barksdale. If an emergency occurred while the cadet had the yoke, the instructor had critical problems regaining control.

The Hudson had another dicey trait. It was a hot airplane to land. It had an extremely narrow landing gear between the two wings. If the landing was not precise, and if you weren't in complete control, the gear could pitch the plane into a ground loop—a radical swerving to the right or left. If the wing touched the tarmac during this out-of-control lurch, the wheel strut could break off and rupture the gas tank, usually igniting a fire. I saw this happen a few times at Barksdale, and while no one was killed, the results were ugly. It was my first intimation of what we were all preparing for. We cadets learned to be especially cautious at the controls of a Hudson.

One time I got involved in a flip-over crisis in that plane. But it was the reverse of the dreaded textbook situation. In this incident, my instructor, Lieutenant Wharton, was flying the plane, and it was I who had to help seize control.

Wharton was trying to show me some of the finer points of landing the Hudson, and he got so absorbed in it that he bounced the plane off the tarmac like it was a basketball. The bounce was so high that the plane went into a stall and lurched crazily toward another airplane. We were ground-looping. Wharton pushed the throttle ahead while I, from my student's seat, threw all my strength into helping him stabilize the rudders. The two of us managed to keep the plane up in the air and get its thrust going in time to avert a crash. It was a harrowingly close call.

The lieutenant didn't say anything to me and I didn't say anything to him. But after we landed, the captain in charge of flight instruction called me into his office. "Morgan," he said, "I saw that near-fiasco that you and your instructor had out there a few minutes ago. So did some other people. I'd like your side of the story."

I may have been a lowly cadet, but it was not in my nature, then or at any time in my military career, to suffer fools, whether or not they wore officers' stripes. I straightened myself and said, "Sir, I'll tell you my side of the story. The instructor let the plane get away from him. Got out of control from him and we darn near crashed. If it hadn't been for both of us, we wouldn't have gotten that airplane back in the air again and we would have hit another airplane. It could have been a real catastrophe. That's my story." I let him absorb this, and then took my stand. "And incidentally, Sir, I don't want to fly with that instructor again."

The captain reddened a little bit. "Whoa, Morgan. You're a cadet. He's an officer."

I refused to take the hint. "Sir, I don't want to fly with that instructor again. You asked me to tell you the story. I told it to you like it was and you can handle it any way you want to. But if I'm called down on this, I want to report to somebody higher up."

A very tense moment or two passed, but in the end, all the captain said was, "You're dismissed." I never heard another word about it. I must have made my point. I never flew with Wharton again.

Thanksgiving passed, the Christmas holidays approached, our graduation from the cadet program was set for December 12, and it seemed as though the brass at Barksdale was mellowing a little. We cadets were getting more leave time, and we used it in the way of young men in uniform since time immemorial. We headed into town and looked for girls.

That's where I and a few of my cadet friends and our dates found ourselves on a balmy, lazy Sunday afternoon at the end of the first week of December, at a nice hotel in downtown Shreveport, at a party, in our civvies. Dancing to Glenn Miller records, enjoying a few drinks, laughing and flirting. I hadn't been seeing anyone special since I arrived at Barksdale—hardly anyone at all, in fact—so I had asked an old flame from my University of Pennsylvania days, Martha Stone, to come down for graduation week. Her late father had been in the Army Air Corps, and I thought the ceremonies would mean something special to her.

We must have had the radio off in the room that afternoon, and nobody else in the hotel thought to disturb us, because it wasn't until we reported back to base that evening—it was December 7—that we had any inkling about what had happened.

When the carload of us pulled up to the gate, the MP saluted us as smartly as I'd ever seen one do at Barksdale. I figured we were finally getting a little respect now that our graduation was near; but then the MP said something that gave the salute an entirely different edge. "We are to give you instructions that you're to get out of your civilian clothes immediately and get into your military uniforms. You will not wear civilian clothes again at any time." Well, that was something new around here. We exchanged glances, and one of us managed to croak out, "Why?" and the young MP replied, "We're at war. The Japanese have attacked Pearl Harbor and President Roosevelt has declared war."

It's hard to describe what goes through a young boy's mind at a moment like that. You might think that we felt fear or at least anxiety. Here we were, due to graduate in five days, poised to enter the Army Air Forces as second lieutenants, all gung-ho—and lo and behold, our country was now in the middle of a world war! No more fantasy, no more larking around the sky in our training craft, daydreaming of some far-off glory. Now it was real. Now we were going to be part of it. Now the fate of the world, and of our own young lives, was in the balance. Some of us were going to get hurt. Some of us were going to be killed. Who at that time could tell whether peaceful, bucolic America could summon the resources and the willpower to prevail over ferocious military aggressors on both sides of the world?

That wasn't what we were feeling at all. None of it. What we felt was exhilaration so intense that it made our breath come short. That, followed pretty quickly by a scalding surge of anger at Japan for hitting us that way. It was a sneak attack, planned for months, so unexpected that on the morning it happened some of our officers at Hawaii were on the golf course. All that planning, that movement of the Japanese carriers across the Pacific to within striking distance of our fleet, had occurred while our State Department had been negotiating in good faith—so it thought—in Washington with representatives of the Imperial government.

The strike at Pearl Harbor offended every virtue, every notion of honor and fair play that my generation of American boys had grown up with, handed down to us from the Western movies, from our schools, from church, from the neighborhood policemen who let us ride around in their cars, from our households. You didn't hit somebody from behind. You didn't sucker-punch your enemy while pretending to talk nice to him.

Besides, what was Japan doing messing with us anyway? We were the *good guys!* We believed in good things. America in 1941 was a nation that could identify with the image of Jack Armstrong, radio's All-American boy, who fought for justice with whistle rings and secret charts and his own innate pluck.

I was a little old to have heard this myself, but I imagine some of the younger guys in the car with me that night at the gate at Barksdale might have been listening to a Jack Armstrong episode broadcast in 1939 over the NBC Blue Network. I came across a transcript of it many, many years later. I think it really summed up all the patriotism and idealism and yes, the innocence, of American kids in those years.

In it, Jack is off on an adventure in the Far East, and he's encountered a Tibetan monk who has this message for him:

> "Tell the boys and girls of the United States this world is theirs. If they have hearts of gold, a glorious new golden age awaits us. If they are honest, riches shall be theirs. If they are kind, they shall save the whole world from malice and meanness. Will you take that message to the boys and girls of the United States, Jack Armstrong?"

Corny? Maybe. But that's who we were, we boys of the 1930s who became the warriors of the 1940s. Our enemies may have prided themselves on how well they thought they knew America—knew it as a sleeping giant—but I don't think they ever picked up on that kind of spirit or took it into their calculations. It cost them plenty, in the end.

What we cadets did after learning the big news was floor that car's accelerator and aim it toward our barracks. We dashed to our rooms, every one of us from that carload, and threw on our military togs, as ordered. Then we converged on the base bar to have a drink and salute the fact that we were now in uniform for the duration.

Scared? Anxious? Worried about the final outcome? No. Proud, and determined, and angry in a way that carried us into the worst kinds of hell that the masterminds of human warfare had ever devised, and on to triumph on the other side. For those of us who lived.

Our graduation ceremonies five days later had a special solemnity. Germany and Italy had declared war on America on December 11, and Japan had followed up Pearl Harbor with bombing attacks on Guam, Wake Island, Hong Kong, Singapore, and the Philippines.

There was no question about it—our diplomas would have some value in the job-market just opening up.

Before we got those sheepskins, the Army had one more hoop for us to jump through. We needed to take our physicals again. After all, it had been twelve whole months. Who knows?—some of us may have gotten too fat or two short!

I had a more realistic fear. That little defect in my left eye, over-looked by the friendly surgeon at Langley, would be in play again. This time, the examiner could well be a little pickier.

Sure enough, I passed every test with ease until they got to my eyes. "Morgan," the flight surgeon said to me, "did you know that you didn't have complete 20/20 vision in your left eye?"

Damn, I thought, *this is it. The end of everything.* I figured I may as well go down swinging. I put a big grin on my face, as if a slightly bum eye were nothing but a pilot's best friend. I said, "Yes, Sir, I did know." And I told him the story about Langley Field and the ice pack.

Call it Morgan's Southern charm, but it worked. The surgeon laughed and said, "You know, I believe your story. I don't know whether that other fella was kidding you or not, but anyway, he passed you." Then the surgeon looked at me seriously. "You know," he said in a quiet voice, "you've got a choice here. I can flunk you on this physical, absolutely on the up-and-up. You can get out of active duty. With all the flying time you've logged, you can become a civilian instructor and make a lot of money.

"Or," he went on, "if you want, I'll overlook this little matter. I'll pass you, and you can go on and become a second lieutenant in the Army Air Forces. What's your choice?"

I barely waited for him to finish. "There's no question about it, Sir," I said. "I've been in the Army Air Forces now for nine months as a cadet. I want to be an officer. I want my wings. I think I'm a good enough pilot to do the job where it needs to be done. I may be crazy, but that's my wish. So, please pass me." He did, and that was the end of all the nonsense about my left eye.

Despite the great sense of mobilization in the air, the officers at Barksdale gave us a graduation ceremony with all the flourishes. We cadets lined up in rows in our dress uniforms, looking razor-sharp. Drum and bugles played "Pomp and Circumstance." The base commander spoke of our great duty and of his high hopes for us. Martha Stone pinned my wings on me. I was now a second lieutenant in the Army Air Forces and I was damned proud of it.

My dad and brother came down for the graduation. They gave me a party. Once again, Martha was at my side. I'd sort of warmed to Martha again. Maybe it was loneliness, maybe it was the enormity of what was to come. Maybe my dead mother was calling out to me. Anyway, Martha and I had talked a little bit. My end of the conversation had gone something like this. "Martha, your dad was in the Air Corps. I know you were fond of him. You seem to be very proud of me. You and I have gotten along well. We've had an affair. Why don't we get married?"

Well, now, what girl could resist a line like that? To my surprise, and maybe hers, she said, "Yes." So, when Dad and Dave came down, I told them, "Martha and I are going to get married." I guess they were used to shocks like that by now, because the only question they had was, "When?" and I said, "Right after I graduate."

So, we did it.

We were married two weeks later in Tampa, Florida. That's where I was to be stationed, at McDill Field. I reported for duty there on December 26. My orders were for the 29th Bomb Group, 52nd Bomb Squadron. We set up housekeeping on Davis Island near the base—Martha, me, and Martha's cocker spaniel, Rags.

I made my first flight at McDill on the day after Christmas 1941. I served as a check pilot on the A-29s and was part of a detail assigned to patrol the Gulf of Mexico, looking out for enemy submarines. The Lockheed was up to its usual tricks. We lost two or three of them in those early days for the usual reasons—ground-looping that caused the landing gear to break up into the gas tank—and some boys were burned pretty bad, although none died.

I also got checked out in the first four-engine airplane I'd ever flown, or seen. Man, it looked big! It was the B-24C, which was called the Liberator. Its nickname was the "Boxcar," because of its rectangular shape.

I could hardly take my eyes off the Liberator's mass. It was overwhelming—far and away the biggest aircraft I'd ever seen. Could one fellow ever fly a machine as huge as that? My amazement continued when I climbed inside its cockpit, and found that I could stand straight up and not bump my head. The controls and instruments in front of me seemed endless. It was like the pilot room of an ocean liner! Suddenly the Lockheed Hudson seemed like a motor-scooter by comparison. I did learn to fly it, of course, even though at first it felt like being at the controls of a house with wings.

Meanwhile, in that little Davis Island apartment, my bride Martha Stone Morgan and I were having some ground-loop problems of our own. Our marriage had touched down, and immediately taken a big bounce. Several bounces.

Martha was a sweet girl, and she looked up to me. But she was so young and inexperienced—and I, well, I'd had a fistful of experiences. Without meaning to, I think I overwhelmed her. The whole whirlwind courtship and marriage scared her to death, actually. Not that I was anything but gentle with her. I have always been gentle with women. But maybe I expected her to be a little more worldly than she was. When I realized that she was not all that worldly, I let myself get all caught up in the Army Air Forces lifestyle—up early, flying all day, staying a little too long at the officers' club at night. And meanwhile Martha was isolated, way out of her familiar world, on an island in Florida. She had few friends and a husband who was always up in the air, in more ways than one.

As the differences between us swam more into focus, we spent more and more time apart. I began to volunteer for cross-country flights. It seemed that I'd rather be almost anywhere than at home feuding with my wife.

Maybe that explains the recurrence of my demon "buzzing" urges one beautiful, sunny January Sunday. I was tooling the Hudson up and down the Gulf coast looking for submarines when the plane passed over St. Petersburg beach. Looking down, I could see a big party of people on the beach between the town and the ocean. They looked like they were having fun, a lot more fun than I was, and I thought I'd drop down and take a closer look at them and see what everybody was wearing and having to drink.

At 1,000 feet it looked like they were having a good time. At 200 feet I was starting to have a pretty good time myself, and I guarantee you I got everybody's attention. If I'd been any lower, somebody could have handed me a mint julep.

I landed the plane pretty tickled with myself about the surprise I caused those folks. But I should not have been surprised myself—though, for some reason, I was—the next morning when I reported in at the operations office and heard the operations officer roar, "Morgan!"

He passed me along to the commanding officer of the 22nd Bomb Squadron, who said, "Morgan! The General would like to see you!" Well, I had never met the General, but I was going to meet him now. I went over to his office, saluted, and walked in. The General said, "Morgan! Were you flying a Lockheed Hudson"—he recited the serial number—"yesterday afternoon, over the Gulf?" I had to admit that I was. "Did you happen to make a low pass at a party on the beach?" I said I believed that possibly I had.

Now the General put his knuckles on the desk and rose up slowly out of his chair. The stars on his collar were damn near blinding. He leaned toward me. "I must tell you," he said, "that I was at that party, and you made a *very* low pass. As a matter of fact, you made *two* low passes at that party." If I could have squeezed my eyes shut and gritted my teeth I would have, but this didn't seem like the time. Instead I murmured, "Yes, Sir." There was nothing else to say.

The General's voice was icy now. "Morgan, I ought to kick you out for that. I ought to dismiss you right now, on the spot. But," he said, "I have found out that you're a pretty good pilot. We've spent a lot of money and time and effort training you, so I'm not going to take that action. But I tell you this. If I can, in any way, influence your future, you will be the oldest second lieutenant in the history of the Army Air Forces. I'll see to it."

"Yes, Sir."

"Dismissed."

That word gave me a start, until I realized he meant dismissed from his office. Once again I'd come within a hair's breadth of being booted out of the service. I felt pretty low for a while.

Like, for about fifteen minutes. Then I perked up. What the heck. They needed me! I was still a pilot. Still going to fly. So, I kept flying.

And, I admit, buzzing.

By the end of January I was a full "first pilot" now on the B-24C, with 60 hours at the controls, and headed—or so I briefly thought—for combat in Africa. Erwin Rommel's second desert offensive had kicked in against the British in Libya, spurred by his dreaded Panzer tank divisions. The Nazis were advancing toward the Egyptian border and the British Eighth Army needed all the Allied support it could get.

That suited me fine; I felt at the top of my form and was itching to get into this war. The prospect made for some tender moments between Martha and me. It gave us something deeper to think about than our own little problems. The day before my unit was supposed to leave McDill for Africa, the brass changed the orders. They decided that they still needed us first pilots at McDill. Instead of sending the first pilots, they upgraded the copilots among us and shipped them off to combat over the Libyan desert in those clunky B-24s. It was only later that I found out the reason. The hard fact was, the

brass was saving us more experienced pilots for a greater challenge—
and a much, much greater flying reward.

They say that life is unfair, and that war is a train of unforeseen
and unsupposed circumstances. I felt for those young just-promoted
copilots who went bravely off to Africa in our place because they
suffered a double dose of bad luck. One, they jumped into hot combat ahead of us—and two, they did not get to savor the sublime satisfaction of sitting at the controls of the miraculous aircraft that we
second lieutenants now found rolling onto the line at McDill and at
our disposal.

Nothing in all my flying experience ever prepared me for the B-17.
All those other planes that had seemed so intoxicating when I was
cutting my teeth on them—the yellow PT-17s, the Lockheed Hudsons, all the rest of them—well, it was almost as if they never existed.
One look at the B-17, silver and elegant and indomitable-looking on
the tarmac, bristling with armature, that massive reassuring tailfin
crowning its splendid architecture, and the world started all over
again. I mean, that airplane was that stupendous to behold. You
could immediately understand what came over that nameless journalist up in Seattle who took one look at the first model to come
wheeling out of the hangar and gasped that it was a "flying fortress."
To me and the thousands of men who flew her, "goddess" would not
have been overdoing it.

Its prototype had been in planning and development at Boeing
since 1934, seven years after Charles Lindbergh's transatlantic flight
had rejuvenated America's waning interest in aviation. The Army had
started to put out requests for a heavy, long-range bomber about
then, and the Boeing engineers had plunged in with designs for a four-
engine craft, nearly unimaginable back then, with an original
wingspan of nearly 150 feet, although by wartime, it had been scaled
back to 103 feet. In a way, the B-17 took form as a hybrid between a
futuristic bomber and several other concepts that Boeing was tinker-
ing with back then. One was a light-skinned, all-metal "Monomail"
craft designed to carry passengers and mail across the continent. Another was a luxury commercial "flying boat" called the Stratoliner,
the first pressurized airliner and the first to make a scheduled transat-

lantic flight, in 1940. Boeing built its Stratoliners for stability and the safety of their passengers. As the military version developed on the drawing board, these features were built into it—as was the light-weight metal skin of the Monomail. The engineers may not have even known what a masterpiece of warmaking they were piecing together. The flying machine they eventually handed the Army turned out to be maneuverable, reliable, and difficult to shoot down.

For all this, the B-17 had a rocky road to the mass-production line. Through the late 1930s it was almost too visionary for its own good. Many experts in government and the military doubted that a craft of its size and expense would ever be needed; Boeing was ordered again and again to slash the price tag, as its 1939 list price of $202,500 was still a few thousand dollars higher than the politicians in Congress were willing to pay.

Right about that time, Adolf Hitler's Spanish Civil War–tested Panzers and Stukas started turning up in Poland, and it was amazing how good this new nonesuch started looking to everybody.

Still, the plane's birth pains persisted. Grew worse, even. When the U.S. sent a number of B-17Cs over to Britain in May 1941, mainly for defensive use, the Royal Air Force—understandably eager to slash at Germany after heroically fending off catastrophe in the Battle of Britain—pushed the planes and their pilots too far too fast. Disregarding American advisors' recommendations for extensive training and formation-flying, the RAF rushed the Fortresses into a series of daylight raids over targets at Brest and Wilhelmshaven. Excessive altitude, engine trouble, frozen machineguns and lack of fighter-escort cover combined to make the raids worse than ineffective. They were simply disastrous. It is said that both the British and the Germans found bitter humor in the apparent uselessness of the new American bomber. British pilots snarlingly called them Flying Targets, and Joseph Goebbels, Hitler's propaganda chief, hit on an even nastier slur. To him, the planes were Flying Coffins.

Well, as we used to say in North Carolina, we'd have to see about that.

I could have told Herr Goebbels, if he'd asked, that this plane sure as hell didn't feel like a flying coffin to me—but that if he was smart, he ought to be looking around for a nice little plot for himself. To all us boys at McDill lucky enough to be piloting it, the B-17 was a life-force. It practically wanted to fly itself. The experience we were building up at the controls every day, from February on through the spring, was assurance that neither we nor our crews nor our commanders would make the kinds of mistakes that our brave but overeager comrades from the RAF had made.

I couldn't wait to get into that cockpit every new day and take one of those beauties up again. This was where I was meant to be. Back in Seattle, Boeing's engineers were constantly at the drawing board, learning from past flaws and miscalculations, and in mid-February the B-17 model E came off the line. Here was the Fortress as it first went to war, that rear dorsal fin expanded to its ultimate, massive height, the fuselage extended another six feet to accommodate a pair of .50-caliber machineguns in the tail, twin "fifties" installed on top of the fuselage and in a ball turret in the bottom of the waist section, all with a maximum speed capability of 318 miles per hour.

Here was the older sister of the *Memphis Belle*.

As far as I was concerned, it was time to get down to business.

CHAPTER

6

I only wish that my life with dear young Martha could have been half as good as my life in the cockpit, but it wasn't—not for her, and not for me. Sometime in that early spring, the two of us faced the inevitable. We agreed that this marriage was not meant to be. To give her credit, Martha was the one who finally took the bold step and said, "Bob, this isn't going to work. Why don't you just give me a divorce?" So I did. The proceedings went through quickly, and soon Martha and Rags were back in Pittsburgh with her mother.

I didn't know it at the time, but Martha and I weren't quite finished with one another yet.

I'm almost embarrassed to admit how easily I slipped back into the bachelor life. I stayed in the cottage on Davis Island. My buddies and I were learning another valuable wartime skill, taking our pleasures as they came, enjoying each day to the maximum with the knowledge that our days might be limited. We understood the value of no regrets.

We would go down to Miami on weekend leaves, and I'm here to tell you that Miami in the 1940s had a thing or two to offer. I had splurged on a brand new Buick convertible. No regrets. I loved driving to Miami, and once, lo and behold, I ran into one of my old college girlfriends there. We painted the town a little bit, but it didn't get serious. Truth to tell, the only lady in my life that counted just then was the one I took up into the sky every day.

By now, I was a check pilot myself—checking out first lieutenants, captains, even majors in the B-17 for instrument approaches. Instrument approaches were a new thing for a lot of these guys. I enjoyed this. It was a real thrill to have the copilot sitting over there, not being able to see anything but the instruments because the windows had a curtain drawn over them. The rules were that you would cut off the instruments and go manual at two hundred feet, never lower. I followed this rule most of the time. But as the pilots got better, I couldn't help pushing the edge with them. I would take the good ones down to one hundred feet and sometimes even to seventy-five and fifty feet. When I got a pilot that really knew what he was doing and was making a beautiful approach, I would put my hands on the yoke and my feet on the rudders and say, "Come on, we'll just go right on down and touch the runway." We bounced the airplane two or three times but I was always in full control of it. I could take over, bank it and go on around if necessary, because I could see and he couldn't. I got to doing this so often that the squadron commander heard about it. "Morgan," he began, and I braced for another chewing out, but all he said was, "Be careful. We don't need any accidents."

In the end, I think, my pushing the edge helped bring these good pilots to an even higher level of skill.

As for me, my time in the B-17 was building up. By the end of March, I had logged a total air time of 660 hours.

In May, the Army Air Forces formed us up into the 91st Bomb Group, 324th Bomb Squadron. The 91st had actually originated in Savannah, Georgia, but it moved to McDill that month. My new squadron commanding officer was one Major Harold Smelser. One look at him and I knew that the fur was going to fly between us sooner or later. As I've mentioned, I was the kind of guy who didn't give a hoot for spit-and-polish—I would just as soon have dressed in overalls every day as in my uniform. Major Smelser carried a swagger-stick, and he had the military swagger to go with it. He knew how to strut sitting down, as the saying went. Right away, we were on a collision course.

That said, I have to give this martinet of an officer credit where it is due. He recognized my ability as a pilot. Right off the bat, he made me a flight leader, one of only three in our whole squadron. For that, I will always respect him.

We did a lot of cross-country flights that spring, to get us ready for the physical and metal requirements of long-range strategic bombing. These flights were designated no-stop trips. We could pick out some American city, fly there and return to McDill, but we were not to land at any of the cities. That was strictly and specifically against regulations.

So of course Morgan had to land his B-17 during a cross-country trip.

It happened on May 31 of 1942. I planned a trip up to Asheville, my hometown. I wanted to fly over the city and just let the folks see a B-17 from the air. It was a beautiful day—just the kind of day when most of Morgan's mischief seemed to occur. We went up at about 15,000 feet, and when we got to Asheville I let us down to 1,000 feet, which was within regulations. Then it occurred to me that nobody in Asheville would know that their hometown boy Morgan was flying this Fortress because I hadn't called anybody to tell them. How to solve this knotty problem?

We flew around the city for a while until I spotted the old airport. It sat right up against the side of one of those steep mountains that ringed the town. I had never been at that airport, I suddenly realized. That didn't seem right, somehow. Maybe I ought to rectify that situation, I thought. It was, after all, a beautiful day.

The airport had a short runway, only about 4,000 feet. We'd been using runways of 6,000 and 7,000 feet at McDill. What the hell. I made a pass over that field at 500 feet just to kind of let them know I was around. Then—did I mention it was a beautiful day?—I decided that I was going to land, and let the homefolks see the airplane on the ground. Boy, what a thrill they would have.

Well, we landed. That was the easy part. Coming to a full stop while we still had some runway, that was the hard part. We were well along toward using up the last of those 4,000 feet when I slammed on the brakes. The plane screeched and the brakes smoked. I got it stopped before we started to climb the side of that mountain, and I jumped out with a big how-y'all-doin' grin for the slightly dazed-looking spectators clustered around the hangar. Behind my nonchalance I knew that Morgan was in another world of trouble.

Sure enough, I had burned up the brakes and burst the expander tube. I did not dare try to taxi or take off without any brakes. I couldn't think of any local grease-monkeys who would know how to do relining work on the brakes of a Flying Fortress, so I gulped down a deep breath and took the only action left open to me, short of taking up the hermit's life in the Great Smokies. I found a telephone and called up Major Smelser, my Squadron Commander at McDill, and told him what had happened.

He burned up the phone lines for a few minutes—I believe the word "Morgan!" came into play—but in the end he was calm. "I'll send a crew up there and we'll change your brakes," he said, "and you will report back to McDill."

Over the next few days I didn't see Major Smelser, in large part because I was making a concerted effort not to. I dodged him as best I could, but when I did run into him, he didn't say a word to me about that flight. Not a word.

I thought maybe I had dodged the bullet once again. I had a second think coming.

June arrived, and we found out that our final training stop would be Walla Walla, Washington. Why they ever picked Walla Walla, I don't know. It wasn't exactly en route to the European war; it was about 3,000 miles in the opposite direction. On the other hand, it would be a chance for me to fly a B-17 all the way from one coast to another, so I was in no mood to complain.

When I went into the Squadron Operations Office, where the airplanes, their assigned pilots, and crews were listed on a giant blackboard, I was shocked. My name was not on the list!

I queried the Operations officer, who tactfully jerked a thumb toward the office of Major Smelser. I got a funny feeling in my throat, but decided to play it deadpan.

"Which B-17 am I flying to Walla Walla, Sir?" I asked as I saluted him in his office. Clearly, this was a moment the Major had looked forward to for quite some time.

"Morgan," he said, tapping that swagger stick of his into the palm of his hand, "you're not flying to Walla Walla." I registered surprise.

The Major bristled. "You remember that incident at Asheville, North Carolina, when you landed against orders and burned out your brakes?"

"Yes, Sir."

"Well, you're not flying to Walla Walla."

"Yes, Sir."

I wanted to ask him how I was supposed to get to Walla Walla if I couldn't fly, but I decided not to give him the satisfaction. After a moment, the Major told me anyway.

"You . . . are going . . . to ride the troop train," he said. "The troop train, Morgan, with all the ground crew members and the infantry. That's how you're going to get to Walla Walla. On the troop train."

The Major had a particularly grating way of spitting out that phrase, "troop train." I had the feeling he'd rehearsed it. But I didn't point that out to him. He might have sent me to Yakima.

As it turned out, the troop train was not a bad way to travel to Walla Walla. I had a pretty good time. Lots of good guys there. We played cards, we shot dice, we had a few drinks, we told jokes and stories. Before it was over, the engineer had called me up and let me ride in the engine for a while. That was all right, except that I couldn't do any ground rolls or stall-outs. I had a good time but I sure was disgusted that I was not flying a B-17 to Walla Walla.

That was not the end of my problems with the Major.

At Walla Walla, even though we had reached the most critical phase of our training, Major Smelser still found time for his new hobby, thinking up the dirtiest work he could for me. He really didn't like me. He didn't like my free spirit. He didn't like how I tended to forget my officer's cap. He didn't like that I had girlfriends—many girlfriends, more girlfriends than Major Smelser had ribbons. Within a few days of getting my bearings in Walla Walla, I'd started dating a girl whose daddy owned thousands of acres of wheat fields. The guys called her the "Wheat Queen." While that was going on, a girlfriend of mine from Tampa sashayed into town for a surprise visit. When she found out I was dating the Wheat Queen, she left again, without so much as a howdy-do to Major Smelser.

I could almost sense that Round Two was about to start.

Meantime, we were still preparing to go to war. I kept building up hours in the B-17, but I also got to check out and fly an attack bomber called the A-20, which we used in pursuit of a towed target ship, to give our gunners some combat-style practice.

The most fun I had during those weeks was when the Major sent me down over the flatlands near Ogden, Utah, to work on blind-landing shots. That was some of the most thrilling, dangerous, and memorable flying I ever did. I'm not exactly sure that the Major intended it as "fun"—hell, he might have figured he'd seen the last of me when he sent me down there, along with my copilot—but I survived it okay, and had some laughs in the process.

I made twenty-five of those landings—instruments only, no visual contact with the ground, all the way down to zero. Got pretty good at it. Always wondered whether Major Smelser was surprised to see me come back.

In July, the Major struck again. This time it was not a fun experience.

Our unit had been doing some night-flight training. One night, one of our B-17s got disoriented and crashed into the side of a mountain. Major Smelser called me and told me to report to the crash sight. My orders were to identify the bodies and supervise their excavation from the wreckage.

This was a rough assignment. I knew some of those kids—not well, but I knew them. My detail had to climb on foot through brush and woods and debris to get to the crash site. Then I had to face those disfigured bodies. Some I had to identify by their dog tags. The airplane had caught fire and burned them beyond recognition. It was a mess. I could almost hear Major Smelser tap-tapping his swagger stick as I groped and choked my way through it. Thank goodness it was the only tragedy our squadron suffered in training.

July 1942, all in all, was a rough month.

August was better. In August it all started to come together.

In August a sharp young copilot joined my B-17 crew, the last link in a team of specialized warriors destined to become a legend in Army Air Forces history. And it was in August when I met the dazzling young woman who invested that legend with a name.

In August came the genesis of the *Memphis Belle*.

Major Smelser was still sorting out flight crews when we'd left McDill Field for Walla Walla, and he continued to assign and reassign gunners, navigators, and communications men in the first weeks there. Soon the crews began to firm up for their final combat designations. A smoothly functioning flight crew was as important to survival and effectiveness in a B-17 as the wiring in its fuselage, and teamwork was the quality that gave meaning to every individual skill. Not just technical teamwork, but the teamwork born of mutual respect, understanding, instinct, and trust.

I'd been pretty impressed with the boys who were signing on, one by one, as permanent members of my crew. It wasn't until a short, quiet college kid from New Haven, Connecticut, reported for duty as my copilot that I started to realize that we were something special.

Jim Verinis would not have joined us if he hadn't been nearly killed a couple of times in North Carolina, trying to fly single-engine planes. He'd lost an engine from a P-40 in flight down there and had to bail out. He was still getting over that experience when his engine conked out on takeoff of another flight, and he saved the plane only by heroic concentration and skill. After that, Jim decided he'd had about as much fun with single-engine planes as he could take. He wanted to fly a plane with more "fans" upfront—engines. He asked to be transferred to bombers for a while. They sent him to me.

If I'd had any worries about his competence based on his close calls back in Charlotte, they were erased the first time up. He caught on to the B-17 right away. In a couple of hours, I had him flying it himself, shooting landings. He took to it so well that I was afraid they might take him away from me and make a first pilot out of him. They might have, if they hadn't run out of B-17s to send over to Europe. Jim's choice was to either hang around stateside and wait for his own plane—maybe weeks, maybe months—or to take an overseas assignment as a copilot. As he later reminisced, that was actually no choice at all—he was physically and mentally ready to go to war. That is how my B-17 took on the man I'd call its "second pilot."

*   *   *

And then, out of nowhere one day—well, out of Memphis, actually—there was Margaret Polk.

She blew in to the base on a visit from Tennessee with her sister, who was married to the flight surgeon in our squadron.

She was tall and dark-haired, and her slight, friendly squint somehow only made her more gorgeous. She was nineteen, and she brought a touch of glamour to our olive-drab world in her wide straw hats and swirling dresses. She even had a family link to American history. Her father, Oscar Boyle Polk, a lawyer who had made a modest fortune as a cotton farmer in Arkansas, was an indirect descendant of James Knox Polk, our eleventh President, and a good ol' North Carolina boy, I might add.

She'd been brought up in a happy, protective world that still bore the genteel traces of the Old South—private schools for girls in the winter, cloistered places with names like Emma Cook's School and Miss Hutchison's School, then, in summertime, carefree wanderings at her parents' country estate at Hickory Valley, Tennessee. At Hickory Valley she frolicked like a tomboy, riding horses, climbing trees, swimming in the cow pond, and picking strawberries in the fields.

From there she'd entered college—still a rarity for a girl in that time and place. She was enrolled at Southwestern College in Memphis when, in July 1942, Margaret found herself in Walla Walla. She arrived there with sister Elizabeth in the family Ford, to keep Elizabeth company on the long trip home after she bade farewell to her husband, Dr. Edward McCarthy, about to ship out with the 91st.

Neither Margaret nor I could ever remember our first encounter. It was probably at "Mack" McCarthy's house off the base, when Mack invited me in for a drink one day. I do recall the episode that drew us close to one another. It involved a date that she kept with another young man. The date was for July 31, my birthday.

I invited her to the party that was being thrown for me, but Margaret had already accepted this other date. She wanted to break it and come to my party. But her sister and brother-in-law refused to let her do it. She kept that other date, seething and pouting every minute of it, or at least that's how I like to think of it. From that night on, we were inseparable.

Margaret brought a kind of sunlit gladness with her, a way of laughing that was so refreshing in these dark, war-addled times. Margaret Polk was about fun and zest and life and hope. She was the kind of gal who seemed to sum up a lot of what was good about America, a lot of what our enemies never understood, or maybe even feared and were trying to crush. Margaret Polk was what we'd soon be fighting for.

But Margaret had something besides her beauty and surface laughter that set her apart from other girls I'd known. Underneath it all, there was a melancholy—some private wound that would never quite let her go. I got to know a lot more about that wound as our romance deepened and took all its unexpected turns through the war and afterward. But just the hint of it was enough to draw me into her as I'd never before been drawn.

Maybe that hint of melancholy explains why, even from the very outset, I approached this young beauty quite differently from my usual lover-boy style. As soon as I met her I knew the Wheat Queen was history. Yet Margaret and I didn't get hot and heavy. We started out almost as buddies, and we stayed buddies for a long while, at least until that birthday party of mine. After that, I managed to be with her some nearly every day—walking along the old Nez Perce Indian trail that was now Main Street, grabbing a movie for twenty-five cents apiece at the old Liberty Theater or dinner at a downtown restaurant, maybe cuddling and smooching a little at the end of the evening. Mainly we enjoyed the way the world around us seemed to take on a special radiance wherever we touched it—so that the city park, or a cluster of kids, or the Blue Mountains on the horizon all seemed memorable, somehow, just because we gazed at them together.

Call me a romantic so-and-so, but I even offered Margaret the ultimate gesture of my sincerest feelings for her—I buzzed her sister's house bright and early every damn morning in my B-17, rattling the windows and shaking dishes off the shelf. It wasn't something I did for just any woman.

Adding to the intensity of it was our knowledge that we'd soon be forced apart. By September, when my squadron was set to be shuttled back across the United States to Bangor, Maine, and Margaret was packing her bags to go back to Tennessee, I knew that I was a goner for this vivacious, wisecracking girl. We held each other and tried to be funny, and we promised we'd write.

Oh, did we write. Did we ever write.

My first letter to her—the first of hundreds—was written a day after she'd left town, on letterhead from the Marcus Whitman Hotel in Walla Walla. Looking back on these words written more than half a century ago, I recognize so much of my younger self—the jumbled emotions of a young man in the throes of his first real passionate love, frustration over the gigantic forces prying us apart as well as the heightened passion that that kind of separation always generated, and, finally, the unmistakable traces of anxiety and doubt. Was this feeling between us for real? What if it wasn't, for her?

Underneath an engraving of the hotel and the legend, MODERN FIREPROOF HOTEL/WASHED AIR COOLING SYSTEM, I wrote:

My dearest "Polky,"

I was going to sit down & write you yesterday, but then I thought that if I waited a full day after you had gone, you would be more inclined to understand how I really feel, and that I am really sincere.

I miss you, "Little One," I miss you more than you'll ever know or understand, and if you ever miss me this much you will come to me. I know I would be on my way to you if I was a civilian once again.

I know now that I have never loved before. I have never felt towards anyone as I do you. If we can't have *our life* before the war is over, I know I shall come to you afterward, providing you still want me.

You may find by now that you have no real love for me. If that is true, please tell me. We said we'd always be frank . . .

Never worry, God will keep me safe till we are together again.

I send you all the love in my heart.

Forever yours,
Bob

My next rendezvous with Margaret came faster than either of us had expected. I ended up flying from Walla Walla to Bangor with a colonel who had scheduled a stopover in Jackson, Mississippi. I fired off a telegram to Margaret.

JACKSON, MISSISSIPPI, ARMY AIR BASE TONIGHT. WILL CALL. LOVE BOB.

When I got there I didn't have to call. As soon as she received the wire, she'd jumped in her car and driven all night to Jackson. In her scrapbook, for the rest of her life, she kept a green DO NOT DISTURB card. It was the card we hung on the door of Room 931 of the Hotel Heidelberg in Jackson.

If only the world at large had paid attention to that card.

At Dow Field in Bangor, the Army Air Forces brought in a fleet of brand-new B-17Fs, fresh off the assembly lines. My crew was assigned Bomber No. 4485. I walked out to where she was parked on the tarmac the first chance I got and gave her the once-over. It was love at first sight.

She was a long and slender lady, like her sister B-17Es that I'd sampled at McDill, but with a few crucial improvements, notably a clear Plexiglas nose for great visibility and some fine-tuning in the propeller design. Olive-drab, covered partly with camouflage paint, her several turrets birstling with machinegun barrels, she seemed the perfect combination of delicate grace and warlike toughness. And she seemed almost to be beckoning me to come on in and have a look around. So I did.

Her interior was a little smaller, more cramped than the E's I'd flown in training. You could not walk through her standing up, and her cockpit afforded hardly any extra room at all. But that was all right—nobody ever pretended that she was a pleasure-craft. Once inside that cockpit, having swung up through her nose, as did the copilot, navigator, bombardier, nosegunner—the rest of the gunners came in through the rear—I felt almost that she was an extension of my own body. That's how intimate it would be with her during our months together over France and Germany.

By the time I met No. 4485, I had accumulated 834 hours and 30 minutes of flying time. I had accumulated senior-pilot status, instructor status, the works. The works include the dubious distinction of being the first pilot in my group to draw gunfire, and probably the first pilot in the history of the world to draw gunfire from a man with a sidearm in the state of Maine.

It happened during one of our routine training flights above the woods not far from Bangor, and it was triggered—I guess that's the term you'd use—by my incorrigible fondness for buzzing. One of my crewmen spotted a fisherman down below us peacefully casting his line into a beautiful river. A sportsman myself, I was seized with an overwhelming curiosity to find out what sort of luck he was having. So I took the B-17 down a few thousand feet. The lower altitude attracted his attention, but it didn't improve my view all that much, so I circled around and came in lower. I imagine that moose and black bear were by now stampeding out of there over a ten-mile radius, but I still couldn't see inside the fellow's creel box. When I came in for a third pass, so low the fisherman could probably count the bolts on my undercarriage, he decided to fight back. He whipped a pistol out of his pocket and fired off a couple of rounds. Honesty compels me to admit that he got us: we found a couple of small holes in the plane's fuselage when we landed. We asked the ground crew to caulk them up and not ask any questions as to where they'd come from.

So now I had everything—lots of flight hours, senior-pilot standing, green card, hell, even a little combat experience.

I had everything but a nickname for my airplane.

Naming planes was one of the great fads of World War II. Not just naming them, but slapping illustrations of the name on the nose and fuselage. Nose jobs, they called them. It was a terrific morale-booster, and the brass went along with it. I guess that the ground troops did it too—decorating their artillery pieces, tanks, helmets. It was a way of holding on to our individuality, or sense of humor, in a war that was overwhelmingly vast, mechanized, and brutal.

It was a little touch of Margaret Polk in all the darkness, is what it was.

Some of the crews went for warlike symbols like fangs, tigers, or lightning bolts. Others favored cartoons—Donald Duck, Uncle Sam, or Adolf Hitler on the run. But the overwhelming favorite choice for nicknames and illustrations was the pinup girl.

Pinup girls had been spicing up the daydreams of American men (and boys) since the early 1930s. The talented illustrators Alberto Vargas and George Petty brought them into prominence—coy, apple-cheeked young women who managed to look almost innocent while exposing a good deal of fleshy real estate to public view. Not quite off-color, but not quite respectable either, these leggy ladies began gracing calendars, movie posters, and racy magazines such as *Esquire* in their bathing suits, lingerie, cowgirl skirts, and other brief costumes that a fellow wasn't too likely to see, say, down at the neighborhood ice-cream social. It was hardly surprising that when the war came, thousands of lonely servicemen adorned their weaponry with an assortment of Suzie Qs and Miss Liberties. To the German fighter pilots homing in on our American bombers, it must have looked sometimes as though they were being attacked by a wave of flying underwear catalogues.

Well, if every other crew was going to decorate its B-17, Bob Morgan's crew was going to do it too. I got the ten of us together one evening and put it to them. "Look," I said, "we need to name our airplane. Any ideas?"

There were ideas all right. Ten of them, one for each crewman. Here was one instance where teamwork just wasn't working. I wasn't being much help—I was trying to figure a good way to get the name of my new girlfriend Margaret Polk onto the nose. I called off the meeting before the guys declared war on one another.

A couple of nights later Jim Verinis and I went to the movies. The main feature was *Lady for a Night,* a John Wayne costume drama set on the Mississippi in the great Southern riverboat era. The leading woman, played by Joan Blondell, was the glamorous owner of a gambling boat called . . . well, you're way ahead of me.

"How about if we name her the *Memphis Belle*?" I asked the guys at our next skull session. Everybody looked at me like I was nuts. I guess my claim on their undying respect and adoration, as pilot of the damn plane, hadn't quite sunk in yet.

I decided to change my tactics. I'd work on that crew one member at a time, if I had to. My first victim was my tailgunner, a stocky red-haired fellow from Yonkers named John Quinlan. I invited J.P., as we

called him, to a place tailor-made for such weighty negotiations, a
beer joint outside Bangor. I stood him to a few brews, and then I
brought up the many virtues of naming our plane the *Memphis Belle.*
J.P. listened carefully to my arguments, and shook his head. I signaled the waitress for another round. J.P. drained his bottle and allowed that it wasn't the worst name he'd ever heard, but it had some
drawbacks. I addressed those drawbacks by standing him to a couple more cold ones. At some point in the evening—just before closing time, as I recall it—Johnny Quinlan began to see the whole thing
from my perspective. "Chief," he said, "I'll go along with you."

Mission accomplished. True to his word, J.P. voted for the *Belle* at
our next meeting. Jim Verinis fell into line like the good copilot he
was, although he wasn't entirely convinced. From there it grew into
a landslide. *Memphis Belle* it would be.

I was so tickled by my victory that I actually called up *Esquire,* got
the phone number of George Petty, tracked him down, identified myself, and told him I'd like him to draw us one of his Petty Girls to go
along with our plane's new name. He was gracious about it, thrilled to
be a part of things, in fact. The drawing that is now familiar to everyone who knows the *Belle,* which originally ran in the April 1941 issue
of *Esquire,* was sent up to Dow Field. An artist in our squadron, Corporal Tony Starcer, executed two faithful copies, one on each side of
the nose. In one of them, the "Belle" is wearing a red bathing suit as
she purrs into her telephone, in the other, a blue one. Starcer obeyed
my orders to the letter. "I don't care what color you put on her bathing
suit, as long as you put a bathing suit on her."

By now my crew was starting to get a sense of its own special
dash and flair. We were good and we knew it, we were cocky, and
we were brimming over with an eagerness to jump into the thick of
things over in Europe. That chance was looming directly ahead of
us. First, in the early days of September, came two special, inaugu-
ral flights for the *Memphis Belle*—one of them authorized, the
other not.

The unscheduled flight came first. We all just climbed into the airplane one day and set off for Memphis, Tennessee. I'd alerted Margaret that we were coming, in a plane named after her, with the idea

that this was really going to seal our romance, and boy, was I right. Polky was at the field, beaming and radiant, as we broke a bottle of champagne over the nose and posed for photographs.

We could not possibly have foreseen it at the time, but this was the beginning of the most-publicized romance of World War II. The national newspaper and magazine boys would leap onto our story of whirlwind courtship interrupted by war, a story enacted thousands of times over by young men and women all across America. What made our version special—or at least highly visible to the media—was that lilting name, and that sexy illustration, emblazoned on the nose of my B-17. That impulsive flight to Memphis sparked the larger-than-life version of Margaret Polk and Bob Morgan.

In ways we could not yet imagine, that spark would burn us both badly before it lost its heat.

Polky and I had to part again, virtually right after we'd arrived. A few hours of sleep for the crew and me, and then we hightailed it back up to Bangor. It was the last time I saw Margaret Polk before coming home from Europe.

The other trip—this one taken with Major Smelser's permission—was to Asheville, my hometown. The pretext was that we were to pick up our top-turret gunner, Gene Atkins, who lived in Johnson City, Tennessee, just over the mountain from Asheville. We stayed a couple of nights. I got to say good-bye to my father and Dave, and then on the fourteenth we were airborne for Mitchel Field on Long Island, New York, our last stateside stop before heading across the Atlantic.

I managed one important bit of personal business at Mitchel. I got myself engaged to Margaret. By mail. I proposed to her by letter about the third week of September, just before we broke for the British Isles, and she accepted by return mail. Both those letters are sadly missing from my files. I put an engagement ring in a package and sent it off to her, along with an ecstatic note handwritten on Mitchel Field letterhead and dated "Any time/Any place."

To: the dearest person in all the world—You—

With this ring you are mine for as long as you love me. God make that forever.

I'll return to make you happy forever.

Yours,
Bob

Then I telegrammed her a message.

CONGRATULATIONS ON OUR ENGAGEMENT I AM THE LUCKIEST PERSON EVER

BOB MORGAN

To Gander, Newfoundland on September 25. We'd hoped to take off for the British Isles the next morning, but were obliged to cool our heels for a few days. A group of B-25s flew in not long after we'd landed, and to our chagrin, they monopolized priority-status for several days. Why? Well, that's what Second Lieutenant Morgan wanted to know, and I brazenly asked the question of Major Smelser.

The Major's answer came back even more acidly than usual. They had priority, Morgan, because President Roosevelt's son Elliot was aboard one of them.

I could live with that reason.

On September 30, we finally began the long transatlantic haul to the British Isles. It was a twelve-hour flight, the longest by far any of us had ever flown at a stretch.

We hit Prestwick field right on schedule. We were in the war now. It wasn't exactly the way I'd dreamed of getting to England and Europe back in Mabel Morgan's vegetable garden. But I was there now, with nine close comrades and a beautiful flying machine with my sweetheart's nickname on it, and I meant to leave some calling cards before I came back home.

CHAPTER

7

The air war had been raging over Europe for two years by the time our elements of the Eighth Air Force began to arrive late in 1942 and deploy across the misty English countryside. With Hitler's tanks and massed infantry bogged down in the Soviet Union's maw, it was about the only active form of combat going. As it raged, it kept on creating and re-creating itself in a furious upward curve, attackers and defenders alike improvising tactics on a round-the-clock basis, ransacking science and engineering for new technology, any kind of edge—new bomber specs and new fighter-plane wrinkles, new calibrations and ever-higher ranges in antiaircraft fire, radar, rockets, machinegunnery. It was a Buck Rogers serial playing at high speed up there, except the gadgets and the death were real.

In early June the Royal Air Force had launched its first thousand-plane assault, a raid on the west German city of Cologne. Most of those planes were two-engine jobs with limited range, and many of them were scrounged from civilian and training stock. The damage was relatively light, but with that strike and a couple more like it at Bremen and the Ruhr, the British flyers were at least delivering some payback for that horrific summer of 1940. They scored a psychological point with the strutting Luftwaffe chieftain, Hermann Goering, who had sneered that if any enemy aircraft ever showed up over Germany, his colleagues could call him by a Jewish name.

Still, the British experience with aerial warfare had so far been mixed, at best. As we were getting used to our Spam-and-powdered-egg mess-hall breakfasts and tepid English beer, a high-level controversy was crackling over how we were to be used in the bloody months just ahead of us.

No one disputed the urgent need for a strategic bombing campaign of unprecedented scope, targeting Nazi war factories, submarine pens, and transportation centers. The Allies would have to depend on this kind of counterthrust to blunt the powerful Wehrmacht until the West could mobilize and mount a massive land invasion of Europe—at least a year in the future. The English landscape, or vast stretches of it from north to south and east to west, was in the process of being given over to the rapid construction of landing strips, hangars, barracks, and officers' quarters.

The issue that divided the American and the British bombing commands centered on the prickly question of daylight bombing as opposed to nighttime raids. The RAF's debacles at Brest and Wilhelmshaven had soured their faith in daylight missions, not to mention the B-17 itself. The Army Air Forces, commanded by Gen. Ira Eaker with Gen. Carl Spaatz as his deputy, had analyzed those debacles and spotted the flaws that led to them. They were convinced not only that higher-level, skillfully executed daylight raids could work, but that night bombing, with its notorious imprecision, would be a catastrophic waste of materiel and energy.

On that matter of precision, we Yanks had a piece of technology that, we were convinced, would let us lay our bombs down as accurately as Bob Feller painting the corners of home plate with his fastball. It was the Norden bombsight, named for its inventor, Carl Norden, back in 1931. The Norden made use of a gyroscope to stabilize the bombardier's telescopic sights and neutralize the airplane's pitches and rolls. It employed a clockwork-like mechanism to synchronize data fed into it by the bombardier—altitude, speed, drift, the weight of the bombs—and signal the exact moment for optimum release. The RAF had not had access to the Norden, and the Germans were licking their chops to lay hands on its makeup. Meanwhile, the Army Air Forces had it and we were itching to show our British friends how it could "drop a bomb down a pickle barrel."

First we had to make a critical adjustment in our bombing-run technique that would allow us to maximize the Norden's potential.

Then we had to persuade the British to let us do our stuff, which entailed warding off a subtle campaign to fold the Army Air Forces into the command of the Royal Air Force.

As these debates swirled above us, we boys who'd carry out the eventual plan were concerned with far weightier questions. Where should we drop our bags? How do you drive on the left? Are English girls prettier than American girls?

The search for billeting turned up a lucky strike for the 91st.

Assigned to a drab, newly built air base called Kimbolton when we touched down, we resigned ourselves to a barracks routine of damp, sterile Quonset huts and scrubby surroundings far out in the countryside.

Then our pilots encountered a happy problem—the runways on this base had been built for fighter planes, not 60,000-pound B-17s. Our big planes were tearing up tarmac as they dropped heavily out of the skies. I say happy because that problem led the 91st's Group Commander, Col. Stanley Wray, to look for more suitable digs for us. He was ordered to do so by none other than General Eaker himself. And Colonel Wray's dutiful search turned up a site that, once we pounced on it, made us the envy of every other group on the whole island of England.

It was all the more delicious for us because technically, we had no business being there.

The place was called Bassingbourn.

The Colonel stumbled across Bassingborn in mid-October. Bassingbourn was as far from a cookie-cutter, built-from-scratch base as you could imagine. It was in fact a delightful, improbable remnant of medieval England. This tidy little parish and village sat toward the western end of Cambridgeshire, near the village of Royston in the ancient kingdom north of London known as East Anglia. The old stone libraries and gaunt towers of Cambridge University, founded in the twelfth century, were just a medium-range bicycle ride away.

Clustered on Bassingbourn's flat green pea-and-barley fields, where sheep grazed in the fine rain and 500-year-old cathedral spires dotted the horizon, were three spacious old redbrick estates, well restored and set behind hedges and flower gardens. They were Bass-ingbourn Richmond Manor and Castles Seymours and Rowsey. Brooding over this peaceful scene was the gothic Church of Sts. Peter and Paul, built in the fourteenth century and housing a register that dated to 1558.

It wasn't the Vanderbilt Estate, but it was a lot closer to that than I'd ever expected to come in the middle of an international shooting war.

In the late 1930s, as England warily viewed the remobilization of its Great War enemy on the Continent, the trustees of these estates had permitted the Royal Air Force to build a spacious airfield, com-plete with hangars and outbuildings, on the village grounds. This was the enchanting enclave that Col. Stanley Wray came upon in what had been merely a humble search for an adequate airfield.

There were some knotty details to unravel. The most vexing was that the RAF had already laid claim to Bassingbourn. This is what General Eaker informed the Colonel, in no uncertain terms, as soon as he had located the site on a military map. "You cannot take over a British base without their permission," he admonished Colonel Wray sternly by telephone, "and I don't have their permission."

Colonel Wray demonstrated exemplary resourcefulness under fire. "Well, Sir," he responded, "we are already moved in here."

"You mean," said the General, "that you've already moved your entire group into those buildings? The planes? Everything?"

"Yes, Sir," said the Colonel.

This was not great news to General Eaker, who already had his hands full trying to soothe the RAF's rancor over the upstart Yanks' de-termination to run the European bombing campaign from British soil. Something about the Colonel's audacity must have appealed to him, be-cause he refrained from a direct order to move out. "You may have to move again," he warned the group leader. "I'll look into this, but I don't know exactly what we can do about it. We'll see."

Whatever the General said worked pretty well. We stayed there for the duration. Bassingbourn became known as a showcase, *the* base for billeting and entertaining visiting dignitaries both military and civil. Politicians came there. Generals. Bob Hope stayed overnight en route to Europe and we did our best to trade wisecracks with him. A waistgunner/trainer named Clark Gable passed through, as did a pretty, young war correspondent whom I escorted to London a couple of times during her stay there.

My three officers and I dived into our new quarters. We claimed the upstairs suites of one of those old estates—warm, comfy bedrooms, good baths, a lounge, even a kitchen in case we needed one. I doubt we could do as well these days if we went through a travel agent.

Both sides might have been improvising this air war as it went along, but everybody played by one rule, the oldest in the history of organized killing. Sheer numbers usually win. In the fall of 1942, England had more or less turned into one big tarmac. Some 55,000 American servicemen and women of the Army Air Forces had arrived—a fraction of the 350,000 who would pass through by war's end.

An appalling percentage of these young men were headed for disaster. The toll on those who flew aloft was horrific. More than 30,000 fliers would be killed or missing, and another 30,000 ended up as prisoners of war. Two out of every three boys who flew missions—and by "boy," I'm talking about an average age of twenty— were killed. The Eighth Air Force took more casualties in World War II than the Marine Corps and the Navy combined.

East Anglia alone—an area about the size of Vermont—was the site of 130 bases. The average population was about 2,500, consisting of pilots and crews, maintenance and repair people, radiomen, cooks, clerks, and medical staff.

Let me tell you about one small group of them. The crew of the *Memphis Belle.*

Capt. Jim Verinis, my "second" pilot, I already mentioned. At twenty-four, he was one of two guys older than me—I was twenty-three then. Jim would be with us only for our first five missions before he got a plane of his own, but I'll always think of him as *the* copilot of the *Belle.*

Jim was an all-state basketball player from Stamford, Connecticut, where he'd developed a deadly two-handed set shot. He went on to the University of Connecticut, and that's where he must have developed his deadly skill at poker. I never saw a man who played a hand better than he did. After the war I went into business with Jim, and at this writing he is still my best friend in the world, closer to me than my blood relatives.

Staff Sgt. Quinlan I mentioned too—the tailgunner. He could sing "The Wabash Cannonball" better than anyone I ever met, he was the guy who swung the *Belle*'s naming vote for me, and now he'd have to keep those Focke-Wulf 190s from running up on the *Belle* from behind with the twin machineguns of his that he called Pete and Repeat. J.P. was born for that task—he loved to shoot. He'd honed his skills potting squirrels and deer on his homestead farm outside Yonkers, New York—land long since swallowed up by suburbia. He used up more ammunition than anybody else on the plane. He'd rack up two confirmed kills during our missions and many more that were not confirmed only because the necessary witnesses were busy fighting. Quinlan was a Jimmy Cagney look-alike with those deep eyes and that tight mouth set high above his chin. "Lucky Horseshoe," I came to call him, because of his way of ducking his head just as a round would pass where it had been an instant ago. He saved the plane a few times, too, with that trademark cry of his—*"Dive, Chief, dive!"*

Our ball turret gunner, the guy down below the fuselage, was Staff Sgt. Cecil Scott, from my home state of North Carolina, a town called Arapahoe that wasn't even on the map. Scotty had the last job I'd want on a bombing crew, hanging down out of that airplane over a combat zone, watching the flak spiral upward and the fighters zoom by, maybe looking to shoot some holes in the nearby bomb bay. But Scotty handled it like the hero he was. A quiet and kind man on the ground, he was the oldest at twenty-six, and also the smallest. Had to be, to curl up inside that little capsule. "Best position on the airplane," he liked to say. "You get to see a lot of action, you're always busy." He had another reason, too: "If the plane catches on fire you know it first because you can see all four engines." I liked a fellow who was able to look at the bright side of things.

Capt. Vincent Evans was our bombardier. Vince was a pure life-force, always into something. If he had his way, there'd be a female involved. The British women loved those babyface Yank features and that sly Texas drawl of his, and married though he was, Vince could seldom resist returning the compliment.

Vince lived out one of the biggest and most glamorous lives I know of before his death in 1980 in—of all things—an airplane accident. Several times married and divorced, a courter of singers and movie starlets, he gravitated to Hollywood after the war and struck up friendships with Ronald Reagan, Jimmy Stewart, Humphrey Bogart, and June Allyson. He acted a little and wrote the screenplays for two Air Force adventure movies—*Chain Lightning,* starring Bogart in 1950, and *Battle Hymn,* with Rock Hudson, in 1957. He drove race cars, ran a cattle ranch and then a famous restaurant and generally reigned as a Southern California legend of the early postwar years. "Kid Wonder," his sister Peggy called him.

More important than any of the glamour, Vince was one of the best bombardiers I have ever seen. How he got to that level at age twenty-two, from running a fleet of trucks in Fort Worth before enlisting, I'll never know. Vince was the man in charge of making the B-17 do what it was made to do, and he did it as well and as precisely as anybody who ever flew over Europe.

Ever know anybody who never seemed to make a mistake? I did. I knew Capt. Charles Leighton from Flint, Michigan, our navigator. A twenty-three-year-old chemistry student out of Ohio Wesleyan, Chuck ran the maps and charts and compasses on our missions, and he never got us lost using that primitive, sun-and-stars-based equipment. In fact, he saved us twice from drifting off course and back into enemy territory. If that sounds like nothing more than the minimum job description, try factoring in these elements: a sky filled with black smoke from bursting flak and whizzing aircraft both enemy and friendly, fierce blasts of wind and weather, false navigational beams being thrown up by the Germans on the ground, voices screaming through your headset phones, and the superhuman need to keep concentrating, concentrating, concentrating after seven to eight hours of trauma-filled flying. Oh, yes, and the need to lend a hand with the machineguns from time to time.

All this from a guy who overcame chronic airsickness so intense that he never flew without an empty milk carton throughout basic training. The carton nearly always filled up.

Boyish, but quiet and scholarly, and always faithful to his young fiancée Jane—he became a teacher and counselor after the war—Chuck had trained to be a pilot, but took up navigating to get to the war sooner. His hallmark was constantly checking and rechecking his configurations. He still found time to prepare for emergency duties outside his area. Never trained in gunnery, he'd fire his machinegun at waves in the Atlantic to improve his aim, and it paid off the day he shot down a German fighter over Wilhelmshaven.

Technical Sgt. Harold P. Loch, a twenty-two-year-old stevedore out of Green Bay, Wisconsin, would have been happy to spend his life up in the north woods hunting and fishing, which he did, after helping win World War II as our engineer and top turret gunner. In addition to trading machinegun fire with swooping German fighters, Harold was our gauge-switch-and-fuse man, the guy who knew the *Belle*'s innards like a surgeon knows the human body. If something went wrong with a B-17 in the midst of a mission—and you could count on several somethings going wrong—you needed a guy who could get the wires reconnected and make the lights go back on in the heat of combat. All this while keeping his gunsights trained on attackers coming in from any direction.

Our radio operator was Technical Sgt. Robert Hanson. Twenty-two, married, a construction worker from Spokane, he held down another key job that called for concentration and precision under pressure. Besides keeping in touch with our command back at the base, Robert was the communications link with all of us inside the plane. He let us know what was going on from his vantage point, he worked in close tandem with the navigator, and he even doubled as the crew's amateur psychologist—keeping everyone relaxed en route to the target with his occasional low-key remarks over the phones.

The "kid" of our crew, the scrubbed teenager with the shy choirboy grin, was Staff Sgt. Casimir Nastal. Less than a year earlier, "Tony" Nastal was trying not to nick himself while shaving, and working at a washing-machine repair shop in Detroit. Now he was a waistgunner, shrewd and cool, and a deadly shot from the midsection of the plane. Conscientious, too—he took care of those guns of his like a guy with a shiny new car.

The other waistgunner was Staff Sgt. Clarence Winchell, twenty-five, a chemist for a paint company in Chicago before joining up. "Winch," or Bill, as we usually called him, was small and frail, but he had a lion's heart and a kind of serenity about him, bolstered, I guess, by the Bible he always carried. The enlisted men all looked up to Winch, and he had a good influence especially on young Tony—he could calm the kid and give him confidence.

There is one other fellow that I have to list as a member of the crew, although he never once left the ground inside the *Memphis Belle*. All he did was keep her flying.

This was a dark-eyed, cloth-capped, gap-toothed, grease-stained, wrench-wielding nonstop miracle-worker from Hulneville, Pennsylvania, named Joe Giambrone. Joe was the *Belle*'s ground-crew chief. If Joe got a night's sleep during 1942 or 1943 I'm not aware of it. He was too busy bringing the *Belle* back from the dead time and time again—he and his crew of ten fanatical bomber-jockeys.

Joe and his crew were the first people we'd see each time we touched down at Bassingbourn after another mission, running pell-mell across the tarmac for the spot where I'd bring the *Belle* to rest. Almost before the propellers stopped turning, these guys would be swarming over the plane—counting flak holes and then caulking them up, assessing wing and motor damage, calculating where they could go to sweet-talk or barter or swipe whatever spare parts were needed to get our increasingly battered plane up in the air one more time.

The *Belle* was the only plane Joe and his boys worked on, and they knew her like a concert violinist knows his Stradivarius. They could change a shot-up engine in four hours. Most crews took the better part of a day. Joe was the best cannibalizer I ever met—he could descend on a grounded or disabled plane, rummage through it and find exactly the gizmo or piece of wiring that had been torn up in our last mission. Sometimes he had to cajole people. Sometimes he had to make deals. He probably had to do things I wouldn't even want to know about, but when he said the plane was ready, it was ready. He'd never lie to us, never cut corners. We knew that every time we took off for another sortie in our bomber, it was as airworthy as the day it rolled off the line.

In the six months that the *Belle* saw combat, Joe Giambrone's crew replaced nine engines, both wings, two tails, both main landing gear and a lot more, not to mention caulking up hundreds of flak and bullet holes. It took him forty-five years to confess to me how he'd solved one crisis, an over-inflated de-icer on my right wing. "Bob, I took an icepick and stabbed it full of holes," he admitted to me over drinks in a bar in London during a reunion one time.

I guess I even got a little spoiled by how good he was. Our B-17's three-bladed propellers were driven by Wright engines, and they were superb. As the losses and damage mounted up in early 1943, we started to get replacement engines made by the Studebaker automobile company. I didn't care for the Studebakers. I would tell Joe, "If it's the last thing in the world you do for me, don't put a Studebaker engine on my plane." Every time, he somehow came up with a Wright.

He never once complained about the damage he'd have to somehow make right. "Gave her a fit today, didn't you, Chief?" was as close as he'd come to assessing the challenge before him and his boys.

When the *Belle* was dedicated and placed in its Mud Island museum in 1987, I took a commercial flight to Memphis for the ceremonies. There to meet me when I stepped off the plane was a familiar-looking figure in a cloth cap, grease-stained work clothes and a bright gleam in his dark eyes. Joe Giambrone had showed up in the same outfit that he'd worn at Bassingbourn.

A few other good men rotated in and out as sometime members of the *Belle*: Leviticus "Levy" Dillon, who flew several missions for us as a top turret gunner; E. Scott Miller, who flew with us on fifteen missions as a waistgunner and then dropped out of sight after the war, for which he gained the nickname "The Lost Crewman"; Eugene Adkins, who flew a few times at top turret before suffering severe frostbite on our tenth mission; the several officers who did turns as copilot after Jim Verinis left.

This crew called me "The Chief." I took that as a point of honor. It meant that they trusted me unconditionally as I piloted them into war.

I trusted them. These boys I'd be flying with were something special, and it didn't take them long to start proving that.

We couldn't have been on the base more than a couple of weeks before Vince Evans started showing us how he could make fresh eggs appear out of thin air. Or out of somewhere. Sure as hell wasn't the mess hall kitchen. Vince had started to explore the countryside around Bassingbourn in his free time, but I can guarantee you he wasn't out there taking pictures of cathedrals or doing rubbings of tombstones. He was making the rounds of the local farms. The farms, you see, had chickens that laid eggs. Some of the farms also had farmer's daughters. Well, our Vince explored these farms until he found just the right combination of the two—a cute farmer's daughter on a farm with chickens that laid eggs—and when he'd reconnoitered that site, he switched on the old Vince Evans crooked-grin charm. From then on, we crewmen of the *Memphis Belle* had fresh eggs for breakfast. Vince would bring a sack of eggs home after every visit to that farm. We had more damn eggs than you ever saw in your life. We had so many eggs that when we would go to London we would take a bunch of eggs down to the restaurants and get them to make us a batch of omelettes. And hold the Spam.

While Vince was flirting in the neighborhood barnyards, I was composing my first letter to Margaret from across the ocean:

> I sit here so many miles from you and write you my first letter from England. It is quite hard to write, darling, for there is so much in my head and it is so hard to put it on paper. You'll no doubt get bored with my letters, but try to understand that I must be careful what I write.
>
> You must always have faith that I'll be back one of these days. You and I have a wonderful life ahead of us and I am sure we will both dream of it much in the near future. Our life was meant to be and it will be, my love . . .

You will love it over here and someday we'll return together, my love.

The "Memphis Belle" will always stick by us and it will make our future secure.

All my love to you, my darling, forever.

We kept on flying practice missions through mid-October. I had now logged 917 hours and 25 minutes of flying time and had been named a flight leader, but I was stuck in my rank of second lieutenant—the only flight leader in our group with that low a ranking. The general whose beach party I'd buzzed back in Florida apparently had let the chain of command know of his wish that I was not to be promoted. Someone was enforcing that wish. Someone who carried a swagger stick, maybe?

It didn't bother me. I was flying a B-17, and itching for combat. Gung-ho. Ready, eager, willing, and able, second lieutenant or not. I had a good group of pilots on my wing. We had committed ourselves to mastering the hair's-breadth skill of tight formations, wingtips literally inches apart up there. We'd been told that tight formations were going to be the secret in combat, giving us that tight cluster of concentrated fire outward toward the enemy fighters. We worked at tight formations, and by God we achieved tight formations. Of course, all this was still pure theory to us—nobody had yet taken a shot at us; well, nobody except for that fisherman in Maine, and we'd never had to fire back at anybody. In fact, at this stage the General himself didn't know any more about the realities of combat than we did. Our training was all trial-and-error. Now we were ready for the next step—trial-and-error combat.

We took that step on November 7, 1942.

It was a propitious moment in the war. Six days earlier Allied tanks and troops under British General Bernard Montgomery had at last broken through Erwin Rommel's meatgrinder lines at El Alamein, in North Africa. Operation Torch, the U.S. invasion of that territory, would begin November 8. In Russia, Hitler's legions were bogged down in the mutual slaughter that was the Battle of Stalingrad.

And now the 91st was going to raise some hell of its own.

One other bomber group from the Mighty Eighth had already flown sorties over France by this time. Our first mission would be to Brest, on the tip of a peninsula on the French coast below the English Channel. The Nazis maintained a huge system of submarine pens there, and knocking them out would help reduce the enormous toll the U-boats were still exacting in the North Atlantic.

Mission Number 1. What a fragile, first-day-of-school sound that phrase had! Number 1 out of how many?

We were subdued on the evening of the sixth. The usual horseplay was missing. We ate quietly. My officers and I dined together, and the six enlisted men ate with one another. No one was looking much at anyone else. I guess nobody was too eager to say what was on his mind, or to hear what the other fellow was thinking, for that matter.

In a lot of ways it was like the night before your first varsity football game. None of us had any idea, really, what to expect, no concept of what it would be like to be shot at. We'd heard all the stories about the losses the RAF had taken—we'd heard the statistics. Still, it was a kind of void for us, a vacancy of specific images or expectations that each of us filled in as best he could. In solitude.

We turned in early. Busy day tomorrow.

A drizzly English sky greeted us the next morning. Clear enough for flying, though. And so this was it.

As soon as we awoke, it was as though we'd all stepped onto some invisible conveyor-belt. Every move we made now, everything we did was drawing us inexorably toward that moment when we would board the *Memphis Belle* and take off into enemy skies that held the prospect of terror, destruction, pain, and violent death.

We assembled in the briefing room as soon as we were dressed. We sat in wooden chairs, our leather flight jackets zipped under fleecy collars, and watched Colonel Wray as he strode back and forth in front of a map of western Europe, brandishing a pointer, revealing to us what our mission was and what we could expect. A big, hearty man, a West Point graduate, he had a way of giving it to us straight, no sugar-coating, no under-estimations of the odds against us to make us feel good, but all leavened with a rough sense of humor.

Colonel Wray's most famous device for getting laughs was the Rigid Digit. If somebody taxied wrong or racked up a slight error on a practice mission or screwed up some minor task on the base or got back late from London, Colonel Wray would point the culprit out at the next briefing and growl, "Okay, pilot, you're awarded the Rigid Digit for that!" Later on, some of us presented him with a glove that had its index finger stuffed so that it stuck straight up. He took it pretty well.

Anyway, Colonel Wray gave us all the intelligence information he could about the target and ground defenses and likely tactics. The Germans would likely put up a smoke screen to cover the target area, he said, if the wind was blowing in the right direction. Then the weather officer got up there and told us what to expect in that area—clear skies and low winds. Weather information was vital to us, but it was not always reliable—we didn't exactly have a lot of input from the folks we were about to bomb. The French Underground sometimes came through for us, Allied sympathizers in the French countryside communicating by code, and since weather generally moved from west to east, we had the benefit of some pretty educated guesses.

Then Colonel Wray took the stage again and reminded us of the fundamentals. *You flight leaders, keep your formations tight; you bombardiers, keep alert to the lead plane, know where it is, you're going to be toggling your bombs out on the lead plane's release.* By that he meant that the lead bombardier in each group would be operating the Norden bombsight, which would trigger an automatic release when its horizontal and vertical hairs crossed on the target site. Everyone behind him would then manually jettison via the "toggle" switch. *If the lead plane is not there, the secondary lead will take over.*

Bombardiers, if you can't see the first target, go to the second. If you can't see the second, go to the third. But don't drop your bombs indiscriminately. If you can't bomb any targets, don't jettison on open cities. Bring your bombs home.

You gunners, don't get caught sleeping. If you think you scored a hit, don't watch him fall. There'll be others coming at you.

You navigators and radiomen, stay in contact with one another. Be ready to take over a gun if somebody gets hit.

All you men—this is your first mission. I expect you to do a good job. I wish you all the best of luck. Keep your intercoms clear. Don't break radio silence unless absolutely necessary.

That's it. Synchronize your watches.

Colonel Wray put down his pointer and left the briefing room with the rest of us. He was no armchair commander—he would personally lead us into our first action, flying copilot with Lt. Duane Jones in the first plane off the ground, *Pandora's Box*. The *Belle* was slated to lift off second.

Breakfast, then, for those who wanted breakfast. A consultation with a minister or a priest or a rabbi for the guys who felt the need for that.

Then we waited.

There was usually an interval of an hour, or an hour and a half, between the briefing and taxi time. On this first morning, the crew of the *Memphis Belle* did what we'd do on each of our succeeding missions. We gathered quietly and ran down the list of each of our duties. It was all low-key and professional. These young men around me, these working-class guys from several corners of America, who liked to drink beer and play cards and flirt with girls—suddenly they had the solemnity and the level gazes of men twice their age. It wasn't fear, although we were all a little anxious. It was ten minds coming into acute focus.

Half an hour before taxi time, all the members of all the crews got into jeeps and made that sobering little ride to the waiting airplanes. If it's going to hit you, it's going to hit you then—whatever peak of fear, anxiety, or urge to turn back, that you're going to feel. Quinlan used to spend those rides fantasizing about ways out. A bomb-hauling truck would hit the jeep, hurting him just badly enough that he'd have to stay home. The plane would veer off the runway and get mired in the mud. Once you're under way, your mind can finally attach itself to the routine tasks at hand, and push the terror deep into the background. Being under way is actually a relief. It's that damn ride to the planes that nearly kills you.

At the last minute before takeoff on that first mission, I rounded my crew into a huddle at the base of the *Belle*. We put our arms around one another, and I talked to them quietly for a couple of minutes.

I can't recall the words I said. The important thing was that this was *our* huddle, our moment to come together among ourselves. To hear one another's breathing, feel one another's hands on our shoulders. To experience that instant when we stopped being ten separate entities, and became one.

At 10:22 A.M. a signal rocket from the Tower arced into the air and burst, and the 91st flew to France.

The best thing I can say about that first mission is that it was a valuable learning experience. We didn't lose a single plane to the enemy, and we didn't even suffer much damage. We only saw one Nazi fighter plane, and he was too far out of range to even bother shooting at. Quinlan shot at him anyway.

We didn't do much damage ourselves. But we learned. We would keep on learning.

What we learned mainly on this first mission was how cold it was up at those altitudes. Cruising at 21,000 feet, we discovered that temperatures of minus 40 degrees could freeze our guns if they weren't properly checked and lubricated. Only the front part of the airplane—the areas where the pilot, copilot, flight engineer, navigator, and bombardier sat—was wired for heating on the B-17, a design shortfall that the gunners did not appreciate! We learned how valuable an oxygen mask was, and what frostbite felt like. Fourteen bombers had taken off from Bassingbourn, each carrying ten 500-pound bombs. Six had to abort the mission because of equipment problems and chilled, oxygen-deprived crewmen. The eight remaining planes mostly missed the submarine pens. The lead bombardier—not our Vince Evans, by the way—had trouble calibrating through the cloud cover and let loose at the wrong time. Everybody else followed suit and made the same error.

None of us knew that at the time, of course. We made our return to Bassingbourn in a pretty cocky mood. We'd bombed Brest, we were in it now, we'd gotten a lick in at Germany. The flak was bad, but we didn't have to deal with any fighter attacks. Hell, if things kept going this way, it looked like a pretty good war.

Things didn't.

The aerial photographs, when they were developed, supported our illusion for a little while. Colonel Wray reviewed them and was impressed. Then the Intelligence guy took a closer look and said, in effect, "Don't start bragging yet." He was right. When the photos were reviewed at General Eaker's office, the word came down. *You guys did not do much of a job today. We're not putting this out for publication, but you basically screwed up.*

Reality had not set in for us yet. On that first mission we must have been like those raw Yankee troops heading down to Manassas, Virginia, for the Battle of Bull Run, full of youthful exuberance. One of our airplane crews even claimed they'd shot a German fighter down. What the hell? Why not? That sort of claim became a sort of joke in those first weeks: Everybody would come back reporting a fighter shot down. Our generals figured out pretty quick that if we'd really shot down all the fighters we claimed, the Luftwaffe was damn near wiped out already. So the generals made it tough. If you wanted credit for shooting down an airplane, it had to be confirmed by two observers. One of them could be on your own plane, but the other had to be from somewhere else in your formation. Well, naturally, most crewmen had other things to do on a mission besides keep tally of Nazi planes falling out of the sky. That's why a lot of good gunners, including several in my crew, didn't get as much credit for kills as they deserved.

For me, that first sortie was about like any practice run. From where I sat in the cockpit, I could not see anything except what was straight in front of me. I'm mostly looking at the instrument panel anyway, or over at the planes on either wing. It was an irony of design, I guess, but in that type of bomber the pilot could see less—at least, of combat—than any other crew member. The best front views on a B-17 bomber belong to the bombardier and the navigator, because they are right in the nose of the plane, surrounded by glass. Me, I just kept my hands on that yoke and my feet on those rudder pedals, and I concentrated on flying straight and level, in tight formation.

My mother, Mabel Morgan,
in the 1930s.

My father, David Morgan Sr.,
in the 1950s.

That's me on the left
at age five, in 1923—
a bomber pilot in training,
down to the same pose and
look on my face as my
wartime portrait, above.

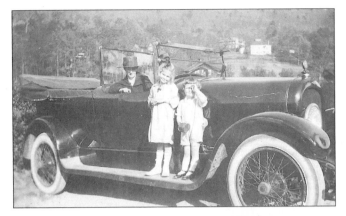

April 24, 1921.
My sister and I
on the running board
of the family
Packard touring car.

April 29, 1924.
My sister and I
in the backyard just
before going to
Cornelia Vanderbilt's
wedding.

Cornelia Vanderbilt's wedding. I believe that's my sister at the far left.
She was one of the flower girls. NORTH CAROLINA COLLECTION,
PACK MEMORIAL PUBLIC LIBRARY, ASHEVILLE, NORTH CAROLINA

July 1941, with a BT-15 for Basic Training at Bush Field
in Augusta, Georgia.

April 17, 1943. The attack on the Focke-Wulf factory over Bremen,
Germany. The white puff on the left is a flak burst. There is a
smokescreen being laid down in the upper right. The bombs fall
and the B-17s fly on in their formation. NATIONAL ARCHIVES

May 17, 1943. We completed our twenty-fifth mission. In this staged publicity photo the crew and I run across the field after returning safely.

Posing with Hollywood director William Wyler (standing, fifth from left) after completing the twenty-fifth mission. Joe Giambrone paints the twenty-fifth bomb on the *Belle*'s nose. INSET: Waistgunners Tony Nastal and Bill Winchell. The fuselage of the 17 was a pretty cramped space.

Copilot Jim Verinis, navigator Chuck Leighton, and I thank
our ground crew just before we return to the States.
Crew chief Joe Giambrone is on the far right.

The *Memphis Belle* and her crew. From left to right, top turret gunner
Harold Loch, ball turret gunner Cecil Scott, radio operator Robert Hanson,
copilot Jim Verinis, me, navigator Chuck Leighton, tailgunner J. P. Quinlan,
waistgunner Tony Nastal, bombardier Vince Evans, and waistgunner
Bill Winchell. NATIONAL ARCHIVES

The *Memphis Belle* leaves England for the last time, headed for the U.S. This is one of her few airborne photos, although there is plenty of movie footage of her in flight. NATIONAL ARCHIVES

After dodging flak and Messerschmitts over Germany, flying a B-17 between the County Court House and Asheville City Hall was a piece of cake, even if I did have to bank the plane on a sixty-degree angle. Rattled a few windows, though.

Boeing
PLANE TALK

READ CAREFULLY
"MEMPHIS BELLE"
"PROGRAM INSTRUC-
TIONS ON PAGE 2

NO. 51

WICHITA, KANSAS, JULY 31, 1943

VOL. 1

"MEMPHIS BELLE" AT PLANTS MONDAY

War-Scarred Memphis Belle Keeps Date With Cupid Here At Joyous Coming-Out Party

Famed Flying Fortress Finds Royal Welcome, Its Pilot Finds His Fiance Upon Arrival At Airport— Thousands Cheer Crew At War Bond Rally

MONEY FOR YOU

Fifty dollars every week the Sun-Telegraph gives for novelties!

If you see or hear of news, call the Novelty Editor, Gilbert 6500.

The editors determine which tips are of the greatest value. Then the checks roll out!

Pittsburgh
Sun-Telegraph

WEDNESDAY, JUNE 30, 1943

RATIONING TIMETABLE

Pittsburgh Toasts 'Memphis Belle' Crew

This ought to give an idea of the grueling schedule we kept on our Public Relations Tour through the summer of 1943. A night on the town in Chicago, top; a crowd gathering to hear us speak at Wright Field in Dayton, Ohio, middle; and addressing the crowd at my old company, the Addressograph Multigraph Corp. in Cleveland. That's our mascot, Stuka, in my arms.

Lame Brain and Jug Head. The real Memphis belle, Margaret Polk, surprised me at our stop in Cleveland.
This photo ran in *Life* magazine on August 2, 1943.

*   *   *

Our crew had two days to rest up from that first taste of World War II, and then on the ninth we were in the air, headed for France again, one of five groups. This time our destination was St. Nazaire, a coastal city farther south than Brest, and the site of another huge cluster of German submarine sheds and pens. This time each plane carried five thousand-pound bombs.

What a different mission from Brest this turned out to be. It was our true indoctrination into the realities of combat, into the realization that people could get killed doing this kind of thing. Could get killed and were getting killed.

On our sortie to Brest, we had flown at 21,000 feet. This time they stacked us vertically. Two of the groups went in at roughly the same altitude—18,000 and 27,000 feet—while the other three swooped in low. The higher groups were decoys, flying about where the Germans expected them to be flying. If the plan worked, they would draw the fighters' fire as they came screaming and chattering downward out of the sun. Meanwhile three lower groups would be unnoticed as they stole toward the target.

The *Belle* led the lowest of the attacking groups. We pilots went in at treetop level till we reached the French coast, hanging on to our rudders and throttles for dear life, and then we kicked it, climbing abruptly to 9,000 feet, our bombing altitude.

True to the plan, we found little fighter opposition. The boys above us were catching all that hell, as the Allied plan coldly anticipated. Our top turret gunners had an unobstructed view of their fiery ordeal as the Nazi hornets converged. Three bombers paid the ultimate price from one group, and one bomber from another. Many more were damaged as the Focke-Wulfs flew wild.

What we did find down there was flak.

It must have been Flak Day in Occupied France. The antiaircraft fire blossomed out as we crossed the coast and gunned into our acceleration, and it never let up. A vast black blanket opened up beneath our wingtips, accented with blazing orange. Not one of our planes escaped damage. A crewman was killed and nine others wounded by exploding fragments. Astoundingly, not one of our planes was lost. We felt the *Belle* shake with two or three concussions from antiaircraft fire. Joe Giambrone counted sixty-three holes when we got back.

Our bombing was good that day. Not outstanding—this would not be our last visit—but enough to leave a pretty good mess amidst those pens and the U-boats trapped inside them. We got congratulated by everybody from Colonel Wray all the way up the chain to Bomber Command headquarters.

Maybe it was the adrenaline still pumping through my system on the way home that led me to take one of the craziest risks I ever took or even heard about in that war. Maybe I was just girl-crazy.

En route back to Bassingbourn in the late afternoon, entertaining myself with thoughts of a certain cuddly young agent from British Intelligence awaiting me in London that evening, I heard the urgent voice of Levy Dillon, our flight engineer that day, on the intercom. He'd discovered an oil line that had been punctured by flak. "We better put her down as soon as we can, Chief," he warned.

I had Bob Hanson radio the RAF base at Exeter, at the edge of Dartmoor just north of the English Channel coast, that we were coming in for an emergency landing. The control tower was all British hospitality.

Once on the ground Levy caulked up the leaky line in no time, but when I went to fire up my engines again for takeoff, a real crisis developed. Engine No. 3 on my right wing refused to start.

I radioed the control tower for help. This time they were a little too British for my tastes. Back came the reply: "Sorry. Tea time. Won't be able to help you out the rest of today, actually. Wouldn't you chaps like to billet here and get a fresh start tomorrow?"

The hell we would. My North Carolina dander was up. It was one thing to fly through the fury and hot steel of the German occupation forces in France and expect that at any moment you might get blown to smithereens. But what really turned my crank that day was the idea that I'd have to miss a hot date in London.

"Everybody out of the plane," I snarled through the intercom. "I'm gonna take her up and get the propeller windmilling.

Then I'll come back and get you-all." There was silence and disbelief from the crew as they started moving toward the hatch.

Then the rational part of my brain regained control. "I'll need a volunteer," I said, "to help me hold the rudders steady on takeoff."

More silence. Even from Verinis, who was supposed to double-date with me that evening. Finally, Levy Dillon spoke up. "I'll go with you, Chief."

With three of our four engines purring and Levy staring ahead wide-eyed in the seat next to me, I aimed the nose of the *Belle* toward the runway. The RAF guy in the control tower looked out his window and immediately put down his teacup.

"Tower to 24485!" he yelled into his microphone. "You *cannot* take off from this base on three engines! Repeat! Permission to take off is denied! Repeat . . ."

It's amazing how much a pilot can improve his concentration on the task at hand sometimes by placing his headset on the floor.

We throttled up and went weaving and fishtailing down the runway, Levy and I bracing the yolk and rudders with all our might to keep the *Belle* from veering off the side, and before you knew it we were in the air. Just as I'd hoped, the force of the air rushing at us started the prop on No. 3 churning—windmilling—and that action ignited the engine.

I stabilized the plane, looped around, landed again, picked up my crew and headed north for a pleasant social evening on the town. To show what a reasonable guy I was, I even refrained from buzzing the Exeter tower.

Verinis and I enjoyed our double-date that night. My dreams, when I finally got to sleep, were rich and vivid.

It wasn't the cuddly Intelligence agent next to me that I was dreaming of. Nor even Margaret, back in Memphis. It was flak.

CHAPTER

8

After the first two missions, it got hairy. Our B-17s started getting shot to pieces and our boys started dying wholesale. The *Memphis Belle* took its first crippling blow. The odds of any of us coming back from a mission took a nosedive.

The *Belle* sat out a mission on November 14, but went back after the submarine pens at St. Nazaire three days later. By now, winter was settling in over Europe and the stratospheric temperatures, frigid in any season, attacked our planes in tandem with the Nazi resistance, which grew in fury and cunning with every new bombing raid. The 91st got twenty planes off that day, and only fourteen made it to the target. Frozen guns and mechanical failure caused the others to abort and turn back.

They didn't miss out on a whole lot of fun. The Germans threw more than 100 fighter planes into the air against us. Their pilots were professionals, the cream of the Luftwaffe, and we would face their cold, calculating fury again and again. Most of them had trained for years, and many had gained combat experience in the Spanish Civil War. They were hardened veterans, men in their thirties and forties going against us ex-college boys and salesmen and truck drivers still learning on the job.

They came at us in their famous Messerschmitts, but their deadliest craft was the newer, faster Focke-Wulf 190, a nasty little hornet that we learned to recognize by the yellow circle painted around its engines. With its light weight—at under 10,000 pounds fully loaded it weighed just one-sixth of a B-17—its BMW engines that could kick it up past 400 miles an hour and its 20-mm cannons mounted in the wings, the 190 could outfly and outshoot anything in the air, including Allied fighter escorts—not that we ever had any fighter escorts beyond the French coast. Their range was too limited until later in the war.

We flew naked except for our own gunners. We flew in tight formation, in clusters of planes nearly wingtip-to-wingtip, our machineguns bristling outward in every direction, like airborne porcupines, fat and slower than our predators at 160 mph on the bombing run, but awfully damn prickly when attacked.

On November 17, the sky was full of predators. On this day we had a whole new kind of war to deal with. Onrushing Nazi planes were everywhere—above, below, to our sides, behind us, and in front of us, slashing suddenly out of the sun. A speck in the distance, then a shape, then a mass of ugly swooping wing and tail, blazing its guns at us in those evil orange flickers. Then gone. All in the space of maybe four seconds. Then another one. Or two. Or three. Then another. And another.

My group was in the middle tier that day, and once again we were lucky. The Germans concentrated their attacks again, and it was the formations above and below us that got chewed up, a B-24 group in particular. Squadrons of fighters diving out of the sky hit the top group, while the planes below were taking it from sidelong attacks. Some of those Focke-Wulfs and Messerschmitts hitting the lower group were knifing directly under us. We could glimpse them as they flew past, see their yellow bands and their swastikas, even briefly make out the figures at the controls. It was something that terrified you and fascinated you at the same time, like a closeup of a bad guy's face in those Westerns I used to eat up back in Asheville.

In moments like those you tried wisecracking, gallows humor, anything that would hold your sanity together. I remember drawling into the intercom, "By gosh, maybe they don't like us or something. They just don't seem to want to shoot us down."

I spoke too soon. A few minutes after that a flak burst tore off a huge chunk of the *Belle*'s left wing. The intercom came alive and we yawed dizzyingly. I fought the rudders back to a compensating angle, and the B-17's magnificent aerodynamics did the rest. We'd been chewed up, but we were still in formation. A bullet that pinged one of my No. 3 engine propellers didn't help matters, but it didn't harm us much either. J. P. Quinlan back in the tail more than evened the score when he nailed a Focke-Wulf with Pete and Repeat, his first confirmed kill of the war.

We bombed at 20,000 feet, Vince toggling his switch on the Number Three ship in our formation because of problems with his Norden sight. Later we learned that our bombing had been good. Not excellent, but good. We also learned that Bomber Command considered good a long way from excellent, and that the whole Mighty Eighth was going to have to close that gap mighty fast, or else.

We lost three airplanes on that run. Six others were heavily damaged by flak over the target. Back at debriefing, we all agreed that this was the first real battle we'd been in up there. Joe Giambrone's boys counted twenty-two flak holes in the *Belle*, as well as the large hole in the left wing, and went to work.

They were still working on it the morning of November 22, and my crew was on the ground, when the rest of the 91st ran a mission so disastrous that it seemed cursed by evil luck.

St. Nazaire was once again the target. Eighteen B-17s taxied into takeoff formation. The first hint of trouble was the fog. Thick, wet, and greenish, it hung over Bassingbourn well after sunup. Finally, two hours behind schedule, the bombers began taking off. Five aborted before they'd made it very far across the Channel. The commander of the 323rd Squadron got lost. The four planes that reached the target found it covered by fog. They proceeded on to their secondary target at Brest. It was covered too.

Then the Focke-Wulf 190s came calling.

Maj. Harold Smelser, my spit-and-polish nemesis, was piloting one of the B-17s as Squadron Commander of the 91st group. The Germans shot out two of his engines. Instantly his plane, *Pandora's Box,* began to lose altitude. The bombers around him slowed down to cover him in order to keep him enveloped within their tight formation. From his cockpit, Major Smelser vigorously waved them on.

He kept dropping, dropping. He dropped until his plane melted into the fog-blanket below. It was the last he, or it, were ever seen.

I thought differently about the Major's martinet attitude after that. The man had taken a personal dislike to me, refused to promote me, hazed me a little, and held me to the strictest guidelines of the military code, but when it came to the moment of truth, he held himself to the same strict standards. He died valiantly. I've sort of missed that swagger stick of his ever since.

Among the other casualties that day was my wingman, the red-headed Lt. Charles Cliburn, one of the best formation fliers I knew. Lieutenant Cliburn was wounded, perhaps as he slowed his plane to protect the Major. He survived, though, and brought his airplane home to England with three other wounded crewmen.

It was our worst mission yet—a miracle that any of the 91st bombers returned at all. I've always wondered how the *Belle* would have fared if she hadn't been out of commission. Once again, our luck had held.

Major Smelser's death eerily liberated me from the bonds of our old feud, in terms of my military rank. A few days after his plane disappeared, some orderlies went through the desk drawers in his office, a routine cleaning-out assignment. In a side drawer they came upon two promotion forms sent to him by the War Department, both of them pertaining to me. One form was for my promotion to first lieutenant. The other, more recent, was to captain. All they needed for final processing was his signature. Yet they had lain for weeks in the drawer unsigned. As I'd suspected, it was the Major who was enforcing the General's vow, back at McDill Field after my buzzing escapade, to keep me locked in forever as a second lieutenant.

The orderlies turned the promotion forms over to Colonel Wray. He and I studied them. The Colonel refrained from any sort of comment—the Major had after all died a hero's death—but Colonel Wray assured me in a quiet voice that things would be taken care of. The next week I was promoted to first lieutenant. The week after that I made captain.

*   *   *

After our return sortie to St. Nazaire we had a respite of nearly three weeks. Our group didn't go out again until December 6. Then we paid a visit to Lille, on the French-Belgian border a hundred forty miles north of Paris. The Germans had built a train factory there to manufacture locomotives for their vast war-materiel transportation system.

The 91st arrived in its stacked tiers again through the frigid winter air, with my group again in the middle. In the midst of the furious action I witnessed one of the most horrible—and yet inescapably fascinating—spectacles of my entire life. I got my first closeup look at a B-17 that had just been shot out of the sky.

Vince Evans called it out on the intercom: *"Airplane coming down from above!"* I craned my neck to the left and looked. The big dark helpless shape passed so close to us we nearly collided. It had begun its fatal spin. I saw no parachutes. The action lasted only a second or two. The vision has lasted more than half a century. I have never stopped seeing it in my dreams.

Once again, our accuracy fell short that day. More bombs missed the target than hit it. Patience was drawing short at Bomber Command, as pressure mounted from the British and from our own War Department to prove that daylight strategic bombing was not a catastrophic folly-in-the-making. Special debriefings were held at air bases all over Great Britain to analyze the results thus far. The results were grim.

The Eighth had been in combat for one month. The damage it had inflicted on German-held targets in France had not come close to crippling Nazi war production. U-boats still streamed out of the pens on the French coast and the railroad transportation system remained intact. Meanwhile, our own losses had steadily increased. We had not even breached the German frontier.

As the generals fretted and debated, our effectiveness was about to change radically for the better. Among the key factors would be that "critical adjustment" I mentioned earlier. It had not yet been made, but its time was drawing close.

On December 15 I wrote a "Happy Birthday" letter to Margaret, who had just turned twenty. Wartime security obliged me to use certain code phrases, such as "worked" and "big game," to hint at bombing missions. I was in a mood both tender and frisky that night, and my writing shows it. Maybe the searing image of that dark shape in the sky, and the prospect of others like it sure to come, explain why.

> My Dearest Darling,
>   You are no longer my little girl. You have grown up, darling, and from now on you are my "little lady."
>   I am sitting here after having won $40 [in a card game]. I am sure the "Petty Girl" got the boys' minds off of the game & I won. I shall put the dough in our trust fund for that trip to Bermuda . . .
>   How does it feel to be out of your teens, my darling? I hope now that you are older, you'll take your fiancé in hand and make him behave—I have been a bad boy!
>   I worked again this week and didn't take a pass to London— therefore I am a tired man—and I have a big game tomorrow . . .
>   The boys in our "Memphis Belle" have always called me the Chief. I act as if I don't like it, but you know it helps my ego and I love it . . .
>   Good night, Margaret. I shall dream of you.

The "big game" actually came five days later, and the stakes were even juicier than the last time. Colonel Wray tapped the blackboard with his swagger stick in the early morning of December 20 and told us we were going to fly directly over Paris to the quaint town of Romilly-sur-Seine, fifty miles to the southeast, which was not so quaint anymore because the Nazis had made it the site of a huge aerodrome for German fighters. It was not only the location of an aerodrome, but the town contained a fighter factory as well, right at its edge.

The 91st Bomber Group was going for both. If we were lucky, we'd hit the aerodrome with a number of German fighter planes lined up on the ground, and we'd blow up the factory in the same run.

I didn't get to admire the Eiffel Tower that day—as my mother and Peggy and Cornelia had just a few years and a whole lifetime earlier—but I saw more German fighters than ever before. Not surprising, I guess, because we were attacking their lair.

The 91st, one of four attacking groups, got seventeen B-17s off the ground in good weather. Thirteen remained aloft. We made landfall well north of the target and the reception committee showed up early. The sheer mass of them was staggering, not to mention their persistence. The Eighth was under fighter attack for two and a half hours on that mission. The Messerschmitts and Focke-Wulfs came at us in two huge waves, diving at us in a steep angle from high overhead, coming out of the midday sun. They looped off into two groups, one to the left and the other to the right, and then they closed in, chattering machinegun rounds. The wave on the left was homing in on our lower bomber group, but the ones from the right were coming right at us. Suddenly we were learning what it was like to be under direct attack.

Everybody was blazing away, Harold Loch up in the top turret, little Cecil Scott curled up in the ball, John Quinlan defending our tail, Clarence Winchell and the kid Tony Nastal in the waist. They were not just firing wildly. They were talking to one another over the intercom as they spun and aimed and squeezed, calling out the position of each new attacking fighter to alert the nearest of their buddies. The *Belle*'s intercom was active that day, but it wasn't disorganized shouting. The teamwork we'd practiced and talked about, the coolness and concentration under heavy fire that we'd wanted to believe we could deliver, was being tested as it had never been tested before. The *Memphis Belle*'s crew was meeting the test.

Vince Evans and Charlie Leighton distinguished themselves especially well. From right down below me in the greenhouse, as we called the nose of the plane, the bombardier and navigator were able to spot most of the attackers before anyone else. These guys had important jobs of their own to do—release the *Belle*'s bomb-load, talk to me about keeping the plane on an unwavering course—but both of them managed somehow to double up as spotters, coolly alerting the other boys to each new streaking blur of German menace.

Vince even got himself a kill that day—the only fighter plane he shot down during the whole war. On top of everything else he had to do, it was almost a superhuman feat. There was only one gun available to the bombardier and navigator, a little machinegun fitted through a slot-hole, almost impossible to maneuver. But Vince seized it against an upcoming Focke-Wulf, held his fire to the last second and squeezed off a dead-on burst, just as he did time and again with his bombsight. I think he may have saved our bacon with that one.

As for me, I just flew the airplane, as usual. Hands on the yoke, feet on the rudder pedals, eyes on the instruments, keeping her steady. I may not have looked it, but I was busy. Not a second of idle time. Eyes roaming from instrument to instrument. The altimeter, that was the main thing. Keep her steady, steady, steady. Don't lose altitude. Don't gain altitude. You're in tight formation. Tight. Tight. Take your eye off the 'meter for two seconds and you're at another altitude—maybe you've bumped a wing next to you. No radical maneuvers, nothing that my wing man couldn't handle that would cause him to run into me.

Then the gyroscope. Keep the wings laid out there flat and parallel. And the fuel gauge, the temperature gauge. All the lights that could go red, signaling trouble.

That was my war, mostly. The instrument panel right in front of my eyes. Steady. Steady. Steady.

I held her steady. I held her steady even after we took a flak burst that knocked out one of our engines and set the plane yawing and lurching for a few wild moments—the second of many, many big hits that failed to bring down the *Memphis Belle*.

I believe that a lot of us young American fliers came to see ourselves as warriors on a par with our seasoned German adversaries over Romilly-sur-Seine. The 91st's machinegunners were magnificent, knocking some twenty-five German fighter planes out of action, and we were all over our ground target. We demolished about a hundred of those sitting-duck fighters on the ground—100 that would never rise to bedevil us again. A popular rumor had it that we hit the German officers' mess hall and even blew up the cellar where they kept their cognac.

We paid a gruesome price, as we always did. The 401st bomb squadron took most of the punishment in our group, losing two planes. Two planes of the 91st were damaged so badly it was a miracle that either of them made it back to the base. One of them crash-landed short of the runway.

In the short, cold days leading up to Christmas Eve, the young fliers of the Eighth Air Force in England got a respite from the bombing runs. That didn't mean we rested. Instead, we flew practice missions.

The idea may sound preposterous—hadn't we already been bloodied in combat?—but it made grim sense. The emphasis on these runs was tight formations. Tight, tighter, and tighter still. The statistics were bearing out the theory. Groups that flew tight—I mean with wingtips overlapping—put out denser cones of machinegun fire, and thus took fewer losses, than the looser groups. One group in particular, the 100th, was noted for not having good formations. It was also noted for losing a lot of airplanes. Soon it received a macabre tag—the Bloody Hundredth.

There were perfectly plausible reasons why our formations sometimes slackened. Flying tight required nerves of steel, mind-breaking concentration and extremes of physical endurance from the pilots. Not every veteran could keep it up hour after hour in the face of shifting wind currents and the sudden terror of fighter attacks. Then, too, our attrition rate was so high that we were constantly absorbing fresh, green pilots from the States who neither understood nor had experienced these requirements. There could be no excuses. The bombers of the Mighty Eighth had to fly tighter than most humans at the controls could manage. Or perish. Period.

It was at about this same time—Christmas 1942—that a conceptual breakthrough swept through the bombing groups of the Eighth Air Force that, almost by itself, transformed the accuracy of our bombing runs. This was the critical adjustment away from the time-honored pilots' prerogative of evasive action and toward fixed, unwavering runs toward the target.

At the outset of the U.S. strategic bombing campaign over Europe, we pilots were free to take evasive action—yank the plane out of an enemy fighter's trajectory or fields of flak—anytime we felt it necessary. Evasive action was always easier said than done. Even at cruising altitudes, any sudden move threatened to disrupt that tiny margin of error that tight formations required, and cause a collision with one of your wing planes. It made a lot less sense once the bombing run had begun. You could screw your bombardier up pretty good if you maneuvered—the motion played havoc with his bombsight. Still, pilots were routinely taking evasive action through the first months of the European bombing campaign. The results were a lot of missed or under-hit targets, a lot of returns to target sites such as St. Nazaire, and a lot of wasted men and airplanes.

It took the arrival late in 1942 of a jowly, scowling young major with the 305th Bomb Group to brush aside that kind of thinking, expose it as worse than useless. This tough young major's name was Curtis LeMay. His acute analysis of this new kind of warfare, as brilliant as it was coldblooded, was already propelling him toward a major-general's stars two years later, and, beyond that, toward becoming a legendary prophet of constant preparedness in a perpetually hostile world. His orbit and my own were destined to cross on the other side of that world.

LeMay was not what anyone would call an evasive action kind of guy. His style, then and for a quarter-century of military and public life afterward, was to plow straight ahead and let the bodies—both hostile and friendly—fall where they may. Almost as soon as he hit the British Isles, this chubby fireplug of a warrior was sounding off against evasive action, and poring through old artillery manuals to support his hunch that a steady course was not only more deadly, but statistically safer. His own pilots blanched on the morning that Curtis LeMay ordered them to go in on a fixed course, but with LeMay himself at the controls of one plane, his unit scored twice as many direct hits as anybody else.

After that, every bomber in the whole Army Air Force came in straight and steady on the target. American bombing suddenly got a lot better.

Unfortunately, it did not get a lot safer for American planes and crewmen.

Our effectiveness had not yet caught up with the strategic doubts of our hosts. At year's end, the bomber commands of both America and England were taking inventory of the entire effort, dating from its inception the previous summer. The British were not at all pleased with the big picture. Noting acidly that American B-17s had yet to fly beyond occupied France and attack the German homeland, the RAF once again raised the prickly question of whether we should give up daylight bombing as a failed idea, and go back to bombing runs under cover of darkness. The controversy moved quickly up the chain of command to the highest military levels. Once again, General Eaker fended off the dreaded order to scuttle the operative strategy. Give us until January, he pleaded with his superiors in Washington. We'll be getting to Germany in January.

In that frame of mind, the Mighty Eighth got set to celebrate Christmas 1942.

Maybe celebrate isn't the right word. Nobody was in a festive mood, not with all those empty tables and chairs at evening mess, the constant awareness of comrades and acquaintances who hadn't made it through another mission, the awareness of death always in our midst. Thirty-six B-17s had crossed the Atlantic from the United States to England to form the original 91st Group. Of these, twenty-nine had now been shot down, a casualty rate of 82 percent. There were a lot of empty chairs at mess in these opening months. A lot of empty chairs.

It was harder on the enlisted men than it was for us officers. We could sequester ourselves in our quarters of that old estate we'd commandeered, our four guys from the *Belle* on the top floor, and four from another squadron on the bottom. Or we could escape to the nighttime pleasures of London. Our chances of having to confront losses among ourselves were relatively low.

The enlisted fellows lived in barracks of maybe forty or fifty. A couple of planes shot down left a crater in their midst, a crater where buddies had slept and shined shoes and horsed around. The enlisted men had to clean out the trunks and closets of their dead young comrades, and so they had that awareness of death a lot more than we did, if you can put any kind of comparison on that kind of thing.

However, they had no monopoly. I lost friends and acquaintances.

I lost them all the time. I'd go back to the bar at night and a few familiar faces wouldn't be there. I would concentrate on the scotch in front of me. That scotch was my instrument panel through those nighttime navigations. I learned to like scotch quite a lot in England during the war. I'd always been a bourbon man until then.

You just didn't talk a lot about it. Not if you were an officer. Oh, we might mutter a little acknowledgement. *God, that was a hell of a sight seeing that crew get shot down today, and only four chutes opening.* Then we'd let it go.

Did we think our own days were numbered as those losses of ours mounted through the fall and winter? Depended on whom you asked, I guess. Each guy had to answer that question separately. And alone.

My answer was to think positively. I never once thought my days were numbered. I believed I was going to make it from the very outset. I felt anxiety, yes. Worry, yes. But I always believed, at rock bottom, that my airplane, my crew, and I were going to make it.

I remember the lesson I learned when we lost the first crew that I had trained with closely. The pilot had flown on my right wing a number of times back in the States. I'd met his wife. I'd heard about his children. We'd gone out on the town together in Shreveport. Now he was dead. I saw him get shot out of the sky. God knew whether or how much he suffered. Suddenly, he just didn't exist anymore.

The lesson I learned after a while was the same one most of the men and women in the Mighty Eighth learned—at least the officers, who had some latitude in the matter. The lesson was, don't fraternize. Don't make any more close friendships than you have to.

Things stopped being like they were back in training. In training, it seemed as though everybody knew everybody else. In war, you knew the men you flew with inside your own plane.

When we went into London, we didn't go with whoever happened to be free that night—even if the train was filled with guys who were free that night. We went as a group of four. It was nothing personal. That was the point—nothing personal.

We learned to stop discussing what was going on with our family or our friends back in the States. To stop asking, Have you heard from Lucy or Martha? If we talked outside our little inner circle, we talked business.

Are you having problems with the damn engines, the damn Studebaker engines they're sending us? I am. First one I got, damn thing lasted about five hours and blew a cylinder.

That kind of business. Like a bunch of truck drivers. Not the shotdown business.

I don't mean that we had grown cold and cynical. On the contrary. It's just that positive thinking was so important in those planes, especially in the presence of the newer guys, whose nerves were always more fragile. You had to have positive thinking, or you were dead, literally.

I watched it happen. You got so you could almost tell when a plane was being flown or navigated by people who had lost their mental edge, or had subconsciously given in to trauma or exhaustion. It was terrible watching one of our airplanes begin to straggle off, like some did after a mission, drifting back in over enemy territory without meaning to. I remember once when we were coming back from St. Nazaire and there was a group off to the right of us. We were over the English Channel, we'd gotten clear of the German fighters, and so we had kind of spread out from our tight formation, relaxing just a little, heading toward England, chow, and a safe night in our beds. Then we noticed that the group on our right had started heading off back east more and more. Chuck Leighton, who never stopped concentrating, was on to it right away. He got on the phones from down in the greenhouse. "Don't follow that group! They're heading right back for France!" Sure enough. As we watched, they wandered right back toward the viper's nest we'd just escaped. We wanted to radio them and alert them to their mistake, but we could not. Military orders strictly forbade breaking radio silence over or near enemy territory. Only in the initial phases of a mission—if an airplane was forced to abort, say—was radio communication permitted.

We watched helplessly as our comrades drifted, and drifted, and finally got the hell shot out of them with antiaircraft guns.

The crew of the *Memphis Belle* devised a little ritual after we'd been on a few missions and seen the losses start to skyrocket. Before each takeoff we would get into that huddle of ours on the tarmac beside the airplane and put our arms on one another's shoulders and recite a pledge. *If only one airplane comes back today, it's going to be us, guys.* I don't know if it did us a bit of good or not, but it kept us from that mind-set of *maybe this is my last mission, maybe I'm going to get it today.* It reminded us that we were no longer ten individuals but one interdependent unit. Each of us is protecting all of us. Each job is to help the other jobs. The gunners are protecting Jim Verinis and me as we fly the plane. We're helping them by keeping it steady. The navigator is our eyes. The radio operator is our ears. And every man on board is ready to switch jobs, grab a machinegun, grab the mike, grab the stick, in a moment of crisis.

Hell, we wouldn't have known how to talk about it anyway. Half a century afterward, and more, most of us who are living still don't know how.

We fought as hard and lived as intensely as we could. We played cards at night, had a few drinks, went helling into London whenever we could get a leave, seeking laughter and swing music and liquor and the comfort of women.

Those London nights helped. In London we could live these make-believe lives for a little while, lives that allowed us to do things other than Not Talk About It.

London. The Ancient City, some of the fliers affectionately called it. London was a gallant battered metropolis during the war, and its Luftwaffe-abused people were models for heroism throughout the Allied world. The city had survived the Battle of Britain from August to September of 1940, its young RAF fighters downing 1,500 Nazi bombers and turning back Hitler's invasion plans, only to endure the vicious carnival of retribution that ran from September 7, 1940, to May 11, 1941, that was known as the Blitz. Fifty-seven consecutive nights of merciless saturation bombing by the Germans, 200,000 tons of explosives dropped on the old capital city, some 20,000 civilians killed, another 1.4 million made homeless, and vast neighborhoods, civic buildings, and historic treasures damaged or destroyed.

The Blitz failed in its Number 1 objective, though, which was to demoralize and panic the British people. The British people took the Blitz and ate it for breakfast. They decided they'd be damned if Hitler's airborne thugs were going to keep them from carrying on their lives and even having a little fun.

Inspired by the sight of Winston Churchill poking his cane through the rubble as he made the rounds of devastation sites, and tipping his homburg to cries of "Winnie! Winnie!", Londoners behaved as if those heavy planes were just another annoying fact of life, like the foggy weather. They pulled the shades down and painted their windows black, but underneath that cover lay a great nighttime carnival of dance halls, ballrooms, restaurants, cinemas, and pubs. Big-time British orchestras were all over town—at the Astoria Ballroom, the Trocadero, the Hammersmith Palais. You could find a three-piece combo in just about any hole-in-the-wall. People dressed themselves up as best their budgets would allow and went dancing. They danced to Billy Cotton and his band playing "Somebody Stole My Gal," and the Sidney Lipton Orchestra, and Mantovani, and Henry Hall and his orchestra playing "It's Just the Time for Dancing," and Harry Roy and his band blowing "The Bugle Call Rag."

The ladies outnumbered the men at these dances, or certainly the young men—most of whom were either flying in the RAF or in the Navy or fighting Rommel on the ground in North Africa—but that didn't stop everyone from having a good time. "The evening air raids came, but no one took any notice," was the way one of them recalled it much later. "As the bombs got closer, the band just played louder."

When Londoners weren't out dancing, they were likely at home listening to war news and music and upbeat personalities on their battery-powered radios. Or they went to the movies. They paid a shilling at the Odeon or the Gaumont to see *Yankee Doodle Dandy* with Jimmy Cagney, or the morale-boosting film *In Which We Serve*, produced by and starring their own Noël Coward.

Maybe they went to pictures with more topical themes. One of the best was an American movie called *Mrs. Miniver*. It starred Greer Garson and Walter Pidgeon, and it had had a big impact on war sentiment back in the States. Some critics later said it helped turn a lot of American isolationists into friends of the British and supporters of the war against Germany. Its plot explored how the Nazi bombing of England in 1940–41 drove one proper middle-class family out of its complacency—trying to ignore the fact that war had come—and into acts of courage and compassion.

There was even a rumor that Churchill had declared, "This film has done more for the war effort than six divisions," and ordered his RAF fliers to drop printed copies of the movie's closing speech over occupied France to encourage the captive citizens to resist.

Many, many years after the war I dug around and came up with the lines of that closing speech. It was delivered by a vicar inside a church that had a bomb-hole in its roof.

> "The homes of many of us have been destroyed, and the lives of old and young have been taken. There's scarcely a household that hasn't been struck to the heart.
> "Why, in all conscience, should these be the ones to suffer? . . . Are these our soldiers? Are these our fighters? Why should they be sacrificed? I shall tell you why. Because this is not only a war of soldiers in uniform, it is a war of the people, and it must be fought not only on the battlefield but in the cities and in the villages, in the factories, and on the farms, in the home and in the heart of every man, woman, and child who loves freedom.
> "This is a people's war, it is our war, we are the fighters, fight it then. Fight it with all that is in us. And may God defend the right."

I can see how a lot of today's moviegoers would find that speech pretty corny. But I'll tell you this, if you don't feel a little tingle of something when you read it, you will have trouble understanding how people felt about things during World War II.

We Yank fliers lost no time diving into London's defiant nightlife. The city was only an hour and a half south of the base by train, and we went there as often as our combat duties allowed us to. Our commander, Colonel Wray, who'd already shown his cavalier side by filching Bassingbourn from the RAF, extended that hell-for-leather attitude to his officers. As long as we reported for duty when our turn for a mission came up, he didn't much care where we spent the rest of our time. When we did report, we invariably reported in uniform, in good condition, and ready for action.

We spent a lot of that time in London's grand hotels.

They were elegant, beautiful old hotels, but we could afford them. Taking advantage of the lopsided exchange rate and our officers' pay, my three best friends and I—Evans, Verinis, and Leighton— pooled our money and hired a suite of rooms at the ritziest hotel London had to offer, the Savoy.

Now, there was a good billet! That great, gray eight-story Victorian palace, a British landmark even back then, was built in 1889 on The Strand near Charing Cross Station, its front entrance overlooking the Thames. With its famous Grill and its Ballroom, the Savoy hung on through the war as a center of London's social and artistic elite. Imagine being locked in life-and-death combat with German fighter planes five miles over France one day and, the next, sharing an elevator ride with the dapper Noël Coward himself, and whiffing the tonic on his slicked-back hair. Or nodding to the legendary novelist Evelyn Waugh as he frowned into the *London Times* on a sofa in the lobby. Or tea-dancing in the late afternoon, as winter fog crept over the Thames and the blackout hour neared.

Tea dances were a tradition at the Savoy, and the management kept them up during wartime, even given that lopsided ratio of ladies to men. Jim, Vince, Chuck, and I did our best to even up that ratio. We were usually on hand, our uniforms nicely pressed, to guide the plucky young women of London around the floor.

It wasn't long before my officers and I had worked out a deal with the base, a deal that let us maximize those London romps. We'd call our operations officer on the phone from the hotel at night and ask, "Are we gonna play baseball tomorrow?" If he said yes, we'd grab the next train back to Bassingbourn.

If he said no, we relaxed and spruced ourselves up for a night of jitterbugging, toasting one another with good Scotch whiskey and chasing those eminently catchable British women.

We'd hop from ballrooms to the smaller clubs, some of them strictly for officers, others for both officers and enlisted men. These were what they called bottle clubs. They didn't serve drinks across the bar. You went in with your own bottle. Liquor was hard to get in wartime London, but we figured out a way. Col. Baskin R. Lawrence, who was the Deputy Commander of the 91st, had a connection with the Coca-Cola company. He arranged it so that when they delivered a shipment of Coke from the U.S. over to the base, they would also ship some scotch or bourbon along with it, unbeknownst to the brass. What was that famous advertising slogan they came up with years later? "Things Go Better With Coke"? I always did like that slogan.

Vince Evans met his wartime sweetheart, Kay, at one of those clubs. She was a cabaret singer, a good one. The night we heard her sing, Vince went into that Casanova act and had her under control in no time. Eventually they found an apartment where they lived while he was in town. He still had that egg connection of his, and he arranged not only to bring her eggs but fresh milk, too, which was as hard to get as liquor. They were so close that Vince seriously thought about going back there and marrying her after the war, but he found some others who were just as eager to marry him. It got complicated, but that's another story.

Christmas brought with it a different mood entirely. The hedonistic spirit of those London nights gave way to something quieter, more pensive. For most of us, this was our first Christmas overseas. And for most of us, this was our first experience with the shock and sorrow that the death of comrades brings.

On Christmas Eve and Christmas Day they had religious services on the base. We didn't go in for boughs of holly or anything like that. There was a Christmas tree in the officers' mess. That was all.

A lot of the guys got Christmas bundles from home. A lot of the guys didn't. The mail delivery was erratic, given the wartime conditions. Many packages addressed to Eighth Air Force boys in England got routed to Africa along with the men and planes and weapons being shipped over there.

We had chicken for our Christmas dinner. They couldn't manage turkey for us.

I guess it was the lack of snow that sent my thoughts back to Biltmore Forest. Christmas and snow went together in my memories. We had big snows when I was a boy in North Carolina. It would snow for ten days at a time, and the snow would stay on the ground for weeks.

On Christmas Eve I sat in my room on the second floor of that old estate at Bassingbourn and wondered a little why I was still alive and thought back to the Christmases of my youth, when my mother was still alive and at the center of our family. She'd supervise the decorations around the house, the big tree and all the candles and the wreaths and the pine boughs we'd put up. The house smelled of sweet tar and needles. We'd thread Christmas carols into that old player piano. I could still see my dad and brother and sister, all bright and excited and pitching in.

I could remember all the extras my mother would do, how she'd trim the dining room table. The whole house would be shimmering in red and gold and pine-green. We would all get up together early on Christmas morning and eat a light breakfast so we'd have room for that big, big Christmas dinner that Mother would have ready for us in mid-afternoon. Then we would all go downstairs into the big living room and Mother would put some Christmas music into that piano and we would sit there and open our presents one at a time. First one kid would open, and then another kid would open, and finally Mother and Dad would open one of theirs. After our big meal we'd go out for an afternoon drive just to see all of the decorations in Biltmore Forest, which were fantastic. The kids would all go sleighing after that, calling to one another as we came out of our different houses in our new Christmas coats and mittens and scarves. Behind the Biltmore house was a four-mile downhill road, with lots of curves, and we would belly-flop onto our sleds and go screaming and careening down that road. At the bottom, the Biltmore staff people had cars waiting to pull us back up. We'd tie our sleds to the rear bumpers of these cars and get a free ride up that hill.

I suspect that childhood Christmas memories were flooding through the minds of just about every man on the base that Christmas Eve. Make that just about every American military man and woman on the whole island of Great Britain. City memories. Small-town memories. Farm memories. Memories of Christmases rich and poor. All different kinds of memories, and every one the same.

While visions of sugarplums danced through their heads, that old line from the yuletide poem goes. I think there must have been a lot of visions of a lot of sugarplums that night.

CHAPTER
9

It wasn't sugarplums that were dancing through the European skies, though, and laying waste to the western regions of a great continent. It was bombs. Bombs, bombs, and more bombs. What had been a dreaded science-fiction fantasy just a few decades earlier was now a full-scale reality for the first time in history. Here was vertical war, fought by men in huge massed long-range warships dropping tons of high explosives down on enemy territory, opposed by men firing powerful guns capable of throwing explosive shells five miles into the sky. Not to mention other men piloting swarms of small, fast fighter planes rising from the enemy's airstrips.

The bombs that American and British planes dropped were deadly and ingenious, and grew more so with each passing month as the war progressed. We dropped bombs filled with TNT and cyclonite and hexogen, and with amatol and picric acid and lead azide and ammonium picrate. We dropped bombs shaped into finned spindles, bombs that looked like teardrops, bombs that looked like tin cans. We dropped bombs singly and bombs bound together, unitary bombs and cluster bombs that spread their submunitions over large areas on the way down. Later in the war, of course, came the incendiaries.

We dropped bombs weighing as little as thirty pounds—a British incendiary, and as much as 8,000 pounds—another RAF device. We dropped fragmentation bombs and bouncing bombs that would skip across an ocean's surface toward a ship, and armor-piercing bombs and bombs that lit up the target in the night. Late in the war a British scientist named Dr. Barnes Wallis eventually came up with two horrific bombs, the massive Tallboy and the even larger Earthquake, whose angled fins made them plummet to earth at the speed of sound, drive nearly 100 feet below the earth's surface, and topple buildings with their shock waves.

The implications of all this were clear, and the implications were terrible. The vertical war would be all-encompassing. Nothing and no one was safe—combatants, civilians, women, children, cities, churches, the great historical monuments. Vertical war meant total war, and eventually no physical or moral boundaries would be able to check the spread of slaughter.

Given these realities, I will always be proud of the restraint shown by the United States Army Air Forces in these early months of the European air war—the time of the *Memphis Belle*. The ordnance carried by the B-17s of the Mighty Eighth reflected the humanitarian hopes of our government and our strictly defined and limited mission, which was to attack only military installations, never civilian centers. Our bombs were "general purpose" missiles of varying weights. TNT-based and non-incendiary, they were designed to wreak havoc with structures such as factories, airfields, railroad yards, and submarine pens, not people. Typically these were the M-30 (100 pounds), the M-43 (500) and the M-44 (1,000). We occasionally took along the M-34, a 2,000-pounder, especially when we were going after those sub pens with their twelve-foot-thick concrete shields. The GP bombs were fitted with quarter-second delay fuses in their tails.

To the best of my knowledge, and despite the near-catastrophic losses we endured, every pilot who flew for the Eighth Army Air Force obeyed these orders to the letter.

It couldn't last, of course. The genie was out of the bottle. The monster had escaped from the mad scientist's lab. The bombs were falling en masse now, and before they stopped falling, their scope of destruction would be virtually unlimited. By the war's end, the Allies would have dropped some 2,700,000 tons of bombs on Europe in more than 1,440,000 bomber sorties. In the process, we laid waste to airfields, munitions and ball-bearing factories, fuel complexes, supply dumps, railroads and other transportation systems. We diverted the fearsome Luftwaffe from its intended role as an offensive power against Allied ground forces, chewed it up in air battles and ultimately defeated it. Unavoidably, we also pulverized dozens of German cities including Hamburg, Dresden, and Berlin. Our bombs destroyed or damaged some 3,600,000 homes. Civilians trapped and annihilated beneath our bombs numbered 593,000, by the most accepted estimate.

It wasn't as though nobody had seen aerial warfare coming, or imagined its worst consequences. Almost from the century's turn, governments had tried to ward it off with laws and conventions, with talk of "humanitarian barriers," even of outlawing air bombardment entirely. How naïve those laws and conventions now seem—all those rules drawn up by the Hague Convention in 1907, the Washington Agreement of 1923, and the Geneva Disarmament Conference of 1932. Did the statesmen actually believe that warmakers would carefully restrict their payloads to military targets? That no Hitler would ever arise to bomb Coventry and London? Or that retaliation against such a fanatical and potent aggressor could refrain from striking back at the enemy's own urban centers?

Yes, the vertical war was a terrible new kind of conflict. We fought it as honorably as we could. We thanked God, in the end, that the terrible damage we inflicted claimed world tyranny as its chief victim.

The *Belle* flew a mission on December 30, to the submarine pens at Lorient, but I didn't fly with it. I was down with a bad cold. Jim Verinis moved over from the second pilot's seat and took the *Belle's* yoke. He flew superbly that day. It turned out to be his farewell mission with our crew. Jim was just too good a talent for the Eighth to keep relegated to second-banana status, especially as our inventory of Number 1 pilots continued to be shredded by the Germans. The brass assigned him to a plane that he quickly named *The Connecticut Yankee.* We shook hands and I told him to be careful up there.

I was glad that Jim was getting his chance to shine, but I hated to lose him. He was irreplaceable. A variety of men took turns in the seat next to me on subsequent missions. Many were fine pilots and earned my respect. But I will always think of Jim Verinis as the second pilot of the *Memphis Belle*.

The New Year, 1943, was only three days old when we flew into the deadliest sheets of destruction the German defenses had yet thrown at us. Our losses on this mission shocked the Eighth from top to bottom and, for the first time, sent serious morale tremors through the ranks of the flying men. How the *Belle* got through it I will never understand. I think it was on this run, through a frigid sky churning with smoke, flames, streaking Nazi fighters and the spiraling debris of my comrades' shattered bombers, that I began to believe that the God I often worshipped in church—my "Command Pilot," as I had begun to think of Him—was cupping this airplane in His hands.

My officers and I had hurried back to the base from London and the Savoy the day before, alerted that something big was in the works. All through that night, into the early hours of January 3, we could hear the muffled sounds of frantic activity out on the tarmac beyond our windows—the engines of trucks hauling loads of bombs to the waiting B-17s, and later the chug and roar of airplane engines warming up. Sure enough, when we staggered out of our warm beds at Bassingbourn and into the chilly gloom of the predawn briefing room, slipping into our chairs and tugging the fleece of our lined flight jackets about our necks, Colonel Wray slapped his pointing stick against the blackboard and uttered the destination that brought groans from some of us and sardonic chuckles from others.

We were going back to St. Nazaire.

This would be our third visit to those teeming coastal submarine pens. We hadn't really hit them square yet, and the Germans had shown amazing determination at repairing what damage we'd inflicted and sending new fleets of U-boats off to bite deeply into Allied shipping in the North Atlantic. So, with a doubtful RAF command looking over our shoulder, not to mention a British public swayed by critical newspaper analysis of our entire daylight bombing strategy, we were going to go back there and hit those pens again.

"Level them," was the steely gist of our orders.

It would have taken a complete fool not to realize that the Germans would be primed and reinforced and waiting for us.

Again, the round of specialized briefings—gunners, bombardiers, navigators. Again, the early-morning breakfasts that dropped like so much lead into our stomachs. Again, the quiet interludes with priests and ministers and rabbis for the boys who felt the need. Doomed boys, many of them.

Again, the waiting. And again, finally, that short—but somehow endless—ride by jeep to the waiting warplanes.

Again, our linked-arms huddle beside the fuselage of the *Belle*. *If only one plane comes back, it's going to be us.*

A cold sun started to spill its milky light onto the flat wet Cambridgeshire landscape.

Then, up and inside, one by one, ten individuals fused into one seamless unit. The cold terror gave way, now, to hyperintense concentration on the duties at hand. Check the guns. Check the ammo. Check the charts. Check the radio. The dials, the gyro, the altimeter, the oxygen masks. Parachutes packed? Intercom working? Check.

Start the engines.

See the black puffs of ignition smoke, hear the tentative chug-chug-chugs of the awakening propellers, and then see the silver blur, hear the roar. My routine was No. 3 engine first, igniting the generator. Then No. 1, then 2, then 4.

All engines running. The *Belle* was stationary yet fidgeting, up and down, impatient to get going. We were at the head of the line this morning. We were leading the entire heavy bombardment wing over to France.

A flare, signaling clearance from the flight tower, as we had to keep radio silence.

I eased the throttle forward and began the taxiing run. There was a lurch of motion and the big hum now, the big vibration as the bomber began its long slow waddle toward takeoff. My hands were on the yoke guiding it, my eyes scanning the instrument dials in front of my face. Each crewman silent, fixed, impassive inside his leather earflapped helmet, goggles up. Another morning at the office. Lots of business to attend to.

Takeoff.

Full throttle forward—the engine whine raised to a scream. The *Belle* was convulsing now, straining, a caged animal ravenous for the hunt. Brake off. Pent-up energy released. The gathering of speed down the runway.

Wheels off. Wheels up. Flight.

The great engine scream fell away as the echoing earth receded. Bassingbourn receded, along with the officers' bar and warm beds, London, England, and all remnants of the amenities, the dailiness, the continuity of human life. Just air in front of us now, and under us, arctic air from the beginning of time, air that would soon be filled with fire and metal. The air of war. Air war.

It was quiet in the *Belle* during the three-hour flight to the target— our duration lengthened by powerful headwinds that slowed our speed to 85 miles per hour, at times, slower than I'd gone in my father's Buick Century. It was usually quiet except for the necessary exchanges of information over the intercom. But this time I thought the quiet had a freighted, pensive quality. We knew what was waiting for us, or at least we thought we did.

Maj. Claude E. Putnam, a Squadron Commander, was flying along as my copilot and observer that day. Major Putnam was an excellent pilot in his own right, a capable and brave man. Graciously, he held back from intervening in my control of the *Belle*.

But, dammit, I missed Jim Verinis. I missed the assurance he'd radiated during those first five missions when he was my second pilot—the absolute personal and military competence he displayed. I missed the bond of brotherhood and trust—no, *faith*—we'd developed, the bond we still share.

With Major Putnam and all the rest of the men who sat to my right, I felt confident enough. With Jim Verinis, I'd felt invincible.

Five groups in all descended on St. Nazaire at midmorning, each group with some twenty-one planes. We had sixteen in our group. As usual, the Messerschmitts and Focke-Wulfs were snarling and buzzing around the target, ready to sting us hard. But it wasn't enemy fighters that tore us up so badly on January 3. Once again, it was the flak.

The Germans had concentrated almost sixty heavy-artillery pieces in the core area around the pens, and they'd brought in several other mobile guns. On this clear day they had no trouble calibrating our altitude, and when those big muzzles opened up on us, hurling shells five miles high and timed to explode within feet of our fuselages, it looked as though you could walk across that sky on the exploding metal. Vince, down below, could see those antiaircraft shells through his bombsight as they spiraled upward. He said afterward that seeing the shells wasn't the bad part. The bad part was bracing for the shells you didn't see.

Even before we dropped into our bombing run the sky around us had started to fill up with the flaming and mutilated bombers of our comrades. The group just to the left of the 91st, in particular, was getting the hell knocked out of it. Some planes, missing a wing or tailsection, spiraled crazily out of control and downward into the sea or the French coast. Others, their engines or fuel lines perforated, would emit telltale streams of thin white smoke. A few simply burst apart in midair, their crews roasted before they could even grasp their parachute rings.

Amidst the carnage around us, jug-eared Chuck Leighton, the navigator, kept feeding me my coordinates in a level voice while the gunners swiveled, scanned, and fired. My own universe had shrunk to the sound of Leighton's voice and the jumping dials in front of me. My legs and arms were straining to keep the *Memphis Belle* in tight formation. When Leighton gave me the word, I throttled us down into our interlude of maximum hell—our run to the target.

This run would be different. On this one, for the first time, all the bombers would conform to Curtis LeMay's dictum of *no evasive action*. To ensure that, the pilots would actually turn their planes over to the bombardier during the moments of the bomb run itself. The bombardier would fly the plane through the Norden bombsight, which could be hooked up electronically to the controls. We pilots would just sit tight and await the word of the bombardier that his payload was cleared and we could start flying again.

As the lead plane, the *Belle* had the privilege of introducing the new tactic. As the pilot, it was my great good fortune—*ahem!*—to be the first to move back from the controls.

I had never been so anxious in all my life. The old Buick Century had sure as hell never prepared me for anything like this.

Most of our bomb runs lasted thirty to forty-five seconds. The longest to date had been a minute. But now, as I relinquished control of the *Memphis Belle* in a sky filled with bullets and shrapnel, and waited for my good pal Vince Evans to give it back to me, I got my first taste of what eternity might be like.

My feet were touching the rudders, but not exerting any pressure. My left hand was poised an inch from the yoke, fingers splayed. My right hand was an inch from the throttle. I sat frozen like this as the seconds ticked off and the *Belle* barreled forward—like a runaway locomotive, it seemed to me. I began to sweat, there in the freezing cockpit. Then the sweat started pouring off me. Was it seconds, now, or minutes? Dammit, I wanted to take that plane back over.

Finally I couldn't stand it any longer. I snatched my mike and barked down at Vince, "When, *when* are you gonna get rid of those bombs? What's wrong?"

Back came that Texas twang of his. "Keep your shirt on, Morgan. I'll let you know when the bombs are gone." Then he went back to work.

Apparently I didn't disrupt his concentration too much. The Bomber Command had defined "target area" as a circle with a radius of 1,000 feet. Photographs from several of our planes later showed that Vince Evans laid those bombs of ours ten or fifteen feet from the target's epicenter. It won him the Distinguished Flying Cross. The other bombardiers, those who had survived, toggled their switches off Vince's release and just simply rained down blazing hell on those trapped U-boats.

Then I grabbed the yoke and rudder back and shoved the throttle forward and we got the hell up and out of there before we got our asses shot off.

A lot of pilots weren't so lucky. The mission lost ten bombers that day. We could glimpse an occasional parachute billowing, then it was gone, but the fate of those jumpers was rarely known to us. The unfortunate group to our left lost four of its first nine planes over the target, and seven in all.

*   *   *

Back at Bassingbourn, Intelligence determined that that "endless" bombing run Vince took us on had consumed a minute and a half.

We did well on that third run to St. Nazaire. We sunk or damaged a number of subs, and left lots of rubble and dirty, oily water.

The *Belle,* once again, was riddled with flak holes, but none of the shrapnel had struck a crewman or damaged a vital element inside the plane.

We paid for our success—as we always did. This was our costliest mission of the war until that time, the mission that brought the casualty rate for the 91st Group up to that almost inconceivable figure of 82 percent of the thirty-five bombers that had flown the North Atlantic in November.

That figure was not typical of the entire Eighth Bomber Command, of course, and it would not be sustained as the campaign moved into the winter and spring of 1943. But that did not mean things were going fine. Losses as a percentage of the entire American presence in England exceeded 6 percent in this phase of the air war— not nearly as dramatic as our early attrition rates, but nonetheless "unacceptable" by U.S. military standards.

It was unacceptable not only to our commanders, but also to us. As 1943 began with no resolution of the air war remotely in sight, morale problems crept into our daily routine. It didn't help that our commanders began to show signs of uncertainty. In the first two weeks of the New Year, we fliers would routinely wake up expecting to go into combat, be briefed for the mission, make our private reckonings with our mortality, taxi out, wait, wait—and then taxi back in, mission canceled. This was not easy on our nerves. Men sometimes erupted into hysterical laughing fits for no apparent reason, or dropped into deep staring silences. Good friends who had backed one another up in the heat of combat could turn on one another in sudden fury.

Our post-mission debriefing sessions began to take on an edge. Fatigued, sometimes traumatized, our minds still tormented with visions of our buddies' planes bursting into fireballs, we absorbed hectorings by our superior officers that we'd let German fighters close in on us without calling out the danger on the intercom. The implication was that somehow our eyes weren't completely open.

Those images of exploding B-17s didn't go away in a hurry. If you'd seen it happen, you'd think of it that evening as you had a drink, maybe had an extra drink, using the extra drink or two or three as an excuse to toast those guys who went down. Then you'd have another drink. There's no question that a lot of us drank to excess between those missions, or that some good pilots and crewmen were ruined by the drinking we did. Perhaps some people, who never sat in a cockpit or a turret, might find the excess drinking morally objectionable. All I knew, and I knew it good and well, was that I was going to remember seeing that plane go down in my dreams, and that a glass or three of scotch might fuzz the dream just enough that I could make it through till reveille.

It didn't help our morale any that the British government and the British military considered us mad for persisting in daylight strategic bombing, that the British press was fanning the flames of this attitude, suggesting day after day that we Americans were wasting our men and what they considered our overmatched B-17s and B-24s in fool's errands of colossal proportions.

Against this tide of pressure, public opinion, strategic-level skepticism and plunging morale, the Eighth Bomber Command drew on a weapon even more devastating than the Norden bombsight. This weapon was our Commander, Gen. Ira Clarence Eaker.

The strapping, dark-browed, purse-lipped Ira Eaker believed in the mission, and he had the stature, nerve, and credentials to blow cigar smoke in the face of anybody who believed otherwise—including the noted cigar-smoker who ran the British government from 10 Downing Street. The son of a Texas tenant farmer born in 1896—the year Ragtime was invented and gold was discovered in the Klondike—he earned his wings in 1918, though he never left the United States during World War I. In 1929 he pioneered the technique of midair refueling, and set an aviation endurance record by staying in the air for 150 hours, nearly a week, getting refueled by planes flying parallel to his. In 1930 he made the first "blind" transcontinental flight, relying solely on instruments. Entering the Army as an enlisted man in 1917, he fought his way into the officers' training program and rose quickly through the Army Air Corps, making Captain in 1920. He filled in his idle hours after that by studying law at Columbia University and picking up a journalism degree.

Assigned to organize the Eighth Bomber Command in January 1942, Brigadier General Eaker arrived at High Wycombe, northwest of London, in February, designated that site his Headquarters, got things up and running by June, and underscored his personal commitment to the air war by hopping into a cockpit and leading the first American bomber strike against Nazi installations on August 17, the railroad center at Rouen.

He braved not only Nazi guns, but even Winston Churchill, Britain's Prime Minister. In several meetings with Churchill, General Eaker boldly made his case for the virtues of daylight strategic bombing. Eaker later recalled that in the wee hours after one such brandy-lubricated meeting, in the fall of 1942, he and Churchill were literally playing war games—with Churchill, as Adolf Hitler, challenging Eaker, in the role of Hermann Goering, to tell him how the Nazis were going to win the war.

He deflected that virulent strain of British press criticism by forthrightly inviting London journalists such as the influential Peter Masefield of the *Sunday Times* of London for a monthlong, no-holds-barred sojourn of the Eighth's day-to-day operations. By the end of those visits, Masefield was not only supporting the American strategy, he flew along on a mission!

Thus it was Ira Eaker, more than any other single force, that kept our American bombers flying in those uncertain months of late 1942 and early 1943.

While the American and British policymakers thrashed out the high-level politics and logic of daylight saturation-bombing, we pilots and crewmen continued to cope with the ceaseless pressures by the most effective means available. As I've already described, these means included the vices of hard drinking, nighttime carousing, and the tender sympathies of the young women of London.

It wasn't all as decadent as it might sound. After all, we were young Americans in a European war, and those carefree days and nights helped us preserve our sense of humanity amidst all the terror and carnage. Like the redbricked estates and spired horizons at Bassingbourn, the Savoy and the London clubs offered us nerve-shattered fliers a healing connection with order, with history, with a civilization worth preserving.

Besides, you never knew who you were going to run into. One afternoon as I was sipping a drink at the Savoy bar, I spied a familiar face. It turned out to be a fellow from my hometown of Asheville—Ray Carter, who'd been a serious rival of mine for the affections of Asheville's Vivien Leigh.

I'd never been all that eager to meet up with Ray back in the prewar days, but now I greeted him as a long-lost friend. It turned out that he was doing some undercover work for the Office of Strategic Services—which became the CIA after the war—nosing around for Nazi sabotage. We had a nice chat. He was an okay fellow when Vivien wasn't around.

Yes, the women were at the center of our off-duty lives in London. "Overpaid, oversexed, and over here," as the British lads grimly put it. Well, they got that part of it right. All three parts.

I'm not going to say that we lived it up at the Savoy, exactly. But I will say that the London air-raid wardens thought they'd accomplished something when they finally persuaded us to quit partying during raids and get down into the bomb shelters with everybody else. That was fine—as long as we could bring the girls along with us.

Through all of these escapades, I kept up my correspondence with Margaret.

It may seem callous that I could write such tender, romantic letters to my fiancée, and then, almost before the ink was dry, be off cavorting in London with my wartime girlfriends. As hard as it might be to understand this, for anyone who has never been in a war far away from home, I meant every word of every letter I wrote to Margaret, and I meant every minute of those London escapades, too.

People might reasonably ask whether my conscience bothered me. It did not. Yes, I was involved—with not one woman in London, but two, at different times. But I was not a married man, and these were not casual conquests. I never indulged in that.

My affairs in London may have been illicit in the eyes of some, but they were genuine romances, on both sides. The scale of evil and terror in the world was pretty vast in those times, and violent death was a real possibility for everyone, by day and by night. To lie in someone's arms for a few hours could be construed as a sin, I suppose, but it was far from the greatest sin going.

My romances never diminished my love for Margaret. Looking back over those old scrawled letters now, I can recover the strong emotions I felt in composing them, and the comfort it gave me to mail them off. Besides the letters, I would send a Western Union telegram to 1095 Poplar Avenue in Memphis on completion of every mission. War censorship prohibited me from even telling her I'd been on a sortie, so we kept those codes of ours going. "THINKING OF YOU ALL THE TIME," "SAFE AND WELL, MISSING YOU" meant I'd come back safely from the "job," or "game," or from "being busy"—but she understood how to read between the lines.

Her feelings meant so much to me. On the same September day I fired off that feverish CONGRATULATIONS telegram from Mitchell Field, I'd sat down at my desk and composed a quieter, more reassuring letter in longhand.

"I am safe and, I can say, happy, for I have you beside me as I do my job," I wrote.

> I can't write you very much, darling, but at least you'll know that I am thinking of you all the time. Our job is a big one and you and I shall do it together. The Memphis Belle will ride the sky safely always, you can be sure . . .

On December 21, the day after Romilly-sur-Seine, I began in a jaunty tone, but after a few lines I let my true emotions show through as I seldom did with anyone.

> I guess that you have been reading all day about our latest game. It was one we shall never forget and I am sure the Huns won't ei-

ther. I feel certain that their respect for "the Fortress" is improving by far . . . You have a just right to be proud, dearest—your plane wasn't even hit all day & we were attacked more than any of the rest, for the "Memphis Belle" was taking her place in the lead, as she has and should, always. I again return with all our crew well and not one injury. That makes me a very proud man, to be flying your plane for us—

Darling, there is no use my denying that I was scared, for I was scared to death. It was one real nightmare, but I guess I have learned now that you are flying with me each time & that God does ride with me & guide me home to safety.

When I landed after the raid I was so tired I could hardly hold my head up. I took a small drink and came to your arms and slept like a baby, just yours.

And then I divulged the good news of a few days earlier:

I have at last received the rank I have always wanted. I am now Captain Morgan, & I am really happy about it—I got my letter from the War Department last night. Now you are able to wear those other earrings, and it will be so much better to marry Captain Morgan, will it not, my darling?

And again, on Christmas Day:

Merry Christmas to the dearest person in all the world. I pray to God that never again will I have to write you a letter on this day; always in the future I'll have you in my arms . . .

Darling, you must know and feel many times how my heart cries out to you from even this distance. You are the one factor in my life that makes me go on to do my duty. But even if I am at my last ounce of strength, I have your smile, your love, and our future to live for, so I have to keep going at all times.

My head is on the table, & so I know you'll excuse me now, my love, so I can go to your arms. Merry Christmas to the sweetest person in all the world. God grant us peace & our own Christmas alone next year.

I suppose there were thousands of letters like those making their way from servicemen to their sweethearts in those melancholy holi-

day weeks of 1942. I am sure they flowed on both sides of this hel-
lacious conflict. Ordinary men and women, caught up in something
bigger and more destructive than they had ever imagined to be possible, reaching out toward one another in simple letters across the
disrupted oceans and the bombed continents, trying to hold on, with
words, to some remnant of a life that once made sense to them.

Thinking of you. Missing you. Merry Christmas. Dearest person
in all the world. I pray to God. Hearts crying out. Nightmares, and
peaceful sleep in the imagined arms of the beloved. Hope for a peace.
Hope for a future. Hope.

The loneliness may have been equal on both sides of the conflict,
and the letters equally poignant, but the aims and the stakes were
not. The leaders of one side were bent on extinguishing the hopes of
ordinary men and women; the leaders of the other—our side—were
fighting on behalf of hope itself. I think every Allied serviceman and
servicewoman understood that. We were in a global fight to save civilization, and the ordinary letters we wrote, and received, amounted
to nothing less than that civilization's sweet, living voice.

CHAPTER
10

Nazi Germany and Imperial Japan pretty much had their brutalizing, murderous way across the Eastern and Western hemispheres throughout 1942, or at least the first several months of it. The year just beginning, 1943, would see the awful weight and force of their momentum checked, ground down to a standstill and finally, incrementally, set back upon its own bloody path.

The cost of this reversal, in the lives, suffering, terror, and resources of the free world's fighting forces and civilians, not to mention the unlucky populations of the Soviet Union and the Axis nations, would be so monumental that today, nearly sixty years and a new century afterward, I still cannot make it fully real in my mind. What is real is my memory of being a part of it, of being there over Europe, in a critical zone of combat, when the momentum started to change.

In the Far East, Japan's rapid onslaught through the Pacific islands after Pearl Harbor had stunned the world, set the Allies scrambling to gain traction for some kind of counteroffensive, and even raised fears of invasion on America's West Coast. By the end of May 1942 the Rising Sun had put its bloody bootprint on Malaya, the Philippines, the Dutch East Indies, the Celebes, Wake Island, Guam, the Gilberts, Thailand, and Burma—the vast area coldly targeted for its "Greater East Asia Co-Prosperity Sphere." Japanese warships had dealt the U.S. Navy a series of defeats, and now, at the beginning of June, had spread their naval strike forces across 2,000 miles of the Pacific, pointed toward the North American continent and a final conquest of the U.S. Pacific Fleet.

In their way stood a resolute Rear Admiral named Chester W. Nimitz, a gaggle of brilliant codebreakers in a basement room at Pearl Harbor, and an outnumbered, hastily-assembled patchwork fleet of destroyers and aircraft carriers. The codebreakers had managed to determine the exact destination of the enemy armada, Nimitz had pulled together his smaller force and placed them in its path, and the aircraft carriers and their cargo did the rest. The Battle of Midway, fought on June 4, 1942, with fighter planes and torpedo bombers from opposing fleets 100 miles apart, broke the back of the Japanese navy. The battle's highlight was the famous "fatal five minutes" late in the day, in which two inspired squadrons of Dauntless dive-bombers screamed down to incinerate four of the six enemy fleet carriers.

From that day forward, the Japanese navy was never again a serious offensive threat, and American naval, Marine, and Army forces could begin the great counter-thrust back across the Pacific.

Meanwhile, the Axis offensive was spreading or holding its own throughout Europe, Africa, and the North Atlantic. Only in Russia, where the German butchery of Jews and partisans reinforced a fanatical resistance by Soviet civilians and guerrillas as well as the regular army, were there signs of stalemate.

By 1942 France and the Low Countries had long since been brought to heel by Hitler's legions, England was battered if not invaded, and German U-boats were churning out of those pens at Brest and St. Nazaire to cripple merchant shipping of food and military supplies. During a five-day stretch in March 1942, known as the Battle of the Atlantic, twenty-seven Allied merchant ships were sunk. By the end of the year Nazi wolf-packs would destroy eight million tons of Allied shipping, and rationing of food and coal swept through Great Britain. In Africa, despite some reversals, German and Italian forces under Field Marshal Erwin Rommel rolled forward along a strategic strip in Libya that gave them potential access to Egypt, French North Africa, and the Near East. In Russia, despite their failure to capture Moscow and a frigid winter that froze tens of thousands of their troops, the Nazis launched a summer offensive, laced with atrocities against Jewish civilians, that for a while seemed to thrust the invaders to the brink of victory. Stalingrad beckoned, fatally.

As for my own corner of the war, these early months had been similarly indecisive for the Allies. We fliers of the 91st had been among the first elements of the Eighth Bomber Command to hit the bases in England and go into action. We'd learned our new trade on the job against hardened, experienced Luftwaffe veterans, we'd made mistakes, we'd been badly shot up, and our missions, despite countless acts of heroism and a few good days, had not yet had much of an impact on German industry or warmaking capacity. Those twelve-foot-thick concrete shields over the U-boat pens at St. Nazaire, for instance, were doing their job against the heaviest of our bombs. Bad weather and the constant sheets of flak and fighter gunfire had kept our bombing accuracy at fairly low levels, despite our tight-formation flying and the Norden bombsight. The sub-zero cold at five-mile heights, worsened by the constant air rush through our open entrance hatches, continued to claim frostbite victims among the crewmen, as did the thin air itself for those who got separated from their oxygen masks.

Finally, we were hamstrung by the limits on inventory. We were not yet flying missions with the great masses of airplanes that our targets and German defenses necessitated. America was still mobilizing through late 1942, still gearing up to full-production capacity for the two-ocean war its young men were fighting. As much as we needed new B-17s in England, not to mention spare parts for our damaged planes and replacement crews for those empty tables and bunks, our forces in the South Pacific needed them too, and in North Africa, and in the Mediterranean. As 1943 began, we were fighting the biggest air war in history on a tight budget. Yet the high-level pressure to extend our bombing from occupied France into the Fatherland—Germany itself—became overwhelming.

Things here—as in combat theaters all over the globe—were starting to change. For some, including us, they would get worse before they got better. But they were starting to change.

Our prospects sure as hell got a boost on January 21 at Casablanca. In that first of several important summits, President

Roosevelt and Winston Churchill strongly ratified the aims and support of strategic bombing over Europe—"the progressive destruction and dislocation of the German military, industrial and economic system, and the undermining of the morale of the German people to a point where their capacity for armed resistance is fatally weakened."

In other words: Keep up what you're doing, fellas, but do it even more.

The top brass even provided us with a blueprint on how to accomplish that. After months of wrangling, the British and Americans finally resolved the daylight-versus-nighttime bombing controversy that had divided them from the start. It was simple. The Americans would keep on bombing by day, and the RAF would take over at night. Round-the-clock saturation bombing, with Germany itself finally in on the fun.

Suddenly, our entire mission in the war had taken on structure. Suddenly the future didn't look quite so endless or so random. We had a goal now, a unified plan, and a new sense of partnership with our RAF comrades. It was at about this time that General Eaker sweetened things even more by issuing his famous incentive—any crew members that survived twenty-five bombing missions for the Eighth Air Force would be entitled to return home to America.

What a masterstroke of psychology that announcement was! Yes, we were hardened veterans in a lethal air war, and our prospects for survival weren't any better than they had been before the General's challenge. But we were young men, too—boys, still, many of us. And like young men, we fastened eagerly on this new incentive. *Twenty-five missions? We can do that!* was a thought that raced through the mind of every pilot, every crewman, most certainly including the pilot and crew of the *Memphis Belle*.

The 91st got two more calls over France before we breached the German frontier, and the second one came as close as any to bringing down the *Belle*.

Our near-disaster came on January 23, just as the *Belle* was pulling out of its bombing run over the submarine pens at Lorient, on the northern coast of the Bay of Biscay.

The danger signals had been flashing well before Vince released his bombs. The 91st managed to get only six planes over the target that day, after starting out with thirteen, so we were more naked than usual going in. We had two groups of three bombers, flying in perilously close formation.

The hit came only seconds after our bomb-bay doors were closed and we were making a left turn up and away from the pens. Vince down below yelled, *"Airplane, 12 o'clock!"* and at that instant a Focke-Wulf came streaking in right for our nose. More than one, actually; there were at least two, maybe more—the images flashed and vanished in split-seconds.

I shoved the throttle forward and sent the *Belle* into a steep climb to prevent a direct hit in the front of our plane. Standard procedure would have been to dive, but that would have smashed us into the bomber group right below us. So I took us upstairs. The airplane whined and lurched, the force of lift ramming all of us rearward. At the same instant I heard J. P. Quinlan's voice screaming through the intercom from his tailgunner slot:

"Chief, the tail is hit, the whole back end is shot off! Chief, it's blazing! The whole tail is leaving the plane!"

The sudden pressure on my yoke and rudder confirmed that something bad had happened. The burst of enemy fire intended for our nose had ripped into our tail instead. I'd prevented an annihilating front-end hit, but maybe we'd lost the plane anyway.

I told Quinlan to calm down—just as Vince Evans had told me to keep my shirt on during that first auto-pilot bombing run—and let me know exactly what the damage was. He looked out his window again and radioed back, "Well gee, it looks like it's all gone! The tail section's probably gone."

That "probably" wasn't much help. "Dog*gone* it, J.P.," I radioed him, "give me a damn report!"

His next news was a lot better. "Oh, the fire's gone out!" That would have been the fabric part of the tail stabilizer. I said, "Well, that's good. Now can you please assess the damage?"

"I can't see the other side of it," he radioed back.

The attacking fighters had streaked far beyond our range by now. I had to find out what the hell had happened to us. Firsthand.

I had never before left my cockpit seat to go back in the plane and look at damage. Combat flying hardly allowed that luxury, and besides, the reports of the crewmen back there were usually precise and informative. This time was different. This time I had to decide whether we were going to have to parachute out.

My copilot that day was a temporary guy, one of several. He was about to get his welcome to the *Memphis Belle*. I unstrapped myself and barked at him, "*Fly* the plane a minute!" As he shot me a stricken look I ranted silently to myself. *Keep it calm, Morgan! Keep it collected! Concentrate! Concentrate!* Panic was out of the question. I could not permit myself the luxury of panic. If I showed signs of terror, it could spread through the entire crew. In the blink of an eye, as I foraged back through the frigid, pitching fuselage, I told myself, *Be scared later. Just find out what's wrong, dammit!*

I got as far as Bob Hanson's radio compartment, where the glass gave me a view of the tail section. Beside Hanson, Chuck Leighton had shoved his navigator's tools to the side and grabbed a .30-caliber machinegun to blaze away at the hovering Focke-Wulfs. In his excitement Chuck missed the rubber-plug opening in the Plexiglas nose and shattered the surface with the barrel. Torrents of wind poured in at forty below zero. As Leighton sprayed the skies around us I noted that the tail damage was considerable. The tail had not left the plane as J.P. had thought, but a huge chunk was torn away. The top of the stabilizer was chewed up, and maybe the bottom as well—I couldn't quite see. The elevator—the fin that caused us to climb—was damaged as well.

Trying to ignore the face-hardening cold and the whine and swoop of fighters around us, I turned and groped my way back to the cockpit. The copilot was only too happy to see me buckle in. He was a selfless guy, not at all interested in hogging the glory.

Right away I could see why. The rudder pedals were haywire. I couldn't summon up their full mobility. I held back from applying pressure to them, for fear that I might snap the cables.

I'd have to fly without rudders. Fine. How would I make turns?

I guided my mangled B-17 along for a while, feeling and touching my way as the German fighters dogged us back north toward the English Channel, swooping in occasionally for a burst at our six-plane group and taking our clustered fire in return. I tried to ignore them and concentrate on keeping us in the sky and on course.

My mind was probing the contours of a dilemma. I knew I could deepen the damage to the airplane by hitting the rudder pedals to make a radical move. If I kept the *Belle* on an unwavering course, the Luftwaffe boys around us would soon notice something unnatural about this lead ship with the lingerie lady on her nose. Then sure as hell, they'd concentrate all their firepower on us, like so many hungry sharks converging on an injured swimmer.

I needed to show them a thing or two. Without a rudder.

Right.

I hit on a couple of ideas. I could improvise turns by manipulating my engine-power. To make a left turn, I'd cut back the power in the two engines on my left and let the right-engine power put us in a turning arc. I didn't figure to make any drastic turns anyway with another bomber tight up against me on each wing.

Another device would be using my yoke to make a "slip turn"—pulling a wing up to go one way, down to go another. Maybe it wouldn't be pretty, but then the Germans weren't handing out bonus points for finesse.

I had the situation figured out as well as possible, based on what I knew. What I did not know—could not know until we landed—was exactly how much of that tail was missing. To put it another way, I was pretty sure that getting the *Belle* back to Bassingbourn didn't figure to be too much of a problem. Getting her landed might be something else.

I knew that the crew was waiting back there for some kind of word from their Chief. Leighton and Evans were below me, in the nose with its jagged hole in the Plexiglas, fighting off frostbite from the arctic wind whipping through there. Quinlan sat in the back, wondering whether the rest of the tail was about to fall on top of him. Everyone else, trigger-fingers ready, was scanning the plane for more damage, wondering if they'd be alive tonight. Waiting for me to tell them.

Finally I clicked on the intercom. "Guys, listen," I said to them. "She's hurt. She's hurt pretty bad. She's hard to maneuver. I have enough alternate methods that I can fly this airplane, and that's what I intend to do. So let's all get back to our jobs. Fend off those fighter planes. Do the same things you've always done, and I'm gonna take you home."

That's exactly what happened. The Focke-Wulfs bade us farewell at the Channel, as usual—they never cared to hang around a neighborhood where those short-range but deadly RAF Spitfires might be lurking—and when we finally got back over Bassingbourn, I apprised the control tower of our damage and asked them to let the other two wing men land ahead of me. I wanted them down safely and the runway cleared so that I could make whatever wild approach and landing might be necessary, without worrying that I'd be leaving debris on the runway for the next plane in.

Was I up to it? Well, they didn't call me Floorboard Freddie for nothing. The approach I made just happened to be tailored to my freewheeling style—fast and hot. The more velocity, the less chance of drift. I knew I still had brakes, and brakes were my friend. We came barreling down on that runway, hit the tarmac with twin sharp puffs of smoke from our wheels, skidded like a taxicab that had just missed its fare, and screeched to a halt as Joe Giambrone's crew came at us on the dead run. They were about to encounter their most challenging repair job of the war thus far, and when he saw that shredded tail section, Joe reacted in his customary deadpan style.

"Gave her a fit today, didn't you, Chief?" he remarked. He got right to work, as usual.

I've thought about that near-disaster a lot since then. People have not let me forget it. In all the decades since the war, talking to high-school kids and reporters and others who want to know what it was like, I've been asked one group of questions pretty consistently. What was the effect of that close call on my nerves? Did it change my attitude about flying those missions? Did it give me the shakes at night?

And, the question that was put most baldly: Was I scared after that?

My answers have always been the same. "No."

It's hard to understand, I guess, for anyone who has never been up there—which means nearly everyone who ever lived. But in my mind—in all our minds, I think—there was never any confusion.

We knew, every time we went up, that it was very possible, likely even, to get hit hard, maybe knocked out of the sky. We might get trapped and roasted at our stations, or riddled with flak or machinegun bullets, or captured and sent to prison camps if we bailed out, provided we survived the trip down. We accepted that knowledge. We accepted it on that day over Lorient, and we accepted it through all the close calls that followed.

We didn't accept it in any grandiose way. It's not as though we thought we were heroes. The word hero had very little meaning to us. Heroes were the men who got shot down, the men who were lost. We hadn't yet faced what those guys faced. We were just a bunch of kids in a bomber doing the job assigned to us.

Doing the job—that was what meant something. Doing the job, doing it right, doing it right under pressure, and expecting everyone else in the crew to be doing their jobs on the same terms. Doing the job *because of* everyone else in the crew, doing it to keep them alive through one more mission.

Hell yes, we knew we'd had a close call, but we looked at it this way—we'd beaten the odds one more time. We were going to keep on beating the odds until we finished those twenty-five missions. Some of us called it the will of God. I was one of those. I was not what you'd call a holy man, or a pious man. Far from it. But I prayed. I meant what I prayed, just as I meant those tender letters home to Margaret, and just as I meant every minute of those wild nights in London.

I prayed to God that He would keep on keeping us safe, that he would let it continue. I imagine there were a lot of prayers being delivered up in those skies, by men and boys on both sides. I imagine that a lot of them were not answered, at least in any way we mortals could understand. I had always been taught that God's will would be done. I was willing to live and die by that.

The other thing that saved us crewmen on the *Belle* from getting

scared was the way these near-death scrapes brought us closer together. With every mission we survived, we were a closer family, a
more tightly-knit team, a stronger, less divisible single entity. Each time
we pulled through we felt more confidence, not less confidence. This
common bond would unite each of us with all of us forever afterward,
through the last moment of every man's last breath. Knighthood must
have been something like this, forging these kinds of bonds. I can't
think of much else that could have come close.

Finally there was our airplane. We came to believe in the *Memphis
Belle* absolutely. Every B-17 that flew in World War II was a miraculous machine, able to withstand damage that would bring down
most other aircraft. But this B-17 in particular—she seemed predes-
tined for surviving those twenty-five missions. You felt it the moment
you swung up through the hatch.

As Feburary 1943 approached, it was time for Allied fliers to pay
some not-so-social visits to the Fatherland.

The *Belle* crew actually missed out on the Mighty Eighth's first
mission over the frontier into Germany on January 27, to Emden
near the coast of the North Sea. We took off with the 91st, but an
oil-pressure problem forced us to turn back after an hour in the air.
The rest of the boys did well on an overcast day, hitting the submarine pens there after bypassing their primary target at Wilhelmshaven. A massive press entourage awaited them on their
return, clamoring for details and personal reactions to this first strike
directly over the Fatherland.

Our own first lick at Germany came on a return sortie to Emden
on February 4. It was a period of heady excitement for the Allied
fighting forces around the world. Just two days earlier, we'd cheered
to the news that a million and a half troops of the encircled German
Sixth Army had surrendered to the Russians at Stalingrad, the first
large-scale defeat of Hitler's forces in the war. Two days later, on
February 6, the U.S. Marines would declare the Pacific island of
Guadalcanal secure after brutal jungle fighting, a major victory in
the American island-hopping surge toward the Japanese home islands. General George Patton, picking up new stars for his collar just

about every other day it seemed, was headed for Tunisia to spear-head a growing rout of the Germans there.

On our own home-base island of Great Britain, unbeknownst to even us active combatants, a certain long-range plan originally known as SLEDGEHAMMER was being thrashed out in the highest strategic circles. Within months it would give way to a more sophis-ticated version known as OVERLORD—the blueprint for a massive Allied thrust across the English Channel and invasion of occupied France.

We still had a long hard war ahead of us. No one doubted that, but our once invincible-seeming adversaries didn't seem quite so in-vincible anymore.

I wish I could say that the *Memphis Belle* boys flew the *Belle* her-self in our first trip across the border, our ninth mission overall, but we didn't. She was still grounded for repairs, and Colonel Wray or-dered my crew to lead a force of fifty-nine bombers in another B-17, the *Jersey Bounce*. With typical leadership, the Colonel joined our crew as Command Pilot. He insisted on being aboard for one of the first trips across the German frontier.

The Germans were not at all pleased to see us. If we'd thought the Luftwaffe was tenacious over occupied France, we now witnessed the fanaticism of veteran fighter pilots defending their homeland. Planes of every conceivable description attacked us in swarms at the coastline and clung to us all the way into the target. The Germans even put up a JU-88, a squat twin-engined dive-bomber that was try-ing to land bombs on our ships from above. It didn't hit anything ex-cept Germany, but it was sure interesting to watch.

Our own bombing on this milestone foray was fair to poor. Thick cloud layers kept the target obscured. The 91st group lost two planes. Most of the rest took heavy damage, and I lost my reliable top-turret gunner, Eugene Adkins, to severe frostbite in his hands. Gene's war, as it turned out, was not finished, only interrupted. He made a heroic return to the service after his fingers partly healed, be-came a gunnery specialist despite his reduced capacity, was restored to duty on combat airplanes, flew two tours of duty in the waist, top, and ball positions as well as a bomb toggler, and retired as a major.

Unfortunately, the *Belle* never got him back. Our first trip to Germany was Gene's last trip with our crew.

We'd been sent a message from our adversaries that day, a message that would be reinforced every time we flew into Germany—if you Yanks thought France was tough, wait till you see what we do to you in our home ballpark. They had plenty reason to be all-out ferocious. We were going after the heart of German war production now—airplane factories, railroad centers, and those ever-popular submarine pens. We even raided the plants that manufactured ball bearings, those innocent-looking little metal spheres that reduce friction in the moving parts of engines and weapons, and thus were critical to the Wehrmacht's combat efficiency.

But even as the volume and the intensity of Nazi fighter attacks leapt upward, we pilots and crews were picking up on a subtle counter-trend. Some of the German pilots weren't quite as good as we'd seen even a few weeks ago. We were still facing some top-flight veterans, but we could discern some newcomers as well—they tended to keep their distance. The Luftwaffe was growing desperate.

The signs were almost imperceptible at first, cloaked in the heavy damage their fighter planes were still inflicting. But they would grow more obvious as winter gave way to spring and then to summer. That odd JU-88 lurching around up there above us, trying to bomb fast-moving aerial targets, was one of the early signals.

The Luftwaffe's talent pool was thinning out. Those seasoned, battle-tested pilots who'd flown against us with such brutal proficiency were slowly but steadily flaming out under our machinegun fire. Their replacements were not men of equal skill. They were younger, and their training hours and average age kept dropping as the war went on and the rate of attrition went up.

At the same time, American war-production factories, unimpeded by enemy attacks, were humming along at maximum capacity. Boeing alone was turning out upward of thirteen of those beautiful B-17s *a day*. And the Army Air Force was turning out pilots and crews with the skills to operate them. Its stateside training programs were augmented by topflight but disabled combat veterans like Gene Adkins, who could transfer both know-how and a sense of awe to those eager young boys.

By May of 1944, after the *Belle* was long gone, the skies over Germany were blanketed with the onslaughts of thousand-plane missions. The Luftwaffe pilots who flew to meet them could expect to survive three weeks, on average, with accidents killing almost as many of them as the Allies.

It was too bad. On the other hand, they started it.

Meanwhile, in the winter of 1943, the Mighty Eighth was still paying in blood and bombers for every mile it flew across the bristling Fatherland.

After ten days of larking in London, we boarded the newly patched-together *Belle* on February 14 and took her on her introductory trip to Germany. It was a little anticlimactic. We flew first to Emden, found the target fogged in, and forged some 150 miles inland to the railroad yards at Hamm, just northeast of the industrial cities of Dusseldorf and Essen. Fog there, too, so we turned around, the Luftwaffe nipping at us till we reached the coast again, and flew home without dropping any bombs. Nor did we jettison them over the ocean. Our orders were to bring our unused bombs home with us. For this reason, our bombs were armed just before they were dropped.

Still, we got credit for a mission.

We had a little business left with occupied France. The 91st paid its fourth visit to the sub pens at St. Nazaire on Feb. 16, a route the planes could probably trace on their own by now. For its troubles, the *Belle* got part of its right wing shot off, along with the No. 4 engine, and took damage to the No. 2 engine, although we didn't shut it down. We decided to let it run rather than try to fly on two engines, which we knew we could do—a B-17 could fly on *one* engine, but only with a severe loss of altitude, and if two people were there to control the rudders.

One engine shot out, part of the tail, part of the wing, another engine damaged—it was a bad day at the office. I guess we were getting used to this sort of thing. So used to it that we chose to pass up, with thanks, the new flak vests that were now being distributed to crewmen of the Eighth. The vests, their insides reinforced with metal, could be dropped over the wearer's head and fastened at the waist and crotch. Since there were not enough of these vests to go around, and since we figured we'd been doing pretty well without them, we opted to turn them down.

Maybe our disregard for the flak vests was a warning signal we should have heeded, a sign that we were getting a little numbed by it all, maybe dangerously so. It was all so routine now, the pressure and fatigue, the close calls, the brushes with death. The crew of the *Memphis Belle* may not have realized it, but we were badly in need of something to raise our spirits, make us laugh a little, and put us back in touch with the gentle things in life.

It was about this time that Stuka dive-bombed her way into our midst, and gave us the lift we needed.

Stuka arrived as a lively, wriggling parcel under the arm of Jim Verinis when he and Chuck Leighton showed up at the base one day after a quick frolic in London. Stuka was a black Scottish terrier puppy. Jim and Chuck had spotted her pressed up against the window of a London pet store, and Jim could not resist the impulse to dash inside, hand the proprietor the equivalent of $50 in American cash, and walk out with the squirming animal under his arm. Although Verinis had his own bomber by now, he still billeted, partied, and played poker with the *Belle* officers. He remained one of us in spirit. Jim installed her in his quarters, took on the challenging job of housebreaking her, and named her after the fearsome German dive-bomber, the Junkers 87.

Stuka never made a combat run on the *Belle*, as has been rumored—the frigid air and the lack of oxygen might have killed her—but she became the adored mascot of the *Belle* crew, wagging her tail and jumping around to greet us after every successful mission. Word has it that Verinis got so attached to her that one night, en route into London for a date, he started to miss that dog. When his train reached the station, he boarded the next one back to Cambridge. Just exactly what that might say about the merits of the young woman Jim was going to see is a question that I never got around to asking him.

Stuka developed a taste for whiskey—who wouldn't, hanging out with our crowd for very long?—and she reached the point where she could hold it pretty well. She was unimpressed by the various movie stars and celebrities who passed through our base—she was one of the few females ever to yawn in the presence of Clark Gable! Most important, though, she gave the crew of the *Memphis Belle* something warm and joyful to come home to after every mission.

Stuka even flew, at lower, safer altitudes, partied, and paraded with us on our national publicity tour after the twenty-fifth mission. She was a favorite of photographers and newsreel cameramen, and she seemed especially to enjoy the parades, playing to the crowd and mugging for attention along with the best of us. After the war, she went home with Jim and was present, wagging her tail, for the birth of his son Steven. If it hadn't been for a stray chicken bone that did her in at about the age of nine, I halfway believe she still might be with us today.

CHAPTER 44

Late winter, and round-the-clock bombing of France and Germany was well established now, with the RAF by night and the Mighty Eighth by day. The British bombers focused their nocturnal attacks on the glowing Ruhr Valley, where the Third Reich's steel industry was concentrated, its furnaces drawing from the largest coal-mining fields in all Europe. Thousands of German civilian workers were obliterated in these raids, and tragically, many thousands of slave laborers perished with them—Poles and Belgians, mostly—the same suffering peoples the Allies were trying to liberate. After dawn the Eighth Bomber Command took over and, with metronomic repetition, punished its own favorite targets—the coastal sub pens, the railroad yards, and the Focke-Wulf factories.

Our bombing campaign over Europe was by now starting to fascinate the American people. The Russian front was remote and abstract—two equally suspicious nations of extreme beliefs grinding one another to bits. The Pacific campaign had not yet produced its defining battles. The African campaign surged back and forth. But the air attack on Hitler's home territory was something else. Here was a phase of the war that Americans could follow with zest and comprehension, especially the millions of Americans who were European immigrants or children of immigrants, many of them refugees from the Reich's uprooting cruelties.

We noticed that more and more U.S. journalists—and British as well—were showing up on our bases in England, writing us up, trying to cadge rides on our sorties.

The "flying" press corps included a couple of kids named Walter Cronkite, then a United Press International correspondent, and a brash *Stars and Stripes* staffer named Andy Rooney. On his first trip Rooney got more action than he'd bargained for. He saw three ships around him get hit and go down, then his own plane, the *Banshee,* took a round in the nose compartment that wounded the navigator a few feet in front of him. Andy helped save the man's life by fitting him with an emergency oxygen bottle.

Another young reporter, Bob Post of *The New York Times,* was aboard a bomber that took a direct hit. He was never seen or heard from again.

The journalists paid particular attention to the planes and crews whose mission totals had started to pile up toward the magical twenty-five. The *Memphis Belle* attracted its share of press attention, especially given its eye-catching human-interest angle—being named for its pilot's girlfriend.

After a few stories about us had appeared in American newspapers, we began to hear versions of a chilling rumor that we laughed off in public, but not alone, late at night—that the Luftwaffe was following those same newspaper accounts, and its pilots had put the *Memphis Belle* at the top of their most-wanted list. They were gunning for us.

It was almost enough to make us want to paint a couple of fur coats over those George Petty drawings on the front of the *Belle.*

Reporters weren't the only noncombatants interested in hitching rides into aerial combat. It was only a matter of time before filmmakers showed up too. Here is where our days at the office in the *Belle* became a part of Hollywood legend.

Along about January 1943 we started catching glimpses of a trim, fairly cocky fellow in an airman's flight-jacket and billed leather cap bustling around Bassingbourn, waving his arms in the air, a cigarette burning from the middle of his lips and a couple of cameramen dogging his footsteps. He wore a Major's uniform, and had a crisp way of ordering everyone around, so I figured he must be quite the VIP. As things turned out, he was a much bigger VIP than I could have imagined—he was a Hollywood film director. He had arrived to make a documentary for the Army Air Force film unit about the effectiveness of daylight strategic bombing over Europe—still a matter of controversy between America and a skeptical Britain in the early weeks of 1943.

His name, somebody said, was Wyler. William Wyler.

I guess I'd seen his name on the screen. I found out he'd directed some of those Bette Davis pictures that Margaret loved to go and cry over, like *Jezebel* and *The Letter*. Sure, Wyler. He'd worked with Henry Fonda and Humphrey Bogart and Mary Astor, too. And years before that, as a kid in the 1920s, I'd probably gobbled up a lot of his early silent Westerns on Saturday afternoons in Asheville—movies with names like *Tenderfoot Courage* and *Galloping Justice* and *The Phantom Outlaw*.

He'd come a long way since then. In fact, not long after he showed up on the base, a little after New Year's, I was reminded where I'd seen his name most recently—under "Directed By" in the credits for *Mrs. Miniver*. I remembered when word got around that the movie had just won him his first Academy Award—one of six the movie itself won, including Best Picture.

You can imagine my surprise when William Wyler bought me a drink one night and said he wanted to make me a star.

Well, that's not exactly the way he put it. What he said to me in his slight European accent in the officers' lounge one evening, between puffs of smoke from that straight-jutting cigarette, was that he wanted to bring his camera on board the *Memphis Belle* and fly some missions with the crew.

He squinted at me—he had a very intense movie director-type of squint—and I looked back at him. I was trying to buy a few seconds to think that one over. Oh, if Mother could only see me now.

The idea was kind of irresistible. I'd already picked up a little of the gossip running around the base about this Wyler. Some of the guys who read movie magazines were talking about his reputation for being excitable, and for ordering major stars like Hank Fonda to do thirty, thirty-five, forty takes of a scene just to get past their actorish mannerisms and give him something from the heart.

One thing I didn't need during a bombing run was for some guy to be crashing around the plane with a camera in one hand and his oxygen bottle in the other, bumping into my gunners and asking my navigator for a closeup. I sure as hell wasn't about to go back and do any retakes for anybody.

"Why us?" I asked him, trying to match that squint of his.

Wyler smiled, and that crinkly squint went deeper, and he took a long thoughtful drag on his cigarette. "Ah," he said as he released the smoke through his nose. "Ah well. That name of your plane. *Memphis Belle.* It has a mystique. Don't you think?" He sipped his drink, swirled the ice a little. "Also, I have asked around, and I've heard that you're a magnificent pilot. How many missions now? Eight? And haven't you led most of those missions? If I flew with you, I'd be right in the center of the action, Captain Morgan. And I'd have a pretty good chance of coming back."

So that was what they meant by "Hollywood charm."

To cover what I feared might be a most un-military blush, I laid it sternly on the line. I took a good belt of the scotch he'd bought me, set the glass down on the bar and said, "You know, Major, we'd have no problem with an eleventh man on the airplane, as long as he stays out of the way. It's crowded in there. Every one of the crew members has a job to do. I've got two waistgunners in the middle of the fuselage backed right up against each other. I've got a bombardier and navigator working in the nose. You try to move among these guys when we're in action, you will interfere with their work and maybe get all of us killed."

Who the hell did I think I was—Dana goddam Andrews? I immediately asked myself. *What am I doing, talking like that to a guy who made Bette Davis leave his movie set in tears and not come back for two weeks?* In the officers' lounge at Bassingbourn Air Base this evening, William Wyler did not show a trace of Hollywood attitude. He was all business, a man's man, and as smooth as the scotch I'd just gulped. "I assure you, Captain," he said, without a trace of sarcasm, "that I will not get in anybody's way."

Well, all right then. He seemed worth the risk. Maybe it would be a kick for the boys in the crew as well. I couldn't help acknowledging to myself a compliment that active combat fliers rarely paid to civilians, which Wyler was in everything but rank. *This guy's got a lot of nerve. With those kind of guts, we can find room for him.* I told him it sounded promising, and that I'd have a final answer for him the next day.

First, I checked him out a little more with Colonel Wray. I learned that Wyler had requested Bassingbourn as his base of operations, and not just because of the cushy living quarters. He'd been impressed with the 91st's reputation. I learned that he'd shown up with about 200 small 16-millimeter film cameras—no microphones, just film—that he handed out to crew members on several airplanes. "Take as much film as you can," he'd told the crewmen. "And after you turn in the film, you can keep the camera."

Later still, much later, after the war was over, I learned some more things about William Wyler that only deepened my respect for him.

The territorial feuds that had triggered bloodshed in western Europe for centuries were woven into his personal history. He'd been born into a Jewish family in 1902 in Mulhouse, in the Alsace, the land between France and Germany that had been coveted by both since the Reformation. As a boy of twelve, in August 1914, he had watched French troops and cavalry stream into the city to liberate it from German annexation at the outset of the Great War. He and his family huddled in their cellar through several weeks of artillery shelling, attacks, and counterattacks as the French and Germans took and retook the city. The Germans claimed it for the war's duration in September, and the boy Willy could hear the thunder of heavy guns from the front lines just a few miles from town. He could see dogfights between German and Allied airplanes from the roof of his house by day, and once rushed to the site of a downed French fighter nearby, cutting a piece of canvas from the airplane's wing.

Perhaps this is where Willy Wyler developed the astonishing coolness under fire that he would display again and again aboard the *Memphis Belle*.

He came to America at age twenty to work for a cousin, Carl Laemmle, a founder of Universal Pictures. Wyler started out writing publicity releases for the studio, then learned the director's trade by grinding out those quickie Westerns that occupied my Saturday afternoons in Asheville, and finally got a shot at directing feature-length movies. He made nearly thirty pictures over the rest of his career, including *Ben Hur* and *Funny Girl*, and most film critics maintained that he never made a bad one.

But what really made William Wyler special to me, I guess, was his courage, and his passion. He wasn't just after cheap thrills or glory in those missions he flew with us—and he flew several. He believed enough in what we were doing to risk his life capturing it on film. That passion—the passion of a European Jew who had seen his world ground under by Hitler and, later, his people exterminated—was a reminder to all of us of what we were fighting for, and against.

That passion damn near got him court-martialed in the process. After he'd been up a few times, it occurred to General Eaker that if Wyler's plane were shot down and he was taken prisoner, the Germans might capitalize on his fame and his Jewishness for propaganda purposes—and also that the director might suffer more than an ordinary prisoner of war. Eaker ordered Wyler grounded.

Wyler's response was to hop on board the next RAF bomber for a night raid over Hamburg. "If anybody wants to court-martial me for doing my job," he snarled, "I'm willing to leave that to the judgment of the readers when they see the headlines."

General Eaker suddenly discovered more important matters that required his attention.

That was the caliber of the eleventh man aboard the *Memphis Belle* for five of her final missions.

He was aboard on Feb. 26, when we attacked one of the key targets of the German war machine—the installations near Wilhelmshaven, on an inlet of the North Sea. Wilhelmshaven was rumored to be a charming resort city, famous for its mud baths, but the 91st wasn't going there for cosmetic reasons. The city was host to the only deep-water seaport in Germany, a key point of egress for U-boats and other elements of the German navy. As such, we were told, it was bound to be heavily defended. It was.

Once again our crew was flying the *Jersey Bounce*. The *Belle* was in for repairs, receiving two new engines and a piece of wing. Once again, our force of fifty-three bombers was swarmed by fighters—about 100 this time—and, later, riddled by heavy flak.

Our own group lost two B-17s and twenty-one men, and nineteen crewmen suffered frostbite, but it was the B-24 group flying with us that really caught hell that day. Though the 24s were bigger planes than ours, and they carried bigger bomb loads, they could not withstand as much damage as the 17s and stay in the air. The Germans knew this—their pilots told us as much after the war—and so they focused on the 24s whenever they could. Once again, our crew was lucky, at the expense of other brave comrades in the air around us.

"How'd you enjoy it?" I asked Wyler when we were back down on the ground.

"Well," he said. He tossed the butt of a cigarette onto the tarmac and carefully flattened it with the toe of his boot. "A lot of action I see. A lot of action."

He may not have enjoyed it, but he came back with us again several times.

Back to the submarine pens at Brest the next day, February 27. An easy mission, no planes lost. Back at the base, Joe Giambrone made a thoughtful circle around the *Memphis Belle,* then turned to me with a quizzical look in his dark, expressive eyes. "Where were you guys?" he wanted to know. "Did you show up for this fight?"

Down for a week. Fatigue and anxiety setting in.

At Lorient on March 6, we recovered a little more of our espirit de corps. Lorient lay on the southern coast of the rugged and fortified Bretagne peninsula. We took the long route there, flying southwest the length of the English Channel, then out over the Atlantic, to keep from crossing that land-mass with its many antiaircraft installations. On a clear day with great visibility, we came looping in low from the Bay of Biscay—surprise!—and climbed rapidly to hit them from 22,000 feet.

Vince, as lead bombardier, had one of his best days ever. He pickle-barreled his bombs precisely over the power plant near the pens. We got a few flak holes, nothing we hadn't seen before.

We got in and out of there pretty cleanly, thanks to our route—a round trip of nine and a half hours, the longest we'd ever experience over Europe. That, plus our bombing success, made us all a little cocky on our trip home.

Every plane on the mission was running short of fuel, thanks to the long curving route and the rapid climb to the bombing run. The group decided that everybody would go their own route, and if some of the pilots wanted to touch down at an airfield near the coast to gas up, that would be fine.

Every plane in the mission ended up touching down at other airfields except one. The *Memphis Belle*. Floorboard Freddie was on the prowl. It had been quite a while since I'd pushed the edges just for the hell of it, and today felt like a good time.

Maj. Eddie Aycock, our new squadron commander, was flying co-pilot with me that day. I knew, as surely as if I could read his mind, that he was quietly wondering about our fuel level. I said, real casually, "Major, you know, I think we can get back to Bassingbourn without stopping." He shot me a doubtful glance. "You do?"

I said, "Yeah. It might be a little close, but I think I could 'lean' these engines out pretty good and we could make it."

I hadn't completely sold him yet. He said, "Do you know what you're doing, Morgan?"

I said, "I think I do." And then I played some hardball. I said, "By the way, there's a big party going on tonight. Do you know that?"

When the Major said, "Yeah," I thought I had him. I knew it for sure when he added, after a thoughtful pause, "As a matter of fact, I've got a girl coming to that party."

I pretended to think this over for a minute. Then I said, "So have I." Another weighty silence while we flew along. "Well," I said, "don't you think we ought to at least make an effort?"

The Major said, "Well, if you think you can do it, let's go ahead and try it."

A while later I checked the fuel gauge and then announced, in my best unconcerned North Carolina drawl, "You know what? I think I'll just shut that Number 3 engine down."

"You think you'll *what?*" Major Aycock shot back.

"Shut ol' Number 3 down," I repeated.

"What for?"

"Oh, I don't know," I said. "I guess I figured out that on three engines, we won't burn as much fuel as we would have with four engines running, and that will save us enough fuel so we'll be sure and make it."

I could almost hear the thought-process ricochet back and forth in the Major's mind—*Girl. Ditch. Girl. Crash-land in a hedgerow. Girl.*

After a while he said, as if our conversation had just recurred to him, "You figured that thing pretty accurately?"

I said, "Well, it makes sense, doesn't it?" He didn't answer. He didn't say another damn word about it. He just sat there. The onus for this one was going to be all on Morgan.

Well, we made it, of course. When Joe Giambrone showed up for the post-flight checkup, I pulled him aside, out of the Major's hearing, and spoke to him discreetly. "Joe," I said, "Check the gas. See how much we've got and let me know tomorrow, will you?"

The next morning, he came over to me with a strange look in his eyes. "I figured," he said, "that you had about eight to ten minutes flying time, at the best."

Well, hell, we'd made it—unlike everybody else, who all took the safe course and landed at other bases. To the victor belong the spoils. That night we had all the girls, all the liquor, all the fun. The morning after was sweetened a little bit by an amazing discovery. Somebody counted up our missions. We'd completed fourteen. All of a sudden, we were more than halfway home.

On March 12, we flew what I would always remember as our "perfect mission." Perfect, because we had fighter backup of our own this time, and the Messerschmitt and Focke-Wulf boys kept their distance.

One ploy that helped make our mission perfect was our unusual flight plan. Across the Channel, the Wing separated itself briefly into three sections, each flying off in a different direction. Our intent was to confuse the Germans, make them think we were branching off toward several targets, and force them to spread thin their squadrons of fighter planes. It worked. After a few minutes of this feint, the

Wing came together again, flanked by an escort of RAF Spitfires. We had the jump on our hastily regrouping foes, and we raced down hard on our single, unlucky target.

This was Rouen, with its massive railway yards, a hub of the Germans' rail transportation. Rouen lay only thirty miles from the English Channel in northern France, less than 100 miles from Brighton across the water. This put it well within range, for a change, of the Spitfires, and they kept us company right through the bomb run. We took full advantage of this luxury, and the eighteen Fortresses of the 91st joined the fun of virtually wiping out those tracks. We figured we could get used to this kind of war.

We paid for our free ride the next day.

We paid for it over Abbeville, a small village even farther up the French coast than Rouen, and closer to Britain. It wasn't the small village we were interested in, it was the big Luftwaffe airfield next to it. Here was the haven where the German aces, the best fliers of the Reich, holed up. Here was our chance to nail a whole cluster of them while they were trapped on the ground. We were practically licking our chops when Colonel Wray tapped Abbeville with his pointer stick in the predawn briefing.

Maybe that eagerness to swat our worst tormentors explains why we got a little too cute for our own good.

The Bomber Command's idea was to lull the Germans into thinking we were headed somewhere else—a variation on the Triangle. "You'll see when you get briefed on navigation," Colonel Wray told our map-and-chart men, "that you will be headed nearly opposite from where you'll end up going. We want to fool them, and make them think we're going up to the northwest. We're going to loop around at the last minute and go to Abbyville. We'll stay low and catch the fighters on the ground if they're still there."

Sounded good in theory. Unfortunately for the practice aspect of it, Chuck Leighton was not the lead navigator that day.

Whoever was leading the mission managed to fool himself and his squadron more than he did the Germans. He not only flew the wrong way, as he was supposed to do—he flew the wrong way *the wrong way.* As usual, Chuck Leighton, spotting from our plane, was onto the mistake the minute the lead squadron drifted off course. *"Don't follow 'em,"* we heard his familiar low-key voice telling us. "They're lost. We'll go in on our own." And so the *Belle,* by default, became the point-plane on the swoop over Abbeville.

How did a navigator make a mistake like that? By not doing the little things. In this case, probably by relying on surface navigation—following landmarks below him based on a map—instead of constantly checking his coordinates, as Chuck always did. It's amazing how much one river or village looks like another in unfamiliar territory. It's easy to go wrong. I've done it myself. I landed once by mistake at the wrong airport in Detroit and later touched down in the wrong city, if you can believe it, in my home state of North Carolina.

I'm aware that anybody can make a mistake. The difference was that I was not at war with Detroit or North Carolina.

Anyway, there were bombers all over the sky after that. We must have looked like the Keystone Kops coming in. Chuck, of course, took the 91st right over the target, and another group followed us in. In spite of the confusion and our diminished numbers, we achieved surprise and did a fair job of blowing up some of the elite pilots' aircraft as it sat on the tarmac. It wasn't the best we could have made of the opportunity. Some days you're perfect and other days you have trouble finding home plate.

My guys had a craving for home plate. That's one thing that made us different. Leighton and Vince Evans down there together in that hatch—what a pair of sticklers they were! Nice fellows, great company, but when it counted, two of the most grimly conscientious men I've ever known. Vince may have been a party guy down on the ground, but on a mission he could be as crabby as your seventh-grade geometry teacher. "You know, if I don't hit the target, all we've got to do is make another mission and come back here again. So rather than do that, let's hit the target the first time." He and Chuck usually did.

Sixteen missions down. Nine to go.

We didn't talk about it. We never talked about it. We spent a lot of time not talking about it.

On March 17 we took off on a sortie to Rouen, a raid that never happened except in the statistics that tabulated the race toward that "magic number" of twenty-five missions completed. Eighteen B-17s took off that morning from the 91st, but all were recalled over the Channel. The reason given was that our scheduled fighter escort of Spitfires had been grounded because of fog—an unusual show of concern for us by Headquarters! The crew of the *Belle* did not get credit for this mission. But in the logic of the record-keepers, the *Memphis Belle* did. It was operational for combat, and therefore worthy of credit. This would prove significant in balancing the number of missions we flew on craft other than the *Belle*.

Five days later, we flew back to Wilhelmshaven, and this one was no mere statistic.

Aside from their deadly submarines and some formidable battleships, the Germans didn't have much of a navy, but our Intelligence had determined that one of their battleships, the *Admiral Scheer,* was in the harbor there. We were to sink it, and, while we were in the neighborhood, bomb the docks and everything else that looked hostile.

Twenty-one B17s took off and three aborted. We took withering flak—the *Belle* had about fifty holes when we got back—but we did what we went there to do. We lit up the *Admiral Scheer*—Vince planted one bomb just off her bow—and left the harbor in ruins. Wyler, hovering behind the pilot/copilot area and the navigator/bombardier station, and making his way the full length of the plane from time to time, got plenty of hot footage.

As on our first mission there, the Germans showed how desperate they had become. More than fifty fighters attacked us, and once again we saw JU-88s trying to bomb us from above. The Nazis shot down three planes from our squadron, including one piloted by my close friend Captain H. C. McClellan. I watched as McClellan's young wife became a widow. Wyler saw it too. He even captured McClellan's spinout on film. He also caught the image of a fighter that sliced in from above and knifed right through our formation. I plunged us into a sudden dive of about 1,200 feet.

The Focke-Wulfs damaged nine other of our ships. One of these was piloted by the superb Red Claiborne, who had been flying as my left wing man from the very beginning. Two of Red's engines were shot out as we left the bombing run, and his oxygen supply was hit, too. He had no choice but to descend to about 10,000 feet so that his crew could breathe. Everyone in the squadron went down with him. It was against the rules, strictly speaking, to go down and cover a plane that had been disabled—you were just letting yourself in for some Luftwaffe target practice—but Red and his crew were too good to just get sacrificed to the wolves. Bomber crews often felt that way about their stricken comrades, and acted accordingly, and paid with their lives. So we dropped along with him, a protective shield of firepower. We took some hits, but nothing serious. Another day at the office.

That's how it was starting to feel in these winter weeks, as the time-interval between our missions decreased and fatigue set in, both mental and physical: another day at the office.

March slogged on. Inhumanly cold in the skies. High casualties. Scanty replacements of men and planes and parts—other war theaters kept up their siphoning drain. Exhaustion among the fliers and the support people on the ground. Not all maintenance crews were as good as Joe Giambrone's, and airplanes were taking off on missions with structural flaws and engine problems that would only become obvious at 20,000 feet. Some of the pilots began to break down under the accumulated strain. Mid-air collisions of friendly bombers, while never commonplace, began to add to the high rate of attrition.

The arctic atmosphere in our planes never let up—it never ceased to take its toll. Our flight jackets and fleece collars and leather helmets may have become glamorous collectors' items in later years, but in actual use they barely kept us alive. For warmth, we relied on exhaust heat from our engines that was funneled through the cockpit. It gave the pilots some warmth, and the bombardier and navigator caught a little of it, and the radio man and top turret gunner, if they were lucky. The other gunners wore electrically heated suits. Sometimes these failed and hypothermia and frostbite would begin their deadly business. Even our firepower suffered from the cold, the guns' oil-based lubrication turning gummy and clogging the moving parts. Gunners would squeeze their triggers at onrushing fighters only to find themselves inside a bad dream, their gelid guns discharging bullets not in rapid bursts but one by one, at horribly languid intervals, as fighters closed in.

The five bomber groups of the Mighty Eighth lost crews wholesale—one group, over several months, lost 113, and more than a thousand men. In March alone, the British-based B-17s flew nine missions and lost ten planes, 100 men. Casualty rates climbed to eight percent per outing. When it was all over, in June of 1945, the Mighty Eighth's losses, from some 200,000 combat crewmen, would total 26,000 killed and 28,000 taken prisoners of war. The 91st alone would have lost 209 planes, and 2,012 crewmen.

The names of missing men, now, were ever-more likely to be the names of men we knew well. We kept hearing stories from survivors of routine heroism and self-sacrifice—of how a damaged ship, its crew on the point of bailing out, elected to remain inside and keep shooting at German fighters, hoping to draw them away from other damaged ships. Of pilots who knew better, insisting on veering off-course to protect afflicted comrades, and being suddenly incinerated by cannon rounds that exploded their gas tanks. Of men, themselves horribly wounded, who groped their way to the guns or the yokes of men wounded even more horribly, or no longer alive.

The chances of any given crew surviving twenty-five missions, a number that had seemed so romantically accessible only a few months earlier, dwindled toward zero.

The *Memphis Belle* kept flying and kept coming back. A few other crews were also edging toward a half-dozen or so missions of the magical number. We tried not to know who they were. We tried not to keep count, to keep score. We tried not to think about it. We went to London and did not think about it.

March 28—back to Rouen. Wyler was with us again. Twenty-two planes got off the ground, and four aborted. It was not a perfect mission this time, but not bad. In fact, Headquarters tried to recall it just as we had locked into our bomb run. They'd learned the railroad yards were overcast and the Spitfire escort we'd been promised could not find us. The Major leading the mission wisely ignored the recall.

The Germans tried a new tactic that day. They came throttling up from below and tried to shoot upward into the formation, into our big, broad bellies. This created some special pressure on Cecil Scott, our little ball turret gunner, down there in his bubble. "They're shooting at me from underneath, and I'm just hanging there," was the way he put it afterward.

But it was the Germans themselves who paid the worst price for their innovation. Their steep climbs left them all but stalled out at the very peak—just hanging there like nice round yellow-tipped melons waiting to be plucked. Our gunners got off some of their best shots of the war that day. Quinlan bagged himself a Focke-Wulf. We noticed that after that, the Germans didn't do too much attacking from underneath. Too bad. We were just starting to get used to it.

We didn't get out of it without any bruises. This was another of our "close-call" missions. J.P. got his guns, Pete and Repeat, knocked out by a burst from a fighter, a round that would have killed him if he hadn't lowered his head just at that instant. A little later he got hit with a piece of flak—a slight flesh wound above his left knee, and the only injury that a crewman on the *Belle* would ever sustain. J.P. didn't even think it was significant enough for a Purple Heart. The Army Air Force made him take one anyway. That same burst tore another hole in our tail section, damaging our elevator and making it hard for me to control my climbing and descending.

Finally, I nearly lost my two waistgunners, Clarence Winchell and Scott Miller, when their oxygen went out. They had lost control of their oxygen bottles, and might have died if I hadn't noticed, in the midst of all the confusion, that I hadn't heard from them in a while. When they did not respond to my direct query over the intercom, I sent Bob Hanson, my radio operator, back to see what was going on back there. He found them nearly unconscious, and managed to re-arrange their masks and get their bottles working again. The team-work we swore by had paid off for us once more.

Through it all, William Wyler kept coolly focused on his own as-signment—shooting film. My fears about him running out of control, or giving in to panic, proved completely unfounded. Many years later, when I worked with his daughter Catherine on that Hollywood feature movie about the *Belle,* she told me she wasn't surprised to hear this. The only times her father truly lost control of himself, she said, were during *real* crises—such as when an actor made a crazy move in front of the camera.

March 31. To Rotterdam, Holland, and the shipyards there. This one was a screwed-up mission from the outset. Two planes got confused in a cloud bank during their formation assembly over the Channel and crashed into each other. Both were lost. Headquarters had ordered a "double diversion" on the way in—lots of planes flying bogus routes to draw off fighters—and that burned up a lot of fuel. The *Belle* had an engine shot out by flak. The target, when we got there, was covered by clouds. We didn't release our bombs. We didn't get credit for a mission. But once again, the *Belle* did.

April 5. We headed to Antwerp, Belgium, in the *Bad Penny* as our plane was in the shop. The mission was to destroy the Luftwaffe's aircraft repair shops there. Twenty B-17s took off, Wyler was with us, and we ran into a tremendous concentration of fighters, between seventy and eighty of them that attacked us in droves. They shot up the lead group and the rear group. We were in the middle, and didn't get hurt very much, but we did some damage. Clarence Winchell got himself a Focke-Wulf—he riddled it with about fifty rounds. Headquarters that day designated Vince Evans as lead bombardier for the group, and promoted him to Captain.

After that, we were down out of action under bad weather for thirteen days. Once again the surreal quality of war took hold. We left those punishing, killing skies over Europe and dived back into the beckoning pleasures of the Ancient City.

This time it was particularly surreal because we had Clark Gable with us.

He had arrived a few days earlier with the 351st Bomb Group. He had enlisted in the war at the age of forty-two, a Hollywood star at the peak of his career, eager to do his part. Too old for serious consideration as an active combatant, he was given the rank of Captain and assigned to make some gunnery training films for Army Air Force use back home. He flew several missions filming crews in action, like Wyler, and serving, at least nominally, as a backup waist-gunner. As with Wyler, the Eighth Bomber Command was a little queasy about having Clark up there. Word had got around that no less a fan than Adolf Hitler himself had offered a reward to any Luftwaffe flier who could bring the big guy down and deliver him to Berlin for a little chat, tough-guy to tough-guy.

Determined to show everyone that he was not just making a star tour, Gable even volunteered to give marksmanship lessons to gunners on the base who were interested. But when he looked at the fuselages on our airplanes and saw the number of swastikas painted on them—each one representing a downed German fighter—he chuckled, loosened up, admitted that he didn't have all that much to teach us, and let us know he was ready to have a little fun. The moviegoers of the 91st were only too happy to oblige.

We invited Clark along with us on our sorties to the West End of London. We showed him our favorite dance halls and officers' clubs over several whirlwind nights. We assured him with absolutely straight faces that if he had any trouble getting dates, we'd be happy to introduce him around. As things turned out, he managed fairly well on his own. He'd had to shave off his trademark mustache for military service, but his famous jug ears and his grinning mouth full of white Hollywood teeth left no doubt as to who he was. His uniform always looked as though it had just been starched and pressed by the wardrobe folks at MGM.

We attracted hordes of women wherever we went. We could hardly step inside a club without the bandleader spotting Clark and motioning his drummer to give us a drumroll and cymbal crash. Vince and Jim and I agreed that it was quite something to stroll into a crowded club with Rhett Butler alongside us—and a whole roomful of Vivien Leighs just waiting to be told he didn't give a damn! For a change, we flyboys of the *Belle* were not the top cats of the joint. But we didn't mind. These were some of the best nights we had. Gable never fell back on his Hollywood credentials—not with us, and not with the girls. He danced, drank whiskey, told tall tales and

whispered sweet nothings to the British ladies like any airman out on
the town. He was both a man's man and an effortless charmer of
women, and it was great just being in his wake—taking the leftovers,
as one of us put it.

That was the damn weirdest stretch of my life, in a lot of ways—
getting shot at with live ammunition by Germans while being filmed
by a Hollywood director one day, then the next nightclub-hopping
in London with the star of *Gone With the Wind* and *It Happened
One Night* and *Mutiny on the Bounty*. I guess it was even more surreal for this genial, likable man who was already nicknamed The
King of Hollywood. The reason Gable had enlisted in the Army Air
Force in the first place was out of grief after his third wife, Carole
Lombard, was killed in January 1942 in a plane crash in Nevada,
while returning from an appearance at a War Bond drive. In what
you'd have to call the most surreal touch of all, the two of them were
seen in a morale-boosting movie called *Show Business at War*, with
dozens of other stars, released in 1943, over a year after her death.

From what I learned of Gable's postwar career, those London
nights on the town with us may in some ways have been the last
good times of his life. He never quite regained the stature of his great
glamour years when he returned to Hollywood. Still wounded over
the death of Carole Lombard, perhaps, and carrying his share of combat memories, he suffered some of the same callous treatment that
awaited many returning veterans. The big studio boys took a look at
his contract and pronounced it "excessive." He never made a truly
great film after that, although a lot of people felt that his 1958 World
War II submarine movie, *Run Silent, Run Deep,* was among the best
of the whole genre. He was dead himself of a heart attack only sixteen years after the war's end.

But Clark Gable never had anything to prove to the crew of the
Memphis Belle. He became one of us during those early-spring
nights in London in 1943. He showed us that he knew what he was
talking about in one of his most famous quoted remarks: "The only
reason they come to see me is that I know that life is great—and they
know I know it."

CHAPTER

12

*J*ust one mission at a time. Just one more mission, then one more.
And then just another one, like any other one. Never mind what
*number it is. Forget about the number. Just go up and do the job.
One more mission. They're all the same. What number? Forget
about it! It's just another mission!*

Everybody was keeping count now, but nobody was admitting it,
including our crew, other crews, the ground crew, the brass at Bassingbourn. Nobody was talking. Nobody wanted to jinx us. That got
to be weird in itself, as the weeks of April ticked by, all our friends,
our commanders, making this big show of Nothing Special. One
thing was sure, though. Everybody wanted to ride with us. Every officer wanted to be my copilot. We could hardly keep Wyler off the
plane if we'd wanted to.

It wasn't hard to figure why anybody would be angling for a little
safety. Our airplanes were getting shot up worse than ever now. The
brass had cut down on our missions by more than half from the
number in March, because the German resistance was growing so
maniacal and replacements were so few and far between.

The *Belle*, it seemed, was taking on that aura of a charmed airplane, an airplane of destiny. I could have told them that. Didn't I
have Margaret's picture up there on the instrument panel to prove it?

April 16. Mission Number 20. The submarine pens at Lorient.
Twenty-one planes in the group took off, eight aborted.

Big experiment on this one. The generals hatched the brilliant idea that if they could get the airplanes up faster to the bombing altitude, it might cut down on exposure to the fighters. So they put out a directive. I will always remember that damn directive, because everybody who read it, including Colonel Wray, said it would be impossible to carry out. The directive told us to climb up to 24,000 feet at 170 miles an hour, our top speed. That was a fine idea except for one thing. Top speed and rapid climbing don't go together. You try to climb a B-17 at 170 miles per hour and you're going to climb real slow, because you can't pull the nose up very much or the plane will stall out in that oxygen-thin higher air. We all tried our best to climb as fast as we could anyway, and what we did was we burnt out the turbo-superchargers in our engines. These devices, like blowers or compressors, were located under the fuselage, and built around a turbine that forced a greater volume of air through the plane's carburetor.

That's why we had eight aborts. It was no day at the beach for the planes that managed to stay in the air. We burnt up a lot of precious fuel in that maneuver, we wandered out of formation, and we arrived at the target low on gas and strung out all over the sky. Luckily for us, the Germans didn't pick up on our exposed condition, and we were able to re-form into tight formations by the time they came after us.

We never practiced rapid climbing again.

April 17. Mission Number 21. A huge objective today—a preview of the massive, deep-penetrating missions the Eighth was about to start pouring into German airspace over the summer and autumn of 1943. Our target was the port city of Bremen on the Weser River in northwest Germany. Bremen would mark our longest journey over enemy territory thus far. Like many targets on both sides, it was a target rich in history, as I later found out. The town had been around since the first century AD. It was steeped in old Teutonic charm, and had even formed the setting for a fable by the Brothers Grimm.

What we were after on this day was no fairy tale. Besides its concentration of shipbuilding and textile plants, Bremen harbored a factory that built those hated and lethal Focke-Wulf 190s—not to mention an airfield where, as our spies and the antifascist Underground informed us, some 200 of Hitler's best fliers and gunners were billeted.

We had no illusions about the kind of hell we would catch over this stronghold. The Germans would throw everything they could think of at us, and then some. The Intelligence officer warned us at briefing that we'd be facing 270 to 300 fighters, not to mention 100 to 150 aerial artillery guns in the target area alone. The chance to prune out some of those demon Focke-Wulfs and their personnel made the prospect bearable. Colonel Wray pumped us up with an extra-fiery pep talk. "This is the target we really want to hit, boys," I remember him saying to us as he smacked that blackboard for emphasis. "Really hit. Really knock 'em out. We've really got to do the job on this one."

In other words, give those Germans the ultimate Rigid Digit.

Thirty-two of the 91st's thirty-six airplanes took off as the lead of four huge groups on the morning of the seventeenth, and only three aborted. The thirty-two were part of a total force numbering more than 100. We needed every ounce of the Colonel's motivating juice.

The flak, when it kicked in, was like nothing any of us had ever seen before. To call it a carpet doesn't begin to do it justice. The sky below us and around us was a boiling black lagoon of exploding metal. It is inconceivable to me, to this day, that any plane made it through that maelstrom without getting riddled to small pieces. A lot of them didn't.

Then the flak stopped—always an ominous sign. It stopped to clear the skies for the fighters.

Here they came, swarms, clouds of them, every make and model you could imagine. "Goering had all his yellow-nose boys up there," was the way one of the crew put it later. Those were the elite 190s, of course, backed up by Messerschmitt 109s; but also a few Messerschmitt 110s, a fighter/attack bomber we hadn't seen too much of before. They even had some more of those JU-88s up above us, trying to drop bombs through the formation. The Germans had begun to realize that they were fighting for the survival of their infrastructure, and they flew and fought like madmen. This was among the roughest of all the *Belle*'s missions.

The atmosphere inside the pitching, roiling *Belle* reflected the fury. The cacophony over the intercom was nonstop. It threatened to get out of control for one of the few times I can recall. Guys were calling out planes coming in, going out, 12 o'clock, 3 o'clock, every o'clock. Often two men were trying to call at one time. I finally had to grab the intercom mike. "Guys, please calm it down back there!" I told them. "We can't understand what you're saying about where they are. Please, one at a time!" It always helped when they heard how calm the Chief was. Except that the Chief himself wasn't too calm that day.

It sure didn't help my nerves when J. P. Quinlan joined the bedlam to report that he had gun trouble again. Just "Repeat" this time— "Pete" was okay—but any falloff in firepower from the tailgunner exposed us to major peril, especially in this kind of madhouse. I recall that I explained to him coolly and precisely just exactly what he had to do. "Johnny," I yelled back, *"get that other gun working somehow!"*

He followed my instructions to the letter. He unjammed "Repeat" and got it firing again. He even nailed his second fighter of the war. I was always glad to be of help like that whenever I could.

A few minutes later Vince Evans returned the favor on J.P.'s behalf.

We'd closed our bomb bay doors after his release, and I had just regained control of the *Belle,* when Vince, who never stopped concentrating, yelled out, *"He's headed right for me! Right for me! He's coming right at me!"* Good Lord, there it was, huge and closing fast, an ugly shape that blotted out the sky. I was pulling the *Belle* up before Vince had stopped yelling, and a good thing, too—the fighter sliced directly beneath us. He would have plowed into us if Vince had not been alert. I don't think it was a suicide ploy—the Germans didn't do that—but the results would have been the same.

The 91st lost six planes out of the twenty-nine. One of them was *Invasion II,* flown by a dear friend of mine from flight school, a blithe spirit named Oscar O'Neill. *Invasion II* had been one of the bombers considered by Wyler's crew as the subject of their documentary. Oscar was one of those people—there were a lot—whose life-trajectories took extreme turns in the war. He wrote poetry and short stories, and he knew some of the Hollywood crowd. He'd even had a fling with Carmen Miranda, the spitfire Brazilian songstress and movie star, "the lady in the tutti-frutti hat." Now Oscar O'Neill had narrowly escaped death by bailing out of a stricken airplane over Germany, only to become a prisoner of war.

Oscar's ordeal had a genuine Hollywood ending. He survived the prison camp, was repatriated after the war, and made his way back to England to marry the girl he'd fallen in love with. The two of them became the parents of movie actress Jennifer O'Neill.

The mission as a whole lost sixteen bombers, the most in any single mission—another hideous gash in the fabric of our remaining veteran crewmen and machines. One squadron lost two-thirds of its planes and men. Not one airplane in our group returned to base without battle damage. The *Belle* landed with eighty-one holes in its fuselage and one engine knocked out. But we'd destroyed half of an extremely productive Focke-Wulf factory. Vince, in addition to his superb bombing, claimed another fighter of his own.

We had planned a party that night—girls, dancing, the works. But this time we let it go. So many of our comrades were dead or missing that nobody was in much of a dancing mood.

That evening in the officers' lounge, after all the military debriefings, William Wyler analyzed this mission from a producer's angle. "I wish I'd put cameras in every airplane up there today," he said. "I would have had enough raw footage to make a feature-length movie."

There were four missions left now for the *Belle*.

The costly attack on Bremen should have punctured a myth that had taken hold in the Eighth Bomber Command's top strategic circles, but it didn't. The myth was that German defenses well inside the country were not as concentrated as they were along the coastlines and submarine pens of the English Channel. The theory had been that once a bomber wing had made it past those coastal defenses, the firepower against it would drop significantly.

In fact the reverse was true. The deeper we penetrated over the Fatherland, the fiercer and more outlandish the resistance. Before long, the Nazi defenders were outdoing themselves in creativity. They threw up not only every make of fighter they could lay hands on, but also rockets, bombs attached to parachutes—everything but the kitchen glockenspiel.

Another development that the Eighth largely ignored, or underplayed, was the rapid advance in the effectiveness of German radar. The electronic-echo breakthrough that had helped the RAF stave off defeat in 1940 was now part of the Luftwaffe's arsenal, and it helped them greatly in concentrating their attacks on our incoming bombers.

It was going to get worse before it got better.

We had a two-week respite after Bremen. The *Belle* officers went down to London, as usual, for two or three days, but somehow the thrill wasn't quite there. Maybe it was fatigue, maybe it was our preoccupation with that topic we weren't supposed to be thinking about. Whatever it was, we spent most of that late-April hiatus hanging around the base. We'd discovered a new outlet for our pent-up anxieties and pressures—softball.

Not baseball, but softball. Maybe we were getting a little sedate in our old age.

May 1. Mission Number 22. Back to the pens at St. Nazaire, and it was an ugly mission from the start. Twenty Flying Fortresses in the group took off, five aborted. There were clouds over the target, and they gave us a bad time. We never really knew whether we hit the target or not—we were toggling individually instead of releasing on the lead bombardier, and suspected that most of our bombs fell into the water. A few others, to our acute regret, landed on the city itself and did considerable damage. There must have been some patriotic French people among the civilian casualties.

We lost an airplane to fighters for our trouble, and the *Belle* had an engine knocked out from flak, and once again we saw the lead navigator from the group in front of us get confused on the way home, and once again I heard Chuck advising me on the intercom, "Don't follow them, they're going back over France." They did, and they lost four of their B-17s to flak. We could not help them. The prohibitions against breaking radio silence, and thus risking a massive, minutely focused attack, were cruelly rigid, but ironclad.

Another day at the office.

May 4. Mission Number 23. Our target was Antwerp, Belgium, and we flew in *The Great Speckled Bird*—the *Belle* was down for repairs. We went there to knock out, of all things, the Ford Motor Company plant. The Germans had seized it to make military trucks. "I hope none of you guys have stock in Ford," I muttered to the crew after the Intelligence guy told us what our target was.

We put twenty-five planes in the air and got twenty-five planes over the target, the first mission we ever had without an abort. It went just as smoothly after that. Few fighters attacked us, the flak was light, and we pulverized that plant—in my notes, I put down "perfect." Everyone thought of it as a breather mission after Bremen, but when I mentioned that to Colonel Wray, he said it wasn't planned that way—the Eighth Bomber Command just wanted to wipe out that Ford plant.

Two to go.

There were no missions for our crew for the next ten days, except in the realm of publicity. Colonel Wray sent Leighton, Quinlan, Hanson, and me down to the BBC studios in London to do a radio broadcast that would be recorded and short-waved back to the states. A morale-boosting program called "The Stars and Stripes in Britain," with Ben Lyon and Bebe Daniels as "master and mistress of ceremonies." It was scheduled to air on the Mutual Network on Sunday, May 23. This sort of request was pretty routine for bomber crews. It gave the folks at home the sense that everybody was doing fine—although of course we could easily have been dead by the time it aired.

We *Belle* fellows were picked for this one because attention had really focused on us now, two missions away from coming home. The interviewer wanted to know how the romance between Margaret Polk and me was going, and I have to admit that I layed it on a little thick. I wanted her to hear it and feel flattered, of course, but it never occurred to me that I was also adding fuel to America's fascination over this storybook romance of ours. In doing so, I was handing over to the public a relationship that still needed lots of private time to find its own way.

Media publicity in those days before television, cable, and the Internet was not what it is today, although with a Hollywood movie director filming us in combat, and interest from radio, newspapers, magazines, and the newsreels, I guess the *Memphis Belle* crew was a few decades ahead of its time. In a few weeks, I would find out just how overwhelming media publicity could be.

Another downside of that little star turn of ours was that the 91st ran two raids while we were in London, and didn't summon us back for either of them. The *Belle* flew on both—to the airplane repair works at Meaulte, France, on May 13, with Lt. C. L. Anderson piloting, and the shipyards at Kiel, Germany, on the fourteenth, with Lt. J. H. Miller at the controls.

I was none too happy about this. The B-17s took intense resistance from fighters on the run to Kiel, and the idea of risking our precious airplane so close to her final run infuriated me, and I let the brass know how I felt. Deep down, I knew I had to accept it. There was a war on, and it was getting hotter by the hour—three missions in three days for the *Belle* was a pretty good index of that. In the end, I had to content myself with the knowledge that she'd come back safely. Moreover, those two missions she flew without us compensated for a couple of the ones she missed when my crew and I were in the air. The calibrations for our twenty-fifth mission were getting pretty complicated, given these separate tallies for the plane and her crew, not to mention the challenge of deciding exactly who the crew consisted of, given the comings and goings of certain members over the months.

May 15. A time of year when the dogwood and the redbud would be out in full force through the Blue Ridge Mountains above Asheville, North Carolina.

This was the penultimate mission, now, for the *Memphis Belle*.

After this run we would be one workday shy of our goal to become the first bomber crew in the Mighty Eighth to finish twenty-five missions and be sent home with their airplane.

It was a promising moment in the war. Just two days earlier, the Allies had accepted the surrender of 275,000 German and Italian troops in North Africa. The Luftwaffe abruptly withdrew from its presence in Tunisia. Suddenly, Churchill and Roosevelt, meeting in Washington, saw their chance to accelerate their plans for an invasion of Sicily and Italy. The surrender had an immediate effect in our corner of the war. It gave the Air Forces generals in England, at long last, the coveted heavy bomber groups that had been diverted to the African campaign. The volume of bomber traffic over Europe was about to explode, so to speak.

In the Atlantic, the beleaguered Nazis were on the brink of suspending U-boat operations, thanks partly to our efforts. The order would come within a week. In the Pacific, the American and British high command was roughing out the final details of Operation Cartwheel, the epic trans-Pacific naval and air thrust that would rout the Japanese from one island cluster after another until, two bloody years later, the Allies were scraping the coasts of the Home Islands.

It was a key moment in the public-opinion phase of the war as well, and we were seizing it. President Roosevelt authorized the release, for the first time, of explicit and disturbing war photographs for publication in the American press. This was to remind the folks at home how deadly this war was, and to help them prepare for its duration. At the same time there were those radio interviews, the flood of inspirational newsreels, the preparation of documentaries by professionals such as Wyler, and the periodic return home of war veterans for parades and speeches and bond-raising efforts.

That was the tantalizing prospect that awaited the crew of the *Memphis Belle*—if only we could survive those two final missions.

Mission Number 24.

An eerie confusion hung about this one, and continues to hang about it today. The scheduled target was Wilhelmshaven. Familiar territory. Halfway across the North Sea, we got word that it was

hopelessly overcast. Our secondary target was Bremen, fifty miles inland to the southeast. But by this time we had used up so much fuel
that the squadron leaders were worried we would end up in the
water on the way home.

Where to go, then?

Confusion reigned through all the bombers for several minutes.
And then some officer—I never learned exactly who—said, "Let's
bomb Helgoland."

Helgoland? Who, what, where was Helgoland? I'd never heard of
it. But somebody in our group had. It turned out that Helgoland was
a tiny island—about 150 acres—in the North Sea about sixteen nau-
tical miles from the German coast, just a little speck of grazing land
out there in the ocean. Like a lot of little specks the world over, Helgoland turned out to have some value in wartime. The Germans had
made it the site of an important naval and submarine base.

So we banked our bomber wing to the left and headed up the sea
to Helgoland. I hear we did a good job. It was never officially ac-
knowledged, even to this day, that we even bombed Helgoland. Officially, the Eighth hit Wilhelmshaven on May 15, 1943.

We did, though. To prove it, we came home with a few holes in
the right wing and some damage to the underpart of the bomb bay
over the target—luckily, Vince Evans had got the bombs away before
the flak hit. The group as a whole lost three planes. Three crews,
thirty-odd boys we'd had breakfast with and wouldn't see for dinner.

There is one eerie footnote to that eerie mission. A year and a half
later—in September 1944—an airplane packed with new, highly explosive flying bombs, or buzz bombs, intended for those same installations on Helgoland, mysteriously exploded while en route to
the island. Both its volunteer pilot and copilot were killed. One of
the two young men was Lt. Joseph P. Kennedy Jr., son of the former
American Ambassador to England and the eldest brother of the future President of the United States.

Twenty-four down, one more to go.

What did it feel like to touch down at your home base after completing all but the very last one of your required bombing missions

over France and Germany in World War II, knowing that you still have one final mission to fly before you are safe and free? What's the first thing you do when the wheels of your Flying Fortress have come to a stop, your propeller blades have stopped turning, and your crew has tumbled out of the hatch?

I'll tell you what you do.

First thing you do is, you sit there.

You just sit there.

You don't move. You let it wash over you for two, or three, or four, or five minutes.

You take a big deep breath. Maybe you clench and unclench your hands a few times. Man, it feels good to have turned loose of that yoke.

You start to slide your feet off those pedals, let your legs go limp a little, and you feel the good pain. It means you're still alive.

And then finally you unstrap yourself and swing down through the hatch, and you amble over to where the boys are standing huddled around the fuselage.

And here comes the ground crew on the run, and the crew chief is up on a stepladder with his paintbrush, slapping the next cartoon bomb at the end of the row with all the others. Number 24.

Now there's nothing left to do out there, so you turn and start the long ambling walk across the tarmac toward the Interrogation Room.

And what do you think about?

I was thinking a lot of things, and I'd continue to think about them that afternoon when I took a pass from having the customary few beers with some of my crew members in the lounge at Bassingbourn, when I went directly to my quarters and stretched out on my bed and began to daydream. I'd think about them on into that night, and the next day, and right up to the moment when I swung back up through that hatch to rev up the *Memphis Belle* and point her toward Germany and our twenty-fifth mission.

I thought about Biltmore Forest through a young boy's eyes, and my mother Mabel Morgan out there in her garden with her big straw hat and her cigarette in its holder. My mother and me spinning wondrous stories amidst the carrots and beets, stories about the journeys we'd go on together, journeys to far-away places like England and France and Germany. That player piano, my crystal radio set. My mother and Cornelia Vanderbilt laughing together in their flapper gowns at some glittering party at the country club, under Japanese lanterns, while the orchestra played.

I recalled hunting and fishing my summers away in the magical woods and streams of the Biltmore estate. Racing my bicycle along with Eddie Nash. Fabulous Western movies on Saturday afternoons. That white shoulder-band and badge I got to wear as a junior high school crossing guard. Those picnics I organized, the spooning, first kiss, first time with a girl, the other times with the other girls. Going to see Clark Gable in *San Francisco* in the summer of 1936. Floorboarding my dad's Buick Century through the Smoky Mountains, startling townsmen off their picket fences with Eddie laughing alongside, headed for Greenville at 110 mph to see my girlfriend Dorothy Beattie.

I sadly remembered the day I got the news that my mother had gone on her ultimate journey without me. And all the feminine companions I tried to substitute for her afterward.

College, tennis, idling it all away, grieving for my mother. Realizing in 1940 that the world was falling apart and that America was going to be sucked into the destruction and that I was going to be a part of it. Those scrapbooks of airplanes I'd kept as a boy.

Then, coming into sharper focus, I flashed back to my start in the Army Air Corps and that physical at Langley. Learning about my bum left eye. The ice pack on the optic nerve. Grinning, shaking hands. To Camden for primary training. First time up in that yellow PT-17 biplane—so *this* is what it's like to be where I belong. First solo, first lesson in humility from Earl Friedell who'd learned to fly with a broomstick. Learning about Pearl Harbor at Shreveport, marrying Martha, breaking up with Martha, my first look at a B-17 at McDill.

To Walla Walla in the troop train, Major Smelser's doghouse. Assembling my crew.

Margaret. The times we had up there. Buddies first, then I was passionately in love with her. Her departure, that first letter of mine to her on hotel stationery—"*I now know that I have never loved before*"—that impulsive flight to Memphis in the airplane I'd named for her.

England. Bassingbourn. The missions. The growing closeness of my crew. The growing horror of it all, the shocking casualties mounting up around us, the loss of friends. The *Belle* under fire, the *Belle* hit, and hit again, and again, and again; the flak, the machine-gun rounds, the rockets, the smashed tail and Quinlan's scream. The helplessness of seeing our friends hit, spin out, explode. The quiet toasts to them at night. The cold, the fatigue, the confusion up there, the relentlessness of the Focke-Wulfs.

London. The London girls.

The letters to Margaret. The letters from Margaret. Margaret's face on the instrument panel in front of me.

The lifetimes I had lived. And one more lifetime yet to live, the day after tomorrow.

Who are you, Bob Morgan?

I wondered if I'd ever find out. Wondered if I'd ever live long enough to find out.

Only one damn thing I knew for sure. I was a long way from Beau-catcher Mountain.

CHAPTER

13

That, more or less, was the life of Bob Morgan up through the late afternoon of Saturday, May 15, 1943.

I had done one other thing after my long reverie there in my quarters. I'd hoisted myself up off the bed—God, but I was exhausted!—and padded over to my desk and typed out a letter to Margaret. Most of my letters to her, I wrote in longhand. Why I typed this one I can't remember any longer. Maybe I was too tired to hold a pen. I was so beat I misdated it 1942.

My dearest heart,

I will try and make some sense out of this letter but if you find that it makes very little sense please just overlook the fact, for I am one tired person today and if it would only get dark I would be in bed now.

The Belle finished her twenty-fourth today and after one more she will be retired from Capt. Robert K. Morgan's hands and given to some other person to carry on with. I am going to have the name painted off though, for I feel that she has done her part and when I begin again somewhere else I will have the Belle the 2nd. You have done your share (known over here as sweating her out) and I know now that I would never be able to finish my tour of duty over here if it hadn't been for the fact that you were behind me at all times. We have done a good job darling and I hope that our life job turns out just as well as this one has.

I made a radio short which you no doubt heard [I was assuming the letter would not arrive until after May 23rd] and I hope that it wasn't as awful as they made it sound. I hope that you didn't mind my using you in it as I did . . .

I still feel that I will be home in June . . . Therefore I feel sure that somehow we will be together, somewhere, soon.

. . . I feel sure now that you did the right thing in making me wait till we saw how things were going to turn out. Now you must realize that the young kid full of hell and stuff isn't the one who is coming back. The war has done many things to me, but I am sure one of them is to make a better man out of me. I hope so if nothing else.

. . . I send all the love in the world to the sweetest person that God ever gave the light of day to.

I waited for the darkness to come. It seemed like the darkness was just a speck in the distance for the longest time that night. Then suddenly there it was, all over me. The navigator didn't even have time to cry out a warning, and I slept.

May 16. A long Sunday. A long, long Sunday. No mission today. But one tomorrow. That made it longer.

Somehow we all found things to do until dinnertime. Then the four of us who had been closest all these months—Vince Evans, Chuck Leighton, Jim Verinis, and myself—went to dinner together. Verinis had not flown on the *Memphis Belle* since December 30, and in fact he had completed his own twenty-fifth mission aboard the *Connecticut Yankee* a few days earlier.

Not that this affection of ours moved him in the slightest during the poker game that followed dinner. It took him less than two hours to coldbloodedly clean all of us out. He took every red cent we brought to the table.

To bed, then, after going to the cleaners. None of us had mentioned it during the game, not once, but none of us had to. Tomorrow shaped up to be a busy day at the office.

Monday, May 17.
They didn't have to wake us up that morning. We'd managed that on our own. They sent somebody around anyway.

Jim Verinis went along with us to the briefing room. He didn't have to, but he did anyway. "Boys," he said, "I hope you get back, and I know you'll get back. Because we're all going home. Remember?" And I said, "Yeah, we are, aren't we, Jim? So you'd better be thinking about us when we're up there." That kind of chatter.

Colonel Wray tapped his pointer against the blackboard and we *Belle* crewmen saw that our final target, one way or another, was going to be another familiar one—the submarine pens at Lorient, France. The Intelligence man told us that it was going to be a lovely day: great visibility. We'd be able to see the Germans just fine. Of course, that meant they'd also have an equally great view of us.

Maj. Eddie Aycock, our squadron commander, invited himself along on that mission as copilot. He said, "I figure I'll go along for good luck, Bob." I looked at him a little sideways and said, "We've had good luck without you." You could get away with wisecracking a Major on a day like this one.

The last thing I did before heading for the shed to suit up was dash off another note to Margaret, this one handwritten:

> I am once again writing you before I taxi the "Belle" out to take off position—I guess this will be the last time for quite awhile. You see, my Angel, this is number <u>25</u>. My whole crew will be finished—a big load off my shoulders & <u>yours</u> too.
>
> There isn't a great deal to say . . . I'll finish this later when I have <u>buzzed</u> the hell out of the field. That is what I have longed to do, my sweetheart. I have both of your ribbons on this morning & darling may God be with <u>us</u> both.
>
> Well sweetheart this is it and so take this kiss & hug & keep me flying darling Angel.

After the briefing and breakfast and suiting-up, I figured I'd better set a tone of matter-of-factness, business-as-usual nonchalance, the kind of thing the crew would expect from the Chief. I got them together in the Operations office for a final pre-mission pow-wow.

For some reason, the first words I heard coming out of my mouth were, "Look. Let's get out to the plane a little early today." Given that we usually got out there about thirty or forty minutes before taxi time, and at this moment we still had an hour to kill, this may not have conveyed exactly the offhand tone I was aiming for. Luckily, everybody else felt exactly the same way.

Everybody except Vince. "Well, don't wait on me," he said, "I'll be there." And headed for the door.

"Okay, fine, Vince," we all said. "No problem. See you out there." We sauntered out to the jeep, and waited for him anyway.

After ten or fifteen minutes we finally saw him trotting toward us. "What was wrong, Vince?" I asked him. "I couldn't find my bomb sight," he replied. It turned out that he didn't keep his Norden bomb sight on the airplane. He kept it in a vault. All the men in his line of work did. Norden bombsights were such high-security mechanisms that bombardiers were authorized to carry .45 sidearms at all times, and shoot anyone, friend or foe, who attempted to examine it.

The thing was that Vince had put his Norden in the wrong vault the previous night.

That would have been a fine howdy-do—Vince showing up over Lorient without his Norden. I doubt that everybody would have waited while he went back and got it.

Finally the jeepful of us was rolling out to the *Belle* in that yellow-green early-morning British light. All around us were the dark shapes of B-17s at ease, noses tilted toward the sky, awaiting their own crews, just like always.

We wheeled up to the *Belle* about fifty minutes before taxi time, and there was Joe Giambrone's ground crew swarming over her—crouched under the fuselage, perched up on scaffolding, giving a propeller blade a speculative little quarter-turn, checking the tire treads, doing a last-minute finger search for uncaulked holes. It hit me that I'd never really kicked back and watched Joe's boys go through their tasks before a takeoff. They looked like so many of Santa's elves in baggy coveralls and billed caps. But as far as I was concerned, no gaggle of squires in tuxedos at Biltmore ever looked more elegant. I wondered, as I often had, where we might be without these guys.

The *Memphis Belle* didn't look too bad herself—like a lady at the hairdresser's, getting ready to go out on a killer date.

"Think she can take us over there and back one more time?" I asked Joe as we both looked up at her. He gave his head a half-shake. "Boy, there's no question about it," he said. "We double-checked everything today. She's just waiting for you."

The crew and I had gathered around under the nose now, as was our custom. I looked around for a certain somebody and spotted him. Sure enough, William Wyler had shown up, and was filming us with his 16 mm camera, as usual.

This morning I was ready for Bill. I had a prop I'd been planning to use, and now I pulled it out of my jacket pocket. It was a Camel cigarette. I lighted it and blew a big puff of smoke in the direction of Wyler's camera.

I didn't smoke. Still don't. In fact, I felt for a minute there as though I might leave my breakfast on the Bassingbourn tarmac. Like I said earlier, I was getting pretty good at this media business. I'd studied those full-page ads in *Life* and the *Saturday Evening Post*— the ones that showed famous ballplayers and movie stars smoking Camels. I figured that if Wyler's camera caught me smoking on that documentary he was making, and if I claimed it was a Camel, I just might get in on some of that endorsement money.

Funny what goes through your mind before your last mission.

Finally the moment arrived when there was no more small-talk, no more horsing around. It was time to get inside the plane.

"This is just another mission," I kept saying to the guys as they swung up through the hatch. "We're at, what, twenty-four? twenty-five? Whatever number, it doesn't matter. Just one more mission." Then I repeated the lucky-charm words, the homeward-angel words that I'd said to the crew since perhaps our second or third sortie together in the *Belle*. "Remember, if only one plane comes back today, it's gonna be us."

Then it was my turn to get inside the plane.

Twenty-four Fortresses took off in our formation. It was even quieter in the plane than usual, it seemed, as we droned across the English Channel. If ever there was an all-or-nothing flight, this was it. I had the spooky sensation that everyone else, in every other B-17, was watching us to see what would happen. That wasn't true, of course. On the other hand, every flier and ground crewman at Bass-ingbourn knew the stakes for the *Memphis Belle* on this day.

The sea below us gave way to coastline. There was no cloud cover, and we donned steel helmets for the rough stuff we knew was about to kick in. The flak, when its ugly black puffs started blossoming around us, seemed somehow lighter that day than usual. Wyler "went Hollywood" on us for the only time on that mission—he asked me if I could steer the airplane closer to one of those big beau-tiful bursts. I had to tell him something in return that I'm sure he never heard from Bette Davis. He took it pretty well. When our re-ception committee of Focke-Wulfs and Messerschmitts arrived to greet us, their ranks seemed thinner—only about fifty of them in all. Once again, they seemed desperate, trying their bizarre air-to-air bombing ploy with the usual lack of success. Most of their fire was directed toward other groups. I had the fleeting thought that maybe, just maybe, on this particular day, they . . . then I got rid of that thought. The Germans didn't do favors. And we didn't either.

Besides, on this mission above all the others, there was no leeway for me to betray any hint of an attitude that the trip was special. On this mission, unlike any of the previous ones, Captain Morgan had a role to play. I absolutely had to behave as though this were just an-other day at the office. By my example, I had to inspire the crew to do likewise.

The fundamental things applied—look out for fighters. Call 'em out. Test your guns. Check the charts.

It was a lie, of course. This was *not* just another mission. I could feel that fact in my mind, in my heart, in my feet, in my legs, all over. I felt it as I looked at Margaret's photograph in front of me. My angel. I felt it as I said a prayer under my breath. *"Lord, let us make this final mission, please. I'm thankful for your guardianship over us through the other twenty-four. Now, please, give us this one more."*

The lie that this was just another mission was a lie that we all had to live out, and me especially. If we didn't live out the lie—if any one of us let down our guard for thirty seconds and got caught up in thoughts of going home—then we'd likely as not face the ultimate moment of truth. We'd all be dead.

We lived the lie so well that we didn't just survive that one, we *prevailed*. Bill Winchell, our wiry little waistgunner, got himself a Focke-Wulf that day—the eighth and final confirmed kill from a gunner on the *Memphis Belle*. The fighter broke apart from the pack and came straight at us, and Winch just lined up the approaching shape in his sights and held the trigger down until he blew that FW to smithereens. The bomb run, with Vince leading the way in our group, was excellent. Again, one of his bombs landed right on the aiming-point. Several others made those Nazi sub pen roofs and storage sheds dance!

Then it was over. No more pretending. No more anxiety. No more praying. It was over.

We swung around in our homeward arc, and this time, we were not just leaving a bombing run behind. We were leaving the air war over Europe behind us. Now fresh infusions of airmen and bombers would pick up where we left off, darkening the skies ever deeper and deeper into Germany with thousand-plane missions for the rest of that summer and fall.

We'd done our fair share. In seven months, between November 7, 1942, and this day, the *Memphis Belle* crew had dropped sixty tons of bombs on France, Germany, and Belgium. Besides those eight confirmed fighter kills, we probably shot down five other fighter planes and damaged more than a dozen. Our airplane got the hell shot out of her, but she protected us. That Purple-Heart scratch of J. P. Quinlan's was the only casualty any crewman sustained. It was one of sixty decorations awarded our crew: each of us received the Distinguished Flying Cross, the Air Medal, and four Oak Leaf Clusters.

Now as we banked away from the European war and set our course one last time for England, I nodded to the photograph of Margaret Polk that I kept fastened to my instrument panel.

"Comin' home, Polky," I whispered.

It was a wild ride home from the English Channel on. The *Belle*'s gun muzzles spent most of it waving around in the high winds, because the crew was all over the airplane, hugging, slapping one another on the back, grinning, crying a little, setting up a cheer when we crested the White Cliffs of Dover for the last time, those cliffs that had been such a harbinger of home to us for the past seven months. All of us were trying to process the fact that the horror and risk were over, that we'd done our duty and survived, and now we could return to America. Strictly speaking, we weren't supposed to be doing that, but God knows, we were entitled. I've never met a braver more disciplined collection of men. If I didn't have to steer the damn airplane, I'd have been back there whooping it up with them, but I had my own plans for a little mischief later on.

Maybe you've seen that famous documentary that came out of William Wyler's filming. If you have, you'll recall the scenes of the ground crews clustered on the tarmac and the officers up in the tower, all of them "sweating it out" as the bombers returning from that mission landed at Bassingbourn. This footage came from some of those cameras that Wyler had handed out. You may recall how the tension mounted as plane after plane touched down—some of them with visible damage, some bearing dead and wounded crewmen, and one of them piloted by a badly wounded man. You may remember how everybody seemed to be scanning the skies and wondering whether the *Memphis Belle* was going to be among the returnees.

Well, that was a little bit of show-biz on Colonel Wray's part. As we approached the landing field, the tower radioed us and told us to stay up in the air until everyone else had come in, so that they could make a special scene out of our grand entrance.

That was fine by us. We hung up there for a while, enjoying the scenery. And when we finally did come swooping in, I could not resist my trademark gesture—I buzzed the hell out of that field. I gave it a grass-cutting you couldn't get these days with a Lawnboy. Somebody said I knocked over a flagpole, but I didn't. I was way too low for anything like that.

The whole base was going wild when the *Belle* finally taxied up to its mark and I cut the engines. Men were cheering, throwing their hats in the air, rushing toward us. Somebody with a movie camera got a great shot of Winchell looking out his window, a grin plastered all over his skinny face, making that little spiral motion with his hand to signal that he'd knocked down a fighter.

The crew came tumbling down through the hatch and stood there, dazed, giddy, watching their buddies greet them, drinking it all in. I sat alone in the cockpit for a few minutes, looking through the Plexiglas at them, enjoying their ecstasy. I smiled as I watched one of them drop to his knees and kiss the ground. In the privacy of my pilot's seat, I made my own blessing—a whispered prayer of thanksgiving. Then I turned my gaze to the photograph of the young girl up there on the instrument panel.

"We did it," I told her quietly. *"We did it, Little One."*

Then I was down out of the airplane too, engulfed by the swarm of airmen and the noise. Somebody showed up with a stepladder and propped it against the plane's nose, and they boosted me up it and I planted a kiss on that illustrated Memphis Belle, and gave her fanny a pat. I damn near pitched over backward in my excitement.

Then here was good old dear old Joe Giambrone coming through. No repairs for Joe today—the *Belle* had made it without a scratch. This was a perfect mission, a mission that had been written by the book. Not a plane lost, not an airman wounded in the entire 91st group of twenty-four planes. It was like we'd had an angel covering us that day. Maybe we had.

Nope—Joe was just there to paint the twenty-fifth bomb on the row that graced our fuselage—the symbol of our last mission.

William Wyler shouldered his way through the crowd and gave me his famous intense squint. He'd already got a cigarette stuck into the very front of his mouth. "I've got news for you, Morgan," he yelled above the din. "We're naming this documentary *The Memphis Belle!*" Well, that was nice—the first time he'd ever mentioned that possibility. At that moment, I was so overcome with excitement and relief at it all being over that I wouldn't have given a damn if he'd decided to name it *"Tinker Belle."*

I smiled and nodded and turned away to speak to somebody else, and then a weird question hit me. I turned back around and said, "Bill? What in the world would you have done if we'd got shot down today, and you hadn't been on board?" Wyler at least had the courtesy to appear to give it some thought. Finally he squinted back at me and said, "Oh, that wouldn't have been a problem. My backup

film crew was working with another airplane that was about to finish its twenty-five missions. *The Hell's Angels.*" He smiled, in a reassuring sort of way. "Well, thanks," I told him. These Hollywood
directors—all heart.

The next comrade I spotted was Jim Verinis. He was holding
Stuka in his arms. Stuka was straining and arfing and wagging her
tail. It looked to me as if Verinis was wagging his tail too.

Oh, Mabel Morgan. If only you could have seen me then.

Well, to tell the truth, I believe she did see me. I believe she was
watching me every time I went up in the *Belle*.

One key member of the 91st that didn't come out to the tarmac to
greet us, sadly enough, was Colonel Wray. He had been a good
group leader and a fine officer, but I think he was already beginning
his jealous streak over the fact that we were going home, taking the
airplane, and he was still here, slugging it out. I guess I couldn't
blame him. Maybe some others felt that way too. It would be only
human—what they had ahead of them was some of the most intense
aerial combat of the entire war. But the *Belle* and its crew had done
our part, lived up to our side of the bargain, and we sure as hell
weren't going home cheap. So we'd just have to accept all the reactions to our achievement as they came. I must say, the overwhelming
attitude from our buddies in the 91st was from the heart—enthusi-
astic, congratulatory, and filled with the respect that only men who
have tasted combat can have for one another.

After a good while the cheering and the celebrating on the tarmac
finally died down. We *Belle* crewmen trooped off to the debriefing,
as we always did. Then we went and got out of our flying clothes,
took big hot showers, went over to the officers' lounge and had a
few drinks, had dinner, and then we played poker.

Damned if that Verinis didn't take us to the cleaners again.

The next few days were more like a homecoming party than a war.
While we got used to our newfound celebrity and accepted the toasts
of our fellow fliers, the brass was busy deciding just which ten men,
out of all who'd flown on the *Memphis Belle*, it was going to select
as the official *Belle* crew. We'd known for some time that if we made

it through, the War Department was going to expect us to do some touring back in the United States. Parades, morale-boosting, exhorting the folks to buy War Bonds, that sort of thing. We'd visit several American cities—the total turned out to be thirty-one—with the plane as a unit. But who, exactly, would the "we" be?

Jim Verinis, of course, was a pretty sure thing. No one had permanently replaced him as my second pilot, and even if they had, everybody understood that Jim was the only choice I would live with. Most of the other choices, though, would be a little tougher than that. Gene Adkins, for example, who'd suffered frozen fingers, had been unable to complete his twenty-five missions. Scott Miller, one of our waistgunners, had flown fifteen missions with the *Belle*—more than some members who were chosen—but then was reassigned, and he, too, had not completed his twenty-five.

Eventually, Colonel Wray and General Eaker settled on the final lineup: Verinis, Evans, Leighton, Hanson, Loch, Scott, Winchell, Quinlan, Nastal, and myself.

We were the golden boys of Bassingbourn, all right. But it didn't take long for us to find out just how big an impact the *Belle*'s triumph had in the larger world beyond our hangars and landing strips.

Early on the morning of May 18—very early, as I recall—the Colonel's office informed us that we were to receive some fairly important visitors around midday, and that officers and enlisted men should put on their full-dress uniforms. Joe's ground crewmen would be allowed to show up in their work clothes, which were the only clothes they had. We all wondered who that could be. The base was already swarming with major journalists from America and England. We were scheduled to go into London later and meet with several high-ranking generals. Who else was there?

It was only several hours later that I got the word from Major Aycock, our squadron leader, as to exactly who these "fairly important visitors" were.

"Morgan," he told me, "the King and Queen of England are coming to visit. They want to meet you and your men and thank you and wish you luck when you return to the States."

The King and Queen of England. Well, that didn't sound like too bad of a deal. The highest-ranking royalty I'd met up till then was Cornelia Vanderbilt.

More seriously, I think every one of us, from tough, worldly men like Vince all the way down to the teenager Tony Nastal, was moved that the Royal Couple was coming to see us. The Royal Couple, with all the cares and anxieties that were on their minds, witnessing their country with its brave people and priceless historic treasures under constant attack from Hitler's Luftwaffe, would find the time to come out to our base and make this gesture. What a gracious thing that was. I know that it raised lumps in all our throats. It reminded us that the grim and terrifying assignments we'd been carrying out all these months had not been simply about two sides of warriors dueling each other for supremacy of the air in a brand-new form of warfare. It had been about history, good against evil, and the survival of humane, civilized institutions.

It had been about the hope that Winston Churchill had raised, referring to der Führer, in one of his immortal House of Commons speeches not long before the Battle of Britain. "If we can stand up to him, all Europe may be free, and the life of the world may move forward into broad, sunlit uplands." Well, by God, the American men of the Army Air Forces, and the Eighth Bomber Command, and the 91st Group, and the *Memphis Belle*, had been there alongside Churchill's brave people as they stood up to Hitler. It was still a little early to tell about those broad, sunlit uplands, but we could sure as hell feel proud of what we'd already done. Prouder still, knowing that the King and Queen of England had noticed our efforts.

A little before noon on Tuesday, May 18, 1943, the crew of the *Belle* stood at strict attention in front of the spiffed-up airplane, lined up in order—officers, enlisted crew, and ground crew. Beside us, their tunics glittering with decorations and insignia, were Colonel Wray and Gen. Haywood Hansell, the Commander of Eighth Bomber Command planning and a personal representative today of Brigadier General Eaker, Commander of the Eighth Air Force. A little farther off, Joe Giambrone's men stood tugging at their smudgy sleeves and pants, making themselves as presentable as possible.

All our eyes were fixed on an entourage of black, long-hooded touring cars that made its way slowly across the landing field from the main entrance gate toward our airplane. The figures inside were indistinct at first, but gradually we could make out the two that counted: an erect, serious-looking man in military tunic and visored cap, and a woman beside him wearing a dramatic feathered hat and powder-blue gown.

There were no bands on hand to play "God Save the Queen," no armed escort, no guards on horseback. Nothing special, really, to announce that these visitors were of any particular magnitude. Just the black cars moving toward us in the sunlight as a breeze whipped up over the expanse of field. It was wartime.

The main open car pulled right up in front of the *Memphis Belle* and its occupants stepped out. Colonel Wray, who had already been introduced to them, presented King George VI and Queen Elizabeth to me. I shook hands with both of them, and then I escorted them down the line, introducing them to each crew member. As Wyler's documentary would mention, the ground crew were a little embarrassed by their work clothes, but the Queen said she thought the outfits were very nice.

King George, I felt, was entirely on his dignity, somewhat aloof and correct. Queen Elizabeth was formal in her bearing, but smiling and quite talkative.

Every single member of the crew was relishing the moment. But it was J. P. Quinlan who registered the most amazement. His amiable round Jimmy Cagney face was flushed, and he couldn't seem to keep his mouth from hanging less than wide open. After it was over he said, "Gee, whiz, I met the Queen and King of England! Wow! I wonder what my Irish-rebel ancestors would have thought about that!"

A couple of days later the *Belle* began the last few missions it would fly over British soil. It was strictly show-business. Wyler needed to take some touchup shots inside and outside the airplane for editing purposes in his documentary, so the crew and I took him up for an hour and a half or so.

It was after the King and Queen's visit that General Eaker and his staff made their final decision about the *Belle*'s next assignment. Perhaps the royal appearance had inspired the General, but at any rate he announced to us soon afterward that we would now embark upon our celebrated twenty-sixth mission—to fly the *Belle* back to the United States and thank the American people for what they were doing. Thank them for their frugal conservation of luxury items and gasoline, and thank them for their inspired, exhausting assembly-line work that built the planes and the bombs and the guns that enabled the fliers of the Eighth Bomber Command to pour merciless punishment on Adolf Hitler's evil industries of war.

It was an assignment that all of us relished. Paradoxically, it was this assignment, more than any I flew over Europe, that drew the most damaging flak.

CHAPTER
14

We didn't go home right away, though. Between May 18 and June 13, when we finally did lift off for America, we had all kinds of obligations—mostly ceremonial, but some military.

The Bomber Command summoned us down to London for a major debriefing on all twenty-five of our missions—what we thought about the targets, formations, flying altitudes; what we remembered about trying to function in combat under subarctic conditions in the stratosphere; what changes we would suggest for improved efficiency in the future. We had plenty of opinions to offer, I can guarantee!

The press crowd was onto us by then. We were a story, and they were at us all the time—the British magazine and newspaper reporters and those ever-popular BBC radio personalities. Some American correspondents too. None of us was very polished about giving interviews, but we got some good basic training here for what we were about to face in America.

It was a giddy, exciting interlude, but it had its melancholy moments as well. I had to say good-bye to my girlfriend Mary Ann from British Intelligence, and Vince Evans had to say a very hard good-bye to Kay, his sweetheart, the cabaret singer. He really wanted to marry that girl, but she told him that if he wanted to marry her, he'd have to come back later. She was a wartime London girl, after all. She knew very well the risks of marrying an active serviceman while a war was still going on.

There were more festivities for us back at Bassingbourn. General

Hansell came back down from Headquarters at High Wycombe to pin the Distinguished Flying Cross on each of us. A few days later, we flew to Bovington Airfield and received the personal well-wishes of Lt. Gen. Jacob L. Devers, who was involved in planning the coming cross-Channel invasion, and of the Eighth Bomber Command's General Eaker himself. It was then that General Eaker formally issued us our twenty-sixth mission orders. "This is your most important mission," the General told us. "You're to go home and thank the American public for what they're doing, and ask them to continue to send us planes and guns and ammunition and all those things they're making in our factories. Remind them that what they have done has made possible what you-all have done. That's your mission. Carry it out."

On May 31 I sent a telegram to Margaret:

SAFE TOUR OF DUTY COMPLETED FINGERS CROSSED ADORE YOU.

BOB

On June 13, 1943, we left for home.

My crew saw to it that Morgan's final trip from the Bassingbourn tarmac to the *Memphis Belle*'s cockpit would be a memorable one. They tackled me, stripped nearly all my clothes off, and then stuffed me into the plane in my undershorts. It was all captured by a Movietone newsreel cameraman—the risqué "European version" of my film career!

Shortly afterward, the *Memphis Belle*'s big wheels retracted for the last time over British soil. It drew a cheer from the ten young men— the ten uncharacteristically relaxed and happy young men—on board. Our eighteen-hour flight west across the Atlantic, with a refueling stop in Greenland, was a curiously mellow, almost dreamlike interlude. There would be plenty of celebrating where we were headed. Now was a time for each of us to draw in a little and try to make sense of the past seven months in our lives—seven months in which we had helped introduce a new scale of aerial warfare into a war-torn world.

We tried to remember, as best we could, just what these cities and towns and neighborhoods were like that we were going back to, these places we had left behind in another lifetime.

Did they still exist? Did the people in them whom we had loved still exist? Did we?

Finally, the East Coast of the United States spread out below us! We landed in virtual anonymity at Westover Field, the Air Force base at Chicopee, Massachusetts, spent the night, refueled, took showers, changed uniforms, filled ourselves with hot coffee, and then throttled off again to our official first destination—Washington, D.C., to receive the official thanks of our own government.

It was a great thrill to ease the *Belle* down into its landing pattern over Washington National Airport. We had a fine clear late-spring day for aerial sightseeing, and every one of us—except for Chuck Leighton and me, I guess—became a tourist for a little while. Faces pressed up against Plexiglas surfaces, the boys called out the great landmarks of our nation's capital—the Washington Monument, the Jefferson and Lincoln Memorials, the newly completed Pentagon, the Capitol building. They seemed to enjoy it a lot more than they had calling out the locations of Focke-Wulfs and Messerschmitts.

Over the airport itself, we could see that a big crowd had gathered to welcome us. I radioed the control tower for landing instructions, and at the end of them I received a special command. "This is direct from General Arnold," a raspy voice informed me. "He has instructed me to order you to buzz the field."

Damn. I guess my reputation had preceded me.

I alerted the boys to grab something and hang on, and I did what the General had told me to do.

Washington National featured a big, open spectators' balcony overlooking the field. It's still there today, even though the airport has been built up around it. That was where everybody had gathered on this day—the dignitaries, the press, the hundreds of spectators, and yes, the Commanding General of the Army Air Forces himself, Henry "Hap" Arnold.

I sort of pointed the *Belle* right for them. It got their attention. They ducked. Interesting sight—they parted on either side of our approach like a field of wheat near Walla Walla, the men hanging on to their homburgs, the women hanging on to whatever was handy.

My impression was that those folks came away with a good working idea of what a fast-moving B-17 Flying Fortress looks and sounds like up close.

When I landed and we got out of the plane, we saw that General Arnold himself was striding across the tarmac toward us from his place on the dais, his aides on either side struggling to keep up. He was a big man, and he knew how to stride. The gleam from his medals was blinding. *If he's mad at us,* I thought to myself, *I'd rather be watching the approach of an FW-190.* But he wasn't mad. The man who'd organized and activated the Army Air Corps for World War II—the legendary airman who had actually learned to fly from Wilbur and Orville Wright in Dayton, Ohio—welcomed the crew home. He walked directly toward me, returned my salute and looked me up and down as I stood at attention.

"Welcome home, Morgan," he finally said. Then he whispered in my ear, *"That was one hell of a buzz job."*

I didn't say a word to contradict him.

We all walked across the tarmac toward the popping flashbulbs and the screaming, waving crowd that had come to see us, toward a world as unreal in its own way as the world of stratospheric combat we had just left behind. It was a world filled with luncheons on fine crystal and linen and microphones on platforms draped in patriotic bunting. A world of people who wanted to touch us, tell us their names, hear our quotes, have us sign pieces of paper. A world of sleek-looking men and women who smelled of hair tonic and perfume and had happy, excited faces, faces that didn't look as though they'd ever seen violent death. A world of young women in pretty hats and nylons and high heels, who looked at us the same way Teresa Wright had looked at her young airman boyfriend in *Mrs. Miniver.*

A world that spoke of us as heroes.

Heroes.

That word again. Was it really us they were talking about? We asked one another that question a lot during the tumult of the next few months. The word felt like a suit of clothes that didn't quite fit. We talked it over among ourselves, and we agreed. "Hero" was not a label any of us felt comfortable wearing.

We weren't heroes. We were just . . . us, a unit of military men who'd been given a job to do and who tried to do it well. We were lucky, that much was sure. We were alive. We lived with our memories of brave men, buddies of ours, who weren't, or whose fates were as yet unknown. Men whose parachutes we'd seen open, or fail to open, when their planes were shot to pieces. Men who'd kept focused on their bombing runs after taking hits they knew they would never survive. Men who steered their planes out of formation to try and protect a damaged ship. Weren't *they* the heroes? We were simply young men who flew bombing missions and played poker and looked out for each other and maybe drank too much and chased too many women sometimes, but who had dreams of coming home and resuming decent, ordinary lives.

Hell, wasn't that enough?

It's hard to explain this wariness about being called a hero to anybody who has not been in combat. Maybe it has something to do with those Western movie and space-cadet radio heroes we all grew up on. Those heroes all seemed invincible, immortal, not to mention really well-dressed—glamorous godlike men who looked and sounded like they'd never had a bad night's sleep or suffered the shakes or did anything the local scoutmaster might not approve of. They never felt pain or grief or remorse, never seemed to wonder why it was that they'd survived when somebody just like them had not made it through. A lot of them could even sing on key.

If that's what being a hero was, sorry, but we just didn't fill the bill. The war had done things to each of us that we couldn't talk about to anyone—not even one another—and that private knowledge gave us our own identities, for which there were no handy labels.

It was probably William Wyler who came the closest to getting it right, this difference between the American people's image of us as heroes and the complicated men we really were.

Wyler—who lost one of his cameramen to German fighter fire, and himself suffered hearing loss from the noise of a bomb concussion over Italy—came back home to direct the greatest war movie I know of. Great, because it was honest about what can happen to the heroes when they return to the people who call them heroes. Rent *The Best Years of Our Lives* sometime, and pay attention to the scene in which Dana Andrews, the out-of-work ex-bombardier, visits a B-17 "graveyard" and seems to wonder if he may not be dead already too. Or the scene in which Harold Russell, a veteran who lost both hands in the movie story and in the actual war as well, struggles with his self-esteem as he reveals his braces and hooks to his sweetheart.

Maybe you will begin to understand why all of us were skeptical about being called heroes.

Heroes or not, the ten of us recognized that we had been given one more job to do, so we concentrated on this twenty-sixth mission that General Eaker had launched us on.

We were given a tour of the Capitol building, shaking hands with high-ranking military brass and civilian members of Roosevelt's cabinet—names I'd previously encountered only in newspaper headlines and the newsreels. We were to have met the President himself, but he had gotten sidetracked with pressing wartime conferences.

We attended a luncheon at a gorgeous private mansion in Chevy Chase, Maryland, an elite suburb of D.C., with a senior editor of the *Washington Post*. He was filled with questions about our experiences, our losses, our memories of buddies who had gone down. This line of inquiry brought up many sad memories for all of us, but we tried our best to answer as well as we could.

Finally, we were thrown a farewell luncheon at the Pentagon hosted by Hap Arnold in full dress uniform. President Roosevelt's elegant Secretary of War, Harold Stimson, a genuine American statesman, joined us, which moved me a lot. J. P. Quinlan was more than moved. "I was so nervous I shook like a leaf," he recalled in later years. Near the end of the luncheon, General Arnold took me aside and offered me, in a low confidential voice, what he must have intended as the ultimate compliment. I sure took it that way.

"Morgan," he said, "don't worry. You can buzz any place you want to while you're on this tour, so have a good time. Just be careful."

*   *   *

I sent a telegram to Margaret dated June 19, 1943.

MEMPHIS BELLE WILL ARRIVE TOMORROW DON'T FORGET THERE ARE 9 OTHER MEN YOU ARE GOING TO HAVE ONE HECK OF A BUSY TIME AM SO TIRED THAT I HOPE THERE WILL BE SOME REST WON'T LEAVE TILL TUESDAY MORNING ADORE YOU

BOB

In the skies over Memphis we spotted fighters at 12 o'clock.

Two Mustangs had been sent up to greet us fifty miles outside Memphis and escort the *Belle* down to the airfield. Well, that was a cute touch, but it got a little less cute when those fighter boys started to peel off, throttle up, do some rolls and loops and other fancy fighter-plane stuff.

That got my blood kind of boiling, to be honest about it. I thought, "Gee whiz, they're gonna show off and we're not." By the time we were over the airport in Memphis—Margaret down there somewhere in the crowd, shading her eyes, for sure—I'd made up my mind that that just would not be the case.

I'll show them a few things, I muttered to myself. To the crew, I said to buckle in. And then I cut the *Memphis Belle* loose.

I put her into some real steep climbs and stalls. I pointed her nose up to heaven and let her float like a wing, like a leaf, back down toward earth. I nearly turned her over on her back. I flipped her rightside up and came roaring down across the airfield at full throttle, then pulled her up to go into another stall.

I kept it up for about half an hour. The guys were going crazy, whooping and hollering and laughing like little kids. We put on quite a show. We were dancing. Yes, it was for Margaret, but it was also for those hotshots in their fighters.

And it was for the simple joy of flying, the joy I hadn't felt since those early days at Camden with Earl Friedell and that yellow PT-17. Earl, with that broomstick of his. This time there were no bullets. No flak. No frigid cold. No death. Just flying. Just flying a beautiful airplane. Now that I look back on it, that half hour above the Memphis airport might have been the last interlude of pure, perfect childlike bliss I ever experienced in my life.

Then we came down to earth and the crowd rushed at us and the rest of my life began.

I made a perfect military landing, and the crew of the *Memphis Belle* came boiling down out of the hatch. We were met by a tremendous crowd. The police had a hard time keeping them back from the airplane. They engulfed us—we were suddenly in the middle of a human sea.

There, moving toward me out of that sea, was Margaret.

I ran to her and hugged her and kissed her, and the crowd went crazy. It let loose a giant roar.

I yelled at her through the noise, "How're you doing, Lame Brain?" She yelled back, "Okay, Jug Head, you sweet thing!" And then we hugged and kissed some more.

While this was going on the newspaper people and the radio people had closed in around us. All of them were trying to interview us at once, and the rest of the crew too. They nearly crushed us. They were yelling in our faces, in our ears, asking questions, yammering for a quote, already writing their stories in their heads about the two sweethearts of the *Memphis Belle*. Already they had us married and with children practically before we got inside the hangar.

They had started owning us. WAR SCARRED MEMPHIS BELLE KEEPS DATE WITH CUPID was typical of the loopy headlines.

In these first few minutes, Margaret and I were starting to lose one another to the damn national myth of ourselves.

We hardly felt it at the moment. We were delirious at being able to hold one another again. I could see that Margaret was happy. Her eyes had practically disappeared in the spread of that wonderful squinty smile of hers. I was happy too. Here was the girl from the photograph in the cockpit of my airplane, come magically to life in my arms.

The only thing left to do was get married, as soon as possible. Before the national publicity tour started in the next few days.

Memphis threw a parade for us and Margaret got to sit in the open car with me. We waved through the confetti and grinned at the folks while the tubas thundered and the bass drums boomed. After it was over I met Margaret's mother, the grand former Ziegfeld Girl, and we took to one another right away. I met her two brothers and liked them too. I paid a quick visit to the house on Poplar Avenue, where all those letters and telegrams of mine had arrived. The house of my bride-to-be.

But not quite yet. As Margaret and I made plans for a hasty, blissful wedding, we were brought up short—not by parents, not by second thoughts, but by the War Department. Yes, the War Department, in the person of an all-business public-relations officer assigned to our tour, a public-relations officer I remember, sourly, after all these years, only as Captain Tom.

Captain Tom took Margaret and me aside and relayed the strong suggestions from on high. There would be no wedding in Memphis. Not just yet. Not until after the national tour of the *Memphis Belle* and her crew was completed. Not for at least another one to two months.

The War Department had thought deeply about this romance between Margaret and me—how nice that it could spare the attention from the war—and had decided that the national interest would be better served if the romance were stretched out a little longer. It would add human interest to every stop along the tour, the War Department figured, if the dashing *Belle* pilot and his sweetheart were *about* to be married, rather than *already* married.

Never mind Margaret's feelings, or mine. There was a war on. And the war demanded, from Bob Morgan, not only twenty-five missions over German territory, but a good story line as well.

We said okay. We talked briefly about eloping, but Margaret was against it. She had always dreamed of a formal wedding. The public's ownership of our romance tightened a little bit more.

Our three and a half days in Memphis had shot by before we knew it. There was Captain Tom ringing my room at the Peabody Hotel, alerting me to get up, get packed, it was time to head for the airport again and take off for Nashville.

Margaret and I were about to part once again, without really having had a chance to be together.

On to Nashville, Bridgeport, Hartford, and Boston, to visit the war factories in those cities, touring the plants, shaking hands with the workers. Parades, speeches to crowds of people, me introducing the crew of the *Belle* again and again from some flag-draped platform with a microphone in the middle. The boys always being charming, humble, brief.

The limousines. The hotels. The good dinners and the drinks that never stopped getting poured.

And the girls.

The girls, girls, girls, girls. The girls in the factories, the girls along the parade routes, the girls in the hospitality suites. Those gorgeous, eager, grateful young American girls. Different from the British girls, somehow. Less worldly-wise, maybe—they hadn't been bombed!—a little more scrubbed, certainly more corn-fed.

Oh, how they wanted to scream and hug us and kiss us and ask us to sign autographs on their dresses and their uniforms. Oh, how overwhelming it was. We suddenly knew how Frank Sinatra had felt at the Paramount, and Benny Goodman after a concert, and Clark Gable in a London music hall. Bobby-soxers were swooning over us! Who would ever have thought it?

We didn't intend it that way. Neither did the girls. Nobody did. It just happened, a spontaneous combustion of all kinds of emotion. For us crewmen of the *Belle,* it was a great bursting of all the tension and anxiety that the war had created. For the girls, those hardworking factory girls who labored to make parts and bullets that went off to the big invisible war halfway around the world, and for the other girls who stayed at home and waited to hear whether their boyfriends and brothers were coming back from that big invisible war—for all of them, it must have been almost like watching gods emerge out of thin air. Not that we were gods. We were boys in uniform who the newspapers told them had done something special, and they treated us that way. God knows we accepted it. We'd just spent seven months killing people and trying to avoid being killed, hoping and praying we wouldn't be killed. Now here we were. Back. Girls. Life. We opened our arms to those girls.

From Nashville to Bridgeport, Connecticut—Jim Verinis's hometown. Then to Hartford, where a factory was turning out a newfangled piece of aircraft that had seen some limited rescue and transportation service. It was called the helicopter. "Heroes," the *Hartford Courant* was calling us, and the girls came rushing.

Then to Boston, and again the greeting was tumultuous. So were my emotions when I ran into a flame out of the past—Dorothy Beattie. Dot was the stunning brunette of my wild Buick Century dashes from Asheville down to Greenville in the summer of 1938. We had some speeches to make downtown, the Mayor had introduced the crew, and out of the crowd came Dot, smiling. She was in Boston to visit relatives, and read of our appearance in the papers. Five years had only added some elegance and snap to her natural beauty. I invited her for a cocktail. Yes, I admit it—I tried to light the fuse again. She joked it off, but it was clear that she remembered the good times too. It was clear to me that if temptation presented itself on this tour, I, an unmarried man fresh from war and ready for love, would succumb.

It wouldn't be with Dot. She eventually married a textile tycoon much, much, much older than herself. Can't win 'em all, I guess.

On to Cleveland, and another bizarre twist in my tortured romance with Margaret.

The Addressograph Multigraph Company, my old employer, had asked the Pentagon to let us make a stop there. The local folks put on quite a reception for us, and once again the crowds were large. What I didn't know was that the company and the War Department had worked out a little surprise for me, a highly public and stage-managed surprise.

As usual on every stop, the *Belle* crew was ushered up onto a stage, where they sat on folding chairs while I introduced them, each crewman saying a few words when I called his name.

I had just finished the introductions when I became aware of a commotion behind me on the platform. I turned around, and there were Margaret and her mother! The folks behind the scenes had flown them up from Memphis for a surprise appearance.

The crowed loved it, of course, and I grabbed Margaret and hugged and kissed her, and hugged and kissed her mother too. The flashbulbs popped and the press got pictures of it all. One of them became a classic that ran in newspapers everywhere and later in *Life* magazine.

What the schmaltz-happy public-relations people hadn't anticipated was the flood of emotions this surprise encounter ignited in me. I was already keyed up beyond description, and now, with dear Polky in my arms again, the dream-vision of all my missions, I lost control. All my deep-seated needs for the constancy of a woman came churning to the surface. I wanted to get married! Now! To hell with the War Department!

Somehow, through all the turbulence and waving to crowds and rushing from venue to venue of that highly public afternoon, I managed to press my case to Margaret. *Come on*, I urged her. *Let's do it. Now, now, while we've got the chance!*

We could have broken through all that red tape and all the suffocating weight of other people's needs, the Pentagon's needs, the nation's needs. But Margaret hesitated. She was twenty, a sheltered, private, conservative, obedient young woman. She knew that we were not supposed to do this. She hesitated.

"I don't have a wedding dress," she countered. It was a stalling tactic and I knew it. I called her bluff. Somehow, in the late afternoon, in the hours leading up to the big scheduled banquet at the Hotel Cleveland, I managed to locate someone who knew a downtown bridal store owner who said he'd be glad to keep his store open for her.

No, said Margaret. She was nearly hysterical by now, I could see. It was simply too sudden, too overwhelming for her. Her people just didn't do things this way.

My yearning now turned to frustration. I held my temper in check with Margaret, but inside of me, a voice I did not particularly like was saying, *Well . . . all right then.*

And so I escorted Margaret to the banquet at the Hotel Cleveland, and we sat together at the speaker's table looking happy and radiant and in love. Afterward, still early in the evening, I escorted Margaret and her mother back to their suite, and wished them a most pleasant good evening . . . and then plunged into the night for a late date with a voluptuous brunette I'd met earlier in the day.

Margaret never caught on. My dad did, though. He and my brother had been shipped up to Cleveland too, for the festivities.

"You rascal, you," was all he said when it dawned on him what I was up to. But I don't think he liked it very much.

Thinking back on it now, I don't like it so much myself, even though I can still recall my jumbled, colliding emotions.

Hell, I never even got the brunette's name.

We continued on to Pittsburgh for a great downtown parade with police escort and sirens. Then to Detroit and a B-24 factory in a nearby suburb. There I met the dark-haired daughter of the president of Chrysler Motors at a cocktail party. That encounter progressed to dinner at her house, and then to a night in which, as I recall it, I just hung on to her as tightly and as long as I could. Fickle Bob Morgan? Incorrigible tomcat? Maybe. Call it what you like. From my point of view, it was night, and somewhere in America in a confusing and turbulent time. I was looking for somebody to hang on to.

On to Dayton, and Wright Field, and yet another encounter with a figure from the past, but not a girlfriend this time. I was on the stand making a speech to thousands of people when I felt a tap on my shoulder from behind. I turned and was flabbergasted to behold the general who'd vowed to me that I would never be more than a second lieutenant because I buzzed his oceanside cocktail party way back there in training at McDill. This time he had a big bygones-be-bygones grin on his face. In front of all those people, he recounted that story into the microphone. Then he said, "I can't keep my promise that you would remain a Second Lieutenant because you're already a Captain, but I'm going to raise it one." With that, he reached over to my tunic and pinned on my Major's leaves. All of a sudden I was Major Morgan. Now I was grinning too.

As thrilling as that moment was, it did not stand as my most memorable encounter in Dayton. That distinction was reserved for the crew's introduction to one of the cofounders of human flight, Orville Wright.

He was introduced to us as a crew in a briefing room at the airport. He was seventy-four then, but still had the boyish twinkle and playfulness about him that many people had remarked on. He would die three years later here in the town where he was born in April 1871, six years after the close of the Civil War. His older brother Wilbur had been dead since 1912—he'd contracted typhoid fever and never lived to see how his and Orville's wondrous flying machine changed the world.

Many years after that meeting, I came upon a copy of a letter that Orville had written in about 1900 to his sister from Kitty Hawk, while the brothers were still in the glider phase of testing their new invention. The sweetness and innocence of it raised a lump in the throat of this veteran of fighter/bomber combat in the stratosphere.

"The machine seemed a rather docile thing," Orville had told his sister, "and we taught it to behave fairly well."

Our next stop was Las Vegas, where, after the customary parade, they put us up in a fancy hotel that had a floor show. Las Vegas wasn't "Vegas" yet in those days. Although gambling had been legal since 1931—Bugsy Siegel wouldn't open his Flamingo Hotel until 1946—the town had started to swing a little.

The star of that floor show was some bright young vocalist on her way up, name of Horne. We'd never heard of anybody named Horne—hadn't caught the films she'd already done cameos in—and when she started her set we were in a bit of a rowdy frame of mind, laughing, kidding, even singing along with her from our seats.

I'll never forget how this young black entertainer stopped the music in the middle of a song and turned her serene gaze directly on us and asked us, sweetly and politely, if we would please mind not making quite so much noise. That got our attention. Who the hell was this woman to—?

Then Lena Horne started to sing again, and this time from where we were sitting you could have heard the proverbial pin drop. She had every one of us guys caught up in that magical voice of hers. Hell, "Honeysuckle Rose" was one of the reasons we were fighting the war!

I started to buy her records after that, and didn't stop until I had them all. I still have them.

*   *   *

Kingsland, Arizona, saw us answering questions about combat firing at a training base for machinegunners. Then to Hobbs, New Mexico, and from there to San Antonio. In San Antonio I met another beautiful brunette, the daughter of a colonel, when I was invited to his house for dinner. The local newspapers got wind of it and ran a story saying we'd gotten engaged. Well, the fact was, we did not get engaged. Not officially anyway. You just can't believe everything you read in the papers.

We flew on to Harlingen, Texas; Laredo; Oklahoma City; Denver. The days and the miles were piling up for us now, as was the heat of the summer out there in the West. All the boys of the crew were showing signs of fatigue. We respected what we were doing and were pleased with all the attention, but we were also homesick, tired of hotel life, bored with the little speeches we had to give all over again in every new city—nineteen, by now, with a dozen more to go.

We were even tired of the glamour, and of how easy it was to get girls. The girls just never stopped being there. Some of the boys were sitting in a hotel bar the night we hit Denver, talking to a bunch of them, and everything was getting kind of cozy, when Jim Verinis asked one young thing, "Would you like to come up to my room and see my dog?" The girl shot him a look as though he was crazy, but then she brightened and said, "Of course I'll go up and see your dog." The two of them hopped off their barstools and headed for Jim's room. When Jim opened the door, there was Stuka, our mascot, wagging her tail. The girl was thunderstruck. She took a step back and gasped, *"You really have a dog!"*

What was she expecting—etchings?

Captain Tom kept asking us on behalf of the Air Force if we minded lengthening the tour a few more weeks, adding another city or two to the list, and we kept saying that was fine, but it was starting to get to us.

We were all wishing for a change.

I didn't know it, but I was about to get what I wished for—in two stages. Two big, convulsive stages that changed the course of my future.

Stage One was the painful one. It was the beginning of the end of my future with Margaret Polk as Mrs. Bob Morgan. Looking back on it, I see that there was no one to blame but Mr. Bob Morgan.

It all kicked in with an innocent phone call.

I'd made it a point to call Margaret from every city we landed in. I did this in Denver, but my choice of time and locale could not have been worse. Like a dummy, I picked up a telephone in the hotel suite where the crew was hosting a cocktail party in full swing, and called her number in Memphis.

As soon as she picked up, she was more interested in the background noises than she was in my sweet nothings. It didn't help that the girls at this party had some of the shrillest laughs west of the Mississippi River. I think there must have been some glasses clinking together too, and a little music, and maybe some drinking. There were girls talking, laughing, and giggling. Of course, all this could be heard over the telephone when I was talking to Margaret.

"What is going on there?" Margaret wanted to know.

"Well, we're having a little party," I was forced to admit.

"It sounds like you're having an awful lot of fun with all that carousing," Margaret replied, with a distinct pout in her voice.

At this point I felt another hand on the receiver. One of the party girls had noticed that I was talking on the phone and was playfully trying to wrestle it from me. "Who're you talking to?" she demanded, laughing loudly.

Her dopey move could not have been timed more badly. I heard Margaret draw in her breath. I tried to regain control of the situation by getting a little high-horse. I said, "You know, Margaret, we're here to entertain the public and the public is here to entertain us." I thought that was a pretty snappy line, at the time. "And of course, females as well as males are doing all this. We're enjoying ourselves. The crew's happy and everybody's having a good time."

She said, "Well it sounds like you're having a good time without me."

I said, "Wait a minute. We're not married yet."

And she said, "I don't think we're going to be married either."

"What do you mean?"

She said, "I think we'd better cool it, Morgan."

Morgan. That didn't sound good. *Morgan* was what people usually called me when they were steamed at me. Usually Margaret called me something far sweeter and more affectionate, like Jug Head.

At any rate, I was in no mood to be lectured by long distance about my social habits. I said, "Well, if that's the way you want it, we'll do that!"

She said, "I think that's the best!"

We hung up.

More painful moments were destined to play themselves out after that. But in essence, that phone call spelled the end of America's Romance between Bob Morgan and his Memphis Belle.

Neither of us bothered to inform *Life* magazine.

CHAPTER

15

Stage Two unfolded in Wichita, our very next stop.

Wichita was the site of a huge Boeing airplane manufacturing plant, the second-largest outside the company's home base at Spokane. A large, cheering throng of Boeing workers turned out to welcome us and hear us speak. Here was a crowd that lifted our spirits and injected some fresh passion into our remarks onstage. Housewives, young working girls, kids from nearby farms, townsmen too old for active duty but not too old to wield a blowtorch—all of them had been putting in ten-hour shifts around the clock for nearly a year to produce warplanes. It was cryptically rumored that they were currently working on a new model of strategic bomber that we *Belle* crewmen couldn't wait to learn more about. Their exhausting, selfless work would later be known in Air Force circles as the "Battle of Kansas," the plant's output soaring from sixty planes a month at the outset toward a mind-boggling 362 a month by March 1944.

Our crew was welcomed to the podium by Brig. Gen. Kenneth B. Wolfe, commander of a newly formed bombardment wing that was likewise shrouded in secrecy. After the ceremonies, the General took me aside and asked me the one question in the world guaranteed to get my undivided attention. "Morgan, would you like to see a brand new airplane?"

He escorted me inside a hangar where a vast shape loomed. Its wingspan stretched half a football field. Its four engines were nearly the size of city buses. Its great smooth nose, Plexiglas-tipped, was as perfectly sculpted as the mouth end of a gargantuan Cuban cigar. Its curving contours seemed to devour the available light.

I couldn't stop gaping.

The General said, "This bomber hasn't had publicity, so you've never even heard of it." I hadn't, beyond those tantalizing, awestruck rumors. "This," General Wolfe said, "is the B-29."

The B-29. I didn't know it then, but I was looking at the machine that would soon make the Japanese wish they had never heard of Pearl Harbor, the magnificent Superfortress that in two years and in two fateful strikes would slam down the curtain on World War II and lift the curtain of the Nuclear Age.

The B-29 had so many futuristic features, it was hard to believe, as I later learned, that it had been on Boeing's design boards since the '30s. The company had submitted a prototype of the bomber to the Army in 1939. Its critical attributes were its flying range and its speed. The Superfortress could cover 5,830 miles in the air, five times the distance of the B-17, at a top speed of 365 miles an hour, seventy mph faster than its smaller sister. It weighed 130,000 pounds fully loaded, more than twice the heft of the Flying Fortress, and carried a bomb load of 20,000 pounds. It took the *Belle* seven months to drop 60,000 pounds. The B-29 could ward off attackers with a dozen .50-caliber machineguns and a 20-millimeter cannon, and was propelled by four 2,200-horsepower turbo-supercharged Wright Double Cyclone engines. Its cabins and crew areas were heated and pressurized, eliminating the need for oxygen masks except in an emergency. It featured a radar system for dropping bombs that replaced the Norden bombsight, and a remote-control firing system so that the gunners did not need to be at their stations holding the guns in their hands. It had about everything, in short, except an in-flight movie, and those hadn't been invented yet.

The B-29 had been a top-secret project until this point—even its air testing had been conducted under conditions of optimal security. Now this splendid lady was ready to make her debut into society. And Major Bob Morgan, once again, was falling in love.

General Wolfe invited me up into the cockpit. For a General, he certainly had a knack for closing a sale. I couldn't believe this environment. I could stand up in it. I could move around it without hunching. The cockpit was four times larger than that of the 17. I suddenly realized that I'd like to have a cockpit like this of my own, and of course the bomber to go with it.

"What's the range on this?" I asked the General, for all the world like a new-car buyer kicking the whitewall tires. When he told me, I looked at him sidewise and said, "H'mm—I guess I know where you're going to use this." He just kind of grinned and said nothing. He and I crawled back through the tunnel, through all those interconnected bomb bays and gunnery compartments. I forget exactly all the things I said, but they probably boiled down to, "oooh" and "ahhh."

As we left the hangar, I said to General Wolfe, "Thank you for letting me see this airplane. I'd like to get into this program." The General didn't seem at all surprised to hear that. He replied, "Well, if you're still interested after you've finished all this public relations touring and your leave at home, get back to me. I'll put you in touch with the right people."

All of a sudden, my future didn't look half as bad as it had a day or so ago. Stage Two of the big change in my life was sure a lot more scintillating than Stage One had been.

I didn't plan it that way, exactly. I didn't mean for this new flying opportunity to replace my romance with Margaret. I hadn't yet given up on her. I was still hoping we could repair the damage from that godawful telephone talk in Denver. I wanted to marry Margaret. I assumed that I *would* marry her. If only all these reporters and all these women and all these airplanes would stop getting in the way.

Let's face it—for all the womanizing I'd done in my young life, I still had not become a very good student of women. I still had a lot to learn about a woman's feelings, the way a woman saw the world, the way a woman in love saw her man and judged his willingness to re-form his life around her own. "Commit to a relationship" is how they phrase it these days. "Straighten up and fly right" is how they phrased it then.

My education began that very evening of the day I set eyes on the

B-29. I called Margaret in Memphis to pitch some woo, but before I knew it I was raving on about this new bomber I'd seen.

I might as well have been describing the curves on a cocktail waitress. "So you think you're going to be flying it?" she asked me in a flat voice.

I was caught off-guard. "Yeah," I said. "I think I might do that."

"Well, what does that mean?" she wanted to know. I was truthful. I told her that since I knew what the airplane was being built for, it probably meant I'd be going to the Pacific.

This time the hurt in Margaret's long-distance voice was even thicker than it had been in Denver. "You mean you're going back to the war again," she managed after a few moments. Yeah, I said. She didn't say much after that. I can imagine now, from the perspective of all these years, what might have been going through the poor girl's mind. Other women, she could maybe hold her own with. The War Department, she could wait out.

Bombers. Those were too much for a bridge-playing girl from Poplar Street.

This un-bylined news item ran in the *Memphis Commercial Appeal* in late July 1943.

Memphis Belle Brings
Disillusionment to Pilot

It's almost certain there will never be another Flying Fortress named Memphis Belle. Not if Bob Morgan has anything to do with it. The original Memphis Belle, Miss Margaret Polk, has just returned the engagement ring, together with one of those you-and-I-will-always-be-good-friends notes. So that's that.

Twenty-five times the Memphis Belle set out from the bomber base and headed for Hitlerland, each trip a victory. One needs only a little imagination to appreciate the thoughts that coursed through the mind of Pilot Morgan as he pointed the nose of the ship eastward. Bombs for Hitler . . . and each bomb bringing nearer the day that he and the other soldiers could get back to hometown belles all over the U.S.A.

Now, only disillusionment. Twenty-five trips in a good cause, to be sure. But the next 25 will not be made with the same zip and zest. What can the girl wish for, anyway? He's been promoted now and is Major Robert K. Morgan. He's a flier . . . a soldier . . . a brave man. What does it take to thrill a girl's heart?

Of course, it is just possible that Morgan was the one that terminated the romance. We can't be sure. Still, from what we know of . . . Perhaps she has just heard of that fellow who dived a plane 780 miles an hour. He's a colonel, too. You never can tell!

At any rate, no more Memphis Belles. If the news gets around, there won't be any more like Sweet Sue, Bright Eyes, or Venus Girl, either. Poetry and romance will be expunged from Fortress christenings. We'll read about gallant deeds by Towser Boy, My Pal Joe, and Brooklyn Dodgers. The war will be won, but not in the adventurous spirit with which it started out.

On to Mobile. I tried to get her to meet me there. PLEASE DON'T REFUSE THIS REQUEST, I telegraphed her. No response. Then to Fort Myers, Florida, and the training air bases in the vicinity—Panama City and Sebring. At Sebring a starry-eyed young ground crewman-in-training approached me and a few other *Belle* crewmen and asked, in reverent tones, "Would you fellows let the guys go over the airplane and be sure everything's in good shape?" We sort of chuckled indulgently—kids trying to touch a little aviation history, and all that—and I was gracious enough to say, "I sure would appreciate it."

Well, that turned out to be a fortunate bit of good manners on my part. Up until that time, we had been so preoccupied getting out of one city and into another on schedule that we hadn't bothered to authorize any maintenance work on the plane. I guess Joe Giambrone and his eager boys had kind of spoiled us. The following day the starry-eyed young trainee got in touch with me. Choosing his words with utmost tact, he said, "I didn't find anything major wrong, Sir— except that your elevators on the tail section needed repairing; they had holes rotted into them, and the trim was in such bad shape that we replaced it. It probably would have been knocked out by a heavy rain storm."

I cleared my throat and thanked him and told him he and his boys had done a fine job. Fine job, hell. They may have saved our lives.

An unscheduled stop, next, that I sure didn't mind, because it was a sentimental journey—Camden, South Carolina, where I started my training in PT-17s, and buzzed my first field. The brass there had begged the Army Air Forces to just let us touch down there. We did, even though the field was still a grass strip and a little dicey for landing a big B-17. I was sorry to find that none of my instructors were still there—how I'd loved to have seen Earl Friedell, and told him that pep talk he gave me went a long way!—but everyone there was thrilled by the visit. We even saw some of the good people of Camden, who'd fed and entertained us while we were still cadets.

I was disappointed that my girlfriend from those training days, Betty, who had expected me to marry her, didn't show up at that greeting. I knew she was in town, but nobody brought her name to my attention. The positive side of that disappointment was, her daddy didn't show up either.

Then Asheville. My homecoming. That was a day that I had really looked forward to. The town where I'd ridden bikes as a boy and driven my dad's Buick as a young man, and the airfield where I'd burnt out the brakes as a B-17 pilot under Major Smelser. As I went into my approach this time, I told myself, "Morgan, for goodness sakes, don't burn out your brakes again." Just to underscore this sense of restraint I'd been talking myself into, I went ahead and buzzed the Biltmore Forest Country Club Golf Course.

I took the *Belle* down by the eighteenth hole, low enough that you could have pinged her underbelly with an eight-iron shot, and I noticed that some of the golfers were heading for the woods. There must have been a lot of penalty strokes that morning.

My buzz also caught the attention of a certain dark-haired young secretary at the country club, one Dorothy Johnson.

Then I landed.

Hot.

My little cautionary talk to myself notwithstanding, I came in like

Floorboard Freddie. We touched down, and because there was no headwind, I quickly saw that if I didn't do something, I was going to run the plane clean off the far end of the runway. Jim Verinis next to me had a very interested expression on his face. I thought fast. I noticed that the grass was thick on the left side of the runway. I thought, "Well, I'll get over there, and that'll slow me down." So I did. I eased off the tarmac onto the grass. It worked, sort of. We were still making pretty good time, so I went ahead and pulled the emergency brake. Verinis was looking more interested in my technique with each passing second.

Finally, after a thrilling skid that kicked up divots behind us, we stopped—about six feet shy of a nice, deep draining ditch. If I'd put the *Belle* in that ditch, and flipped her over onto her back, that certainly would have taken some of the edge off the festivities, but I didn't. The crowd didn't notice. Nobody noticed, except the crew. As we unbuckled and made for the hatch, Jim Verinis shot me an arched-eyebrow look that said, *Well, you were lucky that time, cowboy.*

My father and brother were in the crowd that surged forth to greet us. We had a police escort parade into town, an honor well beyond my childhood thrills of riding with the Biltmore Forest cops, and were put up at the old Battery Park Hotel, the classiest hostelry in town in those days. Dinner at the country club, and you can believe my mind's eye was filled with ghosts—visions of elegant couples waltzing under Japanese lanterns, and my mother in her flapper gown, swirling happily through the night, her friend Cornelia not far away.

Luckily I had some dazzling companionship that evening to help keep the ghosts at bay. Dorothy Johnson, the young Biltmore Forest Country Club secretary, was at my table, and her vivacious smile and flattering attention soon had me laughing and alive, regaling the table with stories about my colorful crew from the *Belle*.

The next day the crew and I visited my father's furniture plant and spoke to his employees, many of whom were friends of mine from the summer days when I worked there.

At the nearby town of Swannanoa, we looked in on a factory that made Beacon blankets. Vince Evans made sure the Beacon workers would always remember him. Vince liked to spice up his remarks in each city with something clever and unusual, and he hit his peak this day. "I want to tell you people I know your blankets real well," he told the assembled workers. "As a matter of fact, I had one in London. I got it for my girlfriend. We'd go out to Picadilly Park and . . . talk, and . . . well, I want to thank you for that Beacon blanket. You do make a great comfortable blanket!" It brought down the house.

On our final night in Asheville, the city fathers had a party and reception for us at the City Hall auditorium. Each crew member spoke. When my turn came, I guess I was still in a sentimental mood. I found myself reminiscing about that good old mountain moonshine that was made up in the Smoky Mountains above Asheville. It was awful good, I told the folks, to get back to town here and have a taste of that real homemade whiskey. Then I made a promise. "After the war, I think I will still be flying, and I will see that this moonshine gets flown around all over the United States so that people will realize what good moonshine we make in our mountains." I think the crew was looking at me a little sidewise by this time, but the homefolks loved it, and it brought a big laugh. I still hear about that speech to this day, from people who were at that meeting. I think some of them are still waiting for me to make good on my promise.

Taking off from the Asheville airport the next day, after a special good-bye to Dorothy Johnson, I found myself once again in the grip of my favorite vice. It was a gorgeous Southern day, not a cloud in the sky, and I turned to Verinis and said, "Jim, I think we'll just drive up over the city and give them a little good-bye salute." Verinis knew what was coming, but other than roll his eyes a little, he said nothing. And so sure enough, we took off to the north and then turned east up over Patton Avenue. Down ahead of us, on a square at the crest of a gradual rise in the center of town, City Hall and the Courthouse stood, separated from one another by not a whole lot of space at all. "Oh boy," I said to myself, as Verinis fixed me with a Surely-you're-not-going-to-try-this look. "Should I go between those buildings?" *Yes,* my self answered. *I think you should.* I figured that a sixty-degree bank would squeeze us through all right. And so, heading east, I banked the plane and put the left wing right down between the Courthouse and City Hall. It was kind of a tight fit, but we made it. Then I turned the *Memphis Belle* left and pulled her up over Sunset Mountain, and we were out of town.

Out of town but not out of trouble, just yet, anyway. It happened that City Hall, at that time, housed the office of the Weather Wing Unit of the Army Air Forces. The Lieutenant Colonel in command of that unit happened to be looking out the window as the *Belle* slanted past—maybe the roar of our engines had aroused his curiosity. He was one of those spit-and-polish Lieutenant Colonels, and before we had even reached our cruising altitude he was on the telephone to the Pentagon, sput-sputtering about how Morgan had damn near taken half of greater municipal Asheville with him on leaving the town. As I understand it, the reply he got thoughtfully addressed all his concerns. "Major Morgan," the Pentagon officer replied, "has been given permission to buzz by Lieutenant General Henry Arnold." The Lieutenant Colonel was not heard from on the subject again.

Columbus. A parade from the airbase into town. Tight formation. Then, interceptors at 3 o'clock. An open convertible drew even with our parade jeep on the right. It was loaded with heavy armament— girls, pretty ones. They were whistling and waving. We were outgunned. I yelled out, "Meet us later!"

They yelled back, "We will!" and peeled off.

And we did meet them later. One of them was from a family involved in the Coca-Cola Bottling Co. I spent the evening with her. She lived alone in a nice house with servants. I got all the free Coca-Cola I wanted that night. Columbus was nice.

Chicago—another unscheduled stop. Captain Tom told us, "Chicago has been put on the tour by request of a gentleman there." The gentleman in question was quite patriotic, and quite wealthy. It turned out that he financed the entire detour himself. He was a friend of my father's, and in a letter to Dad, he'd written, "I want to tell you—I drank so many toasts to your son's health that I think I ruined my own health!" This fellow put the crew up at the famous Drake Hotel a couple blocks from Lake Michigan, threw us some parties and introduced us to some girls. Chicago turned out to be even nicer than Columbus.

Not to mention even weirder, at least as far as some of those women were concerned. Getting ready to leave the hotel the next morning, we were approached by a group of girls in military uniform. Or at least they appeared to be military uniforms. A couple of the girls explained they were Red Cross uniforms. They didn't look like any Red Cross uniforms we'd seen in England, but we figured what the hell—maybe they do uniforms differently in Chicago.

These girls had a request for us. They knew that we were headed next to Los Angeles. Our itinerary included a Hollywood rendezvous with William Wyler, lately promoted to Lieutenant Colonel, who needed us to record some dialogue for the final editing of his documentary, and then the Douglas airplane-manufacturing plant near there. The crew and I were looking forward to that long detour west, the last scheduled stop on our marathon tour. We'd been zigzagging all over the country for three months now, giving three or four speeches on some days, going to cocktail parties, dinners, after-dinner speeches, and on some nights, after-after-dinner-speech rendezvous. We'd been adding stops and postponing our reunions with home and family, and we were exhausted. Maybe now, with the end in sight, we were getting a second wind. Besides, Hollywood was Hollywood. It sure as hell wasn't Wilhelmshaven.

At any rate, the request these girls in uniform had for us was, Can we bum a ride?

They explained that they had some friends in Hollywood. As I say, they were in uniforms of some sort. There were strict regulations against us allowing any civilian to fly on a military plane. How could we argue with gals in uniform?

"Sure," I said. "Come on. Get on board."

I've never been one to believe in jinxes, but these passengers of ours nearly made me a believer. About two hours out of Chicago we lost our No. 3 engine. It threw a jug, as we used to say, and went out on us. I had to shut it down and make a forced landing at Ogden Air

Force Base in Utah, for repairs. When we all deplaned and the Base Commander came out to greet us, his eye fell on our young lady passengers—who were no longer in uniform, whatever that uniform might have been.

"And who are these?" I distinctly recall him asking. When I told him they were passengers, he asked the next logical question. "Are you allowed to carry civilian passengers?"

"They're in some kind of unit for the government," I muttered, my ears burning. I knew it wasn't a convincing answer, and the Base Commander clearly felt the same way. He said nothing more to us—no reprimand—but I found out later that he'd turned in a report to the Pentagon about this incident. It caught up with me finally, through channels, while I was on Saipan. "What's this all about, Morgan?" my commanding officer asked me, holding the dispatch. But I noticed that he was grinning. When I told him the story, he laughed, tore up the report, and threw it in the wastepaper basket. We had more pressing matters to worry about at that time.

Funny thing was, though. I never did find out what kind of uniform it was those girls were wearing.

That was all forgotten when we hit Los Angeles. William Wyler rolled out a Hollywood welcome for us that exceeded our wildest dreams. We were guests of honor at a glittering party at his house at 125 Copa de Oro Road in Bel Air, overlooking Sunset Boulevard, at which movie stars were thicker than the hors d'oeuvres. I hadn't seen the crew looking this alert since our last mission over Lorient! Danny Kaye, Dinah Shore—everywhere you looked, a famous face smiled back at you. Wyler asked each of us which star we'd like to meet. While we were thinking it over, a certain sultry blonde arose from her sofa and announced, "Boys, I'm Veronica Lake." J. P. Quinlan did a Cagney-style double-take, gulped, and stammered, "Ma'am, that's nice. Why don't you sit back down and I'll buy you a drink." I requested a date with Hedy Lamarr, but she was one of the few stars in town who couldn't be on hand, so I had to settle for Olivia de Havilland.

The next day we all reported to the Army Air Forces' First Motion Picture Unit in Culver City, the Hal Roach Studios in peacetime.

There Wyler, puffing on his inevitable cigarette, escorted us to the buildings where he and his people were busily editing the 19,000 feet of silent film that Wyler had shot into the *Memphis Belle* documentary. Everyone looked a little frantic. The War Department had made it clear that this movie was to be out in the theaters on the double.

Seated in soundproof booths, in front of microphones connected to recording equipment, the *Belle* crew and I re-created some of the dialogue that we'd typically use during a mission. We watched the scenes of our actual aerial combat up on the screen and improvised dialogue into our microphones.

I must say that for a bunch of flyboys, we didn't make half-bad actors—especially given that we were playing ourselves in situations still fresh in our memories. If you've seen the film—as far as I know, the first Hollywood documentary ever built on footage taken in actual combat—you'll remember that riveting action montage in the middle: quick shots of Vince releasing his bombs, our gunners firing at enemy fighters, American and German planes being hit, parachutes opening, flak bursts, more swooping planes. Over the dubbed-in drone of engines and chatter of machineguns you can hear our voices. "There's four of 'em! One o'clock high, Chief!"

"They're comin' round—watch 'em!"

"Watch 'em, Scotty!"

"I got my sights on 'em."

"B-17 out of control, three o'clock!"

"Come on, guys, bail out! Come on, get outta there!"

"Keep after 'em, Winchell!"

"I got him!"

"He got him, Chief! Look! He's bailing out!"

And me, in my big dramatic line: "Dammit, don't yell on that inter-phone!"

The dubbed dialogue was not the only fictionalized element of Wyler's documentary. The movie seems to be covering a single mission, a raid by elements of the Eighth Bomber Command over Wilhelmshaven in 1943. In fact it's a composite of footage shot over several missions to various targets, and of various scenes of ground crews at work. This said, though, I have always believed that *The

Memphis Belle delivered an accurate message on the level of truthfulness that Wyler was aiming for—the message of what it looked, sounded, and felt like to be in the center of the air war over Europe in 1943, of what the stakes were for the young Americans who flew those missions, and the significance of those missions to the Allied cause in Europe.

The dialogue may have been fake in that it was recorded afterward, in a sound studio, but when I watch it to this day, I have a hard time distinguishing it from the real thing. The weird part was that it all became real again to us as we went through the process of acting it.

At the outset it was a lark. All of us were laughing, joking, cutting up, just enjoying the hell out of going Hollywood for a little while. But as the hours mounted up, and as Wyler's raw footage kept scrolling before us, our moods began to change. The reality of it all came flooding back to us for the first time since we'd left England. We watched footage of B-17s going down, airplanes that had friends of ours in them, and felt our stomachs tighten. The horror and sadness and sense of helplessness that hit us this time were even harder to take than when it all actually happened, because this time we had no combat tasks to keep our minds busy.

I think that a single realization shot through each of us at some point in William Wyler's production studio. *Gee whiz—we were* there, *weren't we? We were* there. It brought a solemn mood over us, so solemn that we tried to tell a few stories and jokes, and kid one another, to get back to that holiday mood we'd come in with.

I suspect that for some of the boys, as for a lot of World War II veterans, that solemn mood never did go completely away.

The Hollywood interlude had a happy effect on one of us, though. It was at Wyler's party that Vince Evans met his future wife, or one of them—a young actress named Jean Ames. The romance opened up the future for Vince. "Bob," he told me, "I'm going to get into this business when I come back." He meant the movie business. And damned if he didn't. There was hardly any limit on what Vince Evans could accomplish in this world.

A wedding portrait with my new bride, Dorothy,
who gave her name to my B-29.

November 23, 1944. *Dauntless Dotty*'s payload of five-hundred-pound
bombs is being readied on Saipan.

November 24, 1944.
General Emmett
"Rosie" O'Donnell
confers with me before
taking off on the first
B-29 raid on Tokyo.

November 24, 1944. *Dauntless Dotty* is the lead plane
on the first B-29 raid of Tokyo.

Here's what the B-29 looked like when dropping
a bomb load over Japan. ARMY AIR FORCE FILM

An example of the devastation rained on Toyko. NATIONAL ARCHIVES

November 24, 1944. The press clamors around me, General O'Donnell, and Vince Evans after we returned from bombing Tokyo.
NATIONAL ARCHIVES

After our little sojourn over Toyko, the Japanese Zeros on Iwo Jima paid us a visit on Saipan. Although they destroyed a number of B-29s on the ground, they couldn't stop us. NATIONAL ARCHIVES

Dauntless Dotty and crew. From left to right are Col. Stud Wright, group commander; Capt. Vince Evans, bombardier; me; Lt. Ed Lee, flight engineer; Lt. N. S. Alton, navigator; Capt. Andrew Mayse, copilot; T/Sgt. W. B. Sanor, left gun; T/Sgt. C. Burke, right gun; T/Sgt. R. W. Powell, radar; Sgt. P. T. Black, tailgunner; T/Sgt. S. Fritzshall, radio; and Sgt. M. H. Brinkmeyer, crew chief.

The *Memphis Belle* stands on her concrete pedestal outside the
Air National Guard in Memphis, Tennessee. By the mid-1970s,
vandals had plundered her for parts, and the nose cone had been replaced.
I was still glad to see Margaret Polk again, though.
MEMPHIS COMMERCIAL APPEAL

Jim Verinis and I stand on the restored *Belle*'s wing in her Mud Island Pavilic
dome on one of our regular visits. She sure looks nice for an old bird.

My daughter,
Peggy Morgan Partin,
who saved my life.

August 29, 1992. Linda and I
are married in front of the *Belle*.

On a recent trip
to England I got
to meet the
Queen Mother
for the first time in
over fifty years.
But this time there
was no war.
Linda arranged the
whole thing.

It's like riding a bike. Once you learn, you never forget.
I'll always cherish the thrill of flying a B-1 bomber. And having a B-1
renamed *Memphis Belle* by the Georgia Air National Guard and
adorned with the same nose art was a great honor.

Maybe it was those searing memories that William Wyler's footage brought back to us, but as our Hollywood stint wound down, a fresh case of homesickness swept through the entire crew. It was late August 1943 now. We had thrown ourselves into pep talks and War Bond promotion from one end of America to another, we'd been in the air more often than we had over Germany, it seemed, and we'd received just about every accolade and tasted every pleasure that wartime America had to offer. We were tired of that now. We wanted to go home.

Thus, when I met with the crew in our Los Angeles hotel bar one evening and relayed to them Captain Tom's request to add still another month to our tour, I was not surprised when the groaning answer came back unanimously, "No, no, no, no, no, we've had enough!"

And I agreed.

Captain Tom was nothing if not persistent, though. "All right," he said, "we'll scrap that idea. There *is*," he went on as I turned to leave, "one more stop we'd like you guys to make, though. This is a personal invitation from the Bulova Watch Company in Woodside, New York. They've asked us to come to New York City. They want to throw a big celebration for you. And besides," he concluded, clinching the argument, "we've got to go back to the East Coast anyway. You may as well go out with one final bash."

We agreed to go to New York City.

None of us regretted it. New York was a town that very few of us had visited—I'd been there a few times—and in the 1940s, it probably held an even bigger mystique than it does today.

What a whirl we had! The Bulova people knew how to do it right. They put us up at the fabulous Waldorf-Astoria Hotel, gave each of us his own separate suite, and piled those suites high with whiskey, fruit, hors d'oeuvres, the works. After a big bash in the Waldorf ballroom the first night—an orchestra, the press, speeches, a glittering crowd of celebrities on hand—they took us out to the Bulova plant in Queens the next day, where once again we spoke to a cheering workforce. Each crewman received a personal watch, engraved on the back with the word, "Valor." Mine is still a cherished possession in my household.

Then it was a round of Broadway musicals, a visit to the Cotton Club in Harlem where Cab Calloway and his musicians blew wild for us, dinner at the 21 Club, dinner in an elegant restaurant in the Empire State Building, and dinner in the Persian Room at the Plaza Hotel. The filet mignon was impeccable.

New York was our last appearance, but not our last stop. On August 31 we flew on to Bolling Field, an Army Air Forces base across the Potomac from where we'd landed three months earlier at Washington National. There we disbanded. There we left the *Memphis Belle*. It was a sad occasion.

A terrible kind of desolation swept over all of us. We hadn't been ready for this. We never saw it coming, though I guess we should have. All the emotions of the past three months, really the past ten months—the missions, the homecoming, the high-strung surreal world we'd been living in all summer. Now it was *over*. It hit us like a cannon round and left us stunned and tearful.

We parked the *Belle* on the tarmac and swung down through the hatch, one by one, leaving her for the last time, as far as any of us knew. We dragged ourselves into the quarters the Army had made available for us and got through a night there, trying with various degrees of success to sleep.

The next day we met for breakfast. It started out fine, all of us talking about how we were going to get back to our hometowns, even joking a little. Then we found ourselves out on the tarmac again, gathered around the *Belle*. We were quiet and thoughtful for quite a while. All of us. Even J. P. Quinlan, who loved to chatter. Little Clarence Winchell. Vince Evans, whose Texas twang was usually audible. Bob Hanson, the radio man. Serious, thoughtful Chuck Leighton. All of them. Dead silent.

Then, abruptly, without any of us suggesting it, every one of us climbed back through the hatch into the plane. We took the positions that we'd flown missions in. And we sat there in silence for ten or fifteen minutes. It was like a funeral.

I finally broke it by saying to Verinis that somebody should have played taps, because here we were leaving the one indispensable member of our crew—the gal that took us there and brought us back, the gal that's been with us all this time around the country.

We will never see her again, I said, and maybe I was thinking of another gal just then as well. I untaped Margaret's photograph from its place on the control panel and put it in my pocket. I asked Captain Tom where the airplane was going. He shrugged and said he didn't know. I said, "Well, if you find out, drop us a line, will ya?" He promised he would, but he forgot. From that day on for many years, we had to rely on distant rumor to find out what had become of the *Memphis Belle*. We heard that she'd gone to the training command. In later years I met some of the men who'd flown her in training, and they spoke of her with awestruck affection. Then we heard that she was consigned to the scrapyard. Then we stopped hearing anything at all for many years.

At any rate, we all shook hands then, bade the *Belle* farewell, and walked off into our separate futures.

CHAPTER
16

I headed back to Asheville in September feeling as melancholy and disconnected as I'd felt since the day I learned my mother had died. I had a thirty-day leave to think over the next stage of my service to the Army Air Forces and, for that matter, my life. Just now, though, none of it seemed real. It was a time for me of sudden silence, of loneliness, and of memories that pounded at me in the night.

The twenty-sixth mission was over, a transition every bit as jarring in its way as the twenty-fifth had been. I could almost feel the motions of it still surging through my body, like you do when you step from a pitching boat onto a firm dock. We'd never be together again in exactly that same way, under those circumstances. Hell, I even missed Stuka.

And Margaret. That part of my life was over too, it seemed, and it ate at me as I tried to sleep at night in my father's house, or went to the country club, looked up old friends, tried to concentrate on what to do next. Margaret and I had stopped contacting each other now, but the ache for what might have been remained.

Much of it was my fault. I'd behaved badly at crucial times, I understood that, but so much of it had been beyond my control. Our control. I was serious about Margaret. I cared for her. I'd intended to marry her. I'd *lived* to marry her. That photograph of her up there to my right on the instrument panel had been like an angel guiding me homeward through all those terrible air battles over France and Germany. I felt that the two of us had earned the right to our destiny. Then something big and relentless had taken our romance and used it for its own purposes, eaten it up, and spat the two of us in opposite directions. The Hero and his Sweetheart. How I came to detest that word, hero.

My fellow townsman Thomas Wolfe had once found a far more lyrical phrase to describe a lost love. "A face that smiled and vanished on a passing train," he'd written.

In my solitude, and in my unslakable hunger of the heart to be near a woman, I turned to Dorothy Johnson. Despite her high-society connections at the country club, Dorothy was an unpretentious girl, quiet and sincere. She was living with her divorced mother just beyond the northern edge of Asheville in a lovely old home with lots of leafy acreage that we could roam together. I wooed her through that early North Carolina autumn, walking and talking in those peaceful sunny woods, Dot in her bluejeans with the cuffs rolled up—the time of year when the trees, the peaceful trees of my boyhood, began to flare into color. The time of year "when the chinkapins are falling," as Wolfe wrote—the sweet chestnuts. Maybe this is my true destiny right here, I told myself—convinced myself. To come home from the war and live amidst the falling chinkapins. To marry a hometown girl.

That would have been fine with her mother, who liked me, but it was not so fine with her father, who smelled a rat. That was the way it usually broke down with the mothers and the fathers of the women in my life. Maybe I reminded those dads a little too much of themselves! Harry Johnson was a rough-edged man. He owned a pool hall. He came to see me—another familiar pattern—at my office in City Hall, where the Army Air Force had assigned me to write some essays for B-17 training manuals. Harry made it known to me in no uncertain terms that he didn't think I was any good for his little girl and he'd be just as happy if I stopped seeing her. I assured him, as I did all those dads, that my intentions were honorable and that anyway I planned to keep on seeing his daughter.

Harry decided to change his tactics. He figured that maybe he should get to know me better, man to man. His idea of breaking the ice was taking me to a cockfight, the first and last of those bloody illegal spectacles I ever saw. I was disgusted. Having just gotten back from the war, it wasn't as though I needed to see a little violent death. Funny thing—*I* was supposed to be the one with the doubtful character!

It didn't really matter. I was determined to marry Dorothy Johnson and settle down and live the life of a normal human being.

Except that I wasn't finished with the damn war yet, and I knew it.

I could have sat behind a desk for the duration, a decorated Major. I could have played out my active-service commitment by training young fighters here at home. All that had been made clear to me. None of it appealed to me in the slightest. My feelings for Dorothy notwithstanding, I had to get back in the air again and fly missions over enemy territory.

My fascination with this new B-29 was a factor, sure. So was the fresh thrill of patriotism I experienced upon receiving a certain letter dated August 10, 1943, a letter that I still cherish to this day. It was from that gallant warrior Maj. Gen. Ira Eaker, who had turned his attention from his heavy duties commanding the Eighth Air Force to acknowledge the success of that twenty-sixth mission across America that he'd assigned us.

The letter read in part:

> I have seen many press clippings and have talked to several officers . . . who have had an opportunity to observe something of the reception of your crew, the work you were doing and the impression you were creating . . .
>
> All the information leads me to believe that you and your boys are carrying out perfectly the mission we charged you with and creating the most favorable impression.
>
> I know that this is a very difficult assignment and that it is almost, if not as hard upon you and your crew as was your combat assignment here.
>
> Please extend to the crew my appreciation and commendation for the way they have carried out their mission, and urge upon them that they continually bear in mind the great responsibilities they bear . . .

I had always respected General Eaker. After receiving that letter from him, I probably would have flown a mission by myself if he'd asked me to.

These weren't the main reasons I needed to get back in the air again. The main reason came from the part of me that had never forgotten a December 1941 Sunday in Louisiana, when my cadet friends and I had returned to the Barksdale air base from that afternoon of dancing to Glenn Miller records at a Shreveport hotel, and that MP at the gate had saluted us ferociously and told us to get into our military uniforms.

No, the main reason was personal. I had some payback I needed to deliver to the Japanese for what they did to us at Pearl Harbor.

I had nothing against the Japanese as a people. I'd never met a Japanese person in my life. Until Pearl Harbor I had scarcely given Japan a thought. But none of that staunched my anger on that night of December 7—a ripe anger shared by almost every serviceman of my generation that I've talked to. A territory belonging to our country had been violated. Young American men like us had been trapped and slaughtered without warning or justice. The military force that did this showed no restraints against absolute conquest of our homeland. That force had to be met and obliterated. We were happy to oblige.

I got on the telephone and called another Wolfe, the Brigadier General in Wichita who'd remained there for a while to supervise the plane's manufacture. I told him that I'd thought it over and yes, I wanted for sure to be part of the B-29 program. He said, "In what respect?"

I didn't hesitate. "I'd like to have my own bomb squadron."

The General said, "I think that can be arranged."

He advised me to travel down to Marietta, Georgia, where the 58th Bombardment Wing was organizing its first active B-29 units. Because I'd turned my new Buick back in to the finance company before I'd left for England, I unearthed that Ford coupe of mine, traded it in for a used convertible, and hit the road south. At Marietta, I met with another general to plead my case.

Apparently the general liked my credentials. He said, "Morgan, you can have your squadron. There's one group training right now in Pratt, Kansas—the 40th Bomb Group. We'll attach you to that group even though you will not be part of them when they go overseas. They'll be leaving sometime before the year is over. When that happens, you will stay back and form your own squadron."

It sounded good to me. I headed my convertible back to Asheville feeling some of the old tingle returning. I was going to be in action again before long. And I was savoring the prospect of rounding up as many members of the *Belle* crew as I could find to come along with me.

During this time I paid close attention to the air war as it was developing around the globe. The skies of World War II's theaters were filled with fighting airplanes.

Back in England, General Eaker finally received the massive buildup of planes and men that he had so desperately needed since the outset. In June, the same month we went home, his strike capacity was increased by the arrival of the 100th, 381st and 384th Bomb Groups. More American planes in the air did not guarantee a drop in American casualties however. In fact, the reverse was true.

On June 10, 1943, the Allied high command decided that if the European bombing strategy was going to work, something would have to be done about those deadly Focke-Wulfs and Messerschmitts. The bloody strategy it ordered was called Pointblank, and it entailed, simply and brutally, the concentrated destruction of German fighters in the air, and German fighter-building factories on the ground. For American bomber crews, this meant flying deeper and deeper over enemy territory, outdistancing their Spitfire escorts for ever-greater stretches, and aiming at targets that were chosen specifically to get those enemy planes up into the air, en masse, as targets to be shot down. Of course, the targets were fully capable of shooting back, and did, to great and tragic effect.

It also meant the bombing of enemy cities, which had been off-limits to American planes during my time with the Mighty Eighth.

Pointblank reached its peak of intensity late in July—Blitz Week, it was called—with a massive Allied thrust at several urban centers.

After three days of nonstop British and American bombing, Hamburg was turned into a raging furnace with temperatures reaching 1,000 degrees centigrade. At least fifty thousand citizens were killed and nearly a million rendered homeless. The RAF and the Mighty Eighth paid a price—eighty-seven of Britain's 2,592 aircraft shot down, and eighty-eight of 1,720 American planes, or 8.5 percent of its total attackers. So heavy was the carnage that for two weeks afterward, neither England nor the United States put a heavy bomber into the air.

The Allies took another brutal pounding on August 17, as they went back for attacks on two industrial targets dangerously deep in Germany—a Messerschmitt factory in Regensburg and the ball-bearing plants at Schweinfurt. Curtis LeMay himself, now a colonel commanding the Third Air Division, led the thrust over Regensburg. The Third's losses were stunning—24 B-17s shot down from the 127 over the target with fifty more badly damaged. At Schewinfurt, the Mighty Eighth flew in with 188 planes. Thirty-six were shot down, carrying 352 airmen. Three others crash-landed in England and 118 were ripped up by fighters and flak. It was more hellishly clear than ever that without long-range fighter escorts to protect them, the mass-slaughter of young American fliers was going to continue.

But where was that long-range fighter support going to come from?

The situation in the Pacific, where I now knew I was headed, was by this time a good deal more promising for the American forces. Many months of bitter fighting remained, with horrific casualties for our Marines, airmen, and Navy. But with the Battle of Midway having shredded Japan's once-mighty carrier force and much of its elite fighter-plane menace, the Allies in the fall of 1943 could feel the first stirrings of inevitability.

Two great trans-Pacific counteroffensives were gathering their mass, aimed at the epicenter of the Rising Sun—one pointed northward from the Solomon Islands and eastern New Guinea, the other churning west from Pearl Harbor, destined for passage through the Marshalls and the Marianas and an assault on a mysteriously code-named "Island X" before hurling itself at Okinawa. This converging, two-pronged "island-hopping" campaign was designed to take back the widely scattered territories conquered by Japan in its great sweep of 1940 and 1941, and then to storm the fiercely defended home islands themselves, if necessary. American air power would be a key element of a densely interwoven sea, land, and air strategy—bomber and fighter support, launched from carriers, Marine troops swarming ashore from transport ships, merciless aerial and submarine pulverizing of the painfully exposed Japanese merchant ships steaming to resupply the far-flung islands, and, in the latter stages, strategic bombing of Japanese cities.

I spent most of September writing that analytic material about the B-17 for the War Department and romancing Dorothy Johnson, and trying to keep on good terms with Harry without becoming a regular at the local cockfights. He wasn't that bad a guy, actually, when I got to know him. I just had to steel myself, grin and bear it, every time he shot me that dark scowl of his and rumbled, "Morgan, I want you to be honest and serious with me. You and my daughter had better behave yourselves. I don't want any flirtatious romance."

Who, me?

The fact was that as October drew near, and with it my date for heading back to active duty, Dorothy and I were having ourselves quite a romance. We agreed to correspond while I was away, and we did—through phone calls and letters. We looked forward to my next leave, at Christmas, when I would have fifteen days back in Asheville. I was already planning my campaign for those fifteen days.

I got myself back in the war, more or less, by reporting in to the Army airfield near Pratt, Kansas, on October 2, 1943. Pratt Field was three miles south of the small prairie town some sixty-five miles west of Wichita, about halfway between there and Dodge City. They didn't waste any time introducing me to my new airplane. I got a short ride in a B-29 as copilot on the day I arrived, and three days later I logged an hour of first-pilot time.

I didn't get a real taste of the B-29 in those months—they were still scarce and few were expendable for training. But I logged some useful time in the B-26. Some smart engineer or flight conductor or general had noticed that the glide angle for approach to a landing on the B-26 was much like the B-29—quite steep—so we shot a lot of landings in the 26 with that in mind. I notched about forty hours during the month. The rest of the time dragged a little. We watched the dust storms, hung around the officers' club at night, enjoyed the good-natured hospitality of the Pratt folks whenever we could. I flew off to Asheville on every weekend I could manage, to see Dorothy.

I was back in it, and yet I was not back in it. Most of the attention went to the squadron already formed and in active training for its imminent departure for the Pacific. I didn't get to fly a Superfortress again until October 20. By then, it was growing clear that this big new bomber came equipped with big new problems.

I got introduced to the B-29's limitations almost as soon as I first climbed into the pilot's seat and gripped the yoke. The Superfortress may have been a gorgeous specimen of airplane to admire from the outside, and her updated gadgetry could dazzle the mind, but she was not much fun to fly. I guess no combat plane ever built could quite match the B-17 in that department. We pilots used to say, "You trim the 17 and she'll fly by herself." Her younger, bigger sister didn't even come close.

Flying the Superfort was work, pure and simple. Because of its heavy wing and the long, sweeping structure of that wing, it didn't lend itself to the tight, close formations of the sort we flew over Europe. It could not maneuver as quickly as the B-17. It could not react as well to the pilot's hand-and-foot movements—the aileron and the elevators were more sluggish, and as for the rudders, it took far more pressure on the pedals to turn the plane.

All this was understandable, in purely military terms. The B-29 was designed and built in a short period of time for a highly specialized purpose. Its purpose was to haul big bomb loads over tremendously vast distances. But the B-29 was not simply a difficult airplane. She could be a very dangerous one to the men inside her.

As I was to find out very soon in combat, Superforts that had been damaged by fighters or antiaircraft did not hold up well. They simply could not take anywhere near the punishment a 17 would and still fly. That was proved by the losses we were soon to absorb in the Pacific. Nor was it just enemy fire that did these planes in. We lost a lot of them through mechanical failure. The large engines overheated easily because not enough air could get through to cool the cylinders. Many times we taxied our B-29s out with just two engines running, and started the others just before take-off so that we would have at least two reasonably cool engines to get us into the sky. There was also that tricky landing approach—steep, long, and fast, far dicier than you would use on the 17. The Superforts landed on tricycle gear, main wheels first, then the nose field settling to the ground halfway down the runway.

For all these reasons, the B-29 was no fun to fly. She wasn't much fun from the Japanese point of view, either.

The devil finds work for idle hands, they say. Idle minds, too. As the October days at Pratt stretched on without much involvement expected of me, my thoughts drifted back, inevitably, to Margaret. As soon as they did, a longing for her swelled up inside me, as acute and as painful as it had been when the bottom fell out of things.

I called her up at her home in Memphis one lonely Sunday afternoon. I let it spill out of me—my regret at the missteps that pulled us apart, my frustration at her refusal to accept my apologies and refused to work with me in putting it all back together. I followed up that call with a letter. The date was October 17th.

> I have never really used your first name to any degree, have I? I am afraid I am not good at writing you anymore . . .
> Margaret, I can't tell you how much better I feel since I got my speech in. You see I have been carrying that around on my mind & in my heart for two months. It has been hell too . . . We always promised if anything came between us we would talk it over. I failed you there because I let that <u>hero</u> stuff get me down.
> I am Bob Morgan now—the guy who fell in love with you in Walla Walla & who has loved you ever since. He went away in

June & just got back. I was hoping your love which brought him
through combat would be strong enough to take him in your arms
& <u>forgive</u> his mistake and take [him] as your <u>own forever</u>—but
darling you can't see it that way eh? Maybe my love was the
strongest after all . . .

If you change your mind before I go to Kansas in November I'll
be waiting—it is your <u>turn</u> now to swallow your pride. If you do
I'll stay in the U.S. . . .

Forever Yours,
Bob

P.S. We all makes mistakes—I have forgiven people—can't
you?

A few days later I received a breezy reply from Margaret that an-
noyed me even further by its damnable chattiness. From the perspective of years, I can see that she was probably just trying to keep
the dialogue from getting too heavy, as a proper and cautious young
Southern girl might. At the time, though, it worked on me like Chinese water-torture:

> Ah! The weather is so perfect. I just want to go out and play.
> Whee! I bet you are hunting now—yep! I might well say the lazy
> way from a car. How about that exercise the <u>officers</u> (God Bless
> 'em) are supposed to take? Come on—try a few of those new fan-
> gled vitamin pills.
>
> Ah! They are playing "My Ideal" on the radio. They just fin-
> ished "The Dreamer" . . .
>
> Bob, all I can say is what I said Sunday. We are the best of
> friends. If we can ever get that <u>old feeling</u>—well time will tell. I
> have ceased to be surprised with what tomorrow brings. I feel sure
> that everything happens for the best so why worry—it's just too
> pretty a day to think . . .
>
> Have you read the Nov. Woman's Home Companion? Now, it's
> not meant as an insult—the article on P.4. "Rendezvous With He-
> roes" might be interesting . . .

Just
Margaret

P.S. I'm from Mo.

Maybe it was that postscript that drove me up the wall—a reference to a popular slogan of the day, "I'm From Missouri, You've Got to Show Me." At any rate, it coaxed out of me, predictably enough, I guess, this apocalyptic eruption dated October 27.

> I hope that you will forgive me for typing this to you, but since it may be the last letter that I will ever have the honor of writing to you I want a copy of it to put in my scrap book for my future years if there are any.
>
> I must be frank "little one" as we have always been that way except when the public took a tired young man away from you. I love you and never have ceased in the least . . . We kept our love going thru hell and high water . . . I come home. I am made a hero when all I want is you. The public damn near killed me and got me to the point where I wanted to tell all of them where to go. You told me I had a job to do even here in the states. I did it and a damn good job. I made an awful error by blowing up, but I couldn't help it darling. I needed you and your pride kept you from coming to me. I need you now forever. I need you more now than at any time over Germany . . . This is our last chance darling as I can't take it any more . . .
>
> I fought death for you. Sure I let you down, but . . . I need you now and have you ever come to me when I really needed you? You know you haven't. So darling take a good look at yourself and see if your pride wasn't stronger than your love. If it wasn't you will say yes (and we'll be married quietly). The Col. says I can have 15 days if I can talk you into it . . . All I ask is for your decision and cut out this Missouri stuff . . . I am giving up death when I have to live knowing that you let one letter and one phone call and your pride wipe out happiness.

Did I melt her heart? Did my passion cause her to see the error of her ways and pledge her love eternal? Not exactly. Her return letter was written, romantically enough, on the letterhead of the National Liberty Insurance Company of America.

> Happy Halloween—the goblins will get you if—
> Here I sit in the midst of downy cushions. Do I hear you ask why? As usual, I have just returned from the farm. The horse went

one way and I went down and hit rock bottom. Won't I ever learn? O.K. laugh. It's worth it.

I received your letter yesterday. Some parts of it beat the hell out of me. So I must make the next move. Well, here goes. I am asking you to come here so we can have a little talk. There are a few rough spots. If the Colonel will give you 15 days after you "talk me into it," surely he will give you a few days to "talk me into it." Perhaps one of the main difficulties is that we have never been with each other except for a few hours. I think we should have another speaking session, or a good facsimile.

Bob, do you agree with that old axiom now? You really don't realize the value of something until you lose it. If it was of any value in the first place, it should be worth working for. The days of "Pennies from Heaven" are past.

You say you can't go on like this, Bob, if we don't marry I will still be on your mind. I am linked to the most important thing in your life. If we can't talk things over and recover our old feelings, you will always wonder what it would have been like being married to me. Oh, do you want my opinion? O.K., I will save it for future reference. Just as you say, Chief.

Something to tuck you in bed tonight. Have you ever tried to reflect yourself into my place? What would you have done, or would you do now, under existing circumstances? I do hope I will see you soon.

> Sweet dreams,
> Margaret

P.S. People are bursting with curiosity as to what we are doing.

Reasonable enough? Not to a hot-blooded twenty-five-year-old North Carolina romantic with a strong need for a woman's unconditional love.

I waited a few weeks—waited until November 17, in fact, the day I logged my first long-distance flight as a first pilot in the B-29, a stint of five hours—and then composed to her my Noble Farewell. Or at least that's what I thought it was at the time.

I am sorry that I have not written you sooner in answer to your fine letter, but I have been away for a week and just got back this Monday. I am sure you will understand all this.

Yes, I guess I do understand how you felt when you got that telephone call from me when I was in Denver, but I will never feel that you could have loved me as you said and let us go our ways without doing anything about it. If I could feel that you ever really loved me then I'd try to win it back. We have been apart now for a long time and the wound is nearly gone and I feel that we would open it once again if we tried to start over again.

I hope that we will always be friends and that any time I am in Memphis I will give you a call. I hope that you will do the same when you are near wherever I am. I hope that I have as much luck this next trip as I did last time. I guess I am the only member of the 8th Air Force who is crazy enough to go back into combat, but I am fighting for something still.

Good luck Margaret and may our paths cross again soon no matter where. My best to your whole family.

At least my piloting hopes were holding together. By late November I was piling up the hours in the B-29. By January I would have logged more than sixty hours—not to mention several training stints in the B-17 and getting checked out in two additional airplanes, a medium-range bomber called the B-26 and a dive-bomber, the Curtiss Helldiver, designated as the A-25.

Back to Asheville in mid-December, after a cross-country practice flight in the B-26, landing in a certain familiar city.

I began my serious courtship of Dorothy almost immediately. She was doubtful at first. In fact, "No, no, no, no, no!" was one of the ways she put it, as I recall. Me being the kind of guy I was, I took that for a yes. I kept romancing her, kept up my ardent entreaties. I asked her to marry me at least two or three times a day. She kept resisting.

Christmas Day passed with that standoff in place. But I thought I could see her melting a little. At least this Christmas, I had something to dream about besides long-ago Yuletides in Asheville!

Her telephone call came to my father's house two days later. "All right, Morgan. I'll marry you."

Mission accomplished!

One drawback to getting married in North Carolina in those days was the mandatory waiting period. An engaged couple had to wait for an examining doctor to complete a certificate of health.

There was no waiting period in South Carolina, however.

On December 29 Dorothy and I drove a well-worn route for me, down to Greenville, to the air base there. A captain on the base agreed to stand as a witness for us, a hometown boy from Asheville named Babe Malloy. In the base chapel on that day Dorothy Johnson became Dorothy Johnson Morgan.

We drove back to Asheville and spent our wedding night at the Biltmore Forest Country Club. The next day we let our families in on the good news. Her mother and father were not too happy, but my father and brother were pleased—hell, they'd had more practice.

Then off to Pratt, Kansas, where I was due to report by January 1, 1944. We had a terrible time arranging transportation. We finally booked an upper berth on a train headed first to Chicago and then on to Wichita.

I'd written one last letter to Margaret before leaving Asheville. It was on Biltmore Forest Country Club letterhead:

> I am sorry I have not written you sooner, but I have been so very busy & on top of that 15 days leave has left me away from desks.
>
> I was sorry you were not in when I landed in Memphis about 10 days ago—I thought you'd like to see the B-29.
>
> I hope your Christmas was a happy one—I only wish mine had been—I am sure that if it hadn't been for newspapers, etc., my life would be as I want it . . .
>
> I will be back in combat soon & no doubt won't see you again—so may I wish you a Happy New Year & may you get what you want in life. I know you will get it as you have the courage to get that which you <u>desire</u>.
>
> May God end the war soon. We are all proud of the part you already have played and are still playing.
>
> My love to you all.

And then I married Dorothy Johnson.

CHAPTER

17

Few Americans have ever been fully aware of the complexities of aerial warfare in Asia that I was now preparing to join as I trained at Pratt in early 1944.

It was the European theater that most gripped the country's attention. Pearl Harbor may have shocked the nation and demonized Japan as a sinister, alien predator. But aside from the invasion-wary cities of the West Coast, it was Adolf Hitler's Germany that most Americans focused on. This focus grew stronger as the Pacific battles receded farther into the distance and the great Allied invasion saga, from D-Day in 1944 through the Nazi surrender in the spring of 1945, unfolded. After all, Great Britain, our embattled friend, was the fountainhead of our culture. More recently, the over-run countries of Europe had been the homelands to millions of patriotic immigrant citizens.

For another thing, the war in the East was a good deal harder to visualize, to make sense of, for most people. The great battles of Europe were being waged across relatively compact, somewhat well-known, easy-to-follow terrain. The Russian front had been a different matter. Then again, not many Americans cared about what the Russians and the Germans were doing to one another. However, thousands of miles of open ocean separated the small, scattered Pacific islands and straits where the battles occurred. Aside from the families of the young Marines and soldiers and seamen and pilots who were paying with their lives to repel Japan's aggression, most Americans seemed to accept on faith that the Pacific war would sort itself out, sooner or later, in favor of the Allies.

They were both right and wrong.

Right, in that once the heroic triumph at Midway had finally blunted the stunning momentum of Japan's aggression and decimated its carrier fleet, Japan was essentially finished. The great forces of economics, technology, manpower, and mobilization now swung inexorably in America's favor. From mid-1942 onward, victory over Japan would be but a matter of time.

Wrong, in that "a matter of time" hardly began to suggest the stupendous toll of casualties the backpedaling Japanese warlords were ready and willing to inflict—not only on the counter-thrusting Allies, but on their own conscripted, overmatched soldiers. Their early fantasies of dominating a captive East Asia Co-Prosperity Sphere shattered, Japan's ruling military zealots now clung to an even more primitive and bloodthirsty strategy—a defensive war of attrition, in which their doomed island troops would annihilate so many hundreds of thousands of invading Americans that public opinion in the U.S. would swing toward a negotiated peace.

The Allied strategists had no illusions about the degree of the Rising Sun's murderous and suicidal commitment to resist. Nor did they underrate the appalling cost this would mean to American and British servicemen. Even as the two-pronged amphibious invasion force began gearing for its long dual trek across the Pacific, recapturing land masses along the way, Allied commanders furiously probed the possibilities for pulverizing Japan's warmaking power at its roots—a workable strategy for bombing of the Japanese homeland.

The complexities, unlike in Europe, were enormous—as vast as the almost limitless expanse of the Pacific theater.

A bombing strategy required a reliable bomber base. But where? China, a victim of Japan's aggression, offered a receptive mainland site—more or less. The problem was that China was at war not only with the Japanese, but with itself. Chiang Kai-shek's Nationalist army was battling the Communist forces of Mao Tse-tung. Thus, although the Mao-controlled eastern coast of China lay only a tempting 600 to 700 miles from the southwestern tip of Japan, the U.S. was obliged to carve out its airbases at Chentgu, a Nationalist city more than a thousand miles inland, in the south-central province of Szechuan. As early as 1942 the U.S. had sent Gen. Joseph W. Stilwell to assist Chiang. The Allied commander of the "CBI" theater, for China, Burma, and India, was to aid the Nationalists in upgrading and training his army, to pave the way for land and air operations against the Japanese.

The Allies' high hopes for CBI never fully panned out. The highly mechanized military operation needed a massive stream of supplies that rural, divided China could not offer. British-governed India, to the west of Chentgu, might have filled the bill. The United States had even positioned its new Twentieth Bomber Command, under my old Wichita friend General Wolfe, at Kharagpur, to the west of Calcutta. Between India and China lay Burma, and Burma had been overrun by Japan in January 1942. Stillwell's efforts to drive the Japanese out of northern Burma and open an overland supply route met with continual frustration. The alternative gambit—a Kharagpur-Chentgu airlift of 1,300 miles over the hump of the imposing Himalaya Mountains—resulted in many B-29 losses against the cloud-shrouded high peaks, delivering only a fraction of essential materiel.

In the face of these crushing conditions, the United States did in fact manage to get some B-29s over Japanese targets in late 1944— a Japanese steel plant on mainland Manchuria in September, an aircraft factory at Okayama on two raids during October, a similar plant on the home island of Kyushu a day after the second strike at Okayama, and then raids in November against Rangoon, Singapore, and back to Kyushu again. Finally, on December 18, an incendiary-bomb attack hit a Japanese supply base in the mainland city of Hankow—an attack that devastatingly revealed the vulnerability of wood-built Asian cities to the ravages of fire bombs. All these targets, save Manchuria of course, lay in the far western reaches of the Japanese home islands. Tokyo and the great industrial areas around it, farther to the northeast, lay beyond the practical range of CBI operations.

These raids were effective, and dramatically boosted hopes for the B-29. Unfortunately, the Himalayas exacted such excruciating expense, effort, and loss of airplanes that by early 1945 it was clear that a China-based air offensive would be worse than a waste of time. The Twentieth prepared to abandon its base in Kharagpur and move to the one remaining vantage-point for launching air raids against the enemy's home islands—the Pacific.

Until 1944, that sector had not been an option. The chain of small islands called the Marianas stood some 1,500 miles southeast of Tokyo—well within the 5,830-mile capacity of the B-29s. At least two of those islands, Tinian and Saipan, offered ideal terrain for air bases. The problem was that big NO VACANCY sign hung over the islands by the Japanese in their Pacific Blitz.

True, Adm. Chester Nimitz's gigantic Central Pacific fleet was churning west toward the islands with its aircraft carriers and shiploads of Marines and Army men. A conquest of the Marianas seemed likely by mid-summer of 1944. Airstrips on those islands still wouldn't guarantee the Allied bombers a hazard-free ticket to Tokyo—not as long as those deadly swarms of Japanese Zeroes could infest the airlanes halfway to the home islands and halfway back again, rising from an airstrip on an ugly flyspeck of an island called Iwo Jima.

Not that the new B-29s needed enemy gunfire to account for serious operational problems. As I had sensed from the outset, Superforts were glitch-prone, at least the first several hundred off the line in late 1943. Those glitches accounted for many heartbreaking crashes in the ill-fated Chentgu campaign. The very speed of their production back in Kansas, coupled with the high-pitched intricacy of their systems and moving parts, left the Superfortresses vulnerable to breakdowns—faulty cooling systems that could set engines on fire, snafus in the automatic firing control systems, leaking oil, fouled-up fuel transfer systems, even optical illusions caused by the huge curving windshields in front of the pilots. These flaws and malfunctions would be worked out in time. In war, however, time was as precious a commodity as bombs and gasoline.

Dorothy and I set up housekeeping in some rented rooms near the base at Pratt, and I plunged into intensive training in the B-29 in January and Februrary 1944. In February, when the 40th Bomb Group left

Pratt and headed for its combat assignment in India, I was sent to Clovis, New Mexico, for "transition training." They must have thought there'd be a lot of sandstorms in the Pacific, because that was normal weather in Clovis. I was temporarily assigned to the 20th Bomber Command, 409th Bomb Group Headquarters. There I flew an experimental, wide-bodied B-29, focusing on night flying and instrument skills. I also got checked out in the B-25, which is the bomber that Jimmy Doolittle flew in his celebrated raid on Tokyo in 1942. Dorothy and I lived in a hotel in Clovis, and picked the sand-grains out of our meals at the air base. We formed close friendships with some other young fliers and their wives—most memorably Waddy Young, a big, good-natured former football hero from Oklahoma. Waddy was just the kind of engaging, clean-cut kid that America liked to imagine fighting its wars. He proved to be one of my best pilots in the Pacific theater, and I developed a big-brotherly closeness with him, the exact sort of closeness I had trained myself not to develop with the junior officers back at Bassingbourn.

From March onward, when Dorothy and I returned to Pratt, my flying hours grew intensive—practice missions, gunnery missions, dummy bomb missions, even some cross-country flights. I had to subject myself to a new physical, and my old anxiety about my bum left eye resurfaced. Once again the Morgan luck held, and I passed—20/20 vision, it said on the form. At least as nearly as I could make out.

New planes were trickling in now, and I found myself assigned to command the 869th Bomb Squadron, 497th Group, 73rd Wing. My Operations Officer there was Maj. John Carroll, a trusted airman whom I'd known back at Bassingbourn.

Speaking of Bassingbourn, I could not have been more thrilled to follow the news of a white-hot new sidekick that had joined my old outfit, the Mighty Eighth, in its ever-thicker, ever-lengthier penetrations into the industrial heart of Nazi Germany. For more than a year, our bombers had been obliged to face the wrath of those Luftwaffe fighters without fighter escorts of our own, because ours and the RAF's lacked the range. But on January 11, 1944, when the Focke-Wulfs and Messerchmitts flew up to greet a force of 220 B-17s over the plane-assembly factories at Oschersleben and Halberstadt, they were stunned to find fifteen of their own shot down in rapid order, without inflicting a single fighter loss on our boys.

The new kid on the block was the streaking, slashing P-51, the Mustang of Army Air Forces legend. It was not all that new. Its prototype, the North American NA-73, had been in the air since 1940. Everyone had been impressed with its innovative wing design, which allowed it to fly at speeds in excess of 450 mph free of the air-compression stress that limited other fighters. It remained a subsidiary aircraft until an RAF test pilot had the bright idea late in 1943 to suggest replacing its relatively low-performance engine with a Rolls-Royce Merlin, with 1,550 horsepower and a supercharger. When disposable backup fuel canisters—drop-tanks—were fitted to the wings, the Allies suddenly found themselves in possession of a marauding beast with lightning speed, chattering guns, and a range of 2,600 miles. No German territory would be safe from the Allies. The Focke-Wulfs had met their match. The B-17 porcupines had sprouted a few extra quills.

My training at Pratt in 1944 was one of the happiest times of my life. I was making $688.23 a month, including $67.71 for flight pay, good money at the time. The role of Squadron Commander suited me fine. I enjoyed working with those young trainees just out of flying school. They reminded me, as John Wayne said in one of his later movies, of me. Our Group Commander, Col. Stud Wright, was a great fellow who took a liking to me and absolutely doted on Dorothy.

William Wyler's documentary hit the movie theaters that spring. Typical of Wyler's perfectionism, it had taken him and his editors a full year to get its forty-one running minutes just right. One rumor, probably true, had it that the director assembled and discarded twenty versions of the film before he was satisfied. Before releasing it to theaters, the War Department had submitted the film to the White House for a special screening. At its conclusion, President Roosevelt declared, "Every American should see this." Damn near every American did.

It opened on April 13, 1944, in 500 theaters around the country and was an instant sensation. Paramount distributed it on a nonprofit basis.

Moviegoers thrilled not only to the vivid aerial combat scenes that Wyler had recorded and the artful suspense surrounding the twenty-fifth return to base of our plane, but also to the arresting, hardboiled narration, written by the Paramount screenwriter Lester Koenig.

The reviewers raved over it. The *Chicago Daily Tribune* called it "one of the most thrilling and beautiful real-life air movies ever made." *Time Magazine* proclaimed, "The *Belle*'s mission takes its crew among prodigious scenes that have seldom been so well recorded." *Liberty* gushed, "Your heartbeat is tuned to the roar of the motors, the skull-shattering vibration of the guns . . . If you don't come away dizzy from the indescribable impact of air war, we're sorry for you!" *The New York Times* went farther over the top than anybody in its front page review. "No Hollywood producer could do what the United States Army Air Force has done with a film called *The Memphis Belle*."

Maybe not a Hollywood producer, but a Hollywood *director* did.

The Memphis Belle even had its world premier of the film in Memphis, complete with a long list of military and show-business celebrities. Only two of the principal personalities were missing.

The documentary went on to become a recognized classic of its kind. Its influence far outlived its day. Half a century into the future, Steven Spielberg would remark that "From a visual perspective, I was much more influenced by *The Memphis Belle* and John Ford's *The Battle of Midway* than I was by any of Hollywood's representations of the war."

That summer of 1944 was especially happy in another way, too. At Pratt, my bride, Dorothy, became pregnant with our first child.

Toward mid-summer, as I began to think about assembling my B-29 crew for assignment overseas, I got a phone call that sent me reeling right back to the cockpit of the *Memphis Belle*.

It was from Vince Evans. Vince was training bombardiers at Victorville, California. This Texas charmer had taken to the California life during our visit to Wyler's studios, and he was already grooming himself for the big Hollywood life he would lead out there after the war. Vince presently had himself a bit of a problem, and he thought that maybe an extended ride on my B-29 could help him out of it.

"Bob, I need to leave the country for a while," he told me over the phone. "Can you use a good bombardier out there in the Pacific when you go?"

Good bombardier? Vince Evans was the best I'd ever seen or heard of. Damn right I could use him. First I needed to know a little more of what this was all about.

Vince, it seemed, had taken a new bride—the beautiful Hollywood would-be starlet he had met at William Wyler's party named Jean Ames. No problem there, except for the fact that Vince already had himself a bride. He'd met Dinny in Walla Walla about the same time I'd met Margaret, and married her within days. As with a lot of impulsive wartime marriages, Vince and Dinny really did not have time to get to know one another before he shipped out. Two days of married life was all they had. Then all those months had gone by, his war over Europe and then the Twenty-sixth mission, and he'd met Jean on the Paramount lot, and one thing had led to another, and now Dinny was raging that she'd never give him a divorce . . .

Vince decided that on the whole, to paraphrase W. C. Fields, he'd rather be in the far Pacific. At least until things cooled down a little on his homefront, and excited people stopped tossing around the word bigamy.

"Sure, Vince," I said. "I can always use a good bombardier. Let me see what I can do."

I called up Captain Tom at the Pentagon, our public-relations liaison from the tour days. I explained to him what Vince and I needed. He said he'd see what *he* could do.

Colonel Wright called me down to his office a few days later and asked me, smilingly, if I could explain this strange order he was holding in his hand transferring one Captain Vincent Evans from the bombardier's training base at Victorville, California, directly to my squadron. The Colonel let me know that never, in all his military experience, had somebody transferred from one Army Air Forces command to another without going through the entire lengthy channels-and-procedure route. Could I perhaps shed any light on this?

I told him the story about Vince and what he'd accomplished as my bombardier on the *Memphis Belle*. Stud Wright laughed. "Good," he said. "He's accepted then. But believe me, you pulled off something that I've never seen happen before."

Well, that was kind of what we'd done for a living on the *Belle*.

That's how Vince Evans came to be a member of the 869th Bomb Squadron, 497th Group, 73rd Wing. He and Jean arrived at Pratt, Vince grinning that big photogenic grin of his. Dorothy and I put them up in an extra room in our apartment. Jean must have felt like she was in a backwards version of *The Wizard of Oz*—going from the Emerald City to Kansas in a sudden tornado—but she never complained.

There were two other men from the *Belle* I tried to recruit for my Pacific crew. Ideally, of course, I wanted to have every one of them, but that was impossible, and these two were extra-special.

One of them was Jim Verinis. With him as my second pilot I would have aimed my airplane at the moon, if so ordered, and we would have completed the mission. Cool, fearless, intelligent, and professional, Jim was just one of those men who had a glow about him. You were proud to be a friend of a man like Jim, proud to fight alongside him. He probably could have become a high-ranking officer if he'd had the zeal for it.

When I reached my old friend by telephone in his hometown of New Haven, I discovered that Jim had made other plans. He'd accepted an offer by the Army Air Force to attend engineering school at Yale, where he was picking up the additional skills to become a test pilot. "I like it here, Bob," he told me, with affection but firmness. "No war going on around Connecticut. I'm staying put."

He did more than that; he made valuable contributions to the overhauling and air-readiness of many types of plane—the B-25, the B-26, the B-24 as well as the beloved B-17. I respected his decision, and after the war he and I resumed our close friendship.

My other call was to a certain son of Irish rebels who'd been praised by the Queen of England. J. P. Quinlan needed no coaxing. Sure, he'd volunteer to fly again as my tailgunner. I was elated. I'd taken it for granted that the Army Air Force would honor my request that J.P. fly with me.

Bad judgment. J.P. signed up, and the brass promptly assigned him to another crew. There was nothing I could do about it, and I was beside myself. What if my phone call resulted in J.P. getting shot down somewhere in the Pacific with a crew of strangers?

Well, in fact the worst almost did happen. After racking up kills on three Japanese Zeros, J.P. did find himself and his crew bailing out from their crippled B-29 over Manchuria. However, the guy I called "Lucky Horseshoe" was far from finished. Captured by the Japanese—about the worst fate an American flier could imagine—he escaped and found his way to a band of Chinese guerrillas, who handed him a rifle to help them fight their way to a friendly landing strip. He ended his military career with a wall full of medals—the China War Memorial Medal, the Pacific Theater Ribbon with four stars and the Victory Medal to go with all the other honors he had picked up flying on the *Belle* over Europe.

We trained on at Pratt, and enjoyed our social lives, and waited for our chance to rejoin the war. It wasn't long in coming.

All of us had been following the progress of those two massive Allied fleets fighting their way from separate sources toward a convergence south of Japan. Admiral Halsey and Gen. Douglas MacArthur were having great success en route north from the Solomons. Having encircled and neutralized Rabaul with its 100,000-man Japanese garrison, this great force was now closing in on the Philippines. Meanwhile, Admiral Nimitz's fleet was slashing and conquering its way westward, months ahead of its schedule. Having retaken Tarawa and the Gilberts the previous November, the fleet sliced northwest through the eastern and central Marshalls in January 1944, then a month later claimed Eniwetok on the chain's northernmost tip.

Now the Marianas beckoned another thousand miles away, and with them the coveted footing from which to slam destruction against the Japanese home islands.

We read the newspapers, listened to the radio reports and cheered from Pratt as Operation Forager, the invasion of the Marianas, began in mid-June. It was a nasty fight, a prelude of nastier ones to come. Twenty thousand defenders, without a prayer of victory, mounted a suicide resistance that in three weeks resulted in their near-total extermination. Some 4,300 died in the final hours alone, in an insane banzai charge on July 7. Nearly 3,500 young Americans were cut down in the pointless carnage that could have been averted with a surrender.

Now the Marianas belonged to us, and with them, the air bases on the islands of Tinian and Saipan. Now Tokyo could expect visitors.

It was time for Bob Morgan to go back to work.

In early October 1944, the 497th Bomber Group finally received its full compliment of B-29's—twelve of them in each of four squadrons, including the 869th, which I commanded. With the approval of my crew, I christened our airplane the *Dauntless Dotty*, in honor of my pregnant wife.

There were a couple of things I needed to do before I flew west to give the Japanese hell. Neither of them was sanctioned, strictly speaking, by official Air Corps protocol. To put it another way, either one of them could have gotten me court-martialed. But a fellow who buzzed beach parties and Maine fishermen and even his hometown for fun wasn't going to let a thing like that worry him too much.

The first one had been accomplished back in August. I called it my Secret Mission, except that it didn't turn out to be so secret. Before daylight one morning I loaded up Dorothy and all her belongings onto a B-17 assigned to my squadron and flew her back to Asheville. We left early so as not to draw the attention of my commanding officer, Colonel Wright. Civilians in combat aircraft were a no-no, as I already knew from the *Belle* publicity tour.

The other escapade was what became famous in the 869th as the Great Liquor Run.

One of the young lieutenants in my squadron was the nephew of a major liquor distributor and nightclub owner in New York. The lieutenant told me that his liquor-mogul uncle had a proposition for the squadron. If we'd like to take some whiskey along to the Pacific war, we could have all we could carry at cost—if we'd just fly over to Long Island to pick it up. I revealed this sensitive intelligence to my group commander at the next opportunity. He perceived its strategic value at once, and instructed me to scramble into a convenient B-25, which we kept on the base for VIP-type occasions, and fly a preemptive raid on that Long Island liquor warehouse. I followed my orders, and within hours found myself looking on as several large trucks with New York license plates discharged their cargo into the B-25's hold.

Making my approach over the landing field back at Pratt, I heard the voice of our jovial Colonel, Stud Wright, on the radio: "Morgan, you make a real safe, smooth landing." I did as I was told. This was one occasion when Floorboard Freddie kept his foot carefully off the brake.

On October 10th, the 497th Group took wing for the Pacific.

Vince Evans and I suited up, climbed through the hatch of the *Dauntless Dotty,* and joined our crew for the long voyage over. The *Dotty* led the way. Colonel Wright flew with us as a second pilot, backed up by Capt. Andrew Mayse. We laid over at a base near San Francisco for six days, then launched out across the Pacific to Kwajalein, in the Marshall Islands, where the Army Air Force was making good use of a captured Japanese air base. Our next stop would not be India, where the rest of the Twentieth Bomber Command was, but Saipan.

I learned something about Stud Wright during that flight—and about military flying, too, I'm not ashamed to say. Throughout our training at Pratt, I had known the Colonel as a pretty relaxed, fun-loving guy. He'd winked a few times about certain hijinks of mine, he'd seemed amused at the string-pulling we'd done to get Vince Evans into our crew, and he generally softened his authority with a tinge of devil-may-care.

Once we were airborne en route to combat, all of that changed. Now Stud Wright's focus as a commander emerged. A good example of that was his insistence that we fly at our designated altitude—not a few hundred feet above it or below it, but *at that altitude*. I really had not thought about that as very important before. I had lots of occasion to think about it now, as the Colonel corrected me every time I deviated during that long trip across empty ocean. Nor did he let us use the automatic pilot. We kept on a strict three-man piloting rotation throughout the twenty-eight hours in the air to our destination.

I'd liked Colonel Wright for his easy good nature, and now I respected him for his tough discipline when it counted. He was preparing us for the rigors of aerial combat across the wide expanses of the Pacific theater—a form of combat that would require incredible stamina and constant alertness to our position in the air. Many of the very best American officers in the war were a lot like Stud Wright, I think, exacting, iron-willed men when it counted, but never completely divorced from a humane touch with their men.

Our enemies had a different set of attitudes about motivating and commanding men in combat. It's interesting to reflect on which side won.

Finally, on to Saipan. The *Dotty* was the second B-29 to land on the airstrip there, right behind Brig. Gen. Haywood S. "Possum" Hansell Jr., touching down to direct the Twenty-first Bomber Command on its great, historic mission. Gen. Hansell would also command the elements of the Twentieth, my outfit, that were assigned to these islands instead of to the Twentieth's main base at Kharagpur.

We were ready to go to war. All the more so when we checked those whiskey bottles we'd stored in the wing, and found that not a single one of them was broken.

CHAPTER

18

I landed in an island paradise that was also a cauldron of high tension and urgency.

Saipan was beautiful in ways that my old base near Cambridge could never match. A lush, green, mountainous jungle island of some forty-seven square miles, it offered warm ocean breezes instead of fog and mist, sugarcane and coconuts instead of stone fences and scrub-brush, crystal-clear shorewaters, and flaming purple sunsets that could hypnotize you.

Also unlike Cambridge, Saipan harbored some extremely unpleasant neighbors—armed and defiant Japanese resisters were holed up in caves, small in number yet sworn to die before surrendering. Firefights still erupted on the island, and the hardfaced Marines who guarded our airstrip were locked and loaded, ever-alert for a banzai attack.

The tensions ranged well beyond the chance of eating a hostile bullet for breakfast. The purpose of our presence on Saipan was to turn the great aggressor of the Pacific war into a reeling, exposed defender—to carry the war, by air, to the Rising Sun's homeland. The pressure from Washington to commence that task had grown enormous as the great naval fleets closed in. The fiercest proponent was the Commanding General of the Army Air Forces, Henry Arnold—the same Hap Arnold who had smilingly given me permanent buzzing privileges after the *Memphis Belle* had come home. Now, suffering through a string of four serious heart attacks, General Arnold was inundating his operational commanders with torrents of directives. *Bomb the home islands. Now. Massively. Don't tell me about the bad weather, the wind, the malfunctions, the fighter damage. Just bomb the damned islands!*

His vehemence wasn't hard to understand. We were 1,350 miles from those home islands now, with no Japanese navy left to stop us from closing all the way in. As everyone in the Pentagon now well understood, the minute that massed Allied troops hit those home beaches, the calculus would shift again, and shift horribly. The Japanese Imperial Cabinet, that cabal of warlords still in the grip of their morbid samurai-warrior delusions, were prepared to turn those beaches and the lands behind them into slaughtering-fields unmatched in human history. Secret projections already held that the cost of overrunning Japan would be more than a million Allied lives, most of them American.

Every bomb, then, that we could possibly deliver onto a Japanese city would cut that cost in a measurable way. Yes, we would now be unleashing large-scale death and suffering on civilian populations as well as military and industrial targets. As American servicemen trained to respect the interests of noncombatants, we felt grief at what we were now required to do, but we had no choice. The choice rested with the Japanese militarists, not us. Led by their zealot of a premier, Hideki Tojo—the icy bureaucrat famous for his steely gaze behind round spectacles—they had chosen in essence to turn their civilian population into a paramilitary force, by locating war-production centers in the midst of populated areas, and by stipulating that if invaders set foot on the sacred home islands, every citizen would be expected to fight to the death.

Though Tojo had resigned after the fall of Saipan, the mastermind of Pearl Harbor continued to press his countrymen for total war to the finish, drowning out the more temperate voices that had begun to speak of negotiation. One way or another—through strategic bombing attacks, or an invasion, or both—many innocent Japanese people were going to be killed.

As October lengthened into November, Hap Arnold was hearing several excuses as to why we hadn't yet taken the war to the Japanese homeland from our new base on Guam, and they were reasons that tried Hap's nonexistent patience even more.

We simply were not ready. Our pilots were still struggling to master the demands of controlling a B-29 in the best of circumstances, and to avert the many mechanical glitches that could, and did, bring those great fragile birds spiraling into the ocean. On top of that, our fliers had run into an added headache—the swirling demon-winds that seemed to guard the home islands like a mythic beast. It was these winds, in fact, that introduced Allied pilots and thus the rest of the world to the concept of the jet stream.

Japan lay under the path of the great northern jet stream, which circled the globe with its nearly constant flow of westerly winds that could reach velocities of 200 and even 300 miles an hour at altitudes of six to ten miles up. The lower reaches of these infernal streams lay within our flight plans. A head wind of this force could fight an approaching bomber almost to a standstill, and as for bombing accuracy, it could render all our instruments meaningless.

The unhappy carrier of this bad news was the newly arrived General Possum Hansell. Possum was a good young professional officer who lacked a certain edge of fire-breathing aggression, which would soon cost him dearly. In fairness to Possum, he was only relaying information—accurate information—passed on to him by his wing commanders, such as the capable General Emmett "Rosie" O'Donnell.

Those facts didn't make the message any more palatable to the stewing Hap Arnold. The General had reasons to stew that went beyond his hope of crippling Japan's power to resist the planned Allied endgame of invasion. He knew that his Army Air Force was now in a fight for its own legitimacy, its autonomy, and its very future.

Its opponent in this fight was its comrade-in-arms, the U.S. Navy.

It was one of those rivalries among the services that civilians always find it baffling to comprehend, but which have gone on for as long as men have worn uniforms and held weapons. We're all on the same side—right? So why doesn't everybody just pull together and get the job done?

The answer, I suppose, is human nature. The very qualities that make fighting men successful are the ones that make them competitive even with one another.

Admiral Nimitz's Navy had earned its right to strut a little in this operation. After all, this was the force that had destroyed those invincible-seeming Japanese carriers and planes at Midway and blazed its way to victory in every engagement since then. It was the Navy that had conquered the Marianas, along with its land force, the Marines, and some Army troops. So now, naturally, the Navy wanted to lead the charge to the home islands. The Army Air Force? In the Navy's historic view, the Army Air Force was a backup show, a tactical arm of the traditional strategic operations. Hap Arnold was acutely aware of these views. His over-riding anxiety was not simply that his bombers were not yet performing up to full potential, it was that the Air Forces, still under the Army's command chain, by the way, might be facing a fight over its fundamental legitimacy. Would it be allowed to mature into its destiny as a service arm equal to the Navy and the Army—or would its parts be subsumed, picked clean, by the two major branches and relegated forever to a fringe role in the defense of America?

Just now, Hap Arnold could see the needle pulling strongly toward the latter.

We pilots down at ground level sensed these organizational tensions only vaguely. As for the readiness question—well, there *was* no question. *We* were ready. Hell, we always felt ready. That's part of what made us pilots. Since we couldn't just take off and bomb Japan on our own, we concentrated on adapting to our new Pacific-island world.

Vince Evans adapted in a hurry. It didn't take him long—I'd estimate about seven minutes—to discover that Saipan contained a base hospital, and that the base hospital contained nurses. Not long after that, he was hitting me up for the use of my jeep so that he could squire one or another of these young ladies around the island. Same old Vince. It wasn't any of the "same old" for me. I couldn't join my buddy on his new rounds of hijinking, because unlike in Europe, I was no longer just another pilot. My position as Squadron Commander meant that I was constantly in touch with my unit, solving problems, checking on maintenance, and keeping up a strictly-business image. I played some cards and shot some dice with Vince, and we gabbed whenever we could, but outside the airplane, now, we went our separate ways. I take comfort in the assurance, though, that my Texas pal did enough carousing for both of us.

We'd set up tents almost as soon as we'd landed on Saipan, and started preparing for our practice runs. Yes, tents, to house us while Seabees built the Quonset huts. No more of the gracious country-estate living that the Mighty Eighth had enjoyed at Bassingbourn, and no London to visit, either, between missions.

But even under these spartan conditions, the Morgan luck held. Back in Pratt I had taken notice of an enterprising young private in my squadron, a fellow named Herman Ginsburg. Private Ginsburg had demonstrated a knack for such sleight-of-hand as producing nice juicy steaks where no steaks were thought to exist. Now Private Ginsburg made it his mission to see that I had the finest living quarters of anybody on the island. I must admit, the kid had talent. The Squadron Operations Officer, John Carroll, and I had planned to live in the same tent. Private Ginsburg pitched our tent on a scenic point overlooking the ocean, with a long drop down to the beach (off-limits, thanks to those lurking Japanese). Then he put a wood flooring in the tent. Then he found a way to run hot and cold water to it. It wasn't the Savoy, but it wasn't bad. It was better, for instance, than my Commanding Officer's! As for Private Ginsburg, he very quickly became Corporal Ginsburg, and then Sergeant Ginsburg, a reward for his excellent efforts on behalf of the Squadron Commander.

Speaking of the Squadron Commander, he received quite a rude jolt over drinks one night not long after our arrival. Stud Wright took a long sip from his glass, fixed his level gaze on me and said, "By the way, Morgan, you don't think that little trip of yours back to Asheville with Dorothy got by me, do you?" A giant *Uh-oh!* started to form itself in my brain. I could see myself spending the rest of the war humping corrugated tin for the Seabees. Then I noticed that the Colonel was chuckling. "I knew it all along," he said. "I didn't say anything because I wanted to see you get Dot back safely. A car trip would have been hard on her, given her condition."

As I said, that's the kind of officer who makes a guy want to go out and win a war for him. In the end, it wasn't running-water comfort that we were looking for here in the Pacific. It wasn't laughs over drinks. It was action. We didn't have to wait long for that.

The 869th Squadron was in the air on October 28, running a practice mission against the tiny island of Truk, in the chain north of Saipan. With that tuneup under our belts, we took off a few days later for a combat site that would soon become a timeless symbol of American valor—a nasty little chunk of volcanic rock halfway between Saipan and Tokyo that went by the name of Iwo Jima.

For an island of only about eight square miles, Iwo Jima amounted to a continental-sized problem for the advancing Allied forces. Its rocky terrain contained two airstrips on which squadrons of Japanese Zeros lay in wait for the fleets of Superforts that were soon to be flying overhead on their Saipan-Tokyo round trips. That wasn't all. Within a couple months, those same Zeros would be slashing in for hit-and-run attacks against our B-29s on the ground at Saipan, until fighters from our Seventh Air Force struck back and showed them the dangers of a dogfight with American gunslingers.

Iwo Jima had to be neutralized and its airstrips taken. A gigantic Allied force was gathering itself for that task—an armada of some 880 ships carrying 100,000 Marine assault troops, secretly scheduled to cross the Pacific from Hawaii and storm the island with its 22,000 defenders dug deeply into the fortified tunnels that crisscrossed the island. That force would not reach Iwo Jima until mid-February. In the meantime we men of the Twentieth Air Force would have to dodge those Zeros as best we were able, and cause as much damage as we could to Iwo Jima from the air.

We ran our first bombing mission over Iwo on November 5. It turned out to be an easier run than we'd expected. We bombed in daylight at 20,000 feet, and did not see much resistance either from antiaircraft guns or fighters. All our airplanes returned to base. We came back again three days later, and this time we saw some Zeros in attack formation, but they did not press too close. I guess they were measuring us for future sorties.

As practice runs for what lay ahead, these missions did a lot of good. But as the invading Marines were to discover in a few months, our bombs did little damage against the deeply entrenched and heavily armed defenders of the ugly, bristling sulfurous island.

As the 869th settled into its new tropical digs, other squadrons were dropping in from the turquoise sky day by day. The island swarmed with activity—Seabee workers, shirtless in the hot sun, labored to finish off airstrips and build new control towers, hospitals, Quonset barracks, and mess halls to accommodate the rapidly-forming Twentieth and Twenty-first Bomber Commands. Marines, eyes peeled for Japanese snipers, patrolled with their rifles. And the inventory of Superfortresses continued to grow, lengthening their line on the runways, ready to raise hell.

Before that happened, Hap Arnold had a little more hell of his own to raise. The targets were his subordinate generals here in the Marianas.

As delay piled on delay for the onset of our bombing campaign over the home islands, the rumor had spread across the three-island cluster of Saipan, Tinian, and Guam that Possum Hansell's job was on the line. Popularity wasn't the issue—everyone liked this lean, youngish, kindly officer. Nor was it ability, strictly speaking. As a strategic planner, General Hansell was brilliant. His visionary work on the Air War Plan, a précis of how the U.S. would fight World War II in the air and what it would require, had brought him lasting distinction.

The commanders in Washington were looking for a sparkplug, a gladiator, a general who could huff and puff and *blow* those damned Superforts from Saipan to Tokyo, if need be, regardless of the obstacles. The time-interval for Hansell to prove himself as that warrior was drawing dangerously short.

The fact was that Hap Arnold had his eye on such a gladiator, and Hansell's days with the Twenty-first were already numbered. No one, as yet, knew that.

By mid-November, the pilots and crews of the 73rd Wing were itching to kick off on that famously rumored first trip to Japan. We hoped and figured the target would be Tokyo. Late in the second week, word spread that it was finally going to happen, and we started to prepare ourselves and our airplanes.

On the night of November 21 I took a telephone call that made my heart pound with excitement and pride. I learned that we were about to go, but I learned something more than that as well.

The call was from Rosie O'Donnell himself, the raffish ex-football player from West Point who commanded our 73rd Wing. "Morgan," the General said, "we're going to run this mission in the next day or two. When we do, I'd like for you to lead the mission. And I would like to go with you."

I tried to keep my voice detached and military. "Yes, Sir," I responded. "I know you can go on any airplane you want to, General, and I'm honored that you picked mine. I'd appreciate you telling me why, if you don't mind."

General O'Donnell said, "Well, you've had a little experience over Europe, I hear—you got through twenty-five over there. I just hope that we get through the twenty-sixth, if I go with you."

Ah, it was just like the old days! The brass wanting to fly along because of Morgan's reputation. Only the presence of Jim Verinis could have made me any happier.

What I could not have known then, and did not know until years later, was the extreme uncertainty that Rosie O'Donnell was covering with his famous bravado. He was not alone. All up and down the chain of command, anxiety and doubt hovered over this first mission virtually until our bombers' wheels started turning toward the take-off line. Many officers still wondered whether such a mission should be undertaken without participation by the Navy. No one could predict whether the raid would be a success or a catastrophe—not General Arnold in Washington, who was determined to move on Tokyo at all costs, not Possum Hansell, whose hesitations reflected his respect for his subordinate officers down on the flying lines, and certainly not those line officers themselves. Rosie O'Donnell was a brave man who insisted on flying missions with his 73rd Wing. In the hours leading up to this momentous first mission to Tokyo, O'Donnell had expressed his concerns—about weather, the airworthiness of the Superforts, the preparedness of pilots and crew—to General Hansell.

Possum's terse reply settled the question at once. "If you're not willing to lead your Wing on a daylight mission, General, I will turn the Wing over to General Roger Ramey, my deputy, who is anxious to do so."

General O'Donnell never wavered after that.

We lined up to fly to Tokyo early the next day, but the mission was scrubbed because of bad weather. In Washington, Hap Arnold must have hit the ceiling.

Two days later, however, the big four-bladed propellers turned, and nothing stopped us.

Friday, November 24, 1944, came up clear and shimmering across the Pacific. It was a spectacular morning, a golden-purple early tint on the horizon beyond the palm trees. The roar of hundreds of giant R-3350 engines swept across the vast Japanese-built airstrip we'd finished hacking out of the jungle and renamed Isley Field, as pilots began maneuvering 111 enormous B-29s onto the flight line—four groups, sixteen squadrons.

The *Dauntless Dotty* was at the head of the line. With General O'Donnell in the seat beside me, I would pilot the first Allied airplane to release a bombload over Tokyo since Jimmy Doolittle's inspirational bootstrap raid back in 1942.

The anxious questions of the previous days and months had not abated, and tension ran high that morning. Engine overheating remained a major unsolved problem with the Superfortress, and the longer one of them sat on the ground with its propellers turning, the greater that hazard increased. Beyond that, nobody was sure what to expect once we were in the air for our thirteen-hour, 1,350-mile round trip to the target and back. Intelligence had told us to expect fighters. How many? Had they improved since our runs over Iwo Jima? Where would they pick us up? What about ground artillery as we approached the target? What about those swirling, confusing winds that whipped above the great city? Would they waft our bombs away from the critical damage-points?

Would we make it back? Were these new airplanes that reliable?

It was tense, but it was exhilarating too. Those who watched us take off—the ground crews, the officers in the tower, the newspaper people—later agreed that it was an awesome sight—Superfortress after Superfortress getting the go signal, revving its engines to full military power, its huge silvery shape taking on thrust as it barreled toward takeoff. The runway at Isley Field ended at the edge of a cliff over the ocean, a 500-foot dropoff. Those who watched us would never forget the sight of plane after plane clearing that cliff, dropping briefly out of view, to cool off those red-hot engines near the ocean's surface, then reemerging moments later, airborne, lifting, picking up speed, headed for Japan.

Dauntless Dotty in the lead.

Once in flight, we didn't circle and form up, as we had in England. The distance we had to travel made that irrelevant. We simply adjusted our airspeed according to our place in formation, every pilot falling into place, creating a great elongated necklace of bombers. We took our time climbing to our combat altitude of 32,000 feet, six miles up, nearly a mile higher than I'd ever flown in Europe. A hundred miles offshore of Japan left plenty of time for that. Nor did we worry much about tight formation as long as we were over the Pacific. We didn't want that well-known maneuverability problem to exhaust us before we hit our bombing run. A Pacific mission was a hauling job as much as it was a combat job, and the haul was long. Tight formations, like combat altitude, could wait until landfall.

Halfway to the target we passed to the left of Iwo Jima with those notorious airstrips. If Japanese fighters were going to hit us, they were going to hit us now. We tightened up a bit and our gunners scanned the skies. A few Zeros came up to meet us, but they kept a respectable distance.

Japan.

A beautiful strand of elongated islands curving northeastward in the ocean. So peaceful-looking from 32,000 feet, our bombing altitude.

Closer. Tighter in formation. We'd been briefed that more than 3,000 Zeroes were clustered around Tokyo. We kept a sharp lookout for their onslaught. Only a few appeared in the distance, and of these only a handful mounted serious runs at us.

Fuji, now, to our left.

The sacred 10,000-year-old volcano, snow-covered, almost perfectly tapered from its base to the spherical opening of its cone, infinitely beautiful, rising in its two-mile height. The mythical origin of Japanese life, the dwelling-place of the samurai gods. Seldom visible through its thick cloud cover, but visible today, taking the sun. Our lucky day.

Tokyo, embracing its bay. Small but clearly visible beneath us.

We lined up into our bombing run. Eighty-eight of our 111 planes had made it to the target. It was going to be so easy. Hardly any fighters, ineffective flak. We had just flown nearly 1,500 miles to the epicenter, the lair, of an aggressor-nation whose navy and airplanes and infantry had spread terror and bloody domination across half the globe; had caused the peoples of China and America to tremble. We had breached the airspace above its most populous city, and now we were going to bomb it. Simple as that.

How eerily uncomplicated it felt. Almost dreamlike.

The bombardiers of the lead group—my group—would do the actual sighting. As in Europe, the trailing crews would drop on the lead. Once again, my comrade Vince Evans would be the triggering bombardier. His accuracy would determine everyone else's.

I heard Vince's voice coming over my headset on the intercom. He could see the target, but the chronic winds and the crosswinds down below us were going to make it difficult for him to get an accurate bead on the target, even with his trusty Norden bombsight that supplemented the B-29's radar.

The damn crosswinds. I later learned that winds like those had been the salvation of Japan in battles past. A typhoon in 1281 swamped the Mongol armada that would have overrun the islands. A divine wind, the Japanese had called it. "Divine wind"—the meaning of *kamikaze*.

None of that mattered now. We locked into our bomb run.

This would be my first experience attacking an open city. I didn't like that part of the mission, but it could not be helped. Unlike the Germans, the Japanese integrated their industrial and military plants within their civilian districts. Amidst the shops and museums and office buildings of Central Tokyo lay several important manufacturers of war materiel—the Musashino aircraft engine plant, the Fukagawa cylinder plant, the Hitachi complex that made navy accessories, the Mitsubishi steel works that turned out cylinders and steel ingots, and countless smaller shops that contributed to the war effort. They had to be destroyed.

Now we were over the target. Vince had opened the bomb bay doors, and on the instant the needles lined up, our 500-pound demolition bombs fell away. We felt the familiar lurch of an airplane whose weight had just lessened radically. The *Dotty* had dropped the first load on Tokyo since Doolittle. In fact, we were one of only twenty-four planes to hit the primary target. The clouds and winds forced the rest of our bombers toward other sites.

When it was over I put the Superfortress into a left turn—I always remembered that turn, because it took us directly over Mt. Fuji—and we led the Wing away from the target, back to Saipan.

We didn't get out of there scot-free. Two of our planes went down—one due to the B-29's bugaboo, mechanical failure, the other in one of the most bizarre incidents of the Pacific air war. A bomber piloted by Lt. Sam Wagner, of the 870th Squadron, was actually struck by one of the few Zeros that even got close to us. No one who saw it was sure why it occurred. Some believed it was on purpose, a kamikaze attack, others claimed the Zero had been crippled by gunfire and collided with the Superfort accidentally. Whatever the cause, Sam's was the only plane lost to an enemy in combat on that run. There were no parachutes.

There must have been a lot of deep, silent reflection among the pilots and crewmen during those long hours of the return flight to Saipan. There sure was on the *Dotty*. It had been easier than we'd expected, far easier, to deliver this first strike at Japan's war-industry center. "Too quiet," as the cowboy heroes said in the movies when they walked into a seemingly deserted town. The Rising Sun had not been expecting us this time. They would be expecting us from now on.

CHAPTER
19

It didn't take long for the grim realities to set in. At our debriefing on Saipan, we learned that the raid had not been satisfactory in terms of accuracy, a refrain we would hear with mounting vehemence in the ensuing weeks. My squadron was singled out as one of the few that hit its target—Vince had not lost his touch even in those demon-winds. Bomber Command decided we would have to go back there very quickly, on November 27.

I received some good news of a very different sort the day after our return to the base—a letter from Dot informing me that I was a Daddy. Our daughter, Sandra Lea Morgan, had been born. A couple of weeks later Dorothy sent along a clipping that announced Sandra's birth and a newspaper photo of her that I devoured despite its graininess. Two days after that came a fine color photograph of our young princess.

I'd looked forward to that news, but its wallop was even stronger than I'd expected. In a time of violent death on a scale that history had never before known, Bob and Dot Morgan had brought one tiny new life into the world. I thought about that a lot in the ensuing days and weeks as the destruction around me and below me increased beyond belief. I prayed to my Command Pilot that Sandra's world would be a more peaceful one than the hell-on-earth that now boiled around me.

Flying off into combat would never again be quite as easy for me, with the image of this new little angel in my mind.

*   *   *

Our bombing raids to the home islands had been a long time coming, but once we began, our generals poured it on. We sent eighty-one planes back on the twenty-seventh, and on the twenty-ninth we hit them again. I stayed behind on this mission. John Carroll led the group, and an airplane in our squadron had a scary near-miss on the return home. The navigator lost his way, the airplane burnt up nearly all its fuel searching for Saipan, and when it finally did touch down it actually ran out of gas before it could taxi to the parking area.

It was during these early missions that the fighter planes from Iwo Jima strafed our landing fields in the Marianas, destroying a few of our bombers and sending Hap Arnold's blood pressure back into the stratosphere.

If November had shown us how difficult it was going to be to bomb Japan from high altitudes through those twisting, gusting winds, December introduced us to a worse fact of life in the Pacific skies—high casualties.

It was on a December 3 raid on the Musashino aircraft plant in Tokyo that the 73rd wing caught its first real hell from an aroused Japanese fighter force. Six Superfortresses were shot down in a concentrated Zero attack on the 500th Bomb Group, which led the mission. Two colonels in the lead plane parachuted out, were captured, and imprisoned for the duration of the war, not a pleasant prospect with this particular enemy. Fifteen more planes suffered heavy damage among the sixty over the main target, and again the winds scattered our bombs like confetti over the terrain.

An Army Air Forces press release dated December 4 assured American newspapers, in effect, that we were bombing the hell out of Tokyo and Japan. The truth was that we were doing a lousy job and everyone in the Marianas knew it, and everyone knew that something was going to have to change. Including Possum Hansell.

My own work was satisfactory, though, or at least so I thought. On December 6, I was preparing to board the *Dauntless Dotty* on a new and dangerous kind of specialty mission—a three-bomber night-time sortie over Tokyo to analyze the weather conditions and drop some incendiary bombs on the city. This would be our first nighttime raid of any kind over Japan's largest city, and the *Dotty* would fly the lead. As I stood on the airstrip beside the plane with Vince and the rest of my crew, I was surprised to see a jeep carrying Colonel Wright come hurtling toward us and screech to a stop. The Colonel hopped out, marched officiously over to where I was standing, and barked, "Major Morgan will not be allowed to fly this mission!"

I gaped at him. For a moment I was speechless. I wasn't sure I'd heard him right, even though he was just inches from my face. "Could the Colonel please explain," I stammered, trying to stay within the official language of protocol, "why Major Morgan will not be allowed to fly on this mission?"

"Well," Stud Wright snapped, "the reason is that *Lieutenant Colonel* Morgan is going to fly this mission!" He reached out to pump my hand.

That sounded like a good enough reason to me. I climbed inside, glowing from my latest promotion, and set off to provide a very bad night for Tokyo. When we reached the target, we saw that the Japanese had not yet turned off their city lights. There was practically no opposition, the skies were clear and for once we did some serious damage. Too serious, in fact, to bear a lot of thinking. Through the city's frantic searchlights, we could see the results of these firebombs as we banked away. Flames were already starting to ravage the target area. Nasty business. But it had to be done.

Aside from moments of success such as this one, however, the Pacific bombing campaign so far was an exercise in futility.

In the three biggest of our five missions to the Japanese home islands, we had put ninety, eighty-nine, and seventy-eight giant bombers in the air. Of these, seventy-one, sixty-three, and forty-eight had reached their primary targets. This was a stark testament to the rough weather and the temperamental nature of the B-29s, but it was also an index of rapidly increasing fighter opposition—swarms of up to 500 Zeros now, coming up to meet us.

There were the exhausting long-haul hours over the vast Pacific. The constant threat of Japanese fighters prowling above Iwo. The rapidly hardening resistance once we'd reached the home islands. Those damnable swirling jetstream winds that seemed to bat our bombs away from our targets. The rising impatience of Bomber

Command, of the Navy, of the American public to get this ghastly business over with. In Europe, air power was helping to grind the Nazi war machine into fine powder. The Mighty Eighth, my old outfit, was now pulverizing German cities and oil targets with more than 1,800 bombers at a time. The once-potent industries of the Ruhr were smoking rubble. Heavy fighting remained in Europe—the unexpected Battle of the Bulge was about to erupt in the Ardennes— but overall, a sense of the inevitable had begun to animate the Allies.

Why couldn't we hold up our end and close things out here in the Pacific?

It all started to build up in us, the exhaustion, the pressure, the frustration, and good men were suffering from it. We began seeing our first instances of shattered nerves and combat fatigue—crew members asking to be relieved of duty, and not just enlisted men either. A major and a captain from the 870th squadron were among those who asked out.

Half a world removed from the kinds of urban stress-relief that London had offered, growing a little weary of palm trees and gorgeous sunsets, we fliers in the Marianas tried to keep ourselves combat-ready. Of course, we were alert for such pleasures as came our way. On December 16, we celebrated the grand opening of our Squadron Club—a Quonset hut with some tables and chairs. The drink of choice that night was Purple Passion, a concoction of 180-proof grain alcohol and grape juice, and light on the grape juice, please. The alcohol came our way thanks to the estimable Sergeant Ginsburg. Ditto the hangovers. By the eighteenth, the date of our next mission, the hangovers had begun to wear off a little.

The night before that liftoff, my head still throbbing from the Purple Passion, I prayed again. I prayed a lot during that war, but with a new daughter back home, I was praying even more. Nothing complicated. I just asked my Command Pilot to help me. Apparently, the lines of communication up there were holding pretty well.

The 869th got nine planes off on that mission of December 18. We hit the Mitsubishi aircraft plant at Nagoya, which we'd struck before and would again. The bombing was pretty good, but we took a lot of flak. All nine of our squadron's Superforts got home, but the Wing lost four planes on that raid. Forty-four more American boys were added to a casualty list that had no end in sight.

Christmas season was approaching. If Christmas at Bassingbourn had seemed a little bleak sometimes, Christmas on a tropical Pacific island could be downright gloomy. We did the best we could. My diary for December 20, 1944, reads: "Christmas party at Gen. O'Donnell's quarters. Good food. Turkey, etc." It shows that at one point the General remarked to me, "Morgan, we're here for a long time. So don't think about going home anytime soon."

I had already resigned myself to that likelihood. But as much as I respected Rosie O'Donnell, hearing it put that way did not exactly make me want to break into a chorus of "Deck the Halls With Boughs of Holly."

On December 22 we hit Nagoya again. I did not go on this one. Four of the 869th's nine planes had to turn back for mechanical reasons, and it was a poor mission on everybody's part. The next day we all caught hell all along the chain of command, from General O'Donnell on down.

Catching hell was part of our job description, and we took it like men, as usual. But we knew that the generals knew that it wasn't just a question of sloppy execution. There was the whole maintenance problem to consider. Those high-strung, temperamental Superforts needed more close attention on the ground—constant engine changes, for example—than any combat plane ever built, and they just weren't getting it. We did not have enough ground-crew maintenance people, to say nothing of top-line crew chiefs, to assign one group to each airplane, so the crews rotated, going from plane to plane as the need required. They did better than I might have expected, having been spoiled by Joe Giambrone and his boys. They did heroic service, in fact. But they were overmatched by the volume of their tasks, and it showed in the air. Abort. Abort. Abort.

Something was going to have to change, and change drastically. Everyone on the islands knew it.

On Christmas Eve we airmen threw a party with the men of the Second Marine Division. We exchanged many toasts. We thanked them for taking the Mariana island chain, and they thanked us for coming over and bombing Japan. It was an interlude of deeply felt respect and goodwill among men who understood each other's valor and sacrifices.

Christmas Day felt like a big empty room without my wife and the new daughter I had never yet held and kissed. I missed them very badly that day. I missed them even more while a few Japanese planes raided us for about two and a half hours that night. They destroyed a B-29 on the ground, but luckily took no casualties.

Two days later it was business as usual—another mission, another nine-plane liftoff for the 869th. Eight planes hit the target and returned. The missing one was mine. I had to abort two and a half hours out, due to an engine that failed. Colonel Wright was not too happy about it. Neither was I. It was getting to be that kind of war.

The next day, December 29, the unhappiness got amplified. Every squadron and group commander caught hell from a keyed-up General Hansell about the usual topics—poor bombing, the many turn-backs and aborted missions, too few planes over the target. I suppose we deserved it, to an extent. The horrible conditions were affecting the job performance of some of the men. I said as much to the men of my own squadron the next day, New Year's Eve.

On New Year's Day 1945 the Japanese added to everybody's holiday spirits with another social call from Iwo Jima and another B-29 from my squadron strafed and destroyed on the ground.

It was about this time that the Seventh Air Force got busy against these nuisance raids. Of the seven planes that attacked us in January, our fighter boys shot four down, and after that, they didn't visit us too much anymore. Before that, our bombers had flown a couple of missions against the Iwo airfields in December, messing up their runways at least temporarily.

It was too bad that our operations against the home islands could not have gone as well. The fact was that as January 1945 began, our losses and aborts summoned grim comparisons to the attrition rate in the early weeks of the Mighty Eighth's campaign over occupied France.

On January 3, ninety-seven planes of the 73rd Wing took off on an incendiary-bomb raid on Nagoya. Only fifty-seven made it to the target. Of these, five were shot down and more than twenty damaged by a furious fighter attack. This raid featured another grotesque but instructive incident of war. A Plexiglas gunnery blister on one of the bombers got shot away by enemy fire, and the gunner got sucked through the gaping hole. He was saved from death or torture in a prison camp only by a connective harness he had fashioned for himself. He hung outside the plane, whipped and buffeted by the frigid winds, until his fellow crewmen pulled him in. From then on, harnesses were standard equipment for our gunners, and some of them did save lives.

My squadron flew a good mission without me on January 5. Then, four days after that, on a raid against that Musashino aircraft plant in Tokyo, calamity struck again.

The Command sent seventy-two Superforts out. The weather above Japan was so bad that the bombers never managed to achieve a formation. We went in individually. Only eighteen reached our primary targets, thirty-three hit targets of opportunity, but that wasn't the worst.

The 869th really caught it that day. Among the casualties was Waddy Young, the good-natured Oklahoma football player whom Dot and I had befriended at Pratt. His plane was attacked and damaged by Zeros from Iwo Jima on its way home, and Waddy attempted a ditching in the ocean—an almost impossible task for a B-29.

I was sickened when I saw his plane go down. He'd had "Waddy's Wagon" painted on his fuselage. He had this wonderful wife. If I'd had any illusions that I was getting hardened to the deaths of good young men, this one set me straight. After landing at Saipan I sought and received permission from Colonel Wright to fly back out there with my crew and search for Waddy and his men. I thought I had a good fix on where he'd ditched.

We searched for twenty hours. We saw nothing in those waters except a Japanese fishing boat. I don't want to dwell on the memory of what we did to that boat—let's say we were not in the best of moods.

I had to write the letter home informing Waddy's family of the loss. This was one of the things a squadron commander had to do. I'd noticed that I was writing a lot of these letters lately. This one was one of the hardest. I think back on Waddy even today. "Waddy's Wagon." Damn.

We flew a mission on January 14, hitting the Mitsubishi plant in Nagoya. This mission was bad. Upward of 500 Japanese fighters descended on the forty planes that reached the target. Six Superfortresses were shot down, and many others were damaged.

Still others, as usual, did not even make it to the home islands. Among those was a bomber flown by Capt. Leonard Cox. One of his overheated engines caught fire about two and a half hours out of Saipan. Like Waddy, Captain Cox tried to ditch. Like Waddy, he failed. The plane exploded on contact with the water. Only four of the eleven crewmen survived and were rescued. Captain Cox was not among them.

The war had started to stick in my throat. In a little more than a week, I had lost several of my men including two promising, courageous captains. Leonard Cox was a boy cast in my own mold, a playful, fun loving fellow, nonmilitary like me, hard to keep under control. He was always breaking the small rules, and I was always dressing him down in my role as Squadron Commander, but deep down we understood and valued one another. Cox was about life. He'd even had a child born just before he left the States. Now I had another hard letter to write.

I wrote it on January 16, and then I counted the number of such letters I'd had to write since taking command of this squadron. They totaled twenty-eight. My God. Twenty-eight letters to families of lost airmen. We weren't even a measurable drop in the bucket of losses this sector of the war had claimed. From everything we'd been able to learn, the losses were only going to get worse, much worse, before they got better.

To make matters worse, the next day I bade farewell to Vince Evans, my one remaining comrade-in-arms from the Mighty Eighth and the *Memphis Belle*. A good friend of his, Col. Sy Bartlett of the 315th Wing, showed up on Saipan. Bartlett had connections with the Army Air Force public-relations arm back in Washington, and he began talking about the promotional value of a brief trip home for Vince. I got the impression that this hiatus would also give Vince the chance to clean up some of those sticky marital problems he had tried to escape by flying off with me to the Pacific war. At any rate, I could not stand in my friend's way. It was tough seeing him go. I never saw a bombardier the equal of him. Or a ladies' man, either.

Given all of these losses, I was in no mood to fly any more missions the next few days. I was drained.

But not without hope.

A rumor had started making its way around the base two or three days earlier. If it were true, I knew that things would soon be different in this air campaign. If it were true, then God help the Japanese. If it were true, those latter-day Samurai butchers that had seized control of Japan's parliament and declared themselves the supreme warriors of the world were about to meet a warrior who dwarfed even their ferocity. If the rumor were true, Gen. Haywood S. Hansell Jr. had been relieved as commander of the Twenty-first Bomber Command, and would shortly be replaced by Gen. Curtis LeMay.

I respected Possum Hansell, but I knew about LeMay. I'd seen what he had done in Europe during his rapid rise from major to general. I had heard about his exploits in China, getting those B-29s over the hump to nip and tear at Japan. My first thought when I heard the rumor was, *things will be different when he shows up*. I knew that different meant good when LeMay went to work.

The rumors were true. The decision had actually been made on January 6 by Hap Arnold. In the intervening days, LeMay closed out his affairs in the Kharagpur. He arrived in the Marianas on January 19, 1945. Typical of him, he did not blow in with great fanfare, but showed up almost unobtrusively and kept a low profile during the ceremonies organized to welcome him. One officer noticed him trying to conceal his lighted pipe in his pants pocket during photographs. He minimized the embarrassment to Hansell by explaining to the journalists on the base that the move made administrative sense. The CBI bases were being reduced and the Twentieth and Twenty-first Bomber Commands were now to be consolidated as the new Twentieth Bomber Command. LeMay, a Major General at age thirty-nine, outranked Brigadier General Hansell. Possum, for his part, was a gentleman to the last. He recognized LeMay's strengths for what they were. "He may easily be the best combat commander today in the Army Air Forces," he remarked to an aide, and quietly prepared for his transfer of duty back to Washington.

LeMay's arrival was not an immediate hit with everyone on Saipan. Hansell had been a popular and somewhat suave general. LeMay offered a far darker first impression. With his jowly, scowling face, his thick dark hair, and smoldering gaze, he gave many the impression that running a bombing campaign wasn't quite stimulating enough for him, that he wouldn't mind taking apart a few Quonset huts with his bare hands. His speaking style—barely audible sentence fragments murmured through clenched teeth—reinforced his aura as a borderline sociopath. His full-bore command style did nothing to diminish that impression.

In my book, though, he was just what we needed—a scholar-warrior, a thinker as well as a man of action, a canny and aggressive commander who would beat the Japanese by the force of his will, if nothing else. Suddenly the blood was back in my veins. I could sense that some of the boys in my squadron thought maybe I'd had it, and now, reenergized, I decided to prove otherwise. On January 27 I was back in the *Dotty*'s cockpit for that day's mission to Tokyo.

I discovered that the war hadn't gotten any easier since I'd taken my breather.

The Zeros hit us like a rain of meteors. There must have been hundreds of them, swooping in wave after wave for close-encounter attacks. Our losses were the worst of the Pacific campaign to date—nine Superfortresses shot down and many more damaged. The Zeros followed us after we'd left the coast, staying on our tails fifty or sixty miles out over the ocean. Our gunners fired and fired into the thick swarm, and the pickings were easy—sixty-one fighters destroyed, twenty probables, and seventy-eight damaged. Thank God, all six planes in my squadron got back safely.

I sat out the second incendiary raid we flew, on February 3 to Kobe, but I went along two days later. Again the action was close-range and savage. A fighter shot one of the blisters off the *Dotty*.

Our gunner was wearing one of the new harnesses, but he hung out there for several minutes in the frigid air before his buddies could pull him back. That same cold air swept through the plane and we scrambled for our oxygen masks. I actually had the bends for a couple of days after we landed from that one.

A few days after that mission I got my first taste of how Curtis LeMay's regime was going to affect my part of the war, and it wasn't a taste I liked. On February 7 I was nonplussed to learn that Rosie O'Donnell did not want me in the pilot's seat anymore during missions. Nothing personal, the order came from command headquarters. LeMay did not think his squadron commanders should be flying their airplanes. Our job was to direct the performance of the airplanes in our group. I went to O'Donnell and tried to plead my case. He listened to me and told me he understood my displeasure, but orders were orders.

I tried to imagine being in the cockpit of a bomber on a combat mission, not able to control the yoke and rudders. The hell with that. It wasn't in my biological makeup.

I coped with the order the way I coped with most military orders that didn't make any sense to me. I disobeyed it and flew the damn plane anyway. I knew that Colonel Wright knew what I was doing—he knew everything—but I also knew that he would overlook it.

For the first time, now, I began to imagine a scenario that gave me deeply mixed feelings—this war going on without Bob Morgan.

More missions, more frustration and anxiety. On February 11 the Twentieth released 600 bombs over Tokyo, but 325 of them went drifting out of target range. The 73rd Wing lost two planes and the new 313th lost nine. We caught hell from Rosie O'Donnell back at the base. Our rest intervals between sorties were rapidly diminishing now, and it was going to get worse. The Twentieth flew again on the thirteenth, and I was back in the cockpit on the fifteenth.

If we weren't pounding our targets the way the generals wanted us to, it sure as hell wasn't because we weren't trying. During one of our runs, a bombardier on another plane in my group—his name, which I'll never forget, was Lt. Rembert Ebert—found that his bombs were not dropping through the open bomb bay. Lieutenant Ebert crawled back into the wind-tossed bay, an extremely dangerous thing to do, and discovered that his bombs had jammed up. Breathing through his oxygen mask, the lieutenant got a grip on the edge of the bomb bay door and began kicking at the stuck mass of eight quarter-ton bombs. He kicked and shoved with the heel of his foot until the first bomb was dislodged and the others tumbled free. He might not have been quite in Vince Evans's league as a precision-master, but nobody took a backseat to Lieutenant Ebert when it came to courage.

On February 20 we got word that the long-planned invasion of Iwo Jima had commenced the day before, and that the fighting was brutal. The knowledge that Marines were dying to save our B-29s gave us renewed determination. We went out again on the nineteenth, filled with vinegar and resolve, but bombed poorly again, and caught hell for it.

Along about that time, my own little world of the 869th took another jolt. Stud Wright was transferred out of the group. Stud Wright, the capable commander I'd known since Pratt, the man with the agreeable mixture of good humor and common sense and professional discipline, was gone. Worse yet, his replacement was just exactly the sort of officer that had set my teeth on edge from the day I first set eyes on Major Smelser back at McDill.

His name was Col. Arnold P. Johnson. Like Smelser, he was one of those strictly-by-the-book guys. All he lacked was a swagger stick. He was not the kind of officer who would join his men at the bar for a drink and a joke. He did not like officers who got familiar. He did not like the likes of me.

Just as Smelser had done, Colonel Johnson sized me up on the spot as a pilot who did not come up the elite way, as a gung-ho West Point graduate with all the spit-and-polish attitudes that background instilled. He noted my casual regard for my uniform. He noted my flying history as pilot of the *Memphis Belle*—and held that against me because he regarded it as a bogus credential for a squadron commander.

Colonel Johnson knew how to use his power where it did the most damage. He lost no time in letting me know that he expected me to follow General LeMay's orders to the letter. As a squadron leader, I was not, repeat *not,* under any circumstances short of last-ditch emergency, to take that left-hand seat and fly the airplane.

He may as well have thrown a gauntlet at my feet. We'd just have to see about Colonel Johnson's way of doing things.

CHAPTER

20

B y the third week of February 1945 it was starting to seem as if there might be something to that myth of the Divine Wind. Japan's targets were right there, underneath our bomb bays, and yet we couldn't hit them squarely. We'd flown more than 2,000 missions over Japan, with no decisive damage to any important target. This was rubbing General LeMay raw, and back in Washington it was sending Hap Arnold around the bend. LeMay had arrived on Guam as the Commander's own chosen warrior, the wunderkind who could accomplish miracles and make obstacles disappear. But now Arnold was reaching the point where he was as frustrated with General LeMay's results as he had been with General Hansell's. That mission over Tokyo of February 19 was a textbook example—thick clouds, swirling winds, invisible target, radar not much use, indiscriminate bombing, very poor bombing. Everybody was hearing about it, from squadron level right up to General LeMay's office.

We were hearing something else, too. The Navy, never a fan of the B-29 program or the Army Air Forces in general, was finally on the verge of pouncing. Wasn't it time, the Admirals were saying, to face reality and turn the B-29s over to the Fleet as a tactical support arm? Finally there was Gen. Douglas MacArthur. The Supreme Commander of the Southwest Pacific area, fresh from his historic retaking of the Philippines and at the height of his influence, coveted the B-29 program for his own use in the final conquest of Japan.

Clearly, the Twentieth Bomber Command was at a crisis-point—a struggle for its very survival, as was the whole concept of strategic air power in U.S. military philosophy. If something dramatic didn't happen soon, the brilliant Curtis LeMay could very well be relieved of his duty, and Hap Arnold relieved of the whole command structure beneath him. The bright promise of aerial bombing as a coequal component of American defense, along with infantry and navy, would be blunted, its future constricted to auxiliary action.

We needed a miracle from our cigar-chomping miracle worker. And fast.

On February 23, we ran a fifteen-hour mission to Japan. Colonel Johnson rode with me as Command Pilot, observing the action. The visibility over the home islands was good that day, the bombing more successful than usual, the fighter opposition mild, and we did not lose a single airplane. Perhaps, I thought, this was an omen of better things to come.

We returned home to find Isley Field awash in scuttlebutt coming over from Guam, out of General LeMay's own headquarters. As was usually the case with rumor, we could not tell how much of it was true. Some of it had to be—of that there could be no doubt.

A new type of bombing was in the planning stages, a stunningly bold concept being pushed by LeMay himself, to the horrified opposition of some of his generals. It would be radically different from any other approach we had ever tried. The idea was that we'd go in at low altitudes. Very low altitudes. At night. How low, exactly, no one could say for sure. Some of the altitudes we were hearing left us speechless with disbelief.

The 869th was down from March 5 through March 9, an unusually long interval between missions out here. As we waited and listened and questioned and tried out our own theories, I became more and more convinced not only that the general rumor was true, but that it was true in its most extreme versions. LeMay was going to send our bombers over the enemy's homeland, in the dark of night, closer to ground level than any sane person could conceive as anything but suicidal. Our target, once again, was to be Tokyo, the heavily defended capital city. Just to make things interesting, our airplanes were going to carry the biggest bomb loads they could possibly carry. To make things even more interesting, certain crewmen would be cleared out of their stations to make room for these bombs, and most of the machineguns would be stripped along with them.

In other words, LeMay intended to send waves of Superfortresses swooping low over the maniacally defended Japanese home islands to drop their loads, and to assure the biggest loads possible, he was drastically reducing the capacity of those planes to defend themselves.

Perhaps only a warrior of Curtis LeMay's brilliance and blunt intimidating willpower could have persuaded his subordinates to carry out such a plan. The behind-the-scenes confrontations became the stuff of legend. It was later written that in preparation for the sortie, LeMay sent Rosie O'Donnell an order from Guam to Saipan instructing him to take some elements of his 73rd Wing on a radar training mission over a small nearby island at fifty feet above sea level. O'Donnell's shocked return communiqué came back at once: "Altitude in error. Two ciphers missing." When LeMay assured his general that there had been no error, the respected general hopped over to Guam in person and burst in upon his commander to declare, "I cannot fly that mission."

LeMay raised his dark, baleful eyes to meet the glare of his longtime friend and flying-school classmate, and replied in his chillingly soft voice, "You will fly it."

Curtis LeMay was not being totally foolhardy. His plan was far more rational than it at first seemed to his generals. He knew his enemy well. His careful observation of Japanese fighter-planes during his China days had convinced him that they lacked the cutting-edge reactive skills of their German counterparts. He would fly his daring sortie at night to minimize the effect of flak—he'd ordered that fifty-foot-high training mission to convince himself that his radar operators were up to this challenge, and the results had satisfied him. He had shrewdly analyzed the probabilities of surprise, and concluded that the Japanese were simply not prepared yet to anticipate or cope with a low-level raid. By the time they reacted, he figured, even given their radar system, much of their defenses would be twisted, melted scrap-metal.

To assure this sort of meltdown, the bombs to be delivered on this raid would be incendiaries.

The implications of this kind of weapon were such that even LeMay's most war-hardened subordinates found themselves aghast at the news.

Our intelligence had long known that the Japanese urban centers were virtual tinderboxes waiting to be lit. They were vast, densely packed hives constructed in a bygone age from primitive materials. Houses, factories, shrines, shops, and schools alike were built mainly of wood, long since gone brittle, and other organic materials—straw, even forms of paper.

No greater population density existed than in Tokyo, a metropolis of more than seven million people in 1945, set in a larger megalopolis of ten million. More than 90 percent of its population was packed inside a 200-square-mile area. The epicenter of this area was the Kanto Ward, an 11.8-square-mile melange of factories, houses, and shops, with a population density of 103,000 people per square mile, ten times the concentration of an average American city.

It was the Kanto Ward that General LeMay had chosen as our primary target.

We had targeted the Kanto Ward in our earlier, high-altitude runs. It was here that those big warmaking plants were concentrated—Mushashino, Mitsubishi, Hitachi and the rest—and also those smaller shops, where some three hundred thousand subcontractors labored to produce parts and auxiliary products.

Yes, we'd hit the Kanto Ward before, but this was going to be different. If we succeeded, the devastation would beggar anything that had gone before. In human terms, the prospects were nearly unthinkable. Civilians were going to die on this run, die by the tens of thousands. Worse, they were going to be roasted en masse. That's what incendiary bombs were designed to do.

Some of these would be M-69 firebombs with a base of highly flammable magnesium. They were dropped in cannisters containing eighty-three bombs apiece. Released from their clusters by a time-fuse just before contact, they ignited and spread the whitehot-burning alloy over a large area.

Other bombs would be packed with a newer horror—the jellied

gasoline called napalm. Napalm, without question, was one of the cruelest substances unleashed in World War II. Short of the atomic bomb itself, it probably caused more civilian suffering and death than any other kind of ordnance. Composed of gasoline and metallic naptha salt that gave it a gelatinous texture, it formed the payload of the M-17 bombs. When the shell of one of these bombs exploded, it touched off this mass and turned it into an intensely hot fireball that clung fiendishly to whatever surface it was incinerating, whether building-surface or human flesh.

Many Americans, at the time and in the decades following the war, would castigate General LeMay's nightmarish idea, calling it inhumane. It probably was, but so was the Japanese army's genocidal butchery in Nanking in 1938. Inhumanity, sadly enough, was a given in this war. No one wanted to get the inhumanity over with more ardently than we who fought it on behalf of the Allied nations.

As for the dire prediction from his own officers that the Twentieth would absorb terrible losses, General LeMay's solution was equally, icily logical. "They'll just have to send us," he murmured between clenched teeth, "more B-29s."

As we pilots congregated on the fields and in the Quonset clubs to sift these new rumors, we found ourselves more intrigued by the plan than one might have expected. It had an undeniable plausibility, but that didn't diminish the worrisome questions in our minds. What kind of opposition were we going to run into? What kind of bombing were we going to do? If it was radar bombing, could our radar men make it work?

Whatever the eventual answers, one thing was clear. This was Curtis LeMay's brainstorm, Curtis LeMay's show. If it succeeded, he'd be a hero, though LeMay didn't seem to place any more stock in the hero role than I did. If it failed, on the other hand, as many thought likely, he would be stripped of his command. If it proved catastrophic, he could find himself facing a tribunal.

Those were the terms that the tough young general seemed to welcome. We waited on Saipan for the order to suit up and go.

And waited.

March 7 came and went. No orders. We'd been expecting something definite by then, and now the sweating it out grew intense. We played cards, wrote letters, looked at the ocean—anything to make the time pass. London seemed like a city from another life.

In the midst of this tension, a letter arrived from Dorothy back home—a strangely hard and bitter letter from my new wife. I could not fathom the reason why. There was no explanation in her lines. Only months later, after I returned home, would I understand.

Her letter, though, had an unexpected effect on me. It made me think of the people we were soon to bomb, and bomb most horribly. Up until now, I'd hated the Japanese military. I hated them for their cowardly sneak attack on Pearl Harbor. It was one of the most important reasons why I'd decided to keep on fighting after my missions in the *Belle* had been completed—to help pay back Japan. It had seemed so simple and unambiguous at the time.

But now, reading and rereading Dorothy's cryptic, bitter letter, I found myself questioning this hatred of mine for the first time. It's hard to explain why, except that I sensed, without knowing it for sure, that the source of my wife's harsh sentiments had to do, somehow, with this war.

As soon as I grasped this, it all began to back up in me. I hated the Japanese leaders with my head, but now I reminded myself that I did not hate the Japanese people with my heart. Dammit, they were just people who had the misfortune to be in the way, for the most part. They were like all the other people, the objects of hatred, that had suffered and died in this gigantic global holocaust. The frozen and starved Russians. The overrun Poles and Czechs and Lithuanians. The Jews in the concentration camps. Those defiant dance-hall folk of London. The French and German citizens who found themselves under the Eighth Air Force's Norden bombsights. Just people, hated by someone. Or not hated, but just in the way. There was too much hatred. I was tired of it. Suddenly I didn't hate anymore.

That realization did not lessen my discipline or commitment as a bomber pilot, but in other ways, it began to change everything.

Now the rumor was that we were going to run this mission of LeMay's on March 9. The sweating got worse. Still no final answer, no papers, no briefing. Just our own fertile imaginations.

Then the rumors took on more substance. It was going to be a full-strength mission. Three Wings—the 73rd, the 313th, and the 314th—would be involved. Some guys were saying that 300 to 350 Superfortresses would fly. I'd been up on the flight line and I'd seen what they were loading on the airplanes. I'd seen those cylinders that contained the M-16 fire bombs, and I'd seen those napalm canisters. Reliable word had now spread that they were taking out all the machineguns except for the tailguns to make room. Still, there was no telling what the weight was going to be when they'd finished loading the bombs. Only later was it determined that each Superfortress carried six tons of payload. We only figured the weight would be tremendous. More, for certain, than Boeing had ever recommended for the Superforts. Could the B-29s sustain it on liftoff and through all those hours to the target? We'd find out.

Finally, on March 8, I got my hands on our exact orders.

We'd be bombing low, all right. Not the fifty feet of that famous radar run—no one ever expected anything like that in combat. But low enough, thank you. We'd be going in from 5,000 to 7,500 feet, one-sixth the altitude we'd been accustomed to at the lowest level. Low enough. Half as high as the peak of Mt. Fuji.

My squadron, the 869th, would be flying the tail end of Charlie Group in the 73rd Wing. There would be a minimum of 300 B-29s in the air. As rumored, there would be no machineguns or machine-gun ammo, except for the tailgunner.

No formation flying. No reason for it. The planes would fly single file to and from the target. We'd drop our bombs on the fires created by the bombing of a special advance group, a "pathfinder" group that would take off an hour in advance of the rest, at dusk on the ninth. Gen. Thomas Powers, one of LeMay's most trusted generals, would lead the pathfinders and would circle the target at a higher altitude, observing all that followed.

LeMay himself would not fly on this one. Normally, he could be expected to. Only later did we learn that the reason he stayed on Guam was that by now he had been briefed on the details of the Manhattan Project—the atomic bomb—and the Pentagon could not accept even the remote chance of his being shot down and tortured into revealing anything about those secrets.

Then we learned that our target was Tokyo.

My own role would be as Command Pilot of the 896th squadron. This meant, in theory, that I would not be the principal flier of the airplane; that role would belong to my copilot Capt. Andrew Mayse. In practice I would be something else.

We'd be taking off in the dark and bombing in the dark. The prospect gave me a feeling of dread. I remembered the low-level missions that had been tried in Europe, and the results—whole squadrons of B-17s blown out of the sky. I kept reminding myself that this wasn't Europe and that our enemies here weren't the Germans. The Japanese had not achieved great accuracy with their antiaircraft guns. They would be expecting us at high altitudes. We'd be over them and incinerating them before they could adjust. That incineration was going to produce tremendous smoke and heat, and we'd have to fly through it.

There were all kinds of unknown dangers.

I knew that I didn't have to go on this one. Our new Commanding Officer, Colonel Johnson, had offered to fly in my place, but it was out of the question. The men of my squadron were going, so I was going. Scared? I didn't use that word. Apprehensive? You bet I was, but I figured that God had brought me this far. If it was meant to be, I would make this mission and return.

It began at about 6:15 P.M., the great mass exodus of heavy bombers into the air. The 314th Wing, on Guam, went first, with General Powers's "pathfinder" plane in the lead. Fifty-six Superforts took off at 45-second intervals. The 313th went next, from Tinian— 121 big bombers joining the procession just as the sun set on the Pacific. Finally, in darkness cut by the arc of green flares from the control tower, the 162 Superfortresses of our 73rd Wing revved their engines, fell into line and roared down the runway, one by one. Rosie O'Donnell rode the lead plane.

The process of taking off had consumed more than two hours. Airborne, we formed a line that stretched for more than 300 miles.

We stayed low, around 2,000 feet for the first half of the trip. On the *Dauntless Dotty*, Mayse and I shared the flying. We began our climb as we again passed the island of Iwo Jima to our right. The historic thirty-six-day Marine assault on the island was playing out as we flew over. In its endgame phase now, we could see orange flashes of artillery fire. If the famous flag still flew atop Mt. Suribachi, it was beyond our range of vision.

Now we started our climb to bombing altitude. At about 5,800 feet we entered a cloud layer and hoped there were no other B-29s close to our wings.

Several hundred miles offshore of Japan—our lead bombers must have been nearly over the target—we picked up a garishly comic foreshadowing of what was about to happen. We'd been dialing through the Japanese radio-station signals in our cockpit receivers, tired of listening to Tokyo Rose, and just looking for whatever else might be out there on the airwaves.

We found a station playing American music. That wasn't unusual—the Japanese fascination for Western culture was already legendary, even in wartime. It was the selection of songs that transfixed us. Some Tokyo disk jockey, as unaware of what was coming as our sailors had been that Sunday morning at Pearl Harbor, was innocently playing a string of tunes that predicted what we were about to deliver. "Smoke Gets in Your Eyes" was playing when we dialed in. We exchanged grim smiles, and somebody muttered a little tensely that smoke would be in a lot of people's eyes in an hour or two. We couldn't believe it when the disk jockey followed that one up with "My Old Flame." When he spun out "I Don't Want to Set the World on Fire," a few of us started to giggle nervously.

We finally switched that radio off. We didn't know whether we could stand it if he played "There'll Be a Hot Time in the Old Town Tonight."

Now we were getting close. We knew without being able to see it yet that our lead bombers had already begun their deadly low-level business. As the *Dotty* approached the target, and with the consent of my copilot, Mayse, I directly disobeyed the order that Colonel Johnson had given me regarding Curtis LeMay's directive. I took over the left seat. The pilot's seat. To hell with orders and directives. This was Morgan's office.

True to the plan, Tokyo was already an inferno when the *Dotty* arrived. Great plumes of billowing smoke had climbed for miles into the night sky, but down at ground level the raging fires illuminated things, some of which you would rather not see. Curtis LeMay had been right. The Japanese had not expected us at night, this low. Most of the Japanese Zeros and Ginga fighters still sat, some of them melted, on their airstrips. Of those that had managed to get into the air, the thermal windstorms whipped up by the fires tossed them about the skies like helpless kites. As for the ground artillery fire, it was mostly inconsequential, as LeMay had predicted. The guns were calibrated for the wrong altitudes. We were bombing with damn near impunity.

And we were bombing with the very latest in the grim technology of death by fire—the incendiary M-69 and the napalm-packed M-17. Tens of thousands of these projectiles were now falling on the center of Tokyo, turning it into a hell on earth.

Our squadron closed on the target at 7,500, the highest altitude in the Wing, running at between 290 and 310 miles per hour, faster than regulations permitted, but we didn't care. It was nasty down there and in the air around us. Over the flaming city, the *Dotty* was buffeted by the same updrafts that neutralized the fighters—the violent flames were literally burning the oxygen out of the atmosphere. The updrafts brought with them a sickening odor, an odor that I will never be able to get completely out of my nostrils—the smell of roasting human flesh. I later learned that some pilots and crewmen gagged and vomited in reaction to this stench, and that a few had passed out.

Thank God, it was not until years afterward that I learned the full extent of the havoc our bombing had wreaked on those trapped masses down below.

I learned that most Tokyo citizens ignored the air-raid sirens that signaled the onslaught. Sirens by then had become routine sounds in their lives. It probably didn't matter much anyway. When the pellets of jellied gas started erupting, there was nowhere to run.

Squadrons of firemen had battled bravely to contain the blazes during the first fearful minutes of the attack, but they were quickly overwhelmed. Citizens who only a few heartbeats earlier had been eating their evening meals or perhaps attending the theater now milled and surged for their lives. As the fires spread and conjoined, the stampeding crowds grew. They choked the narrow streets, fleeing from one incinerated block only to collide with another throng streaming in the opposite direction. Great tongues of fire reached out to roast them en masse, like the breath of massive dragons.

Some terrified runners commandeered passing cars, but still found themselves penned in, then engulfed. Workers scrambled out of factories, tenants out of apartments. Some stood dazed, or wandered dreamily. All soon gulped for air that was by now too hot to breathe.

As the fires surged into vacuums created by the eaten-up oxygen, wind velocity increased, and scrambling human herds were overtaken by hundred-mile-an-hour firewinds. In their desperation, thousands of men, women, and children flocked toward the rivers and canals that cut through Tokyo, but these only yielded other forms of hideous death. Jumpers drowned, were asphyxiated, or were crushed to death by succeeding waves of jumpers. Soon the steel girders of bridges spanning the waters grew white-hot, forcing refugees to jump into water that was itself beginning to boil.

On a bridge spanning the Kokotoi River, a mob fleeing in one direction collided with a mob headed toward them. Screaming and arguing ensued, each crowd trying to force the other one to retreat. The melee went on for about ten minutes until seven tons of fresh firebombs incinerated the whole vast horde. It was claimed, in later years, that their screams could be heard aboard some of the B-29s trailing in at 7,000 feet.

In the midst of all this, the *Dotty* began her bombing run. My copilot, Captain Mayse, turned to me and said something that I am sure he intended as a little joke. It came out kind of surreal, given the context, one of those oddly bland things you can hear from people in the height of unthinkable chaos.

"We're sure giving the Boeing aircraft a test up here today" is what Mayse said.

I tried to remain focused on keeping the Boeing aircraft in the gusting, buffeting air, and out of another plane's fuselage, and not to think too much about what I was smelling and seeing. The images, God knows, could transfix you—they were the stuff that few human beings who ever lived would witness. Other B-29s around us were outlined in orange from the great groundfires. Hundreds of searchlights swept madly across the skies, the beams mostly eaten up by smoke, like some hellish Hollywood premiere night down there. Antiaircraft shells burst like fireworks, but harmlessly, miles above us. Debris, great jagged shapes of burning things, floated upward toward us along with the smoke. The smoke must have reached five miles into the stratosphere before it thinned out.

Beyond it all, off to the northwest, was perhaps the most surreal sight of all—the ancient Emperor's Palace, serene and untouched, illuminated by the flames of destruction. We'd been instructed not to bomb the Palace. Already, I guess, the high command was thinking ahead to the rebuilding of ties with Japan in peacetime.

Fire and smoke. The universe was fire and smoke. We flew through it, breathing it, engulfed by it, while down in the bomb bay our bombardier hunched over his sight. Our target was coming up, an area south of the city center. The turbulence now was shaking the airplane around as if it were some kind of dodge 'em car at an amusement park. I struggled to hold us on course. Finally the intercom crackled with those blessed and horrifying words, "Bombs away!"

Thank God. Now we could try to find our way out of this inferno and go back home.

It took both Mayse and me pulling on our yokes and rudders to get the *Dotty* turned around to the left. The wind over Japan may have lost its divine properties on this night, but it still had plenty of punishing pull. As we banked her finally in her great homeward arc, we found one great final spectacle filling our view. It was Mt. Fuji, its placid snowcapped volcanic cone glowing in the night with what seemed to us like some kind of elemental anger, or sorrow. Its gods were being vanquished, or at least its false gods were. Fuji would prevail to see its people rise again, in peacetime and prosperity. Just now it was our guidon for the great swing back toward Saipan.

The ocean below calmed us. We let our bodies relax some, and breathed in the simple pleasure of air untainted by flesh. We hadn't been hit, and had plenty of fuel, according to the engineer. We had participated in something awful and historic and yet necessary, something we ourselves would not fully understand perhaps for years, and we were headed—guarded by who knows what angels— for home.

We'd be back.

We arrived back at Saipan with plenty of fuel, as the sun was descending toward the ocean. The early reports on our mission were that more than 282 of our 339 airplanes had made it to the target and that we'd burned out seventeen square miles of Tokyo. The sickening casualty figures only underscored the degree of suffering that Japan's depraved military elite was willing to demand of its own helpless citizens, and would go on demanding beyond the point of reason—83,793 killed, 40,918 injured. More than half of the deaths resulted from suffocation, from the same wind-whipping oxygen-loss that buffeted our planes. More than a million people were left homeless. Some 267,000 buildings were destroyed, and with them, 18 percent of Tokyo's industry.

The mission had lost twenty-seven Superfortresses beyond the usual aborts. Some succumbed to mechanical failure, some to the rapidly readjusted ground artillery guns, and some—about ten—had become victims to the same savage superheated updrafts that our firebombs had created. We took no hits from Japanese fighters. Their pilots' lack of training and the firewinds had seen to that. Our losses were far less than General LeMay's deputy commanders had estimated before the mission.

On the other side of the world, Hap Arnold reacted gallantly, to his credit, when he heard the results. Although Curtis LeMay had not informed him in advance of his low-altitude plans, the recuperating Commander sent LeMay a congratulatory letter over the mission and promised that he would send more B-29s out to the Central Pacific—up to one thousand by July 1.

But Curtis LeMay was in no mood to wait for more bombers.

Our reward for success on this suspense-drenched mission was more of the same, and fast. We hadn't been on the ground eight hours when we were told to scramble for a return trip. This time the target would be Nagoya on the southern coast of Honshu Island. Nagoya was the site of a Mitsubishi aircraft engine plant. Again, more than 300 B-29s would make the run.

I seriously considered foregoing my rest and flying along on that mission, but at the last minute I decided to let John Carroll, my operations officer, lead the group this time. John would assume command of my squadron if anything happened to me, and I figured he could use the leadership experience. I told him good luck and stayed behind on this one.

Like its predecessor a few hours earlier, this raid was a success, if a little less so. The Superforts actually dropped more bombs than we had over Tokyo. This time, LeMay ordered an experiment—spread the bombs a little farther apart, in order to widen the area of damage. It didn't work as well as tight concentration, which stoked the flames more efficiently. But we wrecked that aircraft engine plant, and lost only one plane in the process.

Finally Curtis LeMay had hit upon a strategy that worked, and, gladiator that he was, he bore in now for the kill. Rest and airplane endurance be damned—he'd found a way into the enemy's center, and now he was going to pour fire through it. We hit the home islands again on March 13, the industrial port city of Osaka, Japan's second largest. It was another crowded city where, we were told, our incendiaries would work well. We arrived over a great cloud layer and bombed at 6,000 feet by radar, keeping our hits clustered. The 869th Squadron led the entire 497th Group in effectiveness that night, and I was at the controls over the target. We dropped 1,700 tons, all told. An American prisoner of war on the ground, whose enclave mercifully survived our attack, later wrote that the raid, which lasted through the night, left twenty-five square miles of the city "a smoldering desert." The official report noted that 8.1 square miles were wiped out, including 119 large factories.

"The bombs," he added, "reduced to rubble the homes of the population that supported Osaka's war effort."

By this time, LeMay had approved the reinstallation of some machineguns aboard the Superforts, out of concern that Japanese fighters might quickly adapt to the new nighttime threat, though they hadn't yet. We lost only two airplanes.

We'd wounded Japan badly now, but the stress on our own men was terrific. Many of our crews had now flown three missions in five days, fourteen hours in the air each time. They were exhausted, physically and mentally.

LeMay's response was to pour it on some more.

John Carroll led the 869th to Kobe on the sixteenth. More than 300 planes again, on a bombing run of two hours. This time the Zeros were in the air, more than ever before over the home islands— our crews noted 300 sightings. They still had not learned how to be effective at night. We lost three bombers, none of them to fighter attacks. Again the bombing was excellent, with a fourth of the city bombed out and many industries destroyed.

In the midst of all this death and destruction, a piece of mail arrived March 17 on Saipan from my wife Dorothy—a far more joyful letter than her previous one. It contained another color photograph of our sweet, beautiful little princess Sandra.

The final scorching burst from LeMay's five-mission onslaught came on March 19, a return trip to Nagoya with 290 planes over the target. We bombed by radar through the dense clouds. The *Dauntless Dotty,* piloted again by John Carroll, led fifteen planes of the 869th. Only one went down. Three more square miles were destroyed, and more industry, and more of Japan's dwindling prospects for prevailing in the war it had so wantonly ignited.

Ten nights, five flame-belching low sweeps by our massed bombers over the Rising Sun's sacred homeland. Ten nights, and LeMay's airborne legions had defied the ancient gods, beggared Mt. Fuji's firepower, humiliated the warlords in their own backyard. Ten nights, and four of Japan's greatest cities lay in charred ruins. Ten nights, thirty-three square miles of warmaking industry and urban infrastructure wiped out. Ten nights, some 1,600 individual American sorties, only twenty-one U.S. bombers down.

It would have continued, except that Curtis LeMay had run out of bombs.

To call this sustained raging whirlwind a "success" would be an understatement. LeMay's brutal act of faith in low-level bombing marked the turning-point in our aerial campaign over the home islands. It amounted to nothing less than the beginning of the end of the war.

Only after the fact was it disclosed that General LeMay had set the bombing altitudes of these mission without the knowledge and consent of General Arnold. Later in his career, in his days as founder and head of the Strategic Air Command, LeMay took on a reputation—not a legitimate one, in my opinion—of being a loose cannon, an almost unrestrainable warmonger. Already the seeds of this reputation were starting to germinate—rumors and conjecture swirled about the base as to exactly why the brash young general had dared this extraordinary breach of protocol. Did we have another MacArthur-in-the-making here, a general with visions of unlimited authority?

In postwar conversations, as a guest in his household, I had the chance to ask Curtis LeMay directly about his motives in running the raids his way, without official sanction. His blunt answers made sense to me. He said to me that he didn't tell Hap Arnold of his intentions because he was afraid the Commander might well scrub the missions, and then the efficacy of low-level bombing would never be tested and the final phase of the war would drag out for many more months. If the tactic did prove to be a mistake, LeMay went on with a shrug, "All they could do is fire me."

It was responsibility that LeMay was seeking, not power—responsibility and accountability. As a pilot who had to live or die with the results of LeMay's command style, I will say only this: I admired the heck out of him, even though many did not. As far as I was concerned, he was the greatest Army Air Forces general, and among the greatest of all generals, that America had to offer in World War II.

Now what? we all asked ourselves. As Curtis LeMay fumed and raged at the Navy for under-supplying him with bombs, his fatigued crews wondered what would be in store once he got them. Whatever it was, no airman of the Twentieth doubted that the demands would be superhuman. The reason we had run out of bombs was that Admiral Nimitz had refused to believe what LeMay expected of his airplanes and men—120 hours in the air each month. That equaled 15 eight-hour days, or fully half the month in the air.

Nimitz and his aides had laughed it off, and failed to deliver the quantities of bombs the young general had requested. A hundred twenty hours? Crewmen in Europe were averaging only thirty hours a month. The Twentieth's own military physicians had warned against the effects of more than sixty hours. But Curtis LeMay was not kidding, as Japan and the Allied forces in the Pacific found out. As I found out. I'd flown on two of those March missions and I'd never imagined that my mind or body could withstand that kind of depletion. The men who had flown all five—and they were many— were superhuman, as far as I was concerned.

As our commander chomped his cigar and tapped his foot and waited for the increased flow of bombs that the Navy was suddenly all too happy to provide, we men of the Twentieth "slept fast," as the saying went. We knew very well that we were about to be rewarded again the Curtis LeMay way—by being ordered to perform at an even higher level of impossibility.

CHAPTER
21

While we braced for the next challenge from Curtis LeMay, though, Curtis LeMay was busy trying to dodge a challenge of his own—the latest move to barge in on his Twentieth Bomber Command by his good friends from the U.S. Navy.

Admiral Nimitz and his staff had thought up a new reason to borrow LeMay's Superfortresses while the Army Air Forces awaited those new loads of incendiaries. The admirals wanted the big airships to stop dropping bombs for a while and start dropping mines into Japan's port waters and shipping lanes, including its vital Straits of Shimonoseki, which connected the Pacific Ocean to the teeming harbors of the Inland Sea.

The request had its strong selling points, no question about that. The prospect of face-to-face combat with the massed forces of home-island defenders was drawing ever-closer. Secret projections prepared by our strategists anticipated a year-long fight to subdue the islands, at a cost of a million Allied casualties, most of them American. Small wonder that our admirals and generals were probing every means for softening up those fierce defenders. Japan depended heavily on shipping to import its food and resources. At the war's outset it had been taking in more than six million tons of goods each year. Now, with her major cities and industries largely incinerated, her need was even greater. She was desperate for gasoline, and metals, and food, and hospital supplies from Korea and other subjugated Asian states.

American submarines had already ripped great holes in Japanese supply lines, helping cut her imports to a sixth of that prewar figure by early 1945. Now, in mid-March, with the critical island of Iwo Jima all but conquered and the huge invasion of Okinawa just two weeks away, Nimitz and Admiral Spruance wanted to eliminate even that trickle. The Navy had no airplanes of its own with mine-dropping capabilities. The only alternative was LeMay. LeMay, fresh from his firebombing triumphs, was in no mood to listen. He had plans of his own for his Superforts: to keep pulverizing Japan from the skies until the need for a ground invasion would have—literally—gone up in smoke.

While all this was being resolved, the Army Air Force found plenty to do to keep me busy. On March 23 I flew another mission to Japan. It wasn't a bombing run this time, but a weather-surveying mission. The Twentieth was preparing to resume high-altitude day-light bombing now, while waiting to be resupplied with incendiaries, and the Command needed some firsthand data on those ever-swirling island winds and cloud conditions.

It should have been a routine assignment, forgettable in the after-math of those furious night sorties just concluded. It would have been, except for a mechanical problem on the *Dotty* that set me down, for a few hours, on perhaps the greatest single battle shrine in the war's history.

One of our engines had sputtered out as we circled high above Nagoya. Then another began to lose power. As we headed back across the Pacific, my flight engineer informed me that we could not make it back to Saipan on two engines and a part of a third, given our remaining fuel level. That left us with one choice—one choice more than hundreds of afflicted B-29 pilots had not had available to them until less than a week earlier. We made an emergency landing on Iwo Jima.

The great thirty-six-day battle had officially ended just a week ear-lier, on March 16. Nearly all the 22,000 Japanese defenders had been killed. There were 26,000 Marine casualties including 6,800 killed on the four-mile-long slab of volcanic sand and rock. The *Dotty* touched down on the drab but vital little airstrip that had been the cause of all the carnage. It was no longer a stronghold of Japanese

Zeros, no longer a source of torment for our Superfortresses but a welcoming haven for them.

We spent two nights there while a ground crew changed our disabled engine and tuned up the weakened one. The exhausted, bearded veterans of the epic fight shared their K rations with us. From time to time, as we tried to sleep, we could hear scattered gunfire on the distant rocky slopes—another diehard Rising Sun defender routed out. We also heard some gunfire that was not so distant.

If it had not been for the Marines who sacrificed themselves on the sands of Iwo Jima, the *Dauntless Dotty* and her crew would be at the bottom of the ocean, not resting on a landing field. So would some 800 other crippled Superforts like mine. The strategic bombing campaign from the Marianas would still have been getting shot to pieces as it flew to and from the home islands. Eight hundred planes meant at least 8,000 crewmen whose lives were saved—just about the same total as the American combat deaths in that hideous battle. I said some prayers of thanks for those brave boys that night on Iwo Jima, and I have continued to say them in the many years since.

Maybe, in a way I can't really explain, those prayers were heard. Especially the ones I uttered with that sporadic gunfire in the background. My outlook began to change after I arrived back at Saipan the next day. It changed in subtle ways, ways that seemed destructive at first. A new mood had overtaken me, one of anger, resentment, and suspicion.

Not fear. Fear had no part in it. It wasn't as though I wanted to avoid combat. In many ways I wanted it more than ever, and nothing set me off worse than when I felt my commanding officers were trying to steer me away from it—in particular, that one colonel who had become a real nemesis of mine.

Oddly enough, it was this very mood that eventually—within weeks, in fact—guided me out of harm's way, and back to the bosom of the town and the mountains and the wilderness I'd left behind a lifetime ago.

I have often felt that a Higher Power guided me through that war. Now the angels who looked over me in the Pacific had started working in their mysterious ways to turn me homeward.

I arrived back at Saipan to find that events were accelerating now toward a final decisive onslaught in this war. Inter-service courtesies be damned, and God help the airman, ensign, or rifleman who needed rest in the upcoming weeks. The scent of victory was in the air, and now the merciless momentum had shifted toward the Allies.

The Navy had finally got its way in the great Superfortress wrangle. It took the help of the Joint Chiefs of Staff, but our tough major general relented and handed over the 313th Wing, under Brig. Gen. John "Skip" Davies, for the operation. The results showed that the Navy was right on this one. On March 27, the 313th seeded the Shimonoseki Strait with a thousand one-ton mines, dropped by parachute. The explosions began immediately, but that was just the appetizer course. After most of the 313th returned to its regular bombing runs, one group, the 505th, remained on the task, returning again and again to drop more ordnance than the defenders' overwhelmed minesweepers could possibly cope with. Eighteen merchant ships went to the bottom in April; eighty-five in May; eighty-three in June, taking with them an aggregate half a million tons of shipping. The noose around the warrior-rulers' necks had just jerked tighter.

To his credit, Admiral Nimitz gallantly praised LeMay and his fliers, citing their "phenomenal results." The mining campaign proved yet again that air power had arrived as a coequal force in America's military arsenal, but it didn't stop the Navy from nailing LeMay with another demand.

The invasion of Okinawa was set for April 1, under the overall command of Admiral Spruance. Just 350 miles off the coast of Kyushu, the southernmost home island, Okinawa—with its flat terrain and airstrips—would be the Allied staging-ground for the dreaded final onslaught, projected now for November 1945. Again, the price of conquest would be heavy. Dug in across Okinawa's 60-mile span were 77,000 elite Japanese army troops, backed up by 20,000 locals conscripted as militia and labor personnel—nearly five times the strength that had been deployed on Iwo Jima. Assaulting them would be four divisions of the Army's 24th Corps and the Marine Third Amphibious Corps, under the command of Lt. Gen. Simon B. Buckner Jr.—172,000 combat troops backed by 115,000 service personnel. General Buckner would die a hero's death two and a half months later, the victim of an artillery barrage in the closing hours of the bloody Allied victory.

The operation had actually begun two weeks earlier, with air strikes by the Central Pacific Fleet's Task Force fifty-eight against airfields on Kyushu. The B-29 mining of the Shimoneseki Strait was aimed partly at isolating Okinawa. Now, as March came to an end, some 1,300 Allied ships lay off the island's shores, and a fierce pre-invasion bombardment had commenced.

Spruance and Nimitz wanted that naval bombardment augmented by air strikes. No less an authority than Lauris Norstad, Hap Arnold's Chief of Staff, phoned up LeMay to tell him in effect that Nimitz more or less owned the Twentieth for the duration of the Okinawa campaign. This time, our general recognized the rightness of this order and acceded without protest. His irritation resurfaced only later, toward the end of April, when the Navy used his airplanes to rebomb targets already destroyed instead of returning them to Army Air Forces command for more punishing of Japan's great cities. Curtis LeMay continued fervently to believe that his Superfortresses, if left to do their strategic jobs, could win the war by themselves. He spelled out his conviction in a message to Norstad. "I consider that for the first time strategic air bombardment faces a situation in which its strength is proportionate to the magnitude of its task. I feel that the destruction of Japan's ability to wage war lies within the capability of this command, provided its maximum capacity is exerted unstintingly during the next six months . . ."

History, of course, was about to prove LeMay right, and in just half the time of his own estimate.

I did not see action over Okinawa. That didn't mean I was idle. There was plenty of other work for the groups not involved in that operation, and, under our general's 120-hours-a-month regimen, every airman on Saipan was getting acquainted with the limit of his endurance.

On March 27, not long after my touchdown on Iwo Jima, I flew a daylight raid on a Kyushu airfield. After returning I tried to grab a little needed rest and peace of mind. Instead, I found myself writing yet another condolence letter, this one to a new widow, the wife of a fine young lieutenant named Edward McDonald. This kid had taken a shard of flak deep in his hip on the firebombing raid over Kobe ten days earlier, and he'd finally died from it after lingering in horrible pain. I hated writing that letter. I'd hated writing every letter like it that I'd been obliged to write in this war. But now, with the exhaustion and tension and the fresh memories of that flesh-scented smoke, and with the awareness that so many thousands of young Americans were just days from being slaughtered on the next big island assault— well, all of it sort of backed up on me and left me feeling like my arms and legs were made out of lead, and that the roar of engines and machineguns and artillery was never going to stop. I guess I just didn't quite have the same resilience that I'd had when I was young. I was twenty-six.

On March 30, I was back in it on a bombing run to Nagoya. The next day the 869th flew a rare mine-dropping sortie over the Shimoneseki Strait without me. It was a brutal run—we lost ten airplanes. No time for brooding about it, though. The very next day, as the Allied troops were wading ashore on Okinawa, I was back in the air for another punishing fourteen-hour mission to Tokyo. We went in at 6,800 feet and basically had a terrible run with bad visibility and poor results.

In the bargain we lost another great young pilot, a boy named Edwin Dietzel, and his crew. Like Waddy Young and some of the others, Dietzel had been with me since Pratt. His was another death that hit me harder than the deaths of comrades from what now seemed a thousand years ago, over Europe. It was Dietzel's fifteenth mission and he was a great fellow, a great pilot.

I didn't know it at the time, but that was my final full-fledged combat mission.

My last mission of any sort came on April 4. It was another weather-reconnaissance sortie. I didn't like it. Maybe it was the accumulated exhaustion and stress, but I found myself wondering whether Colonel Johnson liked to see me fly without a squadron. That kind of thinking led nowhere, and I tried to put it aside. Besides, the generals kept insisting that weather missions were as important as bombing assignments. Maybe, but why, then, was this feeling of overall disgust building up in me. Was it losing Dietzel? He was sure on my mind. Maybe Dietzel's death stood for a lot of things. For the first time, it occurred to me to wonder just how much war a man could stand.

A big mission, against the Musashino aircraft engine plant in Tokyo, was scheduled for April 7. It was important enough that the brass had assigned us ninety P-51 escorts from the Seventh Fighter Command now proudly based on Iwo. Fighter escorts—man, what a luxury! I'd always wanted to fly missions with fighter escort. I looked forward to it. I couldn't wait for it. For some reason, tired as I was, disgusted as I was, I wanted to be at those controls.

The mission was a great success. The boys destroyed 101 Japanese planes on the ground. Ours was the only squadron in the Wing to maintain a good formation—it was commented on by General O'Donnell.

But I wasn't part of it. I stayed behind, on the ground. Colonel Johnson wouldn't let me go.

The next morning I stalked into Rosie O'Donnell's office, ready to blow my top. He'd actually made the request for me to come and see him. As soon as I got inside the door I started bellyaching about how I wanted to get flying again in that left seat. O'Donnell gave me a long, measuring look, and quietly said that he would look into it.

I stewed. I followed the news from Okinawa. Our land forces had just started to engage the enemy's inland defense lines. Our fleet, hovering offshore, was catching hell from kamikaze attacks—350 Zeros in the air, with thirty of our ships sunk or damaged in these two days. But by God, our carrier planes sank the *Yamato,* the huge flagship of the Japanese fleet, or what was left of it, plus a cruiser and four destroyers along with it as they were on their way to a suicide attack on our ships.

I wanted some of that action. Dammit, where were my orders? Where was everybody? The top of my head was about to explode. I wanted that yoke in my hands. I wanted . . .

I found myself back in Rosie O'Donnell's office on April 9. He gave me that same look as he had the first time—serious, searching, fatherly. Then he said to me, in a very quiet voice, "Morgan, we might be able to get you back to the States, if you are ready to go."

As soon as the words were out of his mouth I felt a clarifying shudder pass through me. This is what my tension and anxiety and disgust had really been about, even though I had not admitted it to myself. *If you are ready to go,* the General had said. Ready to go? God, yes, I was ready to go! Man, was I ever ready. I was really ready to go.

"Yes, Sir," I said to the General. "If you could look into that. I am ready to go."

The reasons had nothing to do with fear or with doubts about the war's outcome. It was clear now, despite the American blood that still had to be shed, that we had triumphed in the Pacific. Our despised and once-terrifying enemy was a mortally wounded beast, capable only of causing immense needless suffering before her inevitable defeat.

All our enemies were prostrate, in fact. In the European theater, Allied armies were streaming through Germany from the west and Soviet troops were advancing from the east. Adolf Hitler's thoughts were no doubt tending toward his bunker. Unconditional surrender by the Nazis was less than a month away.

It was a time to be joyful, I guess. Proud, certainly. I probably was those things, but I was also a man who wanted to see his wife Dorothy and meet his baby daughter, Sandra Lea, and look at the dogwood and forsythia and azalea blossoms that would be coming out on Beaucatcher Mountain above Asheville about now, and play a little tennis with somebody, and stop dropping bombs on people. I never quite realized all that until Rosie O'Donnell spoke up. I'll forever give that good general credit for this. In the midst of his preoccupations, he had taken a penetrating look inside me, and he had seen an airman at the very razor's edge of his resources—a young man, not so young as his years anymore, who had done his duty and then some, and had earned the right to go home.

"I believe I can get General LeMay's permission to relieve you, Morgan," he said now.

"Yes, Sir," I said. "That would be very good. I would appreciate that, Sir."

He got back to me again two days later, on April 11. He was still working on it and possibly could get me out late in the month. I prayed an awful lot that this would take place.

It wasn't as though I had not earned the right. I'd flown twenty-six missions in the Pacific now, including two historic ones. Twenty-six, to add to those twenty-five I'd flown in Europe. Fifty-one missions in two hemispheres. I guess I could feel assured that I had done my duty.

The following day Colonel Johnson notified me that I had been grounded from all further missions. This time, there was nothing punitive or hostile in his demeanor. The grounding was in consideration of the likelihood that I'd be going home. The Army Air Force didn't want to take any chances that something might happen to me.

On April 12, as we would learn the following day, President Roosevelt died in Warm Springs, Gerogia. His Vice President, a former Missouri senator named Harry Truman, took the oath of office. We all wondered whether Truman would have what it took to get this war over with.

On the night of the thirteenth, 325 B-29s flew to Tokyo and wiped out another 11.4 square miles northwest of the Imperial Palace. Two nights later, they destroyed another six square miles of Tokyo, plus 3.6 square miles of Kawasaki and 1.5 square miles of Yokohama. LeMay might be sharing his bombers with the Navy, but he was getting pretty good use out of the ones they didn't borrow.

Back-to-back missions on the sixteenth and seventeenth. No planes lost from our group. Thank God. Where were those orders sending me home?

A bad mission on the nineteenth. A plane filled with good friends of mine had to ditch. The plane broke up. Several crewmen lost. Bad, bad stuff.

On the twenty-third, another confrontation with Colonel Johnson. The guy was still at me, finding something new every day that I did wrong.

Then finally it happened. On April 26 the orders arrived from General LeMay's office. It was just a few sheets of paper that would carry me out of this hell and back to a civilized world. I was headed home. Headed home. Headed home. Headed home. Headed home.

CHAPTER

22

I left Saipan and the war with two more Distinguished Flying Crosses, one for leading the first B-29 raid on Tokyo, the other for completing twenty-six missions in this tour of duty. I also received five new bronze oak-leaf clusters to place beneath the Air Medal I had won in Europe, each cluster marking five missions completed.

I left with the personal congratulations of General O'Donnell. I had always admired this brilliant and jovial Irishman-by-way-of-Brooklyn, probably the best Air Corps officer in the Pacific aside from LeMay himself. Now I was pleased to learn how deeply my admiration was reciprocated. The General invited me into his office—I was a little more relaxed this time!—to tell me he was glad he was able to arrange for my return home. "I think you've pushed your luck as far as it should be pushed, Morgan," he said. Rosie O'Donnell told me that he was recommending a promotion for me, to Colonel. "It might take some time, but I think that you're going to make it," he said.

I assured the General of the sense of honor I felt—for both the prospect of promotion and for the chance to have served under him. We chatted for a few more minutes, and agreed that after the fire-bombing raids of March, the war couldn't possibly last much longer. We shook hands, I saluted him, and we said good-bye. To my regret I never saw the General again.

The Navy flew me to Honolulu, whose delights I enjoyed for a few days, until some MPs persuaded me toward more contemplative activities. I wangled a bucket-seat on an otherwise filled-up C-54 Skymaster and flew the rest of the way back to mainland America—the America I'd more or less taken for granted as a boy and young man, then spent the past two years of my life defending at altitudes of one to six miles in the air. "*O beautiful for spacious skies,*" we used to sing in school back in Asheville. As my plane began its descent into the San Francisco airport, it hit me that these American skies had never looked so beautiful or so spacious. I hoped their beautiful spaciousness would never, ever be violated by the kind of traffic I'd been a part of over France, Belgium, Germany, and the islands of Japan.

I landed back on home soil on April 30, 1945. It was the day Hitler and his bride Eva Braun committed suicide in their Führerbunker fifty feet underneath Berlin. It was the day after the U.S. Army had liberated the emaciated prisoners at Dachau. In the Pacific the Battle of Okinawa was still raging full force. The Marines' Third Corps and the Army's Twenty-fourth Corps were slugging it out against strong Japanese defenses on the southern part of the island.

Hope and promise were in the air as well. And renewal. The Chicago Cubs and the Detroit Tigers looked like good bets in their respective leagues to win the pennant, I learned from the newspapers. Phil Cavaretta was touted as being ready for a National League batting title. Bob Hope and Bing Crosby were on the "Road to Utopia." Jukeboxes were coming in. Rodgers & Hammerstein's *Carousel* was about to open on Broadway. You could get a good cheeseburger just about anywhere. America was looking pretty good.

It was only when I picked up a telephone in the San Francisco airport to call Dorothy back in Asheville that I realized I had not left the war behind, and would never leave the war behind. I realized that the war would be a living part of all of us who fought it, and all of those who suffered losses from it, forever.

Dorothy was glad to hear from me and eager to welcome me home. But it was in this phone conversation that I finally learned the reason behind the dark, bitter letter I'd received from her a few weeks earlier in Saipan.

Dorothy had had a brother named Harry. He was her only sibling. The two of them were as close-knit as a brother and sister could be. I'd known that. What I hadn't known until Dorothy sobbed it to me just now, over the phone, was that Harry had been killed the previous December in the Battle of the Bulge.

Dorothy wasn't finished unburdening herself. As we talked on, the floodgates of her bitterness and grief opened wide, and she blurted out something to me that left a permanent scar on our marriage. She probably did not mean it the way it sounded—people have trouble putting the right words to pain as deep as what she was feeling. This same kind of anger mixed with anguish was being experienced by tens of thousands of others in those sad times.

Still, I had no way of preparing myself for what she said, or of totally recovering from it afterward. What she said was, *"Why couldn't it have been you instead of my brother?"*

I hung up the telephone feeling as though a flak burst had engulfed me. No, this war was not over for any of us.

I didn't go home to Asheville right away. That was the Army Air Forces' decision, not mine, but it was a lucky one. It gave Dorothy and me a few days' separation, an enforced interval that would allow the sting of her barb to subside a little, in her as well as me. My orders were to report to Fort Bragg, N.C. I did so. There, I was granted a twenty-one-day leave commencing May 7. I used it, quite naturally, to go home.

My face-to-face reunion with Dorothy was warm and tender. I'd missed her terribly. She was a sweet and loving woman, and so I was able to forget—or at least pretend to forget—that outburst of hers on the phone. Of course she had been distraught, I could understand that. I figured, the less said about it, the better. That's the way it worked out, for many years, at least.

Finally, there was Sandra. I couldn't stop looking at her, there in her crib, her mother's arms, my arms, in all her six-month-old innocence. A new life that I'd helped create amidst all the waste and loss and suffering of this terrible war. Maybe Sandra had been my guardian angel all those months in the Pacific. I could not have picked a better one. *Sandra,* I kept repeating, as I put my finger against her soft cheek. *Sandra.*

It was a glorious homecoming, all in all. My father greeted me with great pride and affection, as did my brother David. I renewed friendships from those boyhood years in Biltmore Forest. I wore my uniform nearly every day, and was pleased to discover how proud I was of it. There were parties and dances at the Biltmore Forest Country Club, just like old times—well, almost like old times.

We stayed with Dorothy's divorced mother at her house in downtown Asheville. When Dorothy and I had any time alone, we'd talk about the future, where I might get sent, where we might end up. I discovered that I liked that topic, the future, quite a bit. I sure liked it better than all that moment-to-moment thinking I'd been forced to do the past three years.

That future did not belong to us yet, not quite. The war was still going on—LeMay was sending B-29s in sorties of 400 and more over Japan now—and I still belonged to the U.S. Government. For the first time in my military career, I started to grow aware of what a vast and impersonal bureaucracy the Armed Services could be. Nobody back on Saipan had given me a clue as to what would happen to me once I got back to the States. I'm sure that no one knew, and it wasn't exactly as if they had nothing else on their minds. The only directive I had was to report, after my twenty-one-day leave, to something called the AAF Redistribution Station No. 2, in Miami Beach, Florida, for "processing and reassignment." It sounded a little bit like what might happen to a side of beef that had come through the stockyards at Chicago. I accepted it in stride. There was still a war on.

In Miami Beach, where I arrived on the last day of May 1945, I beheld the spectacle of hundreds of Bob Morgans. Maybe thousands. There was a whole swarming sea of young men in uniform, like me—young men whose eyes were no longer so young. They smoked cigarettes as they sprawled in rows of chairs inside great Quonset huts, or milled on the streets outside under palm trees, or played ping-pong or pool if they could snare a table, or tried to read the paper. These were the guys who had come off the farms and out of the towns and out of college two or three or four years ago to help turn back Hitler and Tojo. Heroes of their generation. Now we were all anonymous anxious faces, just a mass of confused young men waiting to see what would become of us. Trying to figure out which window, which room to go to in order to get that information. Mainly, trying to avoid getting lost in the giant shuffle.

The first thing we all received were "nomenclatures," or numbers, which identified us in relation to the kind of service we had performed. My nomenclature was No. 1093: the designation for Pilot, Very Heavy Bombardment—"Very Heavy" referring to B-29s as opposed to B-17s. That was me, as far as Redistribution knew or cared. For the next few days, or weeks, No. 1093 was going to be more useful to me than all my Distinguished Flying Crosses.

It took nearly a week—the Redistribution folks had a lot of guys besides Bob Morgan to process—but I finally got my set of orders. I'd been reassigned to the Third Air Force, 310th Air Force Base Unit, McDill, Florida.

I had come the full circle, going back to McDill field, where I had first reported for duty with my new bride Martha the day after Christmas 1941, a dewy Second Lieutenant with no clue as to what was about to happen to him, or the world.

Well, that part hadn't changed. Whatever I was supposed to do at McDill this time around was apparently a big secret. I knew that the Army Air Forces still conducted bombardment training there, so I supposed that I'd be expected to help out in that, in one way or another.

We took up residence near McDill. Dorothy and I rented a house on the Gulf, and, more than a year after I'd married her, we began to live as a family. My happiest moments were playing on the beach with Sandra, a peaceful beach on which the only rushing figures were sandpipers, not men with guns.

The problem, it developed, was that the command structure at McDill had no more idea what I was supposed to do there than I did. There was no particular assignment waiting for me. I did a few check-flights just to make sure I'd get my flight pay, but beyond that, I was just . . . there. It was the first time, even counting cadet training, that I had felt so—what?—unnecessary?—around an air base. It was a feeling that took getting used to. Times were changing.

Now the hopscotching began. In late June I received orders to report to Orlando. It was a temporary assignment, so I took Dorothy and Sandra back to Asheville.

At Orlando, I found myself once again a man without a mission. Again, no one knew what to do with me. I hung around a couple of weeks before I was told that my next stop would be New York City and, after that, Washington. I was to be part of a two-week protocol-writing project called 471S, which was described as "Standard Operating Procedure for Very Heavy Bombers Lead Crews." I reported to Army Air Forces headquarters there on July 13th.

I can't recall much about what I contributed to the protocol-writing project, but I do remember well the most astounding thing that happened while I was there—a fiery event that brought the war crashing back into my newly peaceful world.

The Army Air Forces' headquarters was half a block from the Empire State Building on 34th Street near Fifth Avenue. On Saturday, July 28, a foggy morning over New York, an Army Air Forces lieutenant colonel named William F. Smith, a recently returned veteran of 100 combat missions, took off in his unarmed B-25 trainer bomber from his home in Bedford, Massachusetts, headed for the airport at Newark, New Jersey. Lieutenant Colonel Smith intended to pick up his commanding officer there and fly with him to an air base in South Dakota. He was to make an intermediary landing at La Guardia Airport in New York. He never made it past the Empire State Building.

We heard the sudden engine-whine, then the deafening crash, and felt the aftershocks about forty minutes after I'd reported to the office at 9 A.M. that morning. Lieutenant Colonel Smith had lost his bearings in the fog during his descent, attempted to bypass La Guardia and fly on to Newark, narrowly missed the Chrysler building, kicked his right rudder and headed straight for disaster. His last information from the control tower at La Guardia had been, "At the present time I can't see the top of the Empire State Building."

Smith's B-25 slammed into the skyscraper's seventy-ninth floor at

200 miles an hour. It plowed deeply into the building. One of its engines smashed clear through, exited on the 33rd Street side and plunged through the roof of a building nearby.

All of us in the office rushed over to the great building. Thirty-fourth Street and Fifth Avenue were already flooded with people—a complete madhouse. We tried to push through the screaming bystanders and the police, using our military authority to get inside, go up the elevators and be of what assistance we could, but the New York police and firemen weren't letting anyone through. All we could do was stand and watch the rescue efforts, and wonder what the hell had produced this nightmare, with everybody else.

We later learned that fourteen people, including the pilot, had been killed—a mercifully small number, given the population density of the area. But the tragedy was horrific enough. The crashing plane had sent a fireball through the Catholic War Relief Office on the seventy-ninth floor, killing eight office workers.

Just as in war, the crash produced its surreal acts of fate. A badly burned woman named Betty Lou Oliver was given first aid and placed in an elevator car to descend to street level. The weakened cable snapped and the woman plunged seventy-five floors. She survived. The rapidly falling car created an air cushion that slowed its descent as it neared bottom, and the steel cable underneath the car piled up, turning into a giant coiled spring that further absorbed the impact.

Had it been later on a weekday instead of early on a Saturday—had 34th Street been milling with shoppers, and the Empire State Building filled with its customary 15,000 inhabitants instead of the 1,500 it actually held just then—the crash could have produced massive loss of life. Still, I couldn't help thinking, it would have been only a minuscule fraction of what London had experienced night after night during the Blitz. Or Tokyo, for that matter.

But a military plane—a training bomber, a half-block from where I sat in Manhattan? No, the war was not yet over.

I shook off the effects of that trauma as I flew on to Washington for the final phase of my assignment, then got new orders to report to Chatham Field, near Savannah, Georgia, for a stint training B-29 crews there. While there I put in my required flight time—not in a B-29, but in a smaller B-25, the same kind of plane that had hit the Empire State building.

If you were a mystically inclined sort of person, which I was not, you could almost believe that the war had its own sense of humor, though it was a damned macabre one.

It was during that assignment at Chatham that we all gathered around radios on the base at ten P.M. on August 9, to listen to an address to the nation by President Truman.

"The world will note," came the President's raspy Midwestern voice, "that the first atomic bomb was dropped on Hiroshima . . . that attack is only a warning of things to come. If Japan does not surrender, bombs will have to be dropped on her war industries and, unfortunately, thousands of civilian lives will be lost. I urge Japanese civilians to leave industrial cities immediately, and save themselves from destruction . . ."

By the time of that broadcast, the second atomic bomb had also been dropped, on Nagasaki.

The most destructive weapon ever devised had entered human history. Japan was the recipient, and a pair of B-29s had made the delivery. The epochal first bomb had fallen from the *Enola Gay,* piloted by Paul Tibbets, and had exploded with a force equal to 12,500 tons of TNT. It created a heat blanket of up to 1,000 degrees Farenheit, killing 100,000 people almost at once and 140,000 as the months went on.

It was over. The formal surrender aboard the USS *Missouri* would take place in a few weeks, on September 2. But it was over.

Something else was beginning. What, exactly, was too early to say. Perhaps an entirely new way of living life in America, and the world—that was a pretty safe bet. Already, that new way was feeling awfully big and fast and mysterious for a boy who'd grown up not far from Beaucatcher Mountain.

As my thoughts and yearnings turned once again toward home, I couldn't help wonder whether maybe my old fellow townsman Thomas Wolfe might have been right after all. I wondered whether you could go home again.

CHAPTER

23

I t's amazing how quickly a nation can distance itself from a war it
has just fought and won, and how abruptly and thoroughly a
country can grapple with its wartime demons by willing itself to forget.

It never quite works, of course. Nations don't forget their wars. A
war always works its way into the fabrics of the societies that fought
it—the winners as well as the losers. A war changes everything. Half
of America still lived a rural or smalltown life before Pearl Harbor.
The number of farms in this country was at its peak as late as 1935.
Pockets of the country were still unelectrified. Horsedrawn wagons
were not rare. The country was still local in its habits and isolated
by its oceans, or so it thought, from the rest of the world. The pocket
of North Carolina that I'd been privileged to grow up in—a charmed
and ordered society that had been touched by literary legend, fabulous wealth, and limitless natural beauty—had not changed much in
its codes and traditions from the mid-nineteenth century.

All of it was about to change. After the war the GIs came home
and built suburbia. "The great American land rush after 1945," one
historian maintained, "was one of the largest mass movements in
our history." A great general of the war became President and over-
saw the creation of the interstate highway system. The war-fueled
leaps in technology and engineering and communications got transferred to American industry and American commerce. Air travel is
one good example of that. The moral principles, the liberating dem-
ocratic ideals that America fought for—at the cost of 295,000 men

and women killed and wounded—these too received a fresh infusion of postwar passion back here at home—the Civil Rights movement, and what President Johnson called "the War on Poverty."

No, America did not forget World War II. Not with those changes. Not with the monuments, museums, veterans' organizations, the thousands of books written on the subject, the hundreds of movies, the serious and popular music, and now, the Web sites.

America didn't forget. Not exactly. But America tried.

We as a nation tried to forget in the same ways that we had tried to forget the Civil War, when so many of that war's artifacts, including thousands of irreplaceable photographs from the battlefields made on glass-plate negatives, were destroyed. We plunged headlong into the Gilded Age. We tried to forget World War I in the same way, by mostly ignoring those returning doughboys and losing ourselves in the Jazz Age.

We tried to forget World War II the same way we would try to forget Vietnam, including behavior toward our veterans that cut a lot deeper than merely ignoring them ever could.

Let's be honest. No group of Americans tried harder to forget the war than the men and women who fought it. Most of us did everything in our power to behave as if the war had never happened when we got home, but ours was a more complicated kind of forgetting than the rest of America's. We wanted to separate ourselves from what had happened to us, from what we had done, and from our nightmares. Yet we wanted to be remembered, not so much as individuals, but as a fighting force. We wanted to be remembered on behalf of all the airmen and artillerymen and infantrymen and Marines who went into battle and went to their deaths with nothing more to sustain them than the belief that their exploits would be recalled and honored for decades, maybe centuries to come.

How did that set of conflicting passions—to forget, and yet to be remembered—affect the veterans of World War II, not to mention the country they served? One good way to illustrate this would be to trace the postwar fates, the intertwining fates, of Bob Morgan and the *Memphis Belle.*

*   *   *

In the autumn of 1945 the atomic bombs had been dropped, the war was over, and I wanted to get out of the Army Air Forces. I'd never been a gung-ho military man in my own mind—flying was what I loved, and serving my country. I wanted my old life back. Even before the formal Japanese surrender on September 2, I reported to my colonel at Chatham Field in Savannah, Georgia, and told him I wanted to be discharged from active duty.

He looked at me as though he had never heard of such a request before. Maybe he hadn't. "Morgan," he asked me, kind of like an uncle trying to coax a kid who wouldn't brush his teeth, "don't you want to stay in the regular Army Air Force?"

That was an easy one. "No, Sir," I said. "I'd rather not."

He asked me why—I could see he was taking this hard—and I told him.

When I had finished—it didn't take long—the colonel grabbed some papers on his desk and stacked the hell out of them. "Well," he said in a grumpy voice, "I think you should think it over." I said I'd already thought it over. Sir. The colonel stacked some more papers. Finally he said, "Well, we'll see what happens. I don't even know what the process is to get you relieved from active duty." To his great credit, the colonel bothered to find out. On September 1, 1945, the day before that gathering on the USS *Missouri,* the Army Air Forces cut orders sending me to the Separation Center at Fort Bragg. I'd come full circle again. I'd started to notice how often you could travel in circles in the military.

I departed active duty in the Army Air Forces on September 9, having logged 2,035 hours in the air, not to mention a world of experiences and memories that would not fit neatly into military logbooks. I was now a member of the Reserve.

Once again, my homecoming was warm and hospitable. My brother David chartered an airplane to fly down to Fort Bragg and pick me up. Back in Asheville, I doted on Sandra—whom I called my Princess—took up my favorite sport of tennis again, did all the loafing I could manage in the month of paid leave the Forces had given me, and started hunting for a permanent house with Dorothy. I wanted to live in Biltmore Forest, come hell or high water. I wanted to close that four-and-a-half-year gap between my former life and now, so things could continue just as they had before. A house in the Forest, that was the ticket.

Dorothy and I found a charming little rental cottage right next door to the police station—the station I'd hung around as a boy, talking with the officers, cadging rides in their patrol cars. It would not be our permanent dwelling, but it seemed like a good omen. We moved in, set up housekeeping, and I began looking for a place to build.

Maybe we should have paid attention to other omens. Such as the tragic one offered by the *Dauntless Dotty* herself. Like me, the *Dotty* finished out a creditable tour of duty—fifty-three missions, 880 combat hours, 176,000 air miles in combat. Like me, she finally got clearance to go home. Unlike me, she didn't make it.

She left Saipan in early June with a ferry crew commanded by Lt. William Kelly. His copilot was John Neville. They were to fly first to Kwajalein in the Marshall Islands, then to Hawaii, and finally to Mather Field near Sacramento, California. Lieutenant Kelly didn't know that just before he left Saipan his first child, a daughter, had been born.

At a little after three A.M. on June 6, 1945, the *Dotty* took off from Kwajalein with a fresh load of fuel. Forty seconds later she plunged into the Pacific Ocean and spiraled 6,000 feet to the bottom, never to be recovered. Ten of the thirteen crewmen, including Lieutenant Kelly, were killed.

Among the casualties was one Pvt. Lowell Spivey of Windsor, North Carolina. Private Spivey had hitched a ride home aboard the *Dotty* because the War Department had transferred him from active duty in the Pacific theater. The War Department had transferred him under the provisions of a policy. The policy provided that when only one member of a family in the armed services survived, he was eligible for reassignment out of harm's way. Private Spivey was eligible because his two brothers had already been killed in action.

What happened? Different people had differing theories. Some believed that the runway, which dipped down low halfway along its route, had flooded with the incoming early-morning tides and slowed the *Dotty*'s takeoff speed. Others speculated that the bomber lost an engine.

My own theory is somewhat different. I believe Lieutenant Kelly ran afoul of his ingrained wartime habits. In lifting off from Saipan on our bombing missions to Japan, we pilots had routinely taken advantage of the island's 500-foot dropoff over the ocean to cool off those notoriously hot Superfortress engines. We would routinely dip our planes down over the chilly Pacific waters for a few seconds, to let the ocean temperatures act as a coolant.

The end of the runway at Kwajalein was only five feet above sea level. I think that Lieutenant Kelly forgot this in the critical few seconds that spelled doom for the *Dauntless Dotty*.

Along with house-hunting, I also began looking for employment. I'd saved a little money, but a house in the Forest, as I well knew from experience, required a steady job. My father took it for granted that I would come to work for Morgan Manufacturing Company. He and David had expanded the business while I'd been gone. They ran two companies now, Morgan Manufacturing and the Morgan Furniture Company. Morgan Furniture was not quite as domestic as the name implied. My father and brother had secured some contracts to make, among other items, certain graphite products for the Atomic Energy Commission over in Oak Ridge, Tennessee, just outside Knoxville. Those items were top-secret, and I never did learn their exact function.

The Black Mountain plant was also making some more routine products—wooden parts for automobiles, household furniture parts—some of which it shipped over to the Morgan Furniture Company at Woodfin, which assembled the parts into finished furniture for bedrooms, dining rooms, and living rooms. It also produced ammunition boxes and beer boxes for the military.

I hesitated over my father's offer. It appealed to me in many ways, but in other ways it didn't. For one thing, I still wanted to fly airplanes. Not military ones, just . . . airplanes. I'd kept in touch with Vince Evans. If any veteran was going to seize the American future by the throat, it would be my pal Vince. Sure enough, Vince had headed straight back to California after his discharge from the service. He'd gotten his marital problems untangled, was single again and exploited the contacts he had made during our post-production on William Wyler's *Memphis Belle* film. Those contacts had led him in short order to a brooding Hollywood entrepreneur named Howard Hughes. Hughes speculated in two worlds that were of consuming interest to the ex-bombardier from Texas—movies and airplanes. He had produced several motion pictures, a field that Vince was about to plunge into himself. Hughes also owned a controlling interest in a fledgling airline called TWA.

Vince had assured me that if I wanted to become a commercial airline pilot, he could put me in touch with the right people. I was certainly interested, made the calls, and had reached the point where a trip to TWA in California was the next logical step. Before I did that, I wanted to make sure exactly where I stood with the family business. It didn't take me long to figure out that that's where the real intrigue, the risky unknowns lay—not out in Hollywood, but in the family business.

I was facing a hard truth that I'm sure many thousands of my fellow veterans were facing. The hard truth was that life goes on, with or without yesterday's heroes. Business is business. People get hurt in the scramble for the top, and your war ribbons don't mean anything in the ongoing struggle for power and money.

As I looked into the operations of my father's two companies, it struck me that most of the executive decisions were being made by my older brother David. David had not served in the war. He had stayed in Asheville to run the Morgan business. His personnel manager at the company, one Milton Sims, had managed to get Dave an exemption on the basis that some of the work our company was doing was essential to military operations. This was true, particularly at our Woodfin plant. It's also true that someone else could have administered that plant as well as Dave did. He did not have to stay behind. Dave knew this, and I knew it, and he knew I knew it, and it formed the basis of a resentment between us that grew over the years. I know that my brother felt guilty for the rest of his life that he had avoided service. I am sorry about that, but it did not diminish my hard feelings toward him.

My father, as I could see, was getting up in years. A lonely widower, he looked to his few lifelong friends and his hobby of gourmet cooking for fulfillment. He also bore the title of Chairman of the Board of Morgan Manufacturing Company, and proudly performed the task of public relations, traveling about the country to visit our customers who were also his friends. This was a great help to our company, but its primary function was to keep Dad young in spirit. It seemed to work. My father was the first one into the office every morning. He lived on the company grounds at a place we called the Club House, where he gave luncheons for customers when they came to town. I was proud of him for carrying on so ardently in the company he'd founded. When he remarried, in 1951, to a lovely woman named Cumi Palmer, I felt that he had regained most of the things that mattered to him in life.

Running the business itself had grown far too complex for David Morgan Sr., and so he was happy to let David Jr. take control of that end of things. Which Dave was quite happy to do, with his 51 percent controlling interest in the stock.

What neither my father nor I could see clearly just yet was the strong partnership my brother was forging with an old college roommate named Harley Shuford. Harley had money, lots of it. Harley backed David in some of his business investments to the point where David was able to attain his majority stockholder status. David's loyalty had already begun to shift, subtly, away from the family and toward his own financial ambitions.

As it shifted, my resentment took hold. The situation gradually grew clear—Dave had gained control of the company while I was off fighting the war. He'd used those four and a half years to consolidate his own power. It was the sort of fate, sadly enough, that awaited thousands of returning servicemen. That didn't make it any easier to bear.

Dave certainly was not mirroring the wishes of our father. Dad wanted me in the company so badly he was willing to give me all of his stock, which amounted to 30 percent. His good friend Kent

Swift, who had lent Dad the money to restart the business after the Depression, owned 19 percent. Looking back, I can see that Dad was skeptical about my brother's control of the company, but he realized there was nothing he could do about it.

As for David, he was all brisk business and shoeshines. He wanted to make me a vice president and start me out at $18,000 a year, very good money in those days. "We're going to do some public relations using your war record," he told me. He'd come up with a gimmick to boost the company's image—he'd printed a thousand photographs of the *Memphis Belle* crew. He asked me to sign them, and he put them into an advertising brochure for the Morgan Manufacturing Company, along with a calendar, and sent them around to all our customers. He paid me $10,000 for it in addition to my salary.

Ten thousand dollars was a great bonus in those days. Maybe Dave was trying to offer me some compensation for the salaries I missed during those four and a half years in the war. I appreciated the money, but it wasn't the way I intended to earn my living. I wanted to be a working partner in Morgan Manufacturing, not a mascot. I wasn't the kind of person who was going to take a job and then not do his share of the work. My business career was going to be like my military flying career had been. I was going to do a good job of it. Whatever they threw my way at Morgan Furniture, I was going to do a good job.

The TWA piloting opportunity went by the boards. Dot never would have enjoyed that life anyway. She was forthright—California held no allure for her. She yearned to live on in Asheville, where her roots were, and she wanted to raise our children in those beloved Smoky Mountains. I knew that she was right. Asheville was home to me, too. If I went with TWA, I'd have to leave the mountains, leave my personal history and live as an exile, no matter how good the pay. I was home now, and I intended to stay.

"I'm in," I said to my dad and David.

I was on my way now. It was all settled. The future looked fantastic and I even got an airplane out of the deal! David agreed to go partway toward the purchase of an Army-surplus BT-15, which a couple of friends and I located in Norfolk, for a very reasonable price. The official idea was that we'd use it for company-related flights. The real idea was that Bob Morgan would get to keep flying, period.

Before the month was out I even learned that Gen. Rosie O'Donnell had been able to keep his promise—I'd been promoted to full Colonel in the Army Air Forces Reserve. To cap it all, Dot and I bought a lot in Biltmore Forest and began building our dream house on old Park Road, that I knew blindfolded from years ago. Our lot overlooked a playing field where my sister used to ride and play polo, where my boyhood friends and I had played football and baseball, and where the sandboxes and swings of my childhood still stood, just waiting for Sandra.

What better proof could I want that things had not changed, that life would go on as it always had. I didn't know it, but I was acting out the same dream that gripped hundreds of thousands of returning servicemen across America. Get a loan. Build. Put down roots. Establish a little kingdom for the family. Get a job. Be normal. Be average. Get the noise out of your head, if you could—the engines, the gunfire, the screams. Build a house that would withstand the furies of that war, a house that would keep the future connected to the innocent past; that would seal shut that raw gap of four and a half years and keep it shut forever.

In that way, my generation of returning servicemen and I created the 1950s.

But we were never able to build our houses big enough to ward off the changes we had helped create. That raw gap never got sealed. The postwar world was going to be different from our pasts, more different than any of us could ever have dreamed. Perhaps that is one reason why many of us—certainly me—brought with us into civilian life the hard-drinking habits we had acquired in the service. I was never a drunk in the shameful, abusive, falling-down sense of that word. I was never violent nor a public disgrace of any sort, but I drank, and in time my drinking would intensify the heartaches that had worked their way into my life.

*   *   *

While my own postwar life began on a sunlit note, the *Memphis Belle*'s hit rough weather almost immediately.

All of us in the crew assumed that the *Belle* would be returned to combat when the "Twenty-sixth mission" was completed. That had been the intention of the Army Air Forces, and that was what we all assumed would happen when we sadly climbed out of her for the last time on that morning at Bolling Field in Washington.

She was not sent back overseas. Instead, the Army Air Forces decided to use her for training new B-17 crews. They sent the *Belle* to McDill Field in Florida, the Petty Girl illustrations still emblazoned on her nose, where a series of awestruck young pilots climbed into the cockpit seat that had been my airborne domain, and a series of young copilots and navigators and radiomen and bombardiers and gunners went through the routines that had been exalted by men with names like Verinis and Leighton and Hanson and Evans and Quinlan. I'll say this for those young airmen-in-training—they comprehended their airplane's history, and many of them were gallant enough to express it in written testimonies years later. One wrote of the "pure enjoyment of being able to say I flew that beautiful and historic bird." A bombardier recalled the "honor" of it. Another pilot remembered how he "tried to imagine what it must have been like on the *Belle* on one of her raids but my imagination left out many things I was soon to experience in combat."

For all that, she nearly came to a fiery and ignominious end one night at another Florida airfield, when her inexperienced crew, practicing night-flying, found itself without night-lights and without radio transmission to boot. The pilot managed to set her down by trailing another plane onto the tarmac. Then, sitting immobilized with her wheels stuck in the soft sand beside the runway and her tail protruding dangerously out onto it, she was narrowly missed by another incoming plane. Luckily, the pilot gunned his throttle, veered into a low-level turn and avoided disaster.

On Aug. 14, 1945, the world war that created the *Memphis Belle* was over.

The *Belle* became an integer in America's process of forgetting.

Even before the fiery end—a full month before the atomic raids on

Hiroshima and Nagasaki—the *Belle* had been offhandedly reduced from a functioning military aircraft to a piece of salvage. She was flown to an air base at Altus, Oklahoma, joining hundreds of B-17s being rounded up like so much refuse, shipped off to a collective disposal point and stored, pending a bureaucratic decision on her fate. She no longer belonged to any group remotely as dashing as the Mighty Eighth. Now she was the property of something called the Reconstruction Finance Corporation, a government agency created for the sole purpose of getting rid of obsolescent military hardware.

This was the beginning of the *Belle*'s forty-two years years of exile at the fringes of the nation she'd helped defend. This was the beginning of decades in which her dignity, her symbolic memory, and even her continued physical existence were under continual threat. This was the beginning of the *Memphis Belle*'s long search for her own homeward angel.

I started my civilian career riding high. In addition to the airplane, I had the use of a brand-new four-door company Pontiac. I had life insurance, health insurance, perks galore. Dorothy was pregnant again, with our second child. The money was good and promised to get better—thanks in part to a colorful and wealthy business associate of my Dad's named Sam Handel.

Sam was a patriotic fellow who, like me, had been livid over the Japanese attack on Pearl Harbor and outraged at America's enemies on all fronts. Before I left for the Pacific, Sam declared to me that he would pay me $500 for each bomb I dropped. Well, the poor guy had no idea what kind of figures he was dealing with. I did some calculations, and when I added it all up, Sam probably owed me a tidy $250,000. I wasn't about to hold him to a figure like that.

We settled on $175,000. To give you an idea of what kind of money that was in those days, you could buy a brand new 1946 Ford Tudor sedan for about $1,150. We hired a good local architect and got going on the house.

I dedicated myself to becoming a better company man than I'd ever been a military man. I joined the Biltmore Forest Country Club. I brought customers and potential customers out there for relaxation. My game had always been tennis, but I found that our customers didn't play much tennis. They played golf. I took up golf with a vengeance—I didn't like to do anything that I couldn't do reasonably well. The club had a Scottish golf pro by the name of Andy Kay, and he knew his golf. Before long, I was shooting in the middle to upper 80s. I even notched a 79 one time. Eventually I settled into about an 82—good business golf, a good average for the Vice President of Quality Control.

Quality control had actually been my suggestion. David had plans for the company, big plans, multi-million-dollar plans, but the control of quality was not necessarily at the very top of his priorities. David was plugged into the impulses and currents that would transform American business in the second half of the twentieth century—a new kind of dynamic bottom-line style that was mostly foreign to me. Where our father had built the company on personal commitment and the painstaking selection of skilled and trusted employees, David was dazzled by outside professionals like business planners and high-priced consultants. He introduced one of them to me, a sleek-looking man named Emmett Judge, and told me, "Okay, you've gone around the factory and seen the things that we're manufacturing and all. How about taking a look at what our future is with this Emmett? Just sit down and let him use you as a sounding board. See what he's doing and let him show you the blueprints of what we planned, the outline of the financial setup, and our goals for the future. You've got to get the picture."

I wanted to be a good company man, a team player. "Okay, Dave," I said. "I'll work with him. I'll get the picture." For a while, I gave it my best shot.

The picture was that we were going to make furniture. Furniture like Morgan Manufacturing had never made before. Beautiful furniture, quality furniture, high-standard and high-style. Furniture designed by outside designers who'd simply hand us the drawings and plans.

This consultant, this Judge, already had clerks and cost people working for him, planning out the next two to three years of growth, volume, profits, and so on. He had all the facts and figures. His facts and figures astounded me. I didn't necessarily understand them, but they astounded me. After a while, as I continued to look at them, they began to worry me.

They didn't worry David. Emmett Judge had practically hypnotized David. He had convinced my brother that we would make millions of dollars a year in profit. The retail stores were begging for furniture, he assured David. Begging for it. Price didn't mean a thing. Just go, go. Expand. Full steam ahead.

Unfortunately, that was a trap that a lot of postwar businesses, gulled and lulled by consultants, worked themselves into. I couldn't see it then, but I sensed it in my bones. I sensed that it was wrong, it was insane, to go on tooling up as if cost didn't matter. It was crazy to ratchet up your investments and make extravagant claims to sophisticated buyers such as Macy's and Gimbel's that you were delivering quality product on a big scale, especially if you were not delivering quality.

Some of our workers, especially at the Black Mountain plant, were indeed delivering quality. These were former workers just back from the military, qualified men, machinists, and woodworking people. They needed jobs and were willing, like me, to give Morgan Manufacturing the very best that was in them. There were others coming into the firm, new men, money men, whose devotion to craftsmanship was a little more suspect.

My brother liked to bring his friends into business. Nothing wrong with that, if they're qualified. One of these friends, an old Biltmore Forest pal who had made it big in business, was hired as David's sales manager. A sales manager with no specific knowledge of the furniture industry? I didn't pay much attention to it at the time. I did later on, when it was too late.

I had too much else to worry about, trying to learn what Emmett Judge was doing with those figures of his. Judge's line was that if we could just keep the volume up, the selling would take care of itself. After all, furniture was in such a demand at that time that some customers might overlook certain mismatchings of color and grain. I wasn't so sure of that.

The warning signs became clear even to me. I had begun seeing the rejects on my tours of the plants, the furniture returned because of less-than-perfect workmanship. I'd talked with some of the buyers from the big New York stores, who kept telling me, "We need furniture, yes, we've got to have it, *but we've got to have the quality.*"

What would Joe Giambrone have had to say to this?!

I tried the direct approach with my brother. I went to him and said, "Dave, I think quality is going to be one of the most important things in our business." I asked him to let me hire a quality-control manager at the plants, someone to watch our own in-house inspectors, and to visit some of our customers and hear firsthand what they thought of our product.

David went for it, in his slightly distracted way. His mind was on other things. He was borrowing more money from banks to invest in more machinery, more equipment. "That's great, that's a good idea, we'll make you in charge of quality control," he said. "How about that?"

I said it was fine. I hired a good man to run our quality control, a Navy veteran named Jed Davison. I hoped against hope that this would ease my doubts about the company's future.

The *Memphis Belle*'s future was nearly extinguished within weeks of the war's end, when it seemed certain that she would be crushed into unrecognizable scrap metal.

This nearly happened despite the pleas of the Mayor of Memphis, the Honorable Walter Chandler, who wrote to the War Department two weeks after the Japanese surrender on August 25, 1945, to request possession of the airplane on behalf of his city.

Mayor Chandler had been avid to secure the *Belle* as a war memorial well before this moment. He first tried to talk the War Department out of her in the summer of 1943, during our dramatic stopover in Memphis on our Twenty-sixth mission. He was instantly rebuffed— the *Belle* was an active war plane, not a trinket, the Department huffed in effect, and didn't the Mayor know there was a war going on?

Now, in the euphoria of victory, the good Mayor—a veteran himself, having served as a field-artillery Captain in World War I—renewed his plea. He and the city had big plans, he assured the

Department—a permanent hangar that would house the *Belle* as a civic attraction.

This time, the government's reaction was a bureaucratic silence.

Meanwhile, the *Memphis Belle* languished at Altus, Oklahoma, for several weeks, and would have gone from there to the jaws of a metal-crunching factory, had not an alert local newspaper reporter spotted the famous Petty Girl painting on her nose, and phoned Mayor Chandler to let him know the situation.

The Mayor urgently renewed his pleas to the War Department. The Department bumped his petition to the federally run Reconstruction Finance Corporation in Althus. The RFC harrumphed and turned things over to the Civil Aeronautics Administration. An inspector from the CAA visited the *Belle*, looked her up and down, scowled a little, wrote some things down in his clipboard and turned in a report. There was an oil-pressure problem on one engine, and something wrong with the emergency hydraulic system. The throttles were out of synch. Most logical destination for the *Memphis Belle?* The scrapyard.

But the patriotic Mayor was not yet through. He decided to show the governmental pencil-pushers what he thought of their damned red tape.

In March 1946 he made a personal visit to Washington. On March 8, the startled citizens of Memphis awoke to learn that they were now the collective owners of one very used Boeing B-17 long-range bomber with a girl in her underwear painted on each side of her nose. List price—$314,109 new. Resale value considering mileage, wear and tear from flak, cannons, etc.—$350. That is how much Mayor Chandler had forked over to the War Assets Corporation—another bureaucracy—for the title to the plane. Later, a citizen of the town sent the Mayor a check for $350 to relieve Memphis taxpayers of this particular burden. The Mayor tore the check up. The *Belle*, by God, was going to be civic property.

She was tuned up, her faulty systems repaired, and on July 17 of that year she was flown to Memphis. A civic committee in that city had contacted me and asked me to do the piloting, and I happily agreed. Days before the scheduled flight, we encountered labor-union problems at Black Mountain, and I had to cancel, and a Pacific veteran named Robert E. Little sat in very capably at the *Belle*'s controls. He flew her in on three engines, the way I heard it. As it turned out, this was her last flight.

The *Memphis Belle*'s arrival in Memphis should have marked the beginning of her happy-ever-after years as a national icon. As I was finding out, the future didn't always work that way for the veterans of World War II. Instead, on what should have been the cusp of her long postwar glory, the *Belle* began her long exile to the fringes of American life. The process of forgetting had begun.

Mayor Chandler left office that year. His successor was a man ironically named Polk, Sylvanus Polk. He was not related to Margaret, by family or by a sense of history either, it seemed. The new mayor had many urgent priorities for Memphis in the new era of peacetime, but preserving an old bomber was not one of them. People needed housing, not airplanes, was the gist of his rationale for ignoring the *Belle*'s presence—true enough as far as it went, I guess, except that airplanes like the *Belle* had helped ensure that the housing American people lived in would be American-built. The *Belle* sat on the tarmac at the Memphis airport for weeks, until a sympathetic lieutenant colonel of a ferrying command there took pity and brought her into a hangar under his purview.

Then she sat some more.

Things were moving fast in Asheville. Too fast, almost. The house on Park Road had begun to take on a bigger share of my energies—and money—than I'd thought. The architect had suggested a rock exterior, which Dot and I liked. I'd had no idea how expensive rock work could be. We finally decided that, rather than change the design, we would build the house in stages, over the years, completing new sections of it as our income increased and our children were born. We spent all of the $175,000 from Sam Handel on building the house and buying an additional lot.

We'd start with the garage—three-car—and, above it, a master bedroom and two smaller ones, a sitting room, living room, small dining room, and kitchen. Later we would add a hallway connecting the garage with a second section of the house, a full dining room, a larger kitchen, a full basement, and an upstairs master bedroom and bathroom. I figured that as the kids came along, Dot and I would live in the master bedroom and the kids would live in the three bedrooms over the garage.

The company was in full throttle, thanks in part to a new a salesman I'd hired into the company—the dearest friend of my life, Jim Verinis. I'd kept in constant touch with my "other" pilot since the war ended. We'd visited each other and played golf together. He was by now a successful tobacco wholesaler in New England, steady as always, a smart investor of his money, a staunch family man. With the permission of David, I invited Jim to cover the New England territory for the Morgan Furniture Company and Morgan Manufacturing. He jumped at the idea. From the day he took charge, the New England territory showed a great profit. Jim and I even became closer friends than we had been in the Eighth Bomber Command, if such a thing is possible.

My family continued to grow, and Sandra Lea found herself happily presiding over two younger brothers. Robert Jr. was born on May 4, 1946, and Harry Morgan came along on March 18, 1948.

If I wasn't living out the perfect postwar American suburban dream, I don't know who was.

Yet for me, the dream still retained its nightmare edge. It was an edge I shared with hundreds of thousands of veterans, most of whom never talked about it to anyone, not even their wives and children. Sometimes it was those visions of planes falling from the air around me, with good men in them. Sometimes it was that remembered smell of cooking flesh over Tokyo. Sometimes it took the form of a giant question mark in my mind. Why me? Why, why, why me? Why did I survive when all those others did not?

Other times, the nightmare edge took the simple form of loss. Lost time. *Four and a half years. I'd given up four and a half years.* I could not stop comparing David's and my fortunes in that time, could not rid myself of that sense of loss.

She sat for two years, the *Belle* did, while the first of the many vandals to visit her began to pick away at detachable parts to take home for souvenirs. In July 1948 a story in the Memphis *Commercial Appeal* chided the city that the plane was languishing in ignominy.

An Air Force officer—the Army Air Forces had been reorganized as a separate branch of the military—saw the story and suggested, in a helpful spirit I presume, that the answer was to chop the airplane up, preserve a few distinctive parts, and place them in a museum. The rest of the parts, he offered, could be used for training purposes.

No muss, no fuss.

Luckily, an attorney in the city replied to that letter in hot indignation. To do any such thing, he fired back in a letter of his own, would be sacrilege.

It seemed that the *Belle* had a few friends left after all.

That small core of friends, their ranks changing as time went on, would prove to be the salvation of the *Memphis Belle* as she waited forty years for her place of honor in the waning American memory.

A citizens committee was formed back in that July, the first of several, to devise a solution. A pediment in a city park? A coat of clear plastic to prevent rust? No one could quite decide.

The city's newspapers proved another source of support over the years. The influential *Commercial Appeal* editorialized that it was the city's job to find a permanent shelter. Embarrassed, the city's Parks Commission volunteered a site near the famous Pink Palace Museum in Chickasaw Gardens.

Hold on just a minute, the good residents of the leafy neighborhood responded. Why, having the plane here would cause us to be overrun with . . . *tourists*! And besides, the plane is a bit of an . . . ahem . . . eyesore.

There are worse kinds of visitors than tourists to be overrun with, some veterans might have countered, but didn't. As for eyesore, some pretty formidable enemies across the Atlantic would certainly have agreed with that. The Chickasaw Gardens initiative evaporated—an early casualty of "not-in-my-backyard."

After Robert Jr. was born, Dot and I moved into that garage part of the house while the rest of it went up. Things were great. We were flourishing. I was making good money, with lots of perks, and traveling for the company. I was putting in long hours, even working Saturdays. Well, to be honest, Saturdays and some Sundays. Maybe I thought it was a way to get back some of those four and a half years. Maybe I was a little driven.

The strain of it all began to crack through to the surface as the 1950s began.

The 1950s. It's strange, the way America remembers that decade today. The most familiar image of the '50s is a kind of decade-long cartoon—sci-fi movies, the birth of rock 'n' roll, the Cold War and fallout shelters, Lucy and Uncle Miltie on television, Dad with his pipe, Mom in her apron, Sis in her crinoline skirts, Junior in his letter-sweater, and a country that was squeaky-clean, ultra-wholesome, conformist, and idiotically repressed.

There's some truth to that cliché, but to veterans of the war and their families, it conceals as much as it reveals.

If the '50s looked squeaky-clean on the surface, it was partly because we wanted it that way. We'd had enough of the opposite of squeaky-clean. We were trying to forget the worst of what we'd been through, remember, while at the same time wanting our fallen comrades and our collective effort to be remembered by history.

We could not forget, not at night anyway, and the nighttime demons sometimes stayed with us through the days.

The demons got between me and Dot. Like a lot of returning servicemen, I found myself in a marriage that wasn't working the way it was supposed to. The seeds of it were hard to figure. We'd come from the same place, had each been brought up by a hardworking father, and each of us believed in marriage. We loved our kids.

But we were growing apart. Dot loved home and hearth, the ordinary routine of the household. I loved the family, too, but I had a restlessness in me that the house could not contain. I needed to travel, get up in the air, go places, visit our customers in distant cities, socialize at the country club. I loved being around people, I loved laughter, the tinkle of cocktail glasses—all those clues that life was happy and festive again, that things were normal.

Dot and I took some good vacations together—company trips to Hawaii, Bermuda, Jamaica—but I was gone a lot by myself, too, on business. I was traveling at least ten days out of every month, flying off to New York, Chicago, even California. Back in Asheville, I played golf, and spent more and more time at the club.

Our separations were brief, at first. We had several in the early years of the '50s. We would separate for a while and get back together, separate for a while and get back again.

We didn't talk of divorce. That's one thing I didn't want to do. I felt my obligation to my three children. I wanted them to grow up in a household unshattered by divorce. Dot felt the same way. Despite the strains in our marriage, she consecrated her life to her children. She brought a special radiance to her role as a mother. She did her best, I must say, to make our marriage work.

As they came of age, we placed Sandra in the St. Genevieve of the Pines Academy and the two boys in Gibbons Hall, both excellent local private schools. We sent them to camps in the summertime. We took them on trips. We took summer vacations on the beach at Sea Island, Georgia. We did, in short, everything we could to keep the children feeling secure and loved. It worked, I think, but the sad rift between Dorothy and me continued to grow. The separations continued.

Divorce became even more unthinkable, though, with the birth of our fourth child, Peggy, on September 9, 1958. Ten years younger than Harry, our next-youngest, Peggy became the baby of the family, and I doted on her. We named her Peggy after my sister, who had died in England of polio just after the war ended. She had lived there with her British husband for several years, having sold the dress shop in Washington. The separations continued, though. I would move out of the house and into an apartment, move back into the house, move out again and into a small house.

It was during one of these more prolonged separations, in the late 1950s, that I flew to Memphis. It was a business trip. I flew there to visit a plant that was affiliated with our manufacturing concerns. While there, I called Margaret and visited her. For a brief, sad time, our romance was rekindled again.

She hadn't had it easy after the war, either. She had been married in 1950, then divorced. By now, that edge of sorrow that I had noticed in her from the very first, back during our whirlwind romance in Walla Walla, had taken deeper hold of her. She was drinking. In fact, she was an alcoholic. But for a while, she was in my arms again. Polky. My Little One. Just as warm and dear and vibrant as she had ever been.

She had begun training, in her foggy way, for a new career. As I said, it seemed from time to time that the war, which somehow never ended, had its own sense of humor. Margaret was in training to be an airline stewardess.

We saw each other a few times. Arranged some meetings in various places. Wrote letters. Loved. Then argued. Again. It was soon over, as it had to be.

Her alcoholism lasted sixteen years.

Meanwhile, the *Memphis Belle* sat by herself, watching the years pass.

By 1949 the world was really moving on. Americans were buying TV sets by the tens of thousands to watch a funny man in a dress named Milton Berle. Gene Autry was singing "Rudolph the Red-Nosed Reindeer" on the radio. An unknown little nation called Vietnam gained its independence from France within the French Union. Communism had long since replaced Nazism as the national bugaboo. A friendly-looking new kind of car showed up in America, a German car called the Volkswagen, a brainchild of one Adolf Hitler as an inexpensive "people's car." Americans loved its gas-saving features. The Air Force plane in the news these days was called the *Lucky Lady*. It flew all the way around the world nonstop.

As for the *Belle*, she had been evicted from the Air Force hangar and sat out in the open, exposed to the elements.

The proud lady had not been completely deserted. A new ally arose to protect her interests—the Memphis American Legion Post No. 1. In August 1949 its dynamic board of directors took up the *Belle*'s case. The Legionnaires lobbied and won the right to move the airplane from her obscure corner of the airport and into a place of civic honor—the grounds of the National Guard Armory on Central Avenue. The group had actually envisioned an outdoor museum to enfold the airplane and other military mementoes, but it lacked the finances and the clout to achieve that high goal.

It happened. For the first time since she'd rolled off the line at Boeing, the *Belle* was broken down into her component parts. Then she was towed from the airport to the Armory, and reassembled on a concrete pedestal. The date was May 21, 1950.

Her ultimate resting-place? Safe harbor in the shrine she deserved for her legendary status?

Not exactly.

For now she was in plain sight not only to the good people of Memphis, but also to the souvenir-hunters and common vandals of Memphis—to the cheap greediness of some of those whose freedoms she had helped safeguard. As the years stretched on, the predators slipped easily over her protective chainlink fence in the night and helped themselves to pieces of her—instruments and gauges from her panel, chunks of wing, anything that was detachable. Somebody even stole the pilot's yoke out of her cockpit—the same yoke I had gripped to hold her steady over St. Nazaire and Lorient and Wilhelmshaven and Bremen.

I guess this particular defilement, which happened in the late 1950s, proved too shameful even for its perpetrator. A year or two afterward, a package arrived in my office. I opened it to find the missing yoke—accompanied by an unsigned note that said, "My conscience has been bothering me, so I am returning this."

Such second thoughts were all too rare. Some of her admirers began to worry that if nothing were done, the *Belle* might eventually vanish without a trace—the night-people of Memphis accomplishing what legions of German fighter planes had been unable to do.

The 1950s churned on with the Korean War and the Cold War. Jet planes, not propeller-driven bombers, were the new rulers of aerial combat—the F-86H Sabre; the F-84 Thunderstreak. Russia had The Bomb now, and Americans dug fallout shelters. Rock 'n' roll swept aside the jitterbug and swing-dancing of my day, and the star of Memphis now was a babyfaced kid with a ducktail haircut who drove a pink Cadillac and swiveled his hips while singing about heartbreak hotels and blue suede shoes. I often wondered whether

Elvis ever glanced over at the *Belle* as he tooled past it on his way to get a cheeseburger at the Dairy Delight.

I often wondered if anybody did.

It wasn't that Memphis, or America in general, was trying to snub the *Memphis Belle*. Nobody felt that way. It was just that the country had other things on its mind—the future, mainly. Even we veterans were intent on rebuilding our lives, tending our young families, puttering with the backyard patio, getting back to what President Eisenhower called normalcy. The last thing we wanted to do was live in the past.

Still . . .

The *Belle* sat there on her pedestal, watching the century roll by on Central Avenue, invisible in plain sight.

She sat there for twenty-seven years.

Something happened to me in the mid-1950s that yanked me out of my own inertia. Or at least it made me begin the process. I very nearly crashed an airplane filled with friends of mine. Morgan, who'd survived fifty-one combat missions against Germany and Japan, damn near bought the farm with a planeload of duck hunters. The memory of how close I came gives me goosebumps to this day. In the weeks afterward, it gave me something else as well—the determination to start turning my life around.

Every December in those days I took a group of good friends duck hunting on the east coast of North Carolina near a little town called Poplar Branch. I would fly as many of these friends as would fit safely into the Morgan company airplane, and the rest would arrive in cars. On this 1956 trip the company plane was grounded for maintenance. I leased an old World War II craft, an Apache, known commonly as the "bamboo bomber" because of its fabric and wood parts. It held five people.

We took off for the coast on a cold, cloudy, misty day. The Asheville airport had no radar at the time. I filed a flight plan that indicated I would be on top of the clouds at 8,000 feet.

As we climbed to 4,000 feet, though, my wings began to pick up ice. We climbed higher; more ice. Then I discovered that the ice was consolidating around the carburetors of both engines, choking off the fuel supply. The engines began to sputter at 6,000 feet, and the manifold pressure started to drop. The engines were really laboring now, coughing and misfiring. The Apache was not going to make it to 8,000.

I banked her and headed south, hoping to break out of the clouds. We were falling faster now. It took my good friend Bob Schneble and me both to hold the rudders and elevators to keep us from an all-out dive. I had no idea where we were, except that we were in steep mountain country. We kept dropping faster and faster, the plane practically stalled. The terrified men in the plane were bracing for the worst.

Finally, at under 1,000 feet, we broke out of the clouds. Mountains loomed to our right and left, but in front of us there was nothing except the gorgeous smooth tarmac of the small airport at Hendersonville. I made a dead stick landing and six lives were spared.

Someone else besides Bob Schneble, I think, had His hand on the yoke and rudders that day.

CHAPTER
24

By the late 1950s I was starting to feel an urgent need to get in close touch with my Command Pilot. God had pulled me through. He had kept me free from harm in the epicenter of a war in which millions had died. I believed that then, despite behavior that I knew very well was a violation of God's Commandments. I believe it now.

But why? I kept asking myself. Why me? Why a sinner, an unfaithful husband? Why did He bring me back when so many others perished? It surely couldn't have been my clean, virtuous living.

I decided that I was going to find out what that reason was, what God's plan for me might be. I knew that it could take me a long time, and that I might not go about it the right way. But this would be my next mission—to discover who I was in the eyes of my Command Pilot.

Ironically, religion was one of the issues that had helped drive Dorothy and me apart. I'd been born and bred an Episcopalian. Dorothy came from more fundamentalist stock. In the late 1940s she acceded to my wishes by agreeing to join the Calvary Episcopal Church in south Asheville. Calvary was a beautiful church with a beautiful small graveyard. My mother was buried there. The idea was that perhaps this connection to my mother would give me the peace I had been seeking.

Unfortunately, Calvary Episcopal gave Dorothy no peace. As the children grew old enough to worship, she pressed for the right to take them to a church in Asheville that preached the old doctrines that had inspired her family for generations. I didn't like it, but I chose not to interfere. Dot had earned the right, as a tirelessly caring mother, to take her children to a church that gave her comfort. Her efforts paid off. The Morgan children grew up to be splendid adults.

We attended separate churches, and the gulf between us widened.

Then my Command Pilot decided to get in touch with me. He did so via one of his most inspirational apostles of this world, a fellow North Carolinian by the name of Billy Graham.

Billy had soared into national prominence a few years earlier, on the wings of his great Los Angeles Crusade of 1949. In the late 1950s he brought his Crusade to Asheville. At Dorothy's urging, I reluctantly attended it during one of its last days. I was shocked to find that his message touched me deeply. I sought him out—my war record and our shared North Carolina roots helped make a meeting possible—and I even flew to New York to spend a day or two at his famous 1957 Crusade there.

He took an interest in my quest for meaning in my life. He invited me to his home not far from Asheville to discuss religion. We played some golf together—he was the only golfer I ever met who really did play for relaxation, and not for blood or money!

He answered some of my questions. I asked him many blunt ones—about drinking, about a man's choice of church. He said he did not think drinking was a sin. It was what drinking made people do in the way of sin that was the problem. That made a lot of sense. As to church attendance, he said that the choice of a place of worship wasn't as important as being *at* a place of worship. Go where you feel comfortable, he urged me. But go.

I have to give Dorothy credit here—she took my friendship with Billy as a sign of new hope in our family life. In return for my renewed interest in a spiritual life, she agreed to bring our children back to Calvary Episcopal. We became very strong members. I served on the vestry. I became a lay reader and sometimes, with the Bishop's blessing, gave my own sermons. I brought Billy Graham and my Bishop at Calvary Episcopal together for dinner one night, and later I even brought Billy Graham to give a message at Calvary—one of the happiest and most important moments of my life.

Such moments were all too rare. Neither my prayers nor my con-versations with Billy Graham could deflect me from my drinking, which had by now grown heavy. I finally asked to be excused from delivering messages in church anymore. I felt I was not worthy, in my everyday life, to be presenting God's word on Sunday. Dot and I grew further apart, and had separated again. Rather than be a hyp-ocrite, I gave up my time in the pulpit. Finally, to avoid embarrass-ment to my estranged wife on Sunday mornings, I switched my church affiliation to St. Luke's, a small church in a rural section of Asheville.

Mayday. Mayday.

We saw the *Belle* once in a while, the crew and I. We always swung by her when we came to Memphis for a reunion—in 1961, and again in 1967. We got our pictures taken beside her and gave some inter-views to the local TV people. Then we'd leave, and some more years would pass.

My father died of heart problems in 1961 at the age of eighty-four. Soon after his death, the simmering tensions between my brother David and myself turned into unmasked hostility. Dave's plans for the company—which I had sensed, but not known, in recent years—now became crystal-clear. His intention all along had been to build it up in order to sell it off for as much cash as he could wring out of a buyer.

I wasn't part of Dave's plans, and I would not have been a part of them if he'd asked me. My loyalty to my father's vision of the com-pany sealed my fate within it. My brother fired me.

Nothing in my wartime experiences had ever wounded me as deeply as this act. I was utterly deflated, not to say degraded, within my home-town community, my family, and my children. All the years of devo-tion, stewardship, service, and passion I had invested in this beloved enterprise—repudiated, in public, and by my closest blood kin.

Dave's pretext for ousting me drew on my most notorious weak-ness. In 1964, after my latest separation from Dot, I began dating a young woman in the company. Bad for our image, David declared, and booted me out.

It was Billy Graham who again reached out to me and came to my rescue. He helped me to believe that God still loved me even when I was as awash in guilt and remorse as a man could be. He kept me connected to a divine source of light. True to his generous heart, he helped me in more material ways as well.

Billy put me in touch with a wealthy retail-store executive in Charlotte, North Carolina, who was well connected in the business world. This man in turn agreed to back me in an application for a Volkswagen dealership in Martinsville, Virginia, south of Roanoke. Those franchises were highly competitive, but with those friends behind me, I ended up as a dealer of those wildly popular Beetle cars that were sweeping the country. Dot, bless her heart, helped make it possible. She offered some of her deceased father's estate as collateral for me to use in acquiring the business.

Things never got quite so bad that I couldn't laugh, once in a while, at that strange sense of humor that war had. Here I was, a guy who'd bombed a Ford plant as a B-17 pilot over Germany, now making a bundle by selling German cars thought up by Hitler to Americans in Virginia. Only in America.

My new job produced some experiences that went deeper than mere irony. Inevitably, I guess, it led me into contact with some Volkswagen colleagues who had once been associates of mine in a different sort of business.

Once, during one of my periodic visits to Volkswagen headquarters in Wolfsburg, Germany, I found myself on a boat cruise down the Rhine River with a party of American dealers for the company. We passed a village whose gaping rooftops still showed the damage, more than twenty years on, of the bombing that the Eighth Air Force had inflicted on them. One of the dealers in the group, who had learned of my service in the Eighth, passed the information to the boat captain that one of his passengers had helped cause the damage.

Within minutes the captain had made his way back to our group. He was a rugged-looking fellow who had the unmistakable bearing of a veteran. I watched him approach me, half-wondering whether I was about to be pitched into the drink.

Instead, the captain took my hand in his large one, and shook it. And then he asked me a question.

"Do you see that building over there?" he asked, pointing to one edifice that somehow had survived the general rubble. "You knocked all the buildings around it down. How come you didn't knock that one particular building down?" He measured me carefully, while I thought fast. Finally I blurted out, "Well, didn't you notice that that one belonged to the Ford Motor Company?" The captain stared at me a moment, then threw back his head in a roar of laughter. Everyone thought it was quite a joke. Suddenly, instead of wary former enemies, we were all brothers on that cruise boat—survivors of a common horror.

I went on to encounter several of my old adversaries through my work for Volkswagen. The management in Germany felt it was a good thing that I would meet some of the former Luftwaffe pilots, and I had no problems with that. After all, war is war and peace is peace, and it wasn't their fault they were fighting against me, it was Hitler's. I looked forward to these encounters, and sure enough, I finally found myself talking to a former pilot whom I just might have met one day two decades earlier and five miles higher in the sky. We started comparing notes on our war histories. I told him what bombing missions I had flown, and the dates, and he, through an interpreter, told me what his fighter assignments had been. Finally we came across one engagement—it was over the submarine pens at St. Nazaire—that he and I had shared, and perhaps tried to kill one another. Had his Focke-Wulf been one of those blurs past my cockpit window?

We kind of kidded and joked about it, as veterans do, and I asked him a few questions flier-to-flier—about the technique of frontal attacks on our B-17s, and about the Luftwaffe's tendency to veer off from the Flying Fortresses and go after the B-24s when they showed up in our groups. "Oh, *ja*," he said, confirming a long-held suspicion in the Mighty Eighth. "If the B-24s were there, we would attack them, because they were easier to knock down." It was strange, but somehow civilizing, to stand sipping a drink with these middle-aged men, salesmen now, warriors then, and contemplate the shared humanity of people with whom I'd once shared a mutual longing for destruction.

Before long, I was back on my feet again. Along with a highly profitable woodworking plant I was connected with in Bristol, Tennessee, I was soon making about $70,000 a year—major money, back in the 1960s.

That interlude lasted about ten fairly peaceful years. Then the bottom fell out again. In 1978 the last German-made Beetle rolled out of the plant—at Emden, by the way. Volkswagen produced other models, but dealerships like mine, which had leaned heavily on the Bug, went downhill very rapidly. To make matters worse, my woodworking business plummeted as well. As for the stock that I had accumulated in the Morgan family businesses, it had only served to deal me a further debilitating blow. I found that potential buyers were not interested in minority stock from within a family business. I was forced to sell this stock at rock-bottom prices to my brother—who resold it for about three times the amount that he had paid to me.

Meanwhile, I had no options left. I filed for bankruptcy. At about the same time Dorothy filed for divorce. I resisted it as I always had. I wanted us to stay married until the children had finished college. The impasse continued.

I met an Asheville woman, a widow with four children. Elizabeth Thrash.

We began dating. She was reluctant, because I was still married. But Dot and I were emotionally apart forever now.

Dorothy and I were finally divorced on May 24, 1979. She ended up with the house in Biltmore Forest. I ended up broke.

Elizabeth had taken a job at a prominent Asheville realty company, Beverly Hanks. At her suggestion I took an exam and became a broker there too—a job I hold to this day.

In June of 1979 Elizabeth Thrash and I were married. We began a close, affectionate life together. It was, I soon realized, the most genuine love I had ever felt for a woman.

I took this dear woman to England three times. The first time was to sign the famous print of the *Memphis Belle* executed by Robert Taylor, the distinguished British military painter. It was a honeymoon for us, a belated honeymoon.

Our second trip was in 1990, to watch the filming of the Warner Bros. movie, *The Memphis Belle,* produced by William Wyler's daughter Catherine. We had wonderful times with the eight surviving crew members of the *Belle* and their wives. As for the movie itself, I'm afraid I'd have to call it historically incorrect. Although we crewmen volunteered many suggestions regarding authenticity of dialogue and detail to the film's director, Michael Caton-Jones, our ideas were ignored. The crew in the movie came across as a bunch of glamour-boys larking through the air war. That was a far cry from the cool professionalism I observed aboard the *Belle.* One reviewer, noting that "the clichés dropped like bombs," called it "a war movie for teenyboppers," and I'm afraid I can't disagree too much with that assessment. The combat scenes were accurate, though, and I have always been grateful to Ms. Wyler for getting the movie produced.

Our third trip to England was to attend the movie's premiere there.

I will always thank God for the happiness Elizabeth and I enjoyed in that brief span. In 1991 Elizabeth Thrash Morgan contracted lung cancer. She suffered horribly for a year, and then died.

I drank.

The *Memphis Belle,* too, entered her darkest years. In 1976, the city of Memphis decided to sell the land that had been occupied by the National Guard. The buyers announced that there would be no room for the airplane that had helped liberate Europe from Hitler's tyranny. The buyers were the owners of the Memphis Memorial Stadium, the site of—you'll pardon the irony—the Liberty Bowl.

The *Belle,* in short, had been evicted. She now faced the prospect of being homeless, and beyond that, being sold for scrap-metal.

I drank heavily until a guardian angel pulled me out of it.

This angel was my daughter Peggy, my wholesome, bounding, joyful youngest child. I'd watched Peggy grow up happy and athletic, playing tennis, basketball, and field hockey. She enrolled at the University of North Carolina at Charlotte, married her high-school sweetheart—another good athlete named Kenny Partin—got her masters in education, and came back to Asheville as a teacher and athletic coach. She and Ken had three children, Morgan, Caitlin, and Kensley, beautiful girls every one.

Before she accomplished all of this, Peggy saved my life. It happened in 1976, while she was still in college. I was playing awfully hard and drinking a lot then, trying to play and drink my demons away—the falling airplanes, the smell of flesh, Margaret, getting bounced from the family firm by my brother, the bankruptcies, the end of my marriage to Dorothy, the end of my dreams for postwar peace and achievement. I was so deep in my sorrows that I didn't even imagine that anyone was noticing. I felt invisible, but Peggy noticed. While still a college student, she saw what it was doing to my health and to my spirit. And one day she came to me in that frank, no-nonsense way she has, and she said, "Dad, I hate to bring this up, but I want you to be around for my grandchildren. I don't think you will if you keep on drinking."

Talk about a shaft of light. All of a sudden, when Peggy told me that, with all that love and concern and forgiveness in her face, it was as though I were flying the *Belle* again. It was just like in the old days over Europe—all the flak, all the bullets, all the rockets were still whizzing around, but they were missing me now. They couldn't do me any damage anymore. Morgan had come home again, after all. Floorboard Freddie had landed his craft, and he'd kept it on the runway, guided by this latest and dearest of his many angels.

From that moment I was no longer a problem drinker. I gave up scotch, bourbon, vodka—all the hard liquor. Since that day I have drunk only wine, and that in careful moderation.

My personal mission also hit paydirt. Not with wealth or fame, but with contentment. Contentment that has arisen from my humble acceptance of my Command Pilot, and from marriage to the woman who now shares my life, and whom I truly cherish and adore.

It was during her darkest period, those years of neglect capped by eviction, homelessness, and the prospect of oblivion, that the *Memphis Belle* found her own guardian angel.

This guardian angel wasn't nearly as pretty as any of mine. I'd have taken him more for a leprechaun if he weren't so Italian. He was a jolly, broad-faced, silver-haired metallurgist from Memphis by way of Rock Island, Illinois, named Frank Donofrio. I'll guarantee you that if Donofrio were to take off his shirt and show a pair of wings between his shoulder blades, I wouldn't be surprised. Without him, the *Belle* probably wouldn't exist right now, much less be enshrined inside her hallowed dome.

Frank was one of those tens of thousands of people who used to drive past the *Belle* on her pedestal on the National Guard grounds. He drove past her two, sometimes four times a day for years on his way from home to his office at Mid-South Metal Treating Co. and back. Unlike most people, Frank Donofrio noticed her.

Besides being a man of unusual warmth and civic enthusiasm, Frank had some special connections to World War II. As an Army lieutenant, he had instructed young recruits in the techniques of chemical warfare. His two brothers had been Marines. One of them, Arthur, had been a platoon sergeant with G Company, Third Division, the assault force that hit the beaches of Iwo Jima on the third day of the battle. Sgt. Arthur Donofrio died there.

It always bothered Frank Donofrio that nobody had found a more elegant resting-place for the *Memphis Belle*.

In March 1967 Frank was flipping through the pages of *Newsweek* when an article caught his eye. It was a report that some 50,000 military films made during World War II had been put on sale to the public at rock-bottom prices. Most of the stock was miscellaneous training footage, the shortest being a four-minute study of how to put out a cigarette. Donofrio was interested. He was looking for some instructional film on heat-treating to help train his employees.

As Donofrio read on, he saw that some of these surplus films were quite substantial. Among the most fascinating on the list was a forty-one-minute documentary made by the famous Hollywood director William Wyler. Its title was *The Memphis Belle*. The master negative of this forgotten old period-piece had long since been lost, the *Newsweek* article reported. What remained were several cans of forth- and fifth-generation footage—prints of prints of prints.

Donofrio couldn't believe what he'd just stumbled across. He had many good friends in the military, and he picked up a phone and called one of them, a hometown pal from Rockford—Col. Fred Ascani, a decorated World War II bomber pilot. Twenty years earlier Ascani had worked with the test pilot Chuck Yeager at Wright Field in Ohio before Yeager broke the sound barrier in the X-1. Colonel Ascani, later to be a Major General, helped Donofrio track the Wyler film to its storage-place at the U.S. Air Force photography lab in St. Louis.

Donofrio timed his trip to St. Louis well. He went there in July, when the Cardinals were at home and fellow Memphian Tim McCarver was in the lineup as catcher for the Redbirds. Then he visited the photo lab and asked to see what was left of the documentary. When the Commander there learned of Frank's intent—to donate the Wyler film to the Memphis Public Library—he not only gave it to him free, but he took the best-preserved parts from all the footage in stock and edited them into one complete version of the original documentary.

Frank Donofrio hurried back to Memphis, booked a screening of *The Memphis Belle* at the library, and hoped he would attract enough people to fill the auditorium's 178 seats. On a sweltering night in late July, more than 250 crammed their way in.

That marked the beginning of Frank's *Memphis Belle* crusade.

In August 1967 he found himself Acting Chairman of a Memphis Belle Memorial Committee, suggested by a group of citizens. Retiring and modest, Frank could not imagine himself as permanent chairman of anything. For the next eight years, he found himself the *sole* member of the Committee. The chairmanship had been thrust upon him, and he took it seriously. "I never asked for any money from anybody; I paid my own expenses, about $3,500 a year, just so I could say I was Chairman of that Committee," Frank told me once. "I decided I didn't want to be controlled by anyone else's money while I tried to figure out how I was going to save the *Belle*."

In 1977, the year the *Belle* faced extinction, Frank's lonely crusade started to pay off. A Memphis lawyer, George Lewis, who headed up the American Legion local there, and a friend named John Emerson, signed on with him. "We've got to do something about the *Belle*," was the way Lewis put it.

Frank was thrilled. Now was the moment to incorporate the Committee, he sensed. They did, renaming it the Memphis Belle Association. Now the money started to accumulate—a trickle at first, but it was accumulating, and not a moment too soon. In that year the *Belle* was dismantled and shipped back to the airport in parts. Its fate would now depend on the efforts of the Association.

It would also depend on the United States Air Force, which had regained ownership of the *Memphis Belle*. It happened in the early 1970s, when Mayor Wyeth Chandler, a son of the Mayor who had purchased the Belle for $350 in 1946, decided to donate the craft back to the Air Force. Memphis, the Mayor decided, was no longer able to guarantee the plane's upkeep.

The Air Force decided that the city could go on housing the airplane, but it warned that if certain standards of upkeep were not maintained, this piece of military property was subject to removal.

For nine more years, Donofrio and his friends desperately sought a widespread base of funding to meet the Air Force's standards and keep the *Belle* in town. "We never had more than $5,000 in the bank at one time," Frank told a journalist later.

It was during this time that the *Belle* lost one of her sweetest members. In 1980 Vince Evans was killed, in, of all things, a plane crash. Lord, I thought he was going to live forever.

He almost did. He turned his life around after the war, and became a legendary figure in the Santa Ynez Valley north of Los Angeles. He took up acting, wrote a screenplay for Humphrey Bogart, and struck up a close friendship with Ronald Reagan. He married a gorgeous, devoted woman named Margery, an heiress to a Standard Oil Company fortune who tamed him into a family man and bore him a daughter, Venetia. Vince took over management of her properties, realized huge profits, and bought a 900-acre cattle ranch in the Valley in 1959, and in 1965 purchased a landmark restaurant called Pea Soup Andersen's. He and Margery became active supporters of the Santa Barbara Symphony and 4-H activities in the region.

It all ended on April 23, 1980. Vince, Margery, and Venetia were returning to the small airport at Santa Ynez Valley in their private plane from a trip somewhere. An instructor pilot was also aboard. No one ever learned for sure who was at the controls. They were minutes away from landing, flying in and out of clouds, when suddenly they canceled their instrument flight plan and went to a visual plan. Then the airplane reentered a cloud bank. The pilot switched to instruments again—too late to avoid a dead-on crash into the side of a mountain. None of them survived. Venetia was twenty-one. A large piece of the *Memphis Belle*'s heart went down with them.

Frank Donofrio's efforts, and those of the Association, finally awakened the interest of the media. In 1985 a *Commercial Appeal* writer, Barbara Burch, wrote an article warning that unless local citizens got behind the Association's efforts, and fast, the airplane would disappear from the city forever. The Air Force, after all, still owned the airplane; it was on a year-to-year lease to the Association, pending its satisfactory upkeep. Col. Richard Upstrom, Director of the Air Force Museum, had notified the Association that unless they took steps within six months to restore the craft to a presentable condition, it would be moved to the museum in Dayton.

That piece got the attention of Mayor Dick Hackett, who rallied the city's most influential business leaders. The business elite, finally energized, called for a fundraising drive and proposed a new, high-visibility showcase for the *Belle*—Mud Island, just then emerging as a popular and classy historic-interest park.

Some of those executives backed up their ideas with hard cash, most notably Fred Smith, the CEO of Memphis-based Federal Express and a fighter-combat veteran of Vietnam. Smith's company donated a resounding $100,000 in 1986. While the Association was still reeling from that windfall, Smith turned his considerable persuasive powers on the Boeing Corp., which after all had pioneered and manufactured the B-17. Boeing responded with another $100,000. To cap the local outpouring of money, Mayor Hackett presented Donofrio's group with a check for $150,000—the results of a "rider" to a fundraising drive for a memorial to the Rev. Dr. Martin Luther King Jr.

All of a sudden, Frank Donofrio had more than his usual $5,000 in the bank!

Then the drive to enshrine the *Memphis Belle* blossomed from a local to a national crusade. The catalyst was Hugh Downs, the distinguished co-host of ABC's television newsmagazine, *20/20*. Downs, an Army veteran himself, came to Memphis when he heard of the fundraising drive, and reported it in a 1986 telecast that included scenes from Wyler's documentary. Soon, letters were pouring in to Frank Donofrio's steadfast group, 300 a day, with donations ranging from $1 to $5,000. By July 1987 the Association had reached its goal of $600,000. The jolly guardian angel had done his job. The *Memphis Belle* would be saved.

Memphis, Tennessee, in mid-May 1987, had turned itself into a working replica of London and Bassingbourn Air Base combined. Twenty-five thousand excited World War II buffs had descended on the city, and everybody was dancing to the music of '40s-style swing orchestras that had temporarily out-tooted the local blues bands. The crowds converged on Mud Island, in the Mississippi River, where for the past several weeks a kind of military buildup had been going on—bulldozers and cranes tearing up the earth to make way for a parachute-shaped pavilion. Convoys of flatbed trucks rumbled from the island to the city airport ten miles away, from where they returned with massive sections of airplane wings, propellers, fuselage. Ground crews waited for each new part, which they added with welding torches and rivets to the rapidly-emerging finished form of a B-17 bomber. Touch-up artists polished and burnished and painted the surfaces of this great lady, restoring the sweep and luster of her youth. The pinup "Memphis Belle" was repainted on each side of the nose by Tom Starcer, the nephew of Tony Starcer, who had originally executed Geroge Petty's drawing and who had recently died.

Members of Frank Donofrio's committee had arranged for every available B-17 in America—seven of the thirteen that were still airworthy at the time—to fly to Memphis and take part in the ceremonies enshrining the *Memphis Belle* in her permanent pavilion. Think of it—only thirteen Flying Fortresses were left in flying condition. Thirteen, out of an original 12,731 that had rolled off the Boeing assembly lines back in the 1940s. Some 4,000 of those had been lost in combat. The average lifespan of a B-17 in combat was fifty days.

Thirteen left now. And just seven of those available to come to Memphis.

Well, hell. That was enough for a party, anyway.

The *Belle* crew was in town—what was left of us. Vince Evans was gone, of course, and Cecil Scott, too—dead of a heart attack in 1979. J. P. Quinlan couldn't make it—his doctor had told him not to risk the trip. Jim Verinis was on hand, and Charles Leighton, and Bill Winchell, and Bob Hanson, and Casimir Nastal, and Harold Loch.

Good old Joe Giambrone showed up to repaint that symbolic twenty-fifth bomb on the fuselage, as cameras clicked and flashbulbs popped.

I was there, of course. As was Margaret Polk, the original Memphis Belle. Lame Brain and Jug Head, reunited.

Polky was in splendid, smiling form for the occasion. She had pulled herself out of her hard times several years earlier, and had become a great friend and ally of Frank Donofrio. She had gained some new, and deserved, celebrity status for herself as she toured the country with Frank raising money for the airplane. She suffered from a damaged heart valve by now, but she was living quietly and happily, volunteering with the Women's Exchange in Memphis, tending to the raccoons and rabbits and birds that visited her backyard in the house where she'd grown up, working with the Humane Society. Margaret and I were friends by now, real friends, after all these years. I couldn't help but notice that she was quite a gal.

There had been parties, banquets, speeches—just like the old days. The crew and I plunged in and enjoyed it all to the hilt, as we always had. We posed for Moms and Dads with cameras in their hands, handed out autographs to kids, and did a lot of hugging and back-slapping. Told one another a few lies. The day before the big ceremonies, I even got to take the controls of one of those B-17s for an hour or so over Memphis. It was owned by David Tallichet, who'd flown several combat missions in the closing months of the war, and it had "played" the *Belle* in Catherine Wyler's movie.

No buzzing this time. No loops, stalls, or barrel-rolls. Just a few minutes of indescribable pride and fulfillment and memory and gratitude. As usual, I flew that plane despite eye problems, only this time, the problem was tears.

On the big day—May 17—Mud Island was dense with festive humanity. There were American flags, balloons, and children on their fathers' shoulders. Up on the speaker's platform, we all took our bows—the *Belle* crew, Frank Donofrio, and city dignitaries. Margaret was up there with us, radiant and waving to the throng. Dr. Friedman approached the microphone and read a letter that made my heart swell up. It was from Gen. Ira C. Eaker, USAF (Ret.). My old admired commander, the guiding spirit of the Eighth Bomber Command in England, was 91, and could not be there in person. I will never forget the words that opened his letter:

> Vivid in my memory is the day, June 6, 1943, almost 44 years ago, when General Devers, Commander of the European Theater, and I bade you farewell at Bovington—the first 8th Air Force bomber to be sent home upon the completion of 25 combat missions. . . . The *Memphis Belle* shall remain a living memorial.

Damn good thing I wasn't piloting a B-17 when I heard those words read aloud. My vision just then was zero, due to heavy moisture.

Then came the capstone of the ceremonies. Those magnificent B-17s, which had lined up on the runway back at the airport, roared down the tarmac one by one, lifted off into the spacious skies and flew, in perfect formation, above the crowd at Mud Island. At exactly the right moment the lead bomber, *Chuckie,* piloted by "Doc" Hospers of Fort Worth, Texas, opened its bomb bay and released its payload on those assembled onlookers.

Rose petals. Thousands upon thousands of rose petals wafted

down upon the *Belle*'s enclosing canopy, on the speaker's platform, and into the upturned faces and upraised hands of all those beautiful children.

The petals fell, and the crowds cheered, and the *Memphis Belle* sat young-looking and proud in her enveloping shrine. In that bright moment of rosefall I knew, I absolutely knew, that my war, all my wars, were finally over. The *Belle* and I had finally achieved peace beyond anything that a treaty between nations could confer. And I knew that somewhere, far above the roses, a guardian angel in a broad-brimmed straw hat, smoking a cigarette in a holder—surely they have a smoking section in heaven—was looking down upon her happy son, who had come home again.

EPILOGUE

A lot of time has gone by for those of us who fought and won against the Axis Powers. Who among us would ever have believed that we'd be talking about World War II as a conflict that happened "in the last century"?

From where we stood then, these opening years of the new millennium weren't just the future—they were the *distant* future. How wonderful, then—how blessed I am—that I can sit here in the distant future and still look forward to . . . the future!

But that's just what I do, with my amazing wife Linda, our dogs Daisy, Morgan, and Sandy, and our little cat Rascal. There's my real-estate career, my tours of aviation shows, my lectures to groups of schoolkids. I have a lot to look forward to, every day.

I still keep in touch with the crewmen of the *Memphis Belle*, the ones who are still with us. Looking back over the list, I'm gratified that so many of the boys lived out long and fulfilling postwar lives.

Here is the roll call, as of this writing—Labor Day, 2000.

Cecil Scott, our ball turret gunner, went back to Arapahoe, North Carolina, and worked for the Ford Motor Company for thirty years until his death in 1979. His widow Norma represented him at the Memorial ceremonies in 1987.

Vince Evans, I have told you about.

Navigator Charles Leighton enjoyed a long loving marriage to his wartime sweetheart Janet and a wonderful career as a teacher and counselor in Michigan. He died in Bellaire, Michigan, in 1991.

Clarence "Bill" Winchell, who nailed that eighth and final German fighter on the *Belle*'s last mission, went home to a successful career as a chemical engineer. He died in Barrington, Illinois, in 1994, leaving his widow, Laura.

Our second top turret gunner and engineer, Eugene Adkins, who'd suffered frostbite on our tenth mission, retired as a Major after serving as a gunnery specialist with several types of bombers. He died in 1995.

Our first top turret gunner and engineer, Levy Dillon, transferred to the 306th Bomb Group after his stint aboard the *Belle*. On his third mission, Levy took a slight wound in his leg. Back on the ground, he was bandaged by a young volunteer named Adele Astaire—Fred's sister. Levy never mentioned the injury or his brush with a celebrity. He died in 1998.

Joe Giambrone, the man who ran the crew that kept the *Memphis Belle* flying, went back to his native Pennsylvania and enjoyed many years as an office manager in a construction company. He died in 1992.

Tailgunner J. P. Quinlan died while this book was in production, in December 2000.

Margaret died in 1990.

As I write these words, waistgunner Tony Nastal and his wife, Doris, enjoy the sunshine in Apache Junction, Arizona; my "other" pilot, Jim, and Marie Verinis keep in touch from Woodbridge, Connecticut; our third top turret gunner and engineer Harold Loch and his wife, Exie, look back on many good years in real estate at Green Bay, Wisconsin; and radioman Robert Hanson and his wife, Irene, send Christmas cards from Mesa, Arizona.

As for the *Memphis Belle* herself, she remains triumphantly on display inside her special canopy on Mud Island in Memphis. Lately, a few of her caretakers, as well as the Air Force, have grown very concerned about her condition. Like the rest of us, the *Belle* is aging, and even in this safe place her exterior is corroding noticeably under the effects of routine temperature change. Brent Perkins, who until recently was president of The *Memphis Belle* Memorial Association, has spent a number of years trying to raise funds to build a climate controlled building for the *Belle*. He is now spearheading a campaign on what I call the last chance to raise funds for such a building. The association has formed a *Memphis Belle* War Memorial

Foundation to raise this money. If this effort should fail, I hope the Air Force Museum in Dayton, Ohio will take the *Belle* and give her a good home. The hope is that once again the people of America will come to her rescue, as she came to theirs so long ago.

Me? I've got all I can handle here in my hometown. Besides selling real estate at the firm of Beverly Hanks, I relish the opportunity to get around and talk to kids in high school and college about that old war in that century now gone by. I am always astonished that they seem to have gotten their World War II history in a thimble, and scarcely comprehend the magnitude of it and why it was fought and how it created so much of the lives they take for granted. I am also gratified, nearly every time out, at the keen interest that they show in learning about the war. I think that the nation's schools could do worse than build some of their learning curricula around World War II. Think of all the ways you could study it! History . . . literature . . . geography . . . economics. Even cinema. There's a pretty good documentary I could recommend for starters.

The highlights of my life after that glorious May day in 1987 have been many. There was the thrill of seeing the *Memphis Belle*'s exploits made into that feature film in 1990. Granted, the film layed the melodrama on a little thick, but it was quite an experience for us crewmen to see ourselves played by such stars as Matthew Modine, Billy Zane, Eric Stolz, and Harry Connick Jr.

There has been the quiet pleasure of watching my sons and daughters prosper, and enjoying my seven grandchildren.

No highlight can surpass my wedding to the woman who now shares each new day of my life, the former Linda Dickerson.

I first met her at an air show, the Sun 'n Fun show in Lakeland, Florida. As volunteer chair of evening events, she had invited Jim Verinis and me down as guest speakers in April 1991. I was married to Elizabeth then and tending her in her illness, and our acquaintanceship did not progress beyond the cordial.

A year later, a widower now, I met her again—this time at a black-tie dinner at Pope Air Force Base in Fayetteville, North Carolina. She was by then doing public relations for David Tallichet, the owner of the B-17 that had stood in for the *Memphis Belle* in Catherine Wyler's movie. He and his plane were featured attractions at an air show there. I arrived as guest of honor, and there she was—a trim, smart blonde wearing a traditional Southern Belle hoop skirt. I'd soon learn that Linda was as much at home in a skydiver's togs or behind the yoke of a sea plane as in an evening gown, and that she suffered no backtalk from any man or woman, thank you. Not even a Colonel, USAFR (Ret.). Once again, Morgan was dazzled. But I also realized the scope of this challenge. How was I going to approach the first red-blooded, full-fledged feminist of my long romantic career?

Cautious soul that I am in matters of the heart, I took my time wooing this Ms. Dickerson. Would you believe it, I waited all that afternoon and into the evening, while we were swirling around the floor at the big dance, before I dared approach the subject. "Young lady," I whispered to her, "I think I'm falling in love with you. Would you consider marrying me?"

She put me off, believe it or not. After she got over thinking I was pulling a joke, she said she'd have to give it "serious consideration." I decided I'd have to indulge this old-fashioned wish of hers. I followed her around, from air show to air show, and we got more and more comfortable with one another, until we got to Danville, Virginia, a little later in the summer. There I popped the question a good deal more seriously, and there Linda Dickerson, herself a child of the Air Force, a feisty survivor with a heart of gold under her I-can-handle-anything exterior, said Yes.

We were married in August of 1992, in front of the nose of the *Memphis Belle* on Mud Island. Brig. Gen. Paul W. Tibbets Jr., USAF (Ret.), the man who piloted the *Enola Gay* into world history, gave the bride away. I have always referred to that beautiful event as my twenty-seventh and last mission.

Today, Linda is my wife, my partner, and my best friend. In the time we've been together she has helped me organize all of my World War II memorabilia—photographs, letters, flight logs, citations.

She had the imagination and enterprise to set in motion a reunion between me and Queen Mother Elizabeth, and later the Queen herself, in the summer of 1997. The occasion was the Queen's dedication of the $17 million air museum in Duxford, England, to honor the American airmen who served in the war. When we heard about those plans in February of that year, Linda immediately wrote to the Queen asking for the privilege of a meeting with us. Through intermediaries, Linda also set up a visit to the Queen Mother's summer castle at Sandringham, three days before the Duxford ceremonies.

When Linda told me what she was doing, I couldn't suppress a laugh at her audacity. "They'll never agree to anything like this," I told her.

Well, on July 29 we arrived at Sandringham for our scheduled fifteen-minute visit with the Queen Mother, a visit that lasted more than an hour, with many memorable photographs taken. She remembered well our last meeting on the tarmac at Bassingbourn some fifty-four years earlier, and she was overjoyed to gaze at a photograph of that ceremony that Linda and I brought to her. It triggered a lively conversation of reminiscence between us.

Three days later, at Duxford, Queen Elizabeth and her entourage swept up to us. The Queen took both our hands, smiled, and said, "I understand you had a very pleasant visit with my Mum." Linda curtsied, I bowed, and we both replied, "Yes, Your Majesty, we had a wonderful visit!" Prince Philip, second son Prince Andrew, the Duke of Kent, former Prime Minister Margaret Thatcher and other dignitaries were also on hand.

Linda has had occasion to remind me of that "they'll never agree" line of mine plenty of times since then. She always adds her playful needle, "Roger *that*, Morgan!"

Linda has also helped me increase my appearances at air shows, aviation conventions, and similar occasions to the point where we now attend up to twenty or thirty events a year. All this in addition to my real-estate work at Beverly Hanks, the largest such company in western North Carolina, and in addition to her fiercely committed work on behalf of abused domestic animals in the Asheville area. Linda Dickerson Morgan is one lady I'd hate to face if I'd been guilty of kicking a dog around, which, I hasten to add, I have not been!

I'm eighty-two at this writing. I can still fly. I flew three B-17s as recently as last year. Even did a buzz job at Reading, Pennsylvania, not too long ago. In April 1999 I was invited to fly a B-52 at Barksdale Field, the same field where I'd graduated from flying school all those many years ago. I discovered that the Air Force kept a B-52 named the *Memphis Belle* at Barksdale. Learning that was quite a thrill.

The biggest thrill was my getting to fly the B-1. I took the controls of this fantastic machine for the first time in October of 1999, at Robins Air Force Base in Georgia. The fellow who made it possible for me to do so was Sgt. Glenn Parker of the 116th Bomb Wing, 128th Bomb Squadron, Georgia Air National Guard. I will always be grateful to Sergeant Parker and his men for this privilege.

The Georgia Air National Guard later named a B-1 the *Memphis Belle*. Guess you could say the grand old lady has spawned a daughter and a granddaughter.

Linda and I remain active on the air show circuit, where I am constantly reminded that America—or much of America—has not forgotten World War II. Over the years, I've had thousands of people at these shows come up to me to thank me for what I and my fellow men-at-arms did. At the last reunion of the *Belle* crew as of this writing, last September in Nashville, Tennessee, it happened again. Dozens of people, singly and in families, came up to Jim Verinis, Harold Loch, Bob Hanson, and me. We enjoyed a conference telephone chat with J. P. Quinlan and Tony Nastal, who couldn't make it in person. The folks thanked each one of us personally for what we did during World War II, and made such comments as, "We're living the life we're living today because of guys like you." And, "I'm not speaking German today because of guys like you." They all seem very sincere. I did not realize that level of sincerity was still out there in America. It sure means a lot to experience it. In fact, it has answered that old question that haunted me for years after I returned home from the war: *Why me? Why am I still alive?*

This is why. I am still alive to keep on telling the story of the *Belle*, and the war, to people—to people at air shows, and to young people in their schools. I love visiting schools, and talking to students about the airplane, and about the global struggle she helped win, and about the men I knew who fought and died heroically in that great effort, and about how their lives today are enriched by the democracy those heroes helped preserve. Yes, this is "why me." This is why I am still alive.

Now that I know why I am still alive, I also know that I will finally see Mabel again when this life is over.

It means a lot to visit Chatham Field in Savannah, Georgia, where the Eighth Air Force originated and where a fine museum now stands, dedicated to the Mighty Eighth.

I'm going to keep on flying as long as I can pass my physical. If nobody checks that left eye of mine too closely, I can pass it for a few more years now, I'm sure.

Do I still relive my part in World War II and the exploits of the *Memphis Belle*? Of course. Every time I show that William Wyler documentary to friends, every time I go over to Memphis and see her, get up into that cockpit, grip the yoke, put my feet on the rudder pedals, it all comes back to me so vividly. I can feel those old vibrations, hear the sounds of old machineguns firing, and if I glance up at the old photograph on the instrument panel, I can still see that young face there.

And I have to whisper to her, one more time, "Hi, Gal. We did it, didn't we? We did it together."

APPENDIX

Twenty-five Missions in Europe
Unit: 324th Bomb Squadron (H), 91st Bomb Group (H),
1st Combat Wing, 1st Air Division, Eighth Bomber Command
Home base: Bassingbourn, England

Mission/Date	Target	
1: November 7, 1942	Brest, France	U-boat pens
2: November 9, 1942	St. Nazaire, France	U-boat pens
3: November 17, 1942	St. Nazaire, France	U-boat pens
4: December 6, 1942	Lille, France	Locomotive works
5: December 20, 1942	Romilly-sur-Seine, France	German airfield
6: January 3, 1943	St. Nazaire, France	U-boat pens
7: January 13, 1943	Lille, France	Locomotive works
8: January 23, 1943	Lorient, France	U-boat pens
9: February 4, 1943	Emden, Germany	War plant (Ford factory)
10: February 14, 1943	Hamm, Germany	Railway yards
11: February 16, 1943	St. Nazaire, France	U-boat pens
12: February 26, 1943	Wilhelmshaven, Germany	Naval base
13: February 27, 1943	Brest, France	U-boat pens
14: March 6, 1943	Lorient, France	U-boat pens
15: March 12, 1943	Rouen, France	Railway yards
16: March 13, 1943	Abbeville, France	Airfield
17: March 22, 1943	Wilhelmshaven, Germany	Naval base
18: March 28, 1943	Rouen, France	Railway yards
19: April 5, 1943	Antwerp, Belgium	Airplane engine factory

Mission/Date	Target	
20: April 16, 1943	Lorient, France	U-boat pens
21: April 17, 1943	Bremen, Germany	Focke-Wulf factory
22: May 1, 1943	St. Nazaire, France	U-boat pens
23: May 4, 1943	Antwerp, Belgium	Ford truck factory
24: May 15, 1943	Wilhelmshaven, Germany	Naval yards
25: May 17, 1943	Lorient, France	U-boat pens

Stateside Public Relations Tour of the Memphis Belle
(in order of appearance)

From June to August 1943

Washington, D.C.	Las Vegas, NV	Fort Meyers, FL
Memphis, TN	Kingman, AZ	Panama City, FL
Nashville, TN	Roswell, NM	Sebring, FL
Bridgeport, CT	Hobbs, NM	Camden, SC
Hartford, CT	San Antonio, TX	Asheville, NC
Boston, MA	Harlingen, TX	Columbus, OH
Cleveland, OH	Laredo, TX	Chicago, IL
Pittsburgh, PA	Oklahoma City, OK	Los Angeles, CA
Detroit, MI	Denver, CO	New York, NY
Dayton, OH	Wichita, KS	
Akron, OH	Mobile, AL	

The Crew of the Memphis Belle

Pilot:	Capt. Robert Morgan; Asheville, NC
Copilot:	Capt. Jim Verinis; New Haven, CT
Bombardier:	Capt. Vincent B. Evans; Henderson, TX
Navigator:	Capt. Charles B. Leighton; Flint, MI
Radio Operator:	T/Sgt. Robert J. Hanson; Spokane, WA
Top Turret Gunners:	T/Sgt. Leviticus "Levy" Dillon; Providence, VA
.	T/Sgt. Eugene Adkins; Johnson City, TN
	T/Sgt. Harold P. Loch; Green Bay, WI
Left Waistgunner:	S/Sgt. Clarence E. "Bill" Winchell; Oak Park, IL
Right Waistgunners:	S/Sgt. E. Scott Miller; Kingswood, WV
	S/Sgt. Casimir A. "Tony" Nastal; Detroit, MI
Ball Turret Gunner:	S/Sgt. Cecil H. Scott; Arapahoe, NC
Tailgunner:	S/Sgt. John P. Quinlan; Yonkers, NY
Crew Chief:	M/Sgt. Joseph M. Giambrone; Hulneville, PA

Memphis Belle—*Boeing B-17F-10-BO Flying Fortress,
Serial Number 41-24485*

Wing Span: 103'9"
Length: 74'9"
Height: 19'1"
Crew: 10
Weight (empty): 65,500 pounds
Speed: 160 mph @ 25,000 feet
Fuel: 2,520 gallons
Oil: 147.6 gallons
Range: 2,800 miles @ 152 mph
Bomb Load: 8,000 pounds
Guns: Thirteen .50 caliber machineguns
Service ceiling; 37,500 feet
Cost (new): $314,109
Units built: 12,726 (6,981 built by Boeing in various models,
         5,745 built under a nationwide collaborative
         effort by Douglas and Lockheed)

Twenty-six Missions in the Pacific
Unit: 869th Squadron, 497th Bomb Group,
73rd Combat Wing, 20th Bomber Command
Home base: Saipan, Mariana Islands

Mission/Date	Target	
1: October 28, 1944	Truk	Japanese installations
2: October 30, 1944	Truk	Japanese installations
3: November 5, 1944	Iwo Jima	Airstrips
4: November 6, 1944	Iwo Jima	Airstrips
5: November 10, 1944	Tokyo	Reconnaissance
6: November 24, 1944 (first B-29 raid)	Tokyo	Nakajima Aircraft Co.'s Musashi engine plant
7: November 27, 1944	Tokyo	Nakajima Aircraft Co.'s Musashi engine plant
8: December 3, 1944	Tokyo	Musashino aircraft plant
9: December 6–7, 1944	Tokyo	Nighttime incendiary raid
10: December 18, 1944	Nagoya	Mitsubishi aircraft plant
11: December 27, 1944	Tokyo	Aborted mission
12: January 9, 1945	Tokyo	Musashino aircraft plant
13: January 10, 1945	sea search	
14: January 14, 1945	Nagoya	Mitsubishi aircraft plant
15: January 27, 1945	Tokyo	Aircraft engine plant
16: February 4–5, 1945	Kobe	Port
17: February 15, 1945	Nagoya	Aircraft engine plant
18: February 19, 1945	Tokyo	Harbor
19: February 25, 1945	Tokyo	Urban area
20: March 9, 1945	Tokyo	First nighttime low-altitude fire-bomb raid
21: March 13, 1945	Osaka	Nighttime incendiary raid
22: March 23–26, 1945	Nagoya	Weather reconnaissance— landed on Iwo Jima
23: March 27, 1945	Kyushu	Airfield
24: March 30, 1945	Nagoya	Machine shops
25: April 1, 1945	Tokyo	Urban area
26: April 3–4, 1945	Tachikawa	Weather reconnaissance

The crew of the Dauntless Dotty

Pilot:	Lt. Col. Robert Morgan
Copilot:	Capt. Andrew Mayse
Bombardier:	Capt. Vince Evans
Navigator:	Lt. N. S. Alton
Flight Engineer:	Lt. Ed Lee
Radio Operator:	T/Sgt. S. Fritzshall
Radar:	T/Sgt. R. W. Powell
Left Waistgunner:	T/Sgt. W. B. Sanor
Right Waistgunner:	T/Sgt. C. Burke
Tailgunner:	Sgt. P. T. Black
Fire Control:	T/Sgt. E. H. Cordes
Crew Chief:	Sgt. M. H. Brinkmeyer

Dauntless Dotty—*Boeing B-29 Superfortress*
Wing Span: 141'3"
Length: 99'
Maximum height: 27'9"
Crew: 11
Weight: 70,140 pounds empty, 147,000 pounds military load
Cruising speed: 220 mph
Top speed: 365 mph
Fuel: 8,198 gallons
Oil: 340 gallons
Range: 5,830 miles
Bomb Load: 20,000 pounds
Guns: 12 remote controlled .50 caliber machineguns,
        1 20mm cannon
Service ceiling: 31,850 feet
Cost (new): $639,000
Units built: 2,766 by Boeing, 668 by the Bell Aircraft Co.,
        and 536 by the Glenn L. Martin Co.

BIBLIOGRAPHY

Anthony, Elizabeth. Dialogue from *Mrs. Miniver*. Quoted in *Reel Classics: Elizabeth's Classic Movie Homepage*. Http://reelclassics.com (October 19, 2000).

Astor, Gerald. *The Mighty Eighth: The Air War in Europe as Told by the Men Who Fought It*. New York: Dell, 1997.

Coffey, Thomas M. *Iron Eagle: The Turbulent Life of General Curtis LeMay*. New York: Crown, 1986.

Duerksen, Menno. *The Memphis Belle: Home at Last*. Memphis: Castle Books Inc., 1987.

Eaker, Ira C., "Some Memories of Winston Churchill," *Finest Hour 52: Aerospace History* (1972), pp. 120–124.

Haney, Robert E. *Caged Dragons: An American POW in WWII Japan*. Ann Arbor: Sable Press, 1991.

Herman, Jan. *A Talent for Trouble: The Life of Hollywood's Most Acclaimed Director, William Wyler*. New York: Da Capo Press, 1997.

Jackson, Kenneth T. *Crabgrass Frontier: The Suburbanization of the United States*. New York, Oxford: Oxford University Press, 1985.

Roberts, William. "July 28, 1945—Plane Hits Building—Woman Survives 75-Story Fall," *Elevator World* (March 1, 1996).

Col. Robert Morgan, USAFR, Ret., was awarded the Distinguished Flying Cross with two Oak Leaf Clusters and the Air Medal with nine Oak Leaf Clusters. He died in 2004.

Ron Powers is a Pulitzer Prize–winning journalist and cowriter of the #1 *New York Times* bestseller *Flags of Our Fathers*, with James Bradley. He lives in Vermont.